A History of
Ancient Greece

4-7
72-117
118-13
140-164
165-181

182-305

A History of
Ancient Greece

Nancy Demand
Indiana University

OVERTURE
BOOKS

The McGraw-Hill Companies, Inc.

New York   St. Louis   San Francisco   Auckland   Bogotá   Caracas
Lisbon   London   Madrid   Mexico City   Milan   Montreal
New Delhi   San Juan   Singapore   Sydney   Tokyo   Toronto

McGraw-Hill

A Division of The **McGraw·Hill** *Companies*

A HISTORY OF ANCIENT GREECE

Copyright © 1996 by The McGraw-Hill Companies, Inc. All rights reserved.
Printed in the United States of America. Except as permitted under the United
States Copyright Act of 1976, no part of this publication may be reproduced or
distributed in any form or by any means, or stored in a data base or retrieval system, without the prior written permission of the publisher.

Photo Credits appear on pages 383–384 and on this page by reference.

2 3 4 5 6 7 8 9 0   DOC   DOC   9 0 9 8 7 6

ISBN 0-07-016207-7

This book was set in Janson by Ruttle, Shaw & Wetherill, Inc.
R. R. Donnelley & Sons Company was printer and binder.
Maps were prepared by Mapping Specialists, Ltd.

Publisher: Jane Vaicunas
Sponsoring Editor: Leslye Jackson
Editing Supervisor: Peggy Rehberger
Designers: Joseph A. Piliero and Brian H. Crede
Production Supervisor: Kathryn Porzio
Photo Editors: Nancy Dyer and Anne Manning
Photo Researcher: Elyse Rieder

Library of Congress Cataloging-in-Publication Data

Demand, Nancy
        A history of ancient Greece / Nancy Demand.
            p.   cm.
        "Overture books."
        Includes bibliographical references and index.
        ISBN 0-07-016207-7
        1. Greece—History—To 146 B.C.   I. Title.
DF77.D44   1996
938—dc20   95-42782

About the Author

Nancy Demand is a professor of Greek history at Indiana University, Bloomington, Indiana. She received a Ph.D. in Philosophy from the University of Pennsylvania in 1965, an M.A. in Greek from the University of Vermont in 1973, and a Ph.D. in Greek from Bryn Mawr in 1978. She has taught at Trenton State College, Ohio State University, and, since 1979, in the Department of History at Indiana, where she is now a full professor. She has published numerous articles and reviews, and three books: *Thebes in the Fifth Century, Urban Relocation in Archaic and Classical Greece,* and *Birth, Death and Motherhood in Classical Greece,* for which she received a Fellowship from the National Endowment for the Humanities in 1990–1991. She is currently doing research on the origins of the Greek polis and on the role of medicine in fifth-century Greek culture.

To my teachers

Contents

Lists of Maps

Preface

The Greeks have provided us with the best introduction to Greek history in the rich legacy of their literature, art, and architecture, but understanding this legacy requires context. We need to see how these varied sources fit together to tell us their story, what the gaps are, and how historians work to fill in the gaps. This need is usually filled by a history text that presents an overall picture. But while existing texts do usually provide this larger picture, in my teaching I found none that meshed well with the sources. Most of today's college students can use some help in developing the skills to deal with sources in a critical way. In the days of small classes, this could be done on a personal level in class, but the large-lecture format that is becoming more and more the norm today does not provide the best setting for communicating the strategies of critical analysis, which are developed mostly from practice and experiment. And so I began to develop materials that would integrate selections from the sources with the text and guide the reader in working through them, suggesting the sorts of questions a historian might ask. (Too often students assume that what is printed in the textbook is offered as Truth, not to be questioned—or at least not in a friendly way within the context of the course.) The result is this book.

PEDAGOGICAL FEATURES

Students should have copies of Herodotus, Thucydides, and Aristophanes' *Wasps, Knights,* and *Clouds,* which form the basis for many of the Source Analysis sections. Other sources are included in these sections: archaeological plans, illustrations of Geometric pottery, inscriptions (the Theran decree, Drakon's law of homicide, letter of Darius to Gadatas, Troezen inscription), and selections from Tyrtaeus, Solon, Sappho, Plutarch, Plato, Aeschylus, Euripides, Aristotle, Pseudo-Aristotle, *Constitution of Athens,* Lysias, *On the Murder of Eratosthenes,* Demosthenes, *Against Phormio,* Xenophon, *Anabasis,* and Arrian, *Anabasis.* Maps accompanying the various chapters include most of the places mentioned in the chapter. Problems with scale, however, made it impossible to include some far-flung locations, and so a map index is included at the back; here all the places on the maps are listed alphabetically, with the numbers of the maps on which they appear. Each chapter includes at the end a list of the places mentioned in that chapter, which can be used by the student to check up on map knowledge (of course, depending on the students' interest and level, one might want to assign a selection from these lists). Blank outline maps are included at the back of the book, which can be used for various map exercises or for practice of quizzes. A Glossary is also included in the material at the back of the book. Each chapter has a section at the end giving suggestions for further reading, and endnotes documenting statements in the text also provide references for further research.

A NOTE TO STUDENTS

The reader who plays the game will get the most out of this book—it's really important to take the time to do the exercises in the source analyses. But don't stop there—the exercises are intended to get you started and give you an idea of how to approach this material, not to provide a definitive selection of "Great Bits of Greek History." If you have time, read more of the sources. Then if you want to explore other modern interpretations, the suggestions for further reading at the end of each chapter provide some recommendations. The endnotes document the basis for positions taken, or provide more advanced references for those who want to learn more. The list of map places at the conclusion of each chapter is intended to encourage a growing familiarity with the sites of Greek history; assiduously locating each on a map as you study the chapter (using the index of map locations at the back of the book) will undoubtedly increase your understanding of the text, and could result in an astounding knowledge of Greek geography if you really work at it (useful for when you go to Greece to see all these places). The illustrations and plans represent the archaeological sources and are meant to be taken as seriously as the written sources. And, finally, there is a Glossary at the back of the book—when you don't know the meaning of a term, look it up there (if what you need isn't there, write and tell me about it); some of these items might even be useful in an exam!

A note on the spelling of Greek names is traditional in any book dealing with Greek history. The problem arises from the need to transliterate Greek words. For a long period of time this was done by scholars who adopted Latinized forms, and many names became quite familiar in that form (Greek kappas became c's, αι became ae, final -ος became -us, etc.). More recently, however, it has become popular to transliterate directly from the Greek original. Often, however, this results in familiar names taking on a new and (to us) odd-looking form—for example, "Aeschylus" becomes "Aischylos", "Pericles" becomes "Perikles." How much of this any given scholar is willing to engage in varies widely. There really seems no possibility of complete consistency: most of us now keep some Latinized forms that we can't bear to change, and adopt Greek transliteration for the rest. But students will find that names vary in their spelling in different books, and sometimes different spellings even occur within a single book (when quotations are used that employ a different system).

Many people contributed to this book: at McGraw-Hill, Pam Gordon originally suggested that I turn the material I had been using for my classes into a textbook and offered enthusiastic encouragement as I proceeded; Nancy Blaine carried on in the interval between editors; and Leslye Jackson brought the project to completion. I am especially indebted to the scholars who read and commented on the manuscript; they often provided extremely useful suggestions based on their own experiences in teaching, and the book has been greatly shaped by their suggestions. They included Jack Balcer, Ohio State University; Eugene Borza, Penn State University; Elizabeth Carney, Clemson University; Robert Cromey, Virginia Commonwealth University; Roger deLaix, University of Arizona; Gary Ferngren, Oregon State University; Dianne Harris, University of Cincinnati; Paul Harvey, Penn State University; Thomas Kelly, University of Minnesota; Alden Mosshammer, University of California, San Diego; William O'Neal, University of Toledo; and Carol Thomas, University of Washington. Hui-Hua Chang, my research assistant and an enthusiastic devotee of Greek history, provided much appreciated assistance with the Glossary, map lists and general editorial matters.

NANCY DEMAND

List of Common Abbreviations

ANCIENT SOURCES

Ar. = Aristophanes

Arist. = Aristotle

   Ath. Pol. = the *Constitution (Politeia) of the Athenians*

Arr. = Arrian

Dem. = Demosthenes

Diod. Sic. = Diodorus Siculus

Hom. = Homer

   Od. = *Odyssey*

   Il. = *Iliad*

Plut. = Plutarch

   Alex. = *Alexander*

   Lyc. = *Lycurgus*

   Per. = *Pericles*

   Pelop. = *Pelopidas*

Thuc. = Thucydides

Vitr. = Vitruvius

Xen. = Xenophon

   Hell. = *Hellenica*

   Oecon. = *Oeconomicus*

MODERN WORKS

ATL = B. D. Merritt, H. T. Wade-Gery, M. F. McGregor, *The Athenian Tribute Lists* (1939–53) 4 vols.

CAH = *Cambridge Ancient History*

KRS = G. S. Kirk, J. E. Raven, and M. Scholfield, *The Presocratic Philosophers* (1984)

Introduction

reek history rests firmly upon a basis created by the ancient Greeks themselves. In the eighth century B.C. the epic poet Homer told the story of a great war of Greeks against Trojans in the *Iliad* and the *Odyssey*. Scholars still debate whether these poems recall memories of a long vanished heroic age or were works of the poetic imagination, but, in the meantime, thanks to the discoveries of archaeologists, we can walk the streets of Troy and Mycenae, and even read the inventories kept by people who may have been Homer's Achaeans. In the fifth century B.C. Herodotus, called the "Father of History," wrote the first true history, the story of the defense of Greece against the invading Persians. His work is still our best source for both Greek and Persian history of the period. Soon after, the Athenian Thucydides wrote the history of another great war in which most of the Greek world took sides, the war of the Athenians against the Spartans. He was himself a participant in the war he described: he suffered in a great plague that broke out early in the war, later served as general, and finally, exiled because of a military loss, was able to view both sides. The tragedian Aeschylus and the comic poet Aristophanes also left works that provide firsthand perspectives upon these wars. Later historians, such as Arrian with his history of Alexander, carried on the tradition begun by Herodotus and Thucydides, and other works preserved as literature, such as speeches from the law courts, offer us firsthand views of the lives of the Greeks.

Not only are these sources crucial for an understanding of Greek history; they also address questions that are still vital today, despite the vastly larger scale of modern political life and our undoubted technological accomplishments—how to balance individual freedom with reasonable social order within the state, and how the state itself can live amidst competing and rival states without imperialistic domination or self-destructive wars. In fact, the Greeks never achieved a solution to these basic political problems, and the consequences of their failure

1

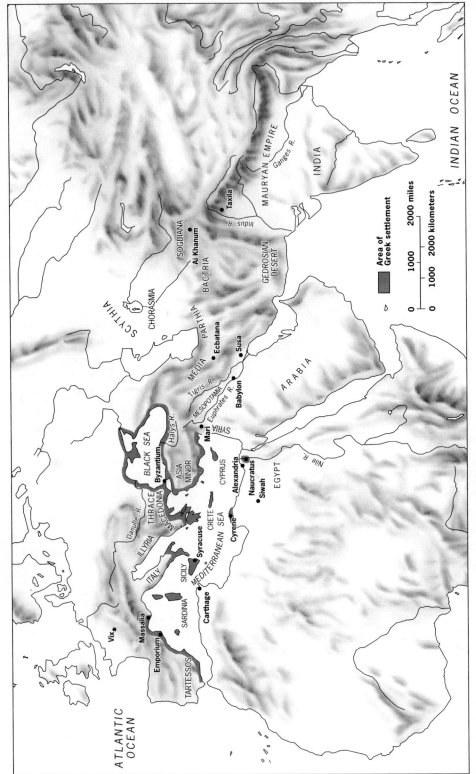

MAP I   The extent of the Greek world at the death of Alexander.

can provide a forewarning to us as we grapple with the same problems. On the other hand, the Greeks had only begun to recognize some of the social and economic problems that we see more clearly today—the exploitation of some members of society so that others can live the "good life" and the structural subordination of the female half of the population. These questions of meaning and value—an intrinsic part of Greek history, whether fully realized or just beginning to surface in the classical period—explain our continued fascination with the Greeks.

The Greek world in antiquity was much larger than it is today—after all, Alexander the Great was called the "Conqueror of the World." Of course, he didn't conquer all the known world, but he did a good job of conquering its most settled and civilized areas, from Greece to the East (his ambition was to reach the Ocean that he believed to lie at the eastern edge of the world—had he lived long enough and continued, he might well have found the Chinese civilization that was developing in a surprisingly parallel fashion on the other side of the globe.

A reasonable view of the lands known to Greeks in the period up to the death of Alexander is represented in Map I. Greeks were living around the shores of the Black Sea, Asia Minor, Cyprus, the northern Aegean coast, much of Sicily, southern Italy, Sardinia, at Naucratus and Cyrene in Africa, and along the shores of Spain and southern France (see shaded areas). Beyond the areas in which they had settled, they had widespread contacts with non-Greeks—Scythians, Phoenicians, the inhabitants of central Europe and even Britain—as they sought tin and other metals, hides and furs, slaves, amber, salt, and timber, and offered in exchange, along with items that left little archaeological trace, Greek drinking vessels, the formal accoutrements of the Greek symposion (elite drinking party), and the wine to go with them. The huge Vix krater (the largest Archaic Greek bronze vessel known) was one such Greek object, given probably as a diplomatic gift by a Greek to a Gallic chief in the sixth century B.C. Alexander extended actual rule and the settlement of Greeks and Macedonians inland to the rugged eastern areas of the former Persian Empire, all the way to India.

We begin our study of Greek history, however, by focusing on the land and the resources of the rugged peninsula of Greece itself, which contributed so much to the formation of the Greek way of life, and the sea that both separated it from and provided an opening to the wider Mediterranean world.

CHAPTER ONE

Greek Environment and Prehistory

THE GREEK ENVIRONMENT[1]

Greece is a land of mountains and sea. The mainland is formed by the Pindos mountain chain, which extends from the European continent toward the southeast until it is submerged by the Aegean Sea, resulting in numerous islands and a jagged coastline. Many of the plains enclosed by the mountains are so small that they could support only a single settlement in ancient times, but a few—such as the great plain of Thessaly in north-central Greece, and the plain of Boeotia in central Greece—are extensive enough to have been shared by several small independent states.

The mountains also create natural regions. At the outer fringes of Greek cultural territory, mountains delimit Macedonia to the northeast and Epirus to the northwest. In the north, the peninsula called the Chalkidike is a naturally defined region, as is Attica in central coastal Greece; in the Peloponnesus, well-defined areas consist of Lakonia, Messenia, the Argolid, and Arkadia. Sometimes the independent states that shared a region were formally organized in a religious federation or a political league, as, for example, the Boeotian League; in other cases, there was no formal organization, as in the peninsula of the Chalkidike before the fifth-century B.C. Chalkidic League, and in Arkadia before the fourth-century B.C. Arkadian League.

From Neolithic times, the ancient inhabitants of Greece lived primarily by farming. The Mediterranean climate in the classical period, with its hot, dry summers and mild, rainy winters, was generally favorable for the production of the "Mediterranean triad": cereals, olives, and vines.[2] Wide variations in climate, however, made success in agriculture difficult. In terms of regional diversity and interannual variability, the climate has not changed appreciably since classical antiquity,[3] and therefore modern figures can give us some idea of the

4

situation that the Greek farmer faced in ancient times. For example, Kavala, on the north coast of the Aegean, had an average annual rainful during the 1960s of 549 millimeters, while rainfall at Athens in the 1950s varied from 216 to 560 millimeters.[4] Barley can be grown with a minimum of 200 millimeters annual rainfall, but the more desirable crop, wheat, requires at least 300 millimeters. Thus we can see that on the north Aegean coast wheat could have been grown every year with reasonable expectation of success, while in Athens the farmer faced years in which even barley harvests might be marginal. Modern human intervention has, of course, changed the agricultural picture in many ways. For example, irrigation, which is central to much agricultural production today, was rarely practiced in antiquity. Moreover, many new crops unknown in antiquity now play important roles in the economy, including cotton, tobacco, and citrus fruits.

Land suitable for farming in ancient Greece was limited and varied in fertility.[5] Much of Greece is rocky and mountainous; plains are often small, and, even when comparatively expansive, may suffer from drainage problems. Terracing extends usable land and allows even fairly steep hillsides to be planted with olives and vines, but making and maintaining terraces is laborious work, adding to the difficulties of farming. Goats and sheep were grazed on land that was even more marginal. Many farmers kept cattle as well, but horses were an expensive luxury raised only by the wealthy few. Meat was not an everyday item in the diet, but was eaten only when sacrifices were made to the gods. Fish provided a source of protein in coastal areas, as did legumes throughout Greece.

Crop diversification helped the Greeks make the best of these difficult conditions. The Greek ideal of self-sufficiency fostered diversity, for each household and each city-state had to produce a range of products. Also, under the Greek system of partible inheritance (an equal part to each son), land was divided among offspring instead of being passed on as one large estate. In some areas and periods land was also used as dowry. As a result, landholdings were often fragmented into scattered plots. Although it may seem inefficient for a single household to work small plots in diverse locations to which family members had to travel, it proved advantageous because even small variations in temperature or precipitation protected against the catastrophic loss of an entire season's harvest. Only in extreme conditions would every crop fail.

In addition to its agricultural potential, the land of Greece also provided some mineral resources. Greece has a number of copper deposits, many conveniently found in rock formations that also provide the most fertile soil; thus, those who settled on good soil were likely to come upon copper as well. Copper was known and used in Greece beginning in the Late Neolithic period, ca. 4800 B.C., although there is no direct evidence that local sources of copper were being used on the mainland until ca. 2700 B.C. Tin, necessary to alloy with copper to produce bronze, does not seem to have been present, however. Silver was concentrated in two areas, in Laurion (in the southern part of Attica) and in the north Aegean in the area around the Strymon River and the island of Thasos. Control of Laurion, and eventually of the northern mines, was a determining factor in Athenian predominance in the fifth century B.C. Other important mineral resources were building stone and marble; timber suitable for the construction of large buildings and large ships was never abundant in southern Greece, although such resources were available in northern Greece and, especially, in Macedonia.

Another useful resource that was lacking in Greece was **obsidian,** a volcanic glass that can take a very sharp edge and was much prized as a cutting tool. The closest source of obsidian was on the Cycladic island of Melos, but as early as 6000 B.C. mainland inhabitants managed to reach the island by boat, and an embryonic system of exchange was even established. The sea, in fact, was as much a determinant of Greek life as the mountainous terrain. Seventy-two percent of the land of Greece is within 25 miles of the sea. People were probably first attracted to the sea by fishing, which led them to fashion small boats. Pursuit of fish migrations took curious and enterprising Greeks to nearby islands, which in turn served as stepping stones to further investigation, including the discovery of obsidian on Melos.

The sea and seafaring skills offered another strategy of survival that had important ramifications for the development of ancient Greek culture and political forms. When pressed by problems at home, the community sometimes sent out some of its members to establish a new settlement elsewhere. The way had been laid for this when the first boat was built and men set out to explore neighboring coasts. By 2000 B.C., the inhabitants of Greece were creating new settlements by collective (not individual) emigration. In the eighth through the sixth centuries,* Greek culture spread by this means as far as Spain, the northern shore of the Black Sea, and the coast of north Africa. As new settlements were established, Greeks gained experience in urban planning and community organization that influenced developments back home; some scholars even attribute the birth of the Greek city-state, or **polis** (pl., **poleis**), to a process of feedback from the colonization experience. In large part it was this expansion of Greek culture that made possible the strong influence of Greek ideas and ideals upon later Western civilizations, beginning with the Romans and extending to our own culture.

It is not surprising that the naturally divided landscape of Greece was politically divided until modern times. While the ancient Greeks recognized that they shared a common language, culture, and religion, they owed their political allegiance to any of a number of small independent states operating under different forms of government: palace-centered kingdoms in the Bronze Age; in later times, city-states, which might take the form of aristocracies, oligarchies (rule of

_____

*All ancient dates are B.C. unless otherwise indicated.

the few), or, by the fifth century B.C., democracies; and *ethne* (sing., *ethnos*), or tribal states.

Variations in the degree of access to the sea helped to create some of these political differences. Those with easy access developed lifestyles, values, and even political structures that were significantly different from those of inland inhabitants. We shall see this clearly in fifth-century B.C. Greece, when Athenian reliance upon the sea led to the development of a radical form of democracy, while inland Sparta's reliance upon the land fostered a conservative oligarchy. **Plato,** an Athenian whose political orientation was decidedly conservative, in fact recommended that the ideal polis be far from the sea. He remarked that the sea "is, in very truth, a briny and bitter neighbor. It fills a city with wholesale traffic and retail huckstering, breeds shifty and distrustful habits of soul, and so makes a society distrustful and unfriendly within itself as well as toward mankind at large."[6]

GREEK PREHISTORY:
THE EARLY NEOLITHIC BACKGROUND

Evidence of human settlement in Greece goes back to at least the nineteenth millennium B.C. and the hunter-gatherer cultures of the Paleolithic Age.

The Franchthi Cave

The best-known very early settlement is the Franchthi Cave, a site in the northeastern Peloponnesus near the Argolid Gulf on the edge of a well-watered coastal plain. The Franchthi Cave was inhabited on at least a seasonal basis from around 18,000 until 3000 B.C., and it provides evidence for the transition from hunting and gathering to settled farming, a transition that is termed the **Neolithic Revolution.**[7]

The first human use of the cave was in the Upper Palaeolithic, when bands of hunters numbering no more than twenty-five to thirty visited it on a seasonal basis. For some reason, however, it was abandoned for a few thousand years around 15,000 B.C. From the twelfth through the eighth millennium B.C. it again sheltered small bands of hunter-gatherers. These people had begun to exploit the sea by fishing, and it is possible that they remained in the cave year-round. They used obsidian, which shows that they had probably begun to construct boats and had achieved considerable mastery of the sea (there are no signs of traveling salesmen in this period).

By the seventh millennium B.C. the Franchthi Cave people were obtaining a significant portion of their diet by catching large tuna. They had also begun to experiment with the cultivation of certain plants, especially lentils. Such experi-

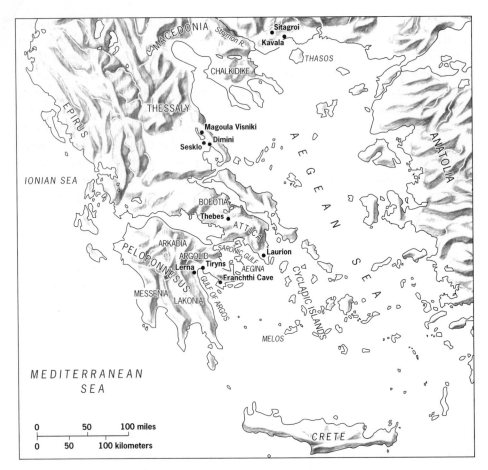

MAP 1 Neolithic and Early Bronze Age Greece.

ments might well have been carried on by the women, who would have been occupied with gathering plants for food while the men were hunting or on fishing
or obsidian-gathering expeditions.

By around 6000 B.C. the full-scale Neolithic Revolution had arrived at
Franchthi. Both plants and animals (sheep, goats, emmer, and einkorn wheat)
had been domesticated. Hunting and fishing dropped off drastically as there was
a shift to food production activities. Population may have increased, as suggested by the building of houses outside the cave. The transition to settled farming would not necessarily have improved health conditions—the Neolithic diet
was less varied than that of hunters and gatherers, and people were more subject
to diseases carried by domesticated animals, with which they now lived in close
proximity—but the number of children that were raised probably increased once
it was no longer necessary for women to restrict themselves to the one small
child at a time that they could carry on gathering trips.

There are no signs that outside contacts were lessened by the demands of farming, however. Obsidian continued to be abundant, and andesite, a stone brought from the Saronic Gulf, was used for millstones. Marble, another nonlocal material, also appears. Even the plants and animals that were domesticated must have been imports, for these species were not present earlier on the site. They were brought to Franchthi, possibly from Anatolia, along with the techniques for their cultivation. The confluence of so many imports suggests that we should envision some sort of network of regional exchange. The Franchthi community seems to have been still an egalitarian group, however, for no evidence of social stratification by wealth or status has been discovered. There are a few figurines and objects of personal adornment, but little to suggest the development of a sense of personal property.

While the Franchthi Cave people continued to make progress in the transition to the Neolithic, the most intensive development in the new style of life came about not in the south but in the north. In the seventh millennium B.C. numerous agricultural villages were established there, in western Macedonia and especially in Thessaly, and for two to three millennia this area was at the forefront of the region's growth and prosperity. The settlements were in contact with each other, and a fairly uniform culture evolved.

THE MIDDLE AND LATE NEOLITHIC BACKGROUND

Two of the best-known Neolithic settlements in Thessaly were Sesklo and Dimini.[8] In archaeological terms, Sesklo and Dimini are *type sites;* that is, each is typical of a number of culturally similar sites, as determined, for the most part, by pottery styles. The name of the particular type site is applied to all sites with a similar material culture, and it also indicates a relative date.

Sesklo

Sesklo was first occupied during the Middle Neolithic, ca. 4800–4400 B.C. Early interpretations of the architectural remains, as reported in Emily Vermeule's widely used book, *Greece in the Bronze Age,* portrayed Sesklo as a small (30 to 50 dwellings, perhaps a maximum of 250 inhabitants), peaceful (as evidenced by the minimal walling), and socially undifferentiated culture (as evidenced by the similarity of house types), which was destroyed by a more warlike people who took over the site and also built the nearby settlement of Dimini.

Subsequent excavations and reinterpretations of the archaeological evidence, however, have considerably modified this picture. They have brought to light the remains of a much larger settlement than Vermeule's reconstruction postulated at Sesklo; it covered 20 to 25 acres, with an estimated population of

Figure 1-1   "Mother-Goddess" figurine.

perhaps 3000. In a central location on the *acropolis* (the defensible hill that forms the nucleus of a city or settlement) stood a prominent building with a courtyard; the plan of this building is of a type called a *megaron* (pl., *megara*): a rectangular building of two rooms having an entrance and a porch on the short side. The degree of social differentiation, if any, indicated by this building is unclear. It may have been the meeting place of a municipal council, but it cannot be characterized as an administrative center. Nevertheless, the regularity and similar orientation of the houses suggest some degree of community organization. This is also supported by the evidence of craft specialization, attested by the high quality of the pottery. The well-made cream-colored pots were decorated with red geometric designs based on a zigzag pattern, revealing their derivation from the designs of weaving. The monochrome pots were innovative as well, with designs created by scraping, impressing, and varying of the color by changes in firing conditions.

The Sesklo clay workers also made figurines, continuing a tradition dating from the Early Neolithic. Similar prehistoric figurines, which often represent a female, sometimes obese or with sexual features emphasized, have been found over a wide geographical area ranging from western Europe to Russia, and over a time span that extends from the Paleolithic period (ca. 25,000 B.C.) to the Bronze Age (ca. 2000 B.C.). The belief that these reveal the worship of a "Great Mother-Goddess" is currently quite popular,[9] but it is not supported by the evidence (Figure 1-1). Those who make such claims focus too much on the female figures while ignoring other figures found in the same contexts, including figures of males, figures without sexual characteristics, and figures of animals. They also overlook the wide variety of female figures. Modern ethnographic studies of tribal peoples suggest that such figurines could have been put to many uses, not all religious. They could have been used as dolls, as teaching devices in initiation ceremonies or before childbirth, in sympathetic magic rituals aimed at inducing pregnancy, as characters in mythological accounts, or in sorcery and black magic.[10] The fact is that we simply don't know how the early peoples used such figurines.

Sesklo, by virtue of its size, organization, and the presence of craft specialization, now appears to have been a small "city" rather than the simple village of the earlier interpretation (Figures 1-2 and 1-3). Moreover, while the walls at Sesklo are not "fortifications," somewhat more imposing defensive measures have been found at other sites of the Sesklo culture. Reporting on the current state of research on Sesklo, D. Theocharis says: "All this greatly changes the traditional picture of the peaceful rural settlements of the 'Sesklo Culture,' and almost entirely destroys the supposed contrast between them and the 'warlike' disposition of the inhabitants of Dimini."[11]

In about 4400 B.C. the settlement at Sesklo was burned and destroyed, and

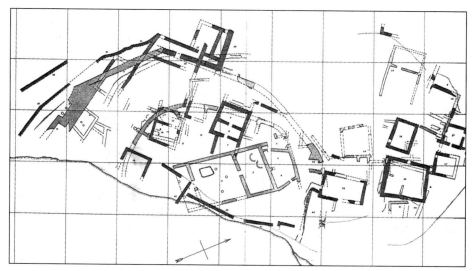

FIGURE 1-2 Site plan of Sesklo.

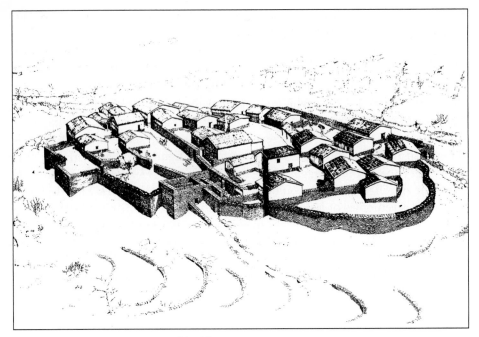

FIGURE 1-3   Reconstruction of Sesklo.

the site remained deserted for about 500 years. A few other settlements of the Sesklo culture also show signs of destruction about this same time, but others remained and underwent a gradual cultural transformation. By 4200 B.C. there were no traces left of the Sesklo culture; the new culture that succeeded it is called simply *pre-Dimini*. It seems to have been considerably less advanced. A less accomplished dark-colored pottery with incised or linear decoration replaced the attractive red on cream of the Sesklo style, the architecture of the buildings was more irregular, and its people made no figurines.

The Dimini Culture

In the Late Neolithic period, ca. 3700 B.C., still another cultural change occurred at the site of Dimini and gave its name to the succeeding period. While this Domini culture was earlier seen as representative of the entire Late Neolithic period in Thessaly, however, it is now recognized as somewhat of an aberration, a peak of development reached in only a small area of eastern Thessaly for a relatively short period of time in the middle of the Late Neolithic period. In this phase the site of Sesklo was reoccupied (on the plan of Sesklo, the buildings of this later, Dimini phase are indicated). There had been a gap in occupation at Sesklo of ca. 500 years, however, and the "Dimini people" cannot be held responsible for the destruction of the earlier Sesklo settlement, as Vermeule's earlier interpretation suggested.

The Dimini culture was notable for the attention it gave to fortifications, as the plan of Dimini shows (Figures 1-4 and 1-5). The central building at Dimini, a megaron in form, occupies a commanding position in the settlement and is much larger than the central building at Sesklo (in the Sesklo stage). It is especially large in proportion to the other buildings at Dimini, which suggests social differentiation. This central building may have been a community hall, or the house of a leader, but it seems clearly to be an architectual expression of some sort of authority or power. A similarly impressive central building is not found again in Greece until the settlement at Lerna, some 1500 years later (see below).

Since the triple concentric rings of fortification found at Dimini are also present at Sesklo, whose acropolis is naturally defended, the presence of a system or standard arrangement is suggested. At another site of Dimini culture, Magoula Visviki (Velestino), there is a megaron whose length is 30 meters, as long as the "Men's Megaron" that we will see in the Late Bronze Age at the Mycenaean palace of Tiryns (Chapter 3).

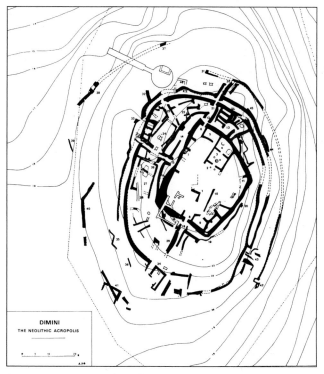

FIGURE 1-4 Site plan of Dimini.

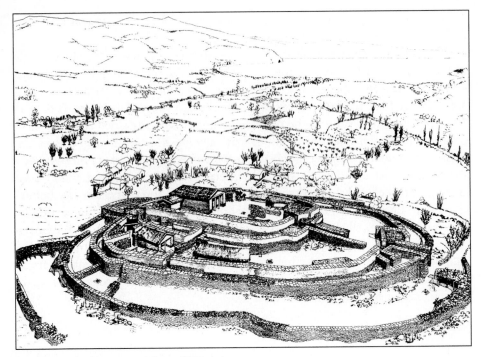

FIGURE 1-5 Reconstruction of Dimini.

The pottery of the Dimini culture was decorated with brown or black geometric designs of meanders, checkerboards, pyramids, or spirals that filled much of the surface (Figure 1-6). Two figurines have been found, one is a seated male and the other a female figure holding an infant that has been called one of the most important Neolithic figurines (Figure 1-7).[12]

Copper axes have been found at Sesklo in the Dimini period, and a site further north, Sitagroi, provided evidence for smelting. Local sources do not seem to have been utilized, however; rather, archaeological finds suggest that the sources for both metal and metallurgical skills at that time were the Balkans and perhaps Anatolia.[13]

There is, however, no evidence of the use of bronze during the Dimini phase, although in the succeeding period it does appear. While bronze came to be increasingly used, it was not used to a degree that affected the economy or social structure. For this reason, the Late Neolithic is called *Chalcolithic* (copper-stone using) rather than *Bronze*.

The notable developments of the Middle and Late Neolithic periods that we have been considering at the sites of Sesklo and Dimini were much more pronounced in that region of Thessaly and the north of Greece than in the south. In the south, which was less fertile and drier, with greater regional fluctuations in rainfall, settlement was sparse until the late fourth millennium B.C. The people in the Franchthi Cave had few neighbors.

The period called *Early Bronze Age I* in Greece (3200–2700 B.C.) is rather oddly named, since it is marked by signs not of an innovation—reliance on bronze—but of a recession. There is a decline in the number of settlements and, most notably, a lack of metal finds. In *Early Bronze Age II* (2700–23/2400 B.C.), however, there was a boom in the use of copper as well as a dramatic rise in settlement numbers in the southern areas. Meanwhile, settlement in the north declined, and the center of innovation shifted permanently to the south. Evidence of the practice of alloying copper with tin to produce the much harder and more useful metal, bronze, also appears for this period. While there were copper resources at Laurion in Attica, most of the mainland probably obtained copper from abroad. Sources of tin, which is not found in Greece, may have been Anatolia, the Balkans, Spain, Afghanistan (via Mesopotamia and Syria), or even Britain.[14]

THE BRONZE AGE

With the introduction of bronze into the Aegean area in the third millennium B.C. (Early Helladic period), settlements increased in number and grew into towns, and some buildings can be called monumental. But the development of these mainland sites was interrupted around 2400 B.C., and a period of cultural

FIGURE 1-6   Dimini pot.

FIGURE 1-7 Figurine of a woman holding an infant, from Dimini.

setbacks followed. The chronology* of the period, which can be only tentative, is given below.[15]

EH II	2900–2570/2410	(Lerna II, III, IV)
EH III	2570/2410–2090/1900	
MH	2090/2050–1600	(arrival of Greeks, 2000?)

The Early Helladic Period and Lerna

The best-known example of the achievements and vicissitudes of the Early Helladic (EH) sites is Lerna, which is situated on the Gulf of Argos (the modern Bay

---

Note: Chronologies throughout the text identify cultural periods as early, middle, or late (e.g., "Early Helladic" or "EH"). In some cases, additional distinctions are made within a period: "EH II" and "EH III." All years are B.C.

of Navplion).[16] Lerna, settled and then abandoned in the Neolithic period, was resettled in EH II by a people who built a row of houses with good-sized square rooms, perhaps along a street or court (Lerna II). They also built a multiroomed monumental building, **Building BG,** having thick mud walls and a schist roof, and they surrounded the whole settlement with a defensive wall. After some time, both Building BG and the wall were destroyed by an intense fire. There was no change of population, however, and the inhabitants gradually recovered, at first building small houses over the site of Building BG (Lerna III). At last they began the construction of another monumental building in the center of the site. This building is called the **House of Tiles** because of its terracotta roof tiles. It measured 25 meters by 12 meters, and consisted of two large rooms and two smaller ones, with exterior corridors accessible from both the inside and outside and used for stairways to an upper floor (Figure 1-8). There appear to have been open balconies on the upper floor, and a light well provided light for the interior rooms on the first floor. The interior walls were carefully plastered, and in the largest room the walls were decorated with rectangular panels. Stairs were fitted with clay treads, and doors were set in wooden jambs. The building was also used for storage, for a large number of seals used to mark containers of stores were found. Moreover, these seals suggest that the people of Lerna had taken the first steps in the development of writing. Red clay benches were set along the two long exterior walls of the building, providing shelter from sun and rain. The functions of display, storage, and public convenience are apparent, and the building is perhaps analogous to the buildings some identify as *protopalaces* in Crete.

Houses of a similar plan, a type called the *Corridor House,* have been found at a number of different sites in mainland Greece, including Thebes in Boeotia and Kolonna on the island of Aegina.[17] Moreover, not far from Lerna, at Tiryns (a later Mycenaean palace site), the remains of a huge round building have been found, about 28 meters in diameter and more than 26 meters in height. The foundation consisted of three thick, concentric ringwalls without connecting doors. If it was ever used as a palace, there must have been access to an upper floor by a ramp of some sort. The most likely suggestion, however, is that it was used as a granary.[18]

To call the Corridor buildings palaces is probably anachronistic, but they do seem to have been built to accommodate large numbers of people and could have provided for differentiation of public and private uses. Vermeule suggests that the best parallel might be with village granges to which all citizens had equal access.[19] Other scholars see them as evidence for the development of a form of social organization called the *chiefdom,* in which power is concentrated in a single leader who effectively controls the community's resources.[20]

Before the House of Tiles was even completed, it fell victim to intruders, and the whole settlement was destroyed in a violent fire, although the inhabitants apparently escaped, as noted earlier. Having destroyed the settlement of

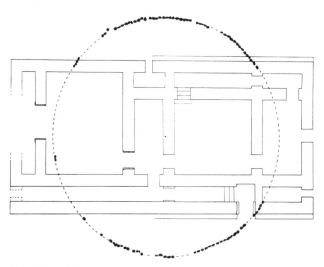

FIGURE 1-8　Site plan of Lerna.

the House of Tiles, the intruders settled down on the site, constructing small irregular buildings of one or two rooms, some with apsidal (round) ends (Lerna IV). Their handmade pottery provides them with a name, the Patterned Ware people. The Patterned Ware people used no seals and had little foreign contact. They did not rebuild the House of Tiles; on the contrary, they heaped up a tumulus over 4 meters high over the remains of the building and marked off its perimeter with a circle of stones, leaving the area inviolate throughout their occupation of the site. Whether they treated the ruins in this way from fear, piety, or some other motivation is a question that cannot be answered. Similar destructions are archaeologically attested at about the same time in a number of other places, yet some of the Corridor Houses, such as those at Thebes and Kolonna, appear simply to have been abandoned, with no signs of fire or other violent destruction. The period that followed, Early Helladic III (EH III), was characterized by small buildings requiring little skill in construction and showing little evidence of specialized function; metals were scarce and craft specialization existed at only a few sites. Moreover, there was a decline in contacts with the Cycladic Islands and a complete break in contact with Crete; life reverted to a simpler, subsistence level.

Historians are divided on the explanation for the rather sudden and widespread appearance of monumental buildings in mainland Greece in EH II. The need to obtain tin required increasing overseas contacts, for which the access to the sea and the seafaring skills that the Greeks along the coasts of the mainland had developed were vital assets. If, as seems likely, sources of tin were found in Afghanistan by way of Mesopotamia and Syria, the contacts with these more advanced cultures may also have been a source of new ideas.[21] Influence from Mesopotamia has been suspected[22] while other scholars prefer to look for evidence of local development.

The Middle Helladic Period and the Arrival of the Greeks

According to the generally accepted account, people speaking an early form of the Greek language entered Greece around 2000 B.C. Their language replaced that of the earlier inhabitants, which nonetheless left its mark on later Greek in the form of commonly used words with the terminations -*nthos* and -*ssos*, such as *olynthos* (a wild fig), *terebinthos* (the turpentine tree), *melissa* (the bee), *thalassa* (the sea), and place names such as Knossos and Corinth(os).

The first Greek speakers have traditionally been called the **Minyans,** after a type of pottery, Minyan ware, that was attributed to them. (Minyas was a legendary king of the area, and the pottery probably has nothing to do with him or his people, the "Minyans.") Minyan ware is a gray (or yellow), wheel-made pottery with a characteristic soapy feel that was made in a limited number of shapes that imitated silver (or gold) vessels. Today we know that Minyan ware was not an innovation brought by invading Greek speakers, but a development of earlier forms by skilled potters using a fast wheel and able to control the conditions of firing.[23] From the evidence of the pottery, therefore, it seems that the EH III settlement of Lerna IV (and of other sites like it) gradually passed into the Middle Helladic period, and these later potters, of greater skill, developed Minyan pottery. There was no sharp break in the pottery tradition such as might signal the intrusion of a new people. But, if that is the case, when did Greek-speaking people enter Greece?

The generally accepted date of ca. 2000 B.C. for the arrival of the Greeks would suggest that the newcomers were the Patterned Ware people, those believed to be responsible for destroying the House of Tiles and building Lerna IV. But nothing in the archaeological record suggests that these people came from some far-distant Indo-European homeland. Rather, they appear to have come from nearby Boeotia.[24]

Another theory, that of Colin Renfrew, suggests that proto Indo-European, the root language out of which Greek and other modern Indo-European languages developed, spread from its original home, probably in Anatolia, carried by the first farmers.[25] Renfrew's argument rests upon the assumption that a new language will prevail over an existing language only if the speakers of the new language have some clear superiority. In the case of Indo-Europeans, the superiority was that of their farming techniques, which allowed far more people to be supported on a given amount of land than hunting and gathering did. Since the beginning of farming in Greece can be traced back beyond 6000 B.C., the Greek language must have developed within Greece for a far longer period than the traditional account assumes.

Renfrew's theory is a complex one, involving a highly specialized subject— the development, change, and dissemination of languages and, in particular, the origin and development of the Indo-European languages. For its evaluation, the historian must await the decision of linguists, but the debate is an interesting and important one to follow, and one that has already generated a great deal of discussion.[26]

CONCLUSION

In the Neolithic period and the early Bronze Age, the mainland of Greece developed gradually and with continual setbacks from the time of the Franchthi Cave people through the village culture of Sesklo and Dimini, and into the beginnings of a more complex society such as we see at Lerna III. During this long span of time, the inhabitants perhaps also assimilated a new population and a new language.

Meanwhile, on the island of Crete, development through the Neolithic period and into the Bronze Age proceeded without such profound interruptions.

The island's location fostered contacts with the seafaring peoples of the Near East, and these people probably served as a source of tin and, perhaps, bronze technology, as well as of ideas about ways to organize the production and distribution of this valuable new metal. By the end of the third millennium B.C. a complex, palace-centered, and literate civilization had developed on the island. This civilization had vital, if indirect, effects on later Greek culture, as well as being important and interesting in itself, and it is to this culture that we turn next.

IMPORTANT PLACES IN CHAPTER 1

On Chapter Map: Aegean, Aegina, Anatolia, Argolid, Arkadia, Attica, Boeotia, Chalkidike, Crete, Cycladic Islands, Dimini, Epirus, Franchthi Cave, Gulf of Argos, Kavala, Lakonia, Lerna, Macedonia, Melos, Messenia, Peloponnesus, Pindos Mountains, Saronic Gulf, Sesklo, Strymon River, Thasos, Thebes, Thessaly, Tiryns

On Other Maps (*Use map index to find these*): Mesopotamia, Syria

SUGGESTIONS FOR FURTHER READING

An easy-to-read account of the ecology of Greece and its effect on the development of Greek culture and history can be found in Robin Osborne, *Classical Landscape with Figures: The Ancient Greek City and Its Countryside* (1987); on the Franchthi Cave, see T. W. Jacobsen, "17,000 Years of Greek Prehistory," *Scientific American* 234 (1976), 76–87; and for a woman's-eye view of prehistory, see M. Ehrenberg, *Women in Prehistory* (1989). On Lerna, see J. Caskey, "The Early Helladic Period in the Argolid," *Hesperia* 29 (1960), 285–303. The arrival of the Greeks is a vexing question; two rather different views are offered: see Colin Renfrew, *Archaeology and Language* (1987), and R. Drews, *The Coming of the Greeks* (1988).

ENDNOTES

1. Robin Osborne, *Classical Landscape with Figures: The Ancient Greek City and Its Countryside* (1987); more-technical books of interest include Thomas W. Gallant, *Risk and Survival in Ancient Greece: Reconstructing the Rural Domestic Economy* (1991); and Peter Garnsey, *Famine and Food Supply in the Graeco-Roman World* (1988).

2. The climate in the Neolithic was cooler and wetter; when the triad began to dominate the agricultural scene is a matter of dispute. See Robert Sallares, *The Ecology of the Ancient Greek World* (1991), 17–18, 32–33.

3. See Sallares (above, n. 2), 35, 390–394; Peter Garnsey, *Famine and Food Supply in the Graeco-Roman World* (1988), 8–14.

4. Osborne (above, n. 1).

5. A good discussion of the problems of farming can be found in Osborne (above, n. 1), chap. 2.

6. Plato, *Laws* 705a, tr. A. E. Taylor, in Edith Hamilton and Huntington Cairns, eds., *The Collected Dialogues of Plato.*

7. T. W. Jacobsen, "17,000 Years of Greek Prehistory," *Scientific American* 234 (1976), 76–87; "The Beginning of Settled Village Life in Greece," *Hesperia* 50 (1981), 303–318.

8. The discussion of these sites by Emily T. Vermeule, *Greece in the Bronze Age* (1972), has been outdated by more recent finds; see now D. Theocharis, *Neolithic Greece* (1973).

9. The work of the archaeologist M. Gimbutas has perhaps done most to further this scenario. See, for example, *The Goddesses and Gods of Old Europe* (1974), and *The Language of the Goddess* (1989). Gimbutas' work has appealed to many in the women's movement and has inspired other books, such as Pamela Berger, *The Goddess Obscured* (1985). Serious criticism is not lacking, but it is more likely to appear in scholarly journals or more specialized publications that get far less publicity, as, for example, Margaret Ehrenberg, *Women in Prehistory* (1989), 63–76.

10. Useful discussions can be found in Ehrenberg, 1989 (above, n. 9), 66–76, and in P. J. Ucko's classic study of figures from Crete, "The Interpretation of Prehistoric Anthropomorphic Figurines," *Journal of the Royal Anthropological Institute of Great Britain and Ireland* 92 (1962), 38–54.

11. Theocharis (above, n. 8), 66.

12. Theocharis (above, n. 8), fig. 56; National Archaeological Museum 5937.

13. On the copper resources of Greece, see V. McGeehan-Liritzis, "The Relationship between Metalwork, Copper Sources and the Evidence for Settlement in the Greek Late Neolithic and Early Bronze Age," *Oxford Journal of Archaeology* 2 (1983), 147–180.

14. On the possible sources of tin, see V. McGeehan-Liritzis and J. W. Taylor, "Yugoslavian Tin Deposits and the Early Bronze Age Industries of the Aegean Region," *Oxford Journal of Archaeology* 6 (1987), 287–300.

15. The archaeological dates are derived from pottery styles and can be only relative; these absolute dates, adopted from Warren and Hankey (1989), 169, with simplifications, are the latest estimates.

16. See J. Caskey, "The Early Helladic Period in the Argolid," *Hesperia* 29 (1960), 285–303.

17. See J. W. Shaw, "The Early Helladic II Corridor House," *American Journal of Archaeology* 91 (1987), 59–79; R. Hägg and D. Konsola, *Early Helladic Architecture and Urbanization* (1986), has a number of articles on the various examples that have been found.

18. See K. Killian, "The Circular Building at Tiryns," in Hägg and Konsola (above, n. 17).

19. Emily T. Vermeule, *Greece in the Bronze Age* (1972), 36.

20. The various views are well represented in Hägg and Konsola (above, n. 17); for an overview, see their conclusion, 95–100.

21. Colin Renfrew discusses the beginnings of civilization in the Aegean, arguing that no single factor was responsible, but that a number of factors interacted in a complex system of feedback, which he calls the *Multiplier Effect*. See his *The Emergence of Civilization: The Cyclades and the Aegean in the Third Millennium* (1972).

22. See Hiller's article in Hägg and Konsola (1986), 85–89.

23. J. B. Rutter, "Fine Gray-Burnished Pottery of the Early Helladic III Period: The Ancestry of Gray Minyan," *Hesperia* 52 (1983), 349.

24. J. B. Rutter, "Review of Aegean Prehistory II: The Prepalatial Bronze Age of the Southern and Central Mainland," *American Journal of Archaeology* 97 (1993), 745–797, 763–767.

25. Colin Renfrew, *Archaeology and Language* (1987).

26. See the series of reviews in *Current Anthropology* 29, 3 (1988), 437–468.

CHAPTER TWO

Myth and Archaeology: Minoan Crete[1]

One of the most fascinating chapters in the history of ancient Greece was provided by a non-Greek people living on the island of Crete. By the second millennium B.C. these people had created a palace civilization that rivaled, in many ways, the older civilizations of Mesopotamia and Egypt. They had elaborate palaces decorated with brightly colored wall paintings. They operated a highly regulated economy of collection and redistribution, keeping written records of even apparently minor transactions. Fine workmanship was perfected, and imported luxury items suggest they maintained diplomatic contacts or trading relationships, or both.

The modern world first learned of this highly sophisticated Cretan civilization through the stories of mythology that were passed down by the classical Greeks. For example, according to the fifth-century B.C. Greek historian Thucydides, Crete was the home of King Minos, the first ruler to control the sea (the Greek word for control over the sea is *thalassocracy*). Plato knew Minos as a wise legislator, although Greek myth also portrayed him as the possessor of the Minotaur, a terrifying monster that was half man, half bull. The Minotaur lived hidden away in the Labyrinth which the fabulous craftsman Daedalus had constructed for him, and every nine years the Athenians were forced to provide seven boys and seven girls to be fed to the beast. Relief came for the Athenians only when Theseus, the son of the king, volunteered to join the sacrificial contingent. Once in Crete, Theseus slew the Minotaur with the help of the Minoan princess Ariadne, with whom he then eloped (but whom he later abandoned). But did any historical truth lie behind the myth of Minos, the Labyrinth, and Minoan thalassocracy?

It is always a question whether, and to what extent, actual historical events

24

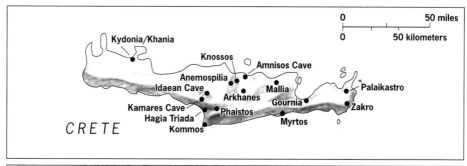

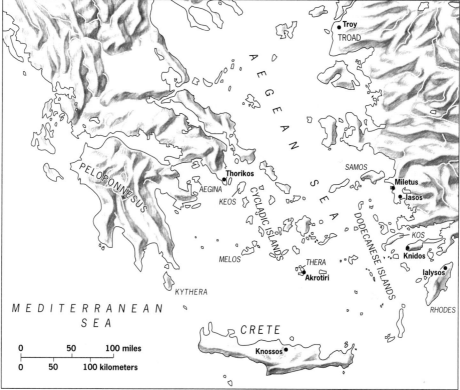

MAP 2   Bronze Age: Minoan Crete.

and situations are reflected and refracted in such oral traditions, and, if they are, how they can be extracted from the fabulous elements. The first suggestions that there might be a kernel of history in the tales of Minos came in the late nineteenth century, when Sir Arthur Evans, a wealthy enthusiast who was investigating hieroglyphic writing on seal stones found in Crete, discovered the remains of a vast labyrinthine palace at Knossos, near modern Heraklion. Evans excavated the complex, which he identified as the Palace of Minos; accordingly, he named the culture *Minoan,* a name that is still applied to the Bronze Age culture of Crete.[2]

Evans' finds seemed to confirm the legend of Minos with startling accuracy. The labyrinthine plan of the palace matched the Labyrinth within which the great Minotaur lived, and the bull played a central role in the imagery used in the wall paintings found in the palace and on seals. Two of the most frequently portrayed symbols are the so-called ***Horns of Consecration,*** which Evans interpreted as stylized bull's horns, and a double axe, possibly the sacrificial instrument (Figures 2-1 and 2-2).

Some sort of bull-leaping game or ritual was also portrayed on frescoes and seals. The acrobatic performers appear to have grasped the bull's horns as it charged, and somersaulted between the horns and over the back of the bull (Figure 2-3). Evans suggested that the large crowds shown watching some sort of spectacle in another fresco were watching bull-leaping (Figure 2-4). It is not known whether the bull-leaper or the bull (if either) was sacrificed in the bull-leaping, but the mythical story of the sacrifice of Athenian youths to the Minotaur suggests that the leapers did not enjoy a long life.

The palace at Knossos was the first of a number of similar building complexes, or palaces, on Crete that have since been found and excavated, including those at Phaistos in the south, near the port of Kommos; at Zakro, on the east-

FIGURE 2-1 Minoan horns of consecration, a frequently found symbol.

FIGURE 2-2   Miniature double axes in gold, another frequently found Minoan symbol; it appears in many forms, from rough inscriptions on pillars to oversize ceremonial models.

ern end of the island; and at Mallia, on the northeast coast.³ Similar complexes may have existed at the port of Khania in the west and at Palaikastro and Arkhanes. In addition, numerous smaller outlying settlements and large country houses, some with palatial features ("minipalaces"), such as Hagia Triada in the vicinity of Phaistos, have been discovered. Excavation of these sites, the study of the written records found in them, and archaeological surveys that document settlement patterns are slowly yielding a still-fragmented and shifting picture of Bronze Age Crete. In the meantime, the colorfully restored ruins of Knossos have become a major tourist attraction, and the spectacular discoveries of a Minoan-Cycladic town buried essentially intact by a volcanic eruption on the nearby island of Thera have contributed to the popular fascination with Minoan Crete. But before we look more closely at King Minos and his subjects, it will be helpful to consider what is known about how this great palace system came into being.

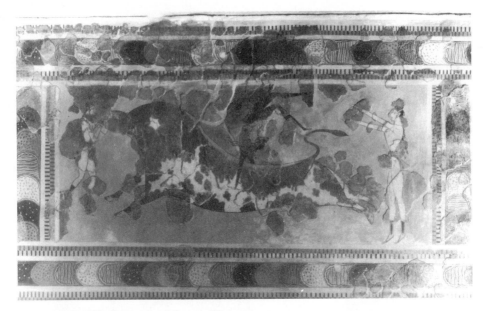

FIGURE 2-3 "Bull-Leaping" fresco, Knossos.

PRE-MINOAN CRETE

By the mid-third millennium B.C. (Early Minoan II, or EM II, see the Appendix on Minoan chronology on pp. 50–51), when the House of Tiles and other large buildings appear on the mainland of Greece, somewhat similar developments were taking place in Crete. In fact, several building complexes believed by some to have been protopalaces (forerunners of the well-known later palaces at Knossos, Mallia, Phaistos, and Zakro) have been discovered. The best known of these is Myrtos,[4] where a cellular building complex of about 100 rooms included an

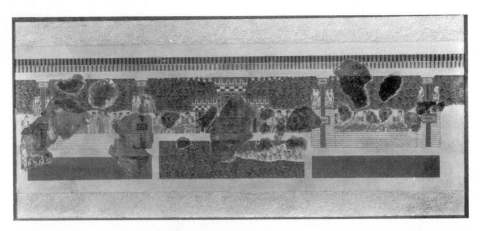

FIGURE 2-4 "Grandstand" fresco, Knossos.

unpaved court, living rooms, kitchens, storerooms with giant clay storage jars, workshops, and a shrine (Figure 2-5). The economy was one of mixed farming and crafts, including specialized production of wine, olive oil, pottery, and textiles. The inhabitants had mastered the arts of making stone vases and cutting seals in stone and ivory. At about the same time, the first Minoan "colony" was also established when a group of Cretans made a settlement on the island of Kythera, off the coast of the Peloponnesus (it may, however, have been only a seasonal fishing camp at first).

Peter Warren interpreted the labyrinthine remains of Myrtos as a miniature prototype of the later Minoan palaces, a nucleus from which the later palace-form developed. And, in fact, the complex at Myrtos did possess some noteworthy architectural features that were characteristic of the later palaces: light wells, use of wall timbers, narrow corridors, storage rooms, central courts, painted walls, wide paved staircases, and intramural wells.

The variety of opinions on the archaeological remains at Myrtos, however, provides a good illustration of some of the difficulties involved in the interpretation of archaeological evidence. While Warren saw the settlement as a protopalace with areas devoted to specialized production and storage, another archaeologist, Tod Whitelaw, interpreted the evidence quite differently. He differentiated periods of occupation, identified the uses of the various rooms, and defined individual houses.[5] As a result, he concluded that only five or six households lived in Myrtos

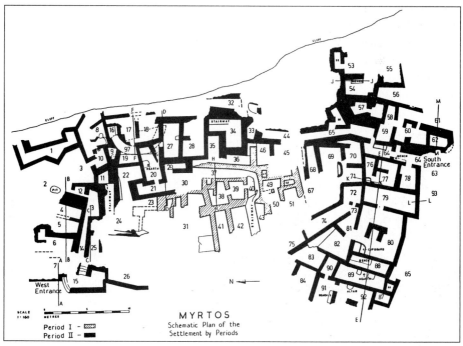

FIGURE 2-5 Site plan of Myrtos (after Warren).

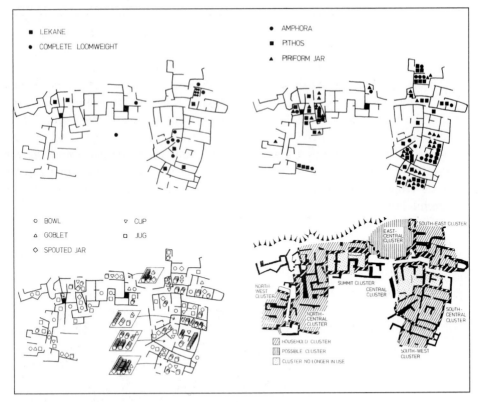

Figure 2-6 Site plan of Myrtos (after Whitelaw).

at any one time, and that production was on a subsistence level, with each household providing for all of its own needs. Therefore, Whitelaw argued that Myrtos could not be seen as a protopalace. Some of Whitelaw's plans are reproduced in Figure 2-6.[6]

In the early Middle Minoan period (MM IA–MM II, 2000–1700 B.C.), the first true palaces were built on Crete using the techniques of monumental *ashlar masonry,* in which buildings were constructed of square-cut and dressed blocks of stone. Writing in a hieroglyphic script began as well. The idea of writing may have originated in Egypt, although the forms of the signs show little dependence on Egyptian hieroglyphics. Other innovations included the potter's wheel and a number of new vase shapes that reflect Near Eastern influence; in particular, animal-shaped libation vessels and bowls with miniature interior figures appear to have been adopted from Near Eastern cult. While palace control over various aspects of life appears to have rapidly escalated during this period, it was not total, for large granaries for communal storage were still located outside the palaces. The period ended about 1700 B.C. with the widespread destruction of the palaces, perhaps by earthquake, perhaps by warfare between the palaces, or by a combination of the two.

S O U R C E   A N A L Y S I S

Examine the plans for the palaces at Knossos, Phaistos, Mallia, and Zakro (Figures 2-7, 2-8, 2-9, and 2-10). Note the similarities and differences between the plans, keeping in mind the scale according to which each was drawn. In particular, note the orientation of each palace and compare the dimensions and proportions of the central courts; find the storage areas, and locate stairways and pillar-and-door construction, which may indicate living quarters. Is similarity in layout good evidence for the exercise of central control over all the palaces?

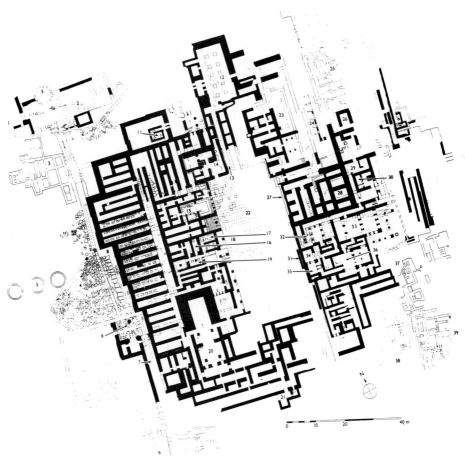

FIGURE 2-7 Site plan of Knossos.

continued

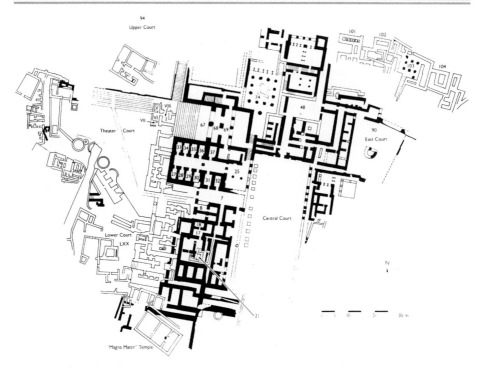

FIGURE 2-8   Site plan of Phaistos.

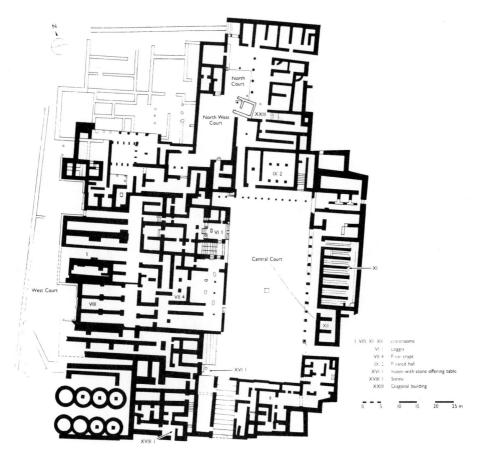

FIGURE 2-9 Site plan of Mallia.

continued

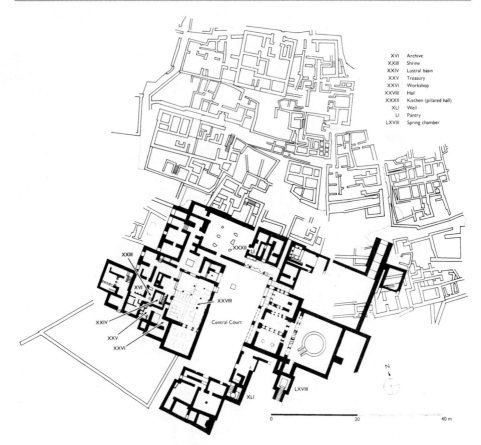

XVI	Archive
XXIII	Shrine
XXIV	Lustral basin
XXV	Treasury
XXVI	Workshop
XXVIII	Hall
XXXII	Kitchen (pillared hall)
XLI	Well
LI	Pantry
LXVIII	Spring chamber

FIGURE 2-10 Site plan of Zakro.

THE NEW PALACES

After the destructions at the palaces at the end of MM II, new palaces were built on the sites of the old palaces, but on a far grander scale. The period from about 1650 to 1450 B.C. (MM IIIB–LM IB) is accordingly often called the *New Palace period*. At Knossos, the "new palace" is the palace that Evans excavated.

Prominent among the features that characterize the New Palaces are the storage areas, which by this time had been moved within the palace. The most typical form of storage was the long, narrow room, or **magazine**, lined with rows of large clay storage jars **(pithoi)**, some as tall as 5 feet, which were used for the storage of grain, oil, wine, and olives. Later, cists were cut in the floor and lined with waterproof material for the storage of fine textiles and other treasures.

Other characteristic elements of the palaces were light wells, often built in conjunction with stairways, and ***pillar-and-door partitions*** (walls made up of a series of pillars with inset doors that could be opened or closed as the weather dictated). Both features provided light and air to the internal rooms of the palace.

All the palaces appear to have been built outward from a central court in a style that has been called *agglutinative*, as if elements were added on as needed to the core feature of the court. The plan extending out from the central court was labyrinthine, as myth would lead us to expect. None of the palaces have external defensive walls.

In addition to the central court, all the palaces have *west courts*, paved areas adjacent to the west facade that were open to the surrounding town, providing a place of interaction between palace and people.[7] The west courts of the Old Palaces were the sites of granaries, and the west wings of the New Palaces contained extensive storage rooms. Storage areas appear to have had religious connections: the double axe is frequently found cut into the pillars and walls of the storerooms, and storerooms communicate directly with rooms identified as shrines, or *crypts* (basement rooms with a central pillar; their religious significance is suggested by double axes or adjacent offering tables). The west wings were also the sites of rooms that are viewed as having had more formal ceremonial or religious uses. At Knossos, these include a throne room with its adjacent ***lustral basin,*** in which a few steps lead down to what has been interpreted as a ritual pool. The apparent religious associations of the storerooms suggest that the divinity was considered to be the recipient and owner of the rooms' contents. Here Cyprus provides a parallel, although from the Late Bronze Age: Cypriot workshops for the production of copper were often located adjacent to shrines, and figures of divinities standing on miniature copper ingots have been identified as images of an Ingot God.[8] In Cyprus, the vital activity of copper production was thus brought under divine protection, and a similar situation may be reflected in the conjunction of storage and workshop facilities and shrines in the Minoan palaces. In three of the west courts, raised walkways were provided, perhaps used by the people of the town to bring offerings to be stored in the palace during a harvest or other religious celebration. This viewpoint supports the model which sees social storage as a key factor in the development of the palace (discussed below).

To the east of the central court at Knossos were apartments that Evans identified as the private living quarters of the ruler.[9] In addition to light wells and pillar-and-door partitions, provisions for comfortable living included bathrooms and flushable toilets connected to the extensive drainage system of the palace. In

keeping with Evans' nineteenth-century assumptions, when there were two similar sets of rooms, one, the larger, has been designated the King's Quarters,
while the smaller suite has been identified as the Queen's.

The wall paintings also provide valuable, if sometimes cryptic, clues to
palace life.[10] Animals appear, especially the bull, and there are numerous scenes
of human activity of a formal nature: processions, dancing, banqueting, bull-
leaping, and a large crowd gathered for a public performance. Scenes including
representations of parts of the palace itself gave Evans clues for his reconstruction. A noteworthy fresco portrays figures identified as tribute bearers; it lines
the walls of the entry corridor at Knossos, perhaps mirroring the anticipated activity of some of those who would use the entrance. The figures resemble those
found in Egyptian tomb paintings that are labeled **Keftiu** (People of the Islands),
thus supporting other evidence of Minoan contact with Egypt.

Many aspects of the scenes raise more questions than they answer. For example, women appear not only in greater numbers than men do, but often as the
largest figures, providing the focus of the scene (in later Greek art, larger size
denotes divinity). In particular, in the assembled crowd in the "Grandstand"
fresco (see Figure 2-4 on page 28) a group of women stand out by virtue of their
prominent position, large size, and carefully detailed portrayal; they were apparently privileged spectators at a public performance attended by masses of people, both men and women. Another well-known fresco of a woman is known as
"La Parisienne"; she is a central female figure who dominates a male banqueting
scene (Figure 2-11). Still unanswered questions include whether the predominance of women in the frescoes reflects the actual position of women in Minoan
society, and whether these figures represent ordinary women, priestesses, or divinities.

All of the frescoes were found in a fragmentary state and required extensive
reconstruction. In some cases, the early reconstructions done by Evans have
been shown by later research to have surpassed the evidence, incorporating assumptions of his own era. For example, Evans identified one figure as the Minoan "Priest-King," yet there is no evidence that the figure was a priest or a
king, or even, for that matter, a male (Figure 2-12).[11] Another revision of Evans'
interpretation involves the "Dolphin" fresco (Figure 2-13). Although there is
nothing intrinsically feminine about the dolphin motif in Minoan iconography,
Evans saw it as feminine and therefore identified the area in which the fragments were found as the Queen's Quarters. He also restored the fresco as a wall
painting. Further study has shown, however, that the fragments had fallen from
the room above, where the fresco had originally decorated the floor. Subsequently, the claim has been made that the dolphin was a Minoan symbol of
priestly power.[12] If this proves to be the case, the fresco may have adorned a
shrine rather than the dressing room of a queen.

In addition to the palaces and their adjoining towns, numerous smaller

FIGURE 2-11 "La Parisienne" fresco, Knossos.

building complexes have been found. Some were located in outlying towns, such as Gournia (Figure 2-14). Other building complexes appear in the countryside, where they seem to have served as both working farms and luxurious homes. Some, such as the complex at Hagia Triada, may have been summer retreats for the inhabitants of nearby palaces.[13]

Linking this hierarchy of architectural forms with the evidence that sealings found at various locations were made by the same seal, historians have concluded that Crete in the New Palace period was organized in a hierarchical network in which local rulers or governors functioned under the central control of the palace at Knossos. This is in contrast with the Old Palace period, when the existence of fortified sites and the evidence of burnt destructions of palaces and other buildings may reflect the presence of several independent and warring states on the island.[14] If this reading of the archaeological evidence is correct,

FIGURE 2-12 "Priest-King" fresco, Knossos. This was the most likely candidate for a portrayal of a ruler, but few now accept this identification.

those unsettled conditions may have given rise to the overlordship of Knossos and to the expression of a hierarchical system of control in a hierarchy of various sites.

Our understanding of the Minoan palaces is based not only upon evidence of architecture and frescoes, but also upon the records that were kept in the palaces. These records were written in a script called **_Linear A._** Linear A was a

FIGURE 2-13 "Dolphin" fresco, Knossos. Restored to the wall of the "Queen's Megaron," it is now known to have fallen from the floor above.

writing system in which the symbols stood for syllables rather than the individual sounds represented in an alphabetic system. It was inscribed on small clay tablets while the clay was still wet; occasionally inscriptions have also been found on portable objects. Even though Linear A cannot yet be read, much information is being teased out of it by detailed study.[15] Many tablets clearly contain accounts of products, for they use ideograms recognizable as indicators for grain, wine, olive oil, and figs. Inscriptions found on storage jars may identify or characterize the contents or indicate the owner or producer.

Linear A script was used for a variety of purposes besides the keeping of economic records. One such use appears to have been religious, as attested by the inscriptions found on portable objects that are similar to later Greek libation vessels and other cultic equipment. The repetition of certain groups of signs on various objects and the resemblance of these objects to later Greek cult equipment suggest their ritual character. No evidence exists for the literary use of Linear A, but it is likely that the tablets that have survived were meant merely for temporary use—only their accidental baking in the fires that destroyed the

SOURCE ANALYSIS

an you locate the "palace" in the site plan of Gournia?

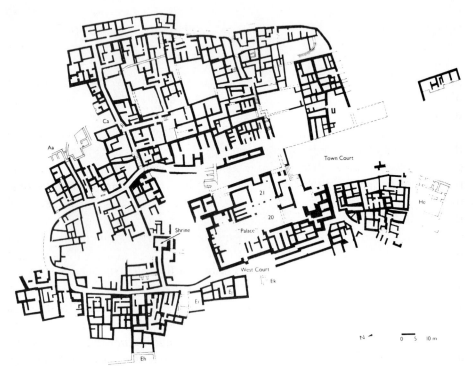

FIGURE 2-14 Site plan of Gournia.

palaces preserved them. More permanent records, and perhaps even literary or religious texts, may have been kept on more valuable, albeit less durable, substances such as papyrus or parchment.

Linear A inscriptions have been found not only in palaces, but also in villa and town sites. The use of the script in so many different locations, and for differing purposes, implies that facility with it was relatively widespread, at least in comparison to that of the later Linear B script. Since Linear A contains fewer than one hundred signs, in contrast to the approximately six hundred signs used in the cuneiform writing of Mesopotamia and the thousand or so signs—out of a repertory of several thousand—that were in common use in Egyptian hiero-glyphics, its use need not have been limited to professional scribes.

From the evidence of extensive storage areas and the finds of Linear A records in the palaces, it is clear that the palaces served as more than just centers of craft production. Grain, oil, wine, wool, flax, metals, and precious materials such as ivory and gold were brought into the palace to be stored; from these stores, food rations went to workers and officials, and raw materials to craft workers, who produced both utilitarian objects (such as weapons and military equipment) and luxury items. All materials entering or being distributed from the palace were carefully documented, as were workers, officials, animal herds, landholdings, and offerings to the gods. A primary function of the Minoan palace was thus as an economic center of collection, storage, and redistribution of the basic necessities of life (although the redistribution may have been mainly to the privileged few).

In their role as the hubs of a palace economy, the Minoan palaces resembled the palaces of the Near East, although the typical Near Eastern institution of a powerful temple paralleling and possibly rivaling the palace is not similarly prominent in Crete. One freestanding temple has been found; it provides dra-matic evidence of a human sacrifice interrupted by an earthquake that destroyed the building, killing the three officiants.[16] But this temple was destroyed in about 1700 B.C., probably in an earthquake that also played a role in the destruc-tion of the Old Palaces, and subsequently the temple form appears incorporated into the New Palaces. In the period of the New Palaces, at least, Cretan reli-gious functions seem to have been carried out in the palace itself and, as we shall see, in outlying sacred spots with palatial connections, rather than in an inde-pendent structure and institution. Shrines, cult equipment, and religious motifs have been identified throughout the palaces, and religious and cult roles seem to have been played by the personnel of the palaces rather than by independent "outsiders." In fact, some have even interpreted the Minoan "palace" itself as a cult center—a temple-palace or palace-temple.[17]

MINOAN RELIGION IN THE LIFE OF THE PEOPLE

The central role played by religion in the palace system could have been instru-mental in solidifying the authority of the ruler only insofar as it extended be-yond the palace to the people themselves. That it did play such a role, linking the concerns of ordinary people with those of the palace, is suggested by the ex-istence of extrapalatial shrines, centered on natural features such as caves, peaks, and trees, that exhibit signs of palatial connections.[18]

About 45 "peak" sanctuaries have been identified in Crete. They tend to be on rather easily accessible sites located between 350 and 1000 meters above sea level and are usually in summer grazing zones. They may have begun as the sacred places of shepherds, for votive offerings included many miniature terracotta sheep and goats, but most are close to, and visible from, a settlement. There is evidence that fire played a central role in the cult, and nighttime ceremonies with giant fires would have provided an impressive spectacle viewed from the nearby settlement. Votives included replicas of creatures helpful to the farmers who lived in such villages, such as weasels (which eat mice) and beetles (which aerate the soil). That the divinities also served the popular role of healers is also suggested by offerings of replicas of human arms, legs, heads, and torsos.

The peak shrines appeared at the same time as the Old Palaces, and each palace had a major peak shrine in its near vicinity. There is evidence that the relationship between the sanctuaries and the palaces increased over time. In the New Palace period, ashlar masonry building techniques characteristic of palace construction were used in monumental buildings at the shrines, and prestigious votives such as the collection of miniature gold axes (see Figure 2-2) and offering tables inscribed in Linear A attest to a palatial presence among the worshippers.[19] Such a shrine is pictured on a stone ritual vessel from the palace of Zakros, on which mountain goats gambol about a fine ashlar masonry shrine adorned with Horns of Consecration.

Caves were also favored places of devotion and such shrines were frequented by both the exalted and the humble. Evidence of worship has been found in at least fifteen caves. A number of different gods, each with a specific function, appear to have been worshipped in these caves. In some, the dedications, such as prestigious weapons and collections of miniature double axes in gold, attest palatial connections. This fits well with the tradition reported by Plato that King Minos sought out Zeus in the Idaean Cave every eight years in order to renew his royal power.[20] In contrast, in one of the more famous cave shrines, at Amnisos, only humble pottery figurines were offered to the goddess of childbirth, *Eileithyia* (the later Greek name).

Another type of extrapalatial cult place was the countryside tree shrine. Since the remains of such shrines would usually be slight and isolated, and therefore unlikely to be found by archaeologists, most of our evidence for them comes from portrayals on gold rings and seals. In these sanctuaries, a large tree was the central feature. It was usually enclosed by a wall, which often also enclosed an altar or even a temple building. Ecstatic activity or dancing around the tree is frequently portrayed. Such shrines, despite their rural locations, could not have been only places of peasant worship, for the evidence of their existence comes from objects of great value.

The overall picture of Minoan religion is one of local religious practices that were institutionalized in support of the power of the palaces. Cult activities were brought into the palaces or, when this was not possible, were associated with them by monumental architecture and ceremonies in which prestigious offerings were made to the divinity.

THE QUESTION OF ORIGINS

The similarity of the Minoan palaces to palaces in the Near East and the fact that the Old Palaces appear to have sprung up very suddenly in about 1900 B.C. have naturally raised the question of Near Eastern influence on the development of the palaces, and a variety of interpretations of the type and degree of influence has been offered. On the other hand, some scholars argue for independent development. We will consider some of the arguments for each of these views.

Perhaps the strongest case for Near Eastern influence is the sudden appearance in Crete not only of palaces but of a cluster of features associated with the palatial buildings of the Near East, especially Syria: monumental structures build in ashlar masonry, specialized production, writing, and an extensive administrative system of seal usage. A comparison of the palace at Mari in Syria (Figure 2-15) with the Cretan palace at Mallia (Figure 2-9) reveals both similarities and differences.

Although the Minoan palaces share many features with the Near Eastern palace as exemplified by Mari, there are some fundamental differences that rule out a simple cookie-cutter model of influence. The most basic architectural difference is that the palace at Mari was strongly fortified; the defensive outer walls had priority and served as the determining factor for the interior plan of the palace. That is, the palace was built from the outside in. In contrast, Minoan palaces lack defensive external walls and seem to have been built from the inside out, with a notable lack of concern for symmetry and formal order, giving the effect of spontaneous growth. Nevertheless, similarities in the various Cretan palaces suggest that the builders did follow at least a general plan.

Arguments for the indigenous origin of the palaces include that of Peter Warren, noted above, who argued that Myrtos was a *protopalace*, a form from which later palaces could have been developed. Another such explanation involves the model of social storage as argued by P. M. Halstead.[21] Halstead reasoned that people in Crete, which is characterized by a high degree of localized climatic variation, had adopted the strategy of communal food storage and exchange to protect against localized crop failures: if everyone put his harvest into storage, then everyone could share in the common resources, even those unlucky individuals whose crops had failed that season. Exchanges with neighboring communities would have extended the safety network. An added advantage was that some of the harvest of good years could be stored against the possibility of a more generalized bad year for the community. Surplus could also be stored

S O U R C E   A N A L Y S I S

C ompare the plans for the palace at Mari with those of the Minoan palaces. What similarities do you see? What differences?

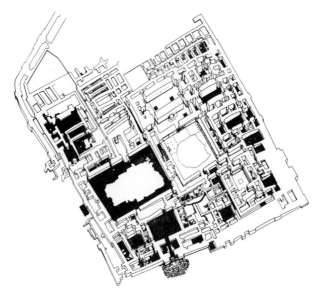

Figure 2-15   Site plan of Mari.

"on the hoof"—that is, by being fed to sheep. The animals could be eaten if necessary, but under normal conditions they would provide wool to make cloth, a desirable item for trade. The large storage facilities of the palaces, including the communal granaries outside the Old Palaces, and the large numbers of sheep (about 100,000) documented in the records of the last stage of the palaces' existence provide evidence that the Minoans did make use of such survival strategies. Once the stores were created, of course, control over their distribution became a source of power in itself. Those who were able to exercise this control were able to determine the utilization and distribution of community resources, and they could use those resources to obtain not only bronze for weapons but also other valuable imports that would enhance their own status. Moreover, as caretakers of the grain and animal resources, they appeared as the human assistants of the divinities of fertility, a role that sanctioned their control of the resources. We do seem to see such a situation in the New Palaces, where storage was brought into the palace and associated with religious symbols and with the throne room itself.

At this time, we have no definitive answer to the question of the origins of the palaces on Crete. Probably, however, the question should not be framed in terms of indigenous versus foreign influence. While similarities between the situation on Crete and the Near Eastern kingdoms are too striking to ignore, Cretan awareness of the Near Eastern palaces, through trade contacts or otherwise, cannot account for the development of an entire palace economy in Crete. A people do not just decide to build palaces and organize their economy around them because they have seen others do this. Certain local conditions are necessary first. There must be a sufficiently strong economic base—a large enough population to furnish the labor force for monumental building, and a surplus capable of sustaining that working force along with the nonworking elite—as well as a system of social control that sanctions gross disparities in status and living conditions. Thus, foreign influence and indigenous development must have worked together; neither alone can provide an adequate explanation.

WAS THERE A MINOAN THALASSOCRACY?

The ancient Greek historian Thucydides claimed that King Minos was the first to establish a navy, conquer and colonize the Cycladic Islands, and free the sea from pirates, exercising a thalassocracy (Thuc. 1.4). Evans accepted this idea. But was Thucydides right? Working in the fifth century B.C., without the evidence revealed by modern archaeology, Thucydides had little to go on beyond mythological tales. Did the tradition of a Minoan thalassocracy contain a kernel of historical truth, or was it simply a fairy tale, or perhaps even a fifth-century B.C. invention to justify Athens' own naval empire?[22]

The widespread distribution of Minoan pottery, which has been found at sites throughout the eastern Mediterranean and as far west as the Lipari Islands north of Sicily, seems at first consideration to support the hypothesis of a thalassocracy. But *thalassocracy* means "command of the seas," and that, given ancient sailing conditions, means control over landing spots and harbors, which, in turn, suggests settlement. Pots may have been simply items of trade, carried by others besides Minoans; they need not attest the presence of Minoans either as traders or as settlers, let alone as masters of the seas. Stronger evidence for settlement is provided by finds of the artifacts of daily living: ordinary kitchen pottery, Minoan techniques in building construction or architectural features, frescoes in the Minoan style, Minoan cult practices and burial customs, or Linear A tablets (not necessarily all at any one site).

Most of the evidence supporting the notion of overseas contact comes from the palatial periods, and most impressively from the New Palace period. Nevertheless, evidence for Minoan settlement overseas begins in the prepalatial period, when archaeological finds on the island of Kythera, off the southern coast of the Peloponnesus, attest that Minoans established themselves, having driven out the original inhabitants. In the New Palace period, this settlement was revived and enlarged; moreover, a Minoan presence becomes evident on a number of Aegean islands.

Why would the Minoans have left their fertile land for the relatively infertile Greek islands? One clue may be found on the island of Keos, which lies off the Attic coast opposite the Laurion mines and their deposits of silver, lead, and copper. Evidence confirms that copper was smelted on Keos, and there was also a significant Minoan presence there.[23] In the Bronze Age, large supplies of bronze were essential to national security, just as oil is essential to the running of the modern economy, and Crete lacked both tin and significant sources of copper, necessary ingredients for bronze production. There were also copper deposits on some of the Cycladic Islands and in the southern Peloponnesus. These deposits may explain the Minoan interest in these places, or rather, in island stepping stones to them, such as Kythera, Keos, Thera, and Melos.

The Minoans, to find tin, had to go further afield. Sources existed in southeastern Anatolia, although it is still unclear whether they were in use at this time; more likely is a source in Elam, supplied via the Syrian state of Mari, and, after Mari's destruction by Hammurabi in 1757 B.C., via Aleppo. Minoans consequently settled in the chain of the Dodecanese Islands and on Rhodes, creating settlements that provided stopping places on the voyage east. The settlers might also have been visited by itinerant Syrian merchants carrying tin and copper. The Late Bronze Age shipwreck off the southern coast of Turkey, discussed in the next chapter, provides a later example of such merchants who traveled to various ports with supplies of copper and tin and metalworking tools to sell metal and to produce items to order.[24] In the same area, copper was also available on nearby Cyprus. While the lead isotope evidence for Minoan use of Cypriot copper at this period is not strong, the fact that the script used on Cyprus was a form of Minoan Linear A must reflect significant early relations between the two peoples.[25]

Another metal route went up the east Anatolian coast to Troy and the Troad, another possible source of copper or bronze.[26] Evidence of a Minoan presence has been found at a number of staging points along this route: the Anatolian sites of Knidos, Miletus, Iasos, and the islands of Kos and Samos. Whether these were full-scale colonies or small enclaves of traders settled among local people is still not clear.

The evidence for a Minoan presence on the island of Thera is particularly important because of the size and prosperity of the Bronze Age city of Akrotiri and its sudden destruction by a volcanic eruption.[27] Thera is the southernmost of the Cycladic Islands, lying about 60 miles to the north of Crete. Today it has the form of a steep, rocky semicircle, part of the rim of a volcanic *caldera*, or cone. In LM IA, a major eruption caused the center of the volcanic island to collapse, leaving only parts of the rim exposed above the water, and burying Akrotiri beneath layers of pumice and ash up to 60 meters deep. The absolute date of the eruption is a hotly contested matter among archaeologists, as we note in the discussion of chronology in the Appendix on pp. 50–51. For a long time it was dated ca. 1500 B.C., but recent evidence from ice cores in Greenland and tree rings in the United States and Ireland suggests a much earlier date, ca. 1628 B.C., and this is now widely accepted.[28]

In 1967, the Greek archaeologist Spyridon Marinatos began the excavation of Akrotiri on the basis of sporadic local finds, including masses of stone that obstructed ploughing. The excavations have revealed seventeen buildings to date, ten of which have been explored, and the limits of the city have so far not been discovered.

Akrotiri lay at a focal point on all of the metal routes and must have possessed a south-facing port that was capable of provisioning ships and crews and serving as a base for assembling ships to sail in convoy. The houses that have been excavated are those of a prosperous people. Many have two or three stories, and the walls are often decorated with frescoes. Apparently the inhabitants had some warning of the impending disaster and were able to escape, for no signs of bodies or abandoned treasures have been found. However, the remains of a great deal of pottery and stored food, and the impressions left by wooden furniture, as well as the frescoes, provide evidence of the nature of life in Akrotiri.

Analyses of the architecture, pottery, and wall paintings of Thera have provided a picture of strong Minoan influence upon a basically Cycladic Island culture. Typical Minoan features appear in the architecture: a lustral basin, one apparent light well (but since the houses were freestanding, the need for light wells might not have been great), pillar-and-door construction, large central pillars, frescoes, the use of timber in wall construction to lessen earthquake damage, and a drainage system. Other evidence of Minoan influence on Thera includes the use of a Minoan system of weights, some inscriptions in Minoan Linear A script on jars (but no tablets), Minoan symbols such as the Horns of Consecration, and more Minoan pottery than at any other site, even on Crete itself, with the exception of Knossos.

The Akrotiri frescoes confirm this picture. While the style of the paintings is Minoan, it has a Cycladic bent: the approach is more naturalistic and less conventionalized than the Minoan frescoes. Human figures appear in apparently nonceremonial contexts; among these are fishermen, children boxing (if this is not a puberty rite),[29] and the various scenes of expedition activity in and around settlements.[30] But the differences between Theran and Cretan frescoes may also reflect the fact that the Theran paintings decorated private homes, while most of the Cretan paintings were found on palace sites.

The most interesting of the Theran frescoes in terms of the question of a

Figure 2-16 "Expedition" fresco, Thera.

Minoan thalassocracy is the miniature "Expedition" fresco, which decorated the walls of a room in the West House (Figure 2-16).[31] It depicts a fleet of eight ships, accompanied by many smaller boats, about to arrive at a (Minoan?) town, having passed by a river landscape reminiscent of the Nile, after leaving another town (in Africa?); a raid on still another town is also portrayed. The rowers of the ships are Minoan in dress and appearance, but some scholars identify the soldiers as a people of mainland Greece, the Mycenaeans.[32] An adjoining room in the same house is decorated with frescoes portraying the cabin of a ship that appears in the Expedition Fresco, and the house has therefore been identified as that of the ship's captain.[33] Were the mainland Mycenaeans serving as mercenaries for the people of Thera? If the fresco represents a military-commercial expedition, it might be evidence for a Minoan thalassocracy. Caution in forming conclusions is suggested, however, by another reading of the scenes in the fresco. Striking similarities have been pointed out between these scenes and themes familiar from Homeric poetry: the juxtaposition of a city at war and in peace, the cattle raid, the attack on a city, Egypt as a land of fantasy.[34] Evidence that epic poetry began as early as the Mycenaean and Minoan periods is growing, and the Expedition Fresco may contribute to this. The events it portrays may not have been a biographical record of the life of the owner of the house, but episodes in a favorite epic poem, recited for the Theran men who gathered in this room to drink and listen to bards sing of far-off adventures.

The Theran picture is one of a strong Minoan cultural veneer overlying a basically Cycladic community; in this it is typical of a number of other, smaller Cycladic communities. The question is whether these Cycladic peoples were simply adopting Minoan fashions as a result of frequent contacts with a richer, more sophisticated culture, or whether Minoans were actually living on the site, and, if they were living there, whether they were present unofficially, perhaps as traders, or officially, in order to control a subject people.

The case for an exercise of Minoan control has been made recently by M. H. Wiener, who argued that the differences in population, resources, and organization on Crete as compared with the smaller Cycladic communities would have made Minoan control likely.[35] Signs of the exercise of central control on Crete itself might be seen in the relative size of the palace at Knossos and its cultural hegemony as expressed in architecture and pottery, and the impressions of sealings made by the same seals at various locations in Crete. There are also signs that peaceful conditions were being maintained by forceful methods— roads guarded by watchtowers, Minoan expertise in the manufacture of bronze weapons, and portrayals of battles on the Expedition Fresco.[36] Moreover, Wiener points to the wealth of luxury goods and copper ingots stored at the port site of Zakro as a reflection of the Minoans' dependence upon imports for copper, tin, and bronze, and their interest in Near Eastern luxury items, all of which depended upon the safety of the seas. But was it the Minoans who policed the seas through the exercise of a thalassocracy?

A recent discovery adds new evidence, and new puzzles, to the picture of Minoan overseas contacts. At a site in the Egyptian delta called *Tell ed-Daba'a*, frescoes portraying Minoan-style scenes of bull-leaping have been discovered. These frescoes have been dated towards the end of the sixteenth century B.C., and during the period of Hyksos rule in Egypt.[37] It is not yet clear whether the paintings were created by Minoan craftsmen or whether they were imitations of Minoan work, or why someone chose to have them painted at this Egyptian site. At this point there is no other evidence that would indicate the presence of a Minoan settlement at the site, but it has been suggested that the scenes were painted for a Minoan princess who had been sent to Egypt for a dynastic marriage. If that were the case, it would show that the Egyptian royal house considered the Minoans of sufficient significance to forge a diplomatic marriage tie with them. Added to passages in Egyptian documents that refer to Crete and the "Islands in the Middle of the Great Green" as a single entity, this would tend to support the arguments for a Minoan thalassocracy.[38]

MINOAN SOCIETY—CONVENTIONAL VIEWS

The picture of Minoan society that has traditionally been drawn from the evidence of the palaces, frescoes, and pottery is one of a happy, carefree people living peacefully in comfortable, light-filled palaces, luxuriating in a flourishing natural landscape and seascape, and celebrating a goddess whose central position enabled human females as well to enjoy high regard and play a central role in society. Perhaps the Cretan landscape and climate, so appealing to archaeologists—many of whom are used to the harsher environments of northern Europe and the United States—also contributed in luring scholars to draw this utopian picture of Minoan life. But some cautions are in order.

The Minoan peace may have been less complete than we assume. While it seems that the New Palaces lacked conventional defensive walls, signs of fortification of the Old Palaces suggest that an early period of strife was brought to an end by the establishment of the central power of Knossos. Moreover, in the New Palace period, as we have seen, suggestions of the use of force and the exercise of sea power, such as the "Expedition" fresco may offer, do exist, even though it is still unclear whether Minoan activities reached a level that could be deemed a thalassocracy.

Most of the frescoes portray an apparently carefree people, and the palaces seem to have been designed to provide comfort and a pleasant environment for their inhabitants. But the frescoes and palaces were designed for the rulers. The bull-leapers in the fresco may not have been enjoying the "sport," and we do not know how happy and carefree the workers were who lived under the control of the palaces, or how comfortable and convenient their homes were. Nor do we know that all women shared in the apparent high status and freedom of those portrayed as central figures in the frescoes, who probably are to be identified as priestesses or nobility, if not as divinities. While it is true that the palaces and artifacts of the Minoan rulers present an enticing vision of life, it is *their* vision. The historian needs to assess it for what it is, remaining always on the lookout for the small clues that may enable him or her to see beneath the palatial facade.

APPENDIX: THE CHRONOLOGY OF THE BRONZE AGE

When Sir Evans excavated the palace at Knossos, he established a tripartite system of dating that still forms the basis of Bronze Age chronology. It provides a series of relative dates based on pottery sequences; absolute dates are then derived from the correlation of pottery sequences with datable Near Eastern objects and events. The result is a division of Bronze Age Crete into *Early Minoan*, *Middle Minoan*, and *Late Minoan* periods (EM, MM, and LM), each of which is in turn subdivided into three, and then further subdivided as needed. This results in designations such as MM II A1. Similar tripartite schemes have been developed for the mainland (Early, Middle, and Late Helladic: EH, MH, and LH) and the islands (Early, Middle, and Late Cycladic: EC, MC, and LC).

It is important to be familiar with this system of pottery dating as well as with the corresponding absolute dates. In many archaeological publications only

the relative dates are given because, in this early period, the connections between the relative and the absolute dates are few and are subject to change with
new evidence. For example, recent debate about the dating of the eruption of
the volcanic island of Thera seriously challenges the current absolute dates for
the pottery series. If, as seems to be the case, it is established that the eruption
occurred over a hundred years earlier than was believed, the dates of pottery
preserved in the destruction will also have to be moved back. And since the conventional dating of this pottery series is tied to the dates of Near Eastern objects
and events, these in turn will have to be recalculated. Accordingly, it will be
some time before a new consensus on dating for the Bronze Age is reached. But
whatever happens to the absolute dating, the relative series will remain. Thus it
is useful to think in terms of both types of dating.

The chronologies given below are the traditional dates; the new alternative
dating of the eruption of Thera is indicated, but no attempt has been made to
revise the whole series of dates.[39] One suggested new chronology is given in the
Endnotes.[40]

Traditional Minoan Dates

All Dates B.C.

EM (Early Minoan)   **3000–1550**

MM (Middle Minoan)   **2050–1550**
    MM IA   2050–1900 (Arrival of Greek-speakers on mainland ca. 2000?)
    MM IB   1900–1800 (Old Palace 1900–1700)
    MM II   1800–1700
    MM III   1700–1550 (New Palace 1700–1375; eruption of Thera 1630–1625)

LM (Late Minoan)   **1550–1100**
    LM IA   1550–1500
    LM IB   1500–1450
    LM II   1450–1375
    LM IIIA   1375–1300
    LM IIIB   1300–1200 (Trojan War 1250?)
    LM IIIC   1200–1100

IMPORTANT PLACES IN CHAPTER 2

On Chapter Map: *Crete:* Amnisos Cave, Anemospilia, Arkhanes, Gournia, Hagia Triada,
Idaean Cave, Kamares Cave, Knossos, Kommos, Kydonia/Khania, Mallia, Myrtos, Palaikastro, Phaistos, Zakro

Sites elsewhere relevant to Minoans: Cycladic Islands, Dodecanese Islands, Ialysos, Iasos, Keos, Knidos, Kos, Kythera, Melos, Miletus, Rhodes, Samos, Thera/Akrotiri, Thorikos, Troad, Troy

On Other Maps *(Use map index to find these):* Cyprus, Iskenderum, Lipari Islands, Mari, Mersin, Sicily, Tell-ed-Daba'a (Egypt), Ulu Burun

SUGGESTIONS FOR FURTHER READING

R. Higgins, *The Archaeology of Minoan Crete* (1973) is a brief illustrated book organized around discussions of the sites and their discovery. N. Platon, *Crete* (1966), which is also well illustrated, is organized chronologically and contains interesting discussions of the problems of excavation and restoration. Unfortunately, the recent books by Rodney Castleden, *The Knossos Labyrinth: A New View of the "Palace of Minos" at Knossos* (1989), and *Minoans: Life in Bronze Age Crete* (1990), should be used with caution because of Castleden's idiosyncratic interpretation of the palaces as temples.

ENDNOTES

1. Some useful books and collections of articles on the Minoans, which are frequently referred to in the notes below, are O. Krzyszkowska and L. Nixon, *Minoan Society* (1983); R. Hägg and N. Marinatos, eds., *The Function of the Minoan Palaces* (1987); R. Hägg and N. Marinatos, eds., *The Minoan Thalassocracy: Myth and Reality* (1984); and N. Marinatos, *Minoan Religion* (1993).

2. On Evans's excavations, see his *The Palace of Minos at Knossos* (1921–1935).

3. For a discussion of the palaces, see Gerald Cadogan, *Palaces of Minoan Crete* (1976); and Hägg and Marinatos, 1987 (above, n. 1). Aerial photographs of sites and complete bibliographies can be found in J. Wilson, E. E. Myers, and G. Cadogan, *The Aerial Atlas of Ancient Crete* (1992).

4. Peter Warren, *Myrtos* (1972); for the buildings at Vasiliki and Palaikastro, see Keith Branigan, *Pre-Palatial: The Foundations of Palatial Crete* (2d rev. ed., 1988), 242 and bibliography.

5. Todd M. Whitelaw, "The Settlement at Fournou Korifi Myrtos and Aspects of Early Minoan Social Organization," in Krzyszkowska and Nixon, 1983 (above, n. 1).

6. Whitelaw's interpretation is widely accepted; see John Cherry, "Evolution, Revolution, and the Origins of Complex Society in Minoan Crete," in Krzyszkowska and Nixon (above, n. 1), and Branigan (above, n. 4), 45–49, 235–236, 242, although Branigan questions a similar interpretation of another of these sites, the House on the Hill at Vasiliki.

7. See R. Hägg, "On the Reconstruction of the West Facade of the Palace at Knossos," in Hägg and Marinatos, 1987 (above, n. 1), 129–134; and, in the same volume, D. J. I. Begg, "Continuity in the West Wing at Knossos," 178–184.

8. See A. B. Knapp, *Copper Production and Divine Protection: Archaeology, Ideology and Social Complexity on Bronze Age Cyprus* (1986).

9. The residential use of these apartments is questioned by some; see, for example, A. C. Nordfeldt, "Residential Quarters and Lustral Basins," in Hägg and Marinatos, 1987 (above, n. 1), 187–194.

10. The paintings in the palace of Knossos, however, date from the final phase of the palace and may thus reflect Minoan motifs as interpreted by the Mycenaean overlords who were then in control.

11. For another interpretation, see W. D. Niemeier, "The 'Priest-King' Fresco from Knossos: A New Reconstruction and Interpretation," in *Problems in Greek History*, E. B. French and K. A. Wardle, eds. (1988), 235–244.

12. See Marinatos, 1993 (above, n. 1), 131–132.

13. S. Hood, "The 'Country House' and Minoan Society," in Krzyszkowska and Nixon, 1983 (above n. 1), 129–135; L. Nixon, "Neopalatial Outlying Settlements and the Function of the Minoan Palaces," in Hägg and Marinatos, 1987 (above, n. 1), 95–99.

14. Hood, 1983 (above, n. 13), 131.

15. See John Chadwick, *Linear B*, chap. 5, reprinted in *Reading the Past* (1990), 178–182.

16. See Y. Sakellarakis and E. Sapouna-Sakellaraki, "Drama of Death in a Minoan Temple," *National Geographic* (Feb. 1981), 205–222; W. A. MacDonald and C. Thomas, *Progress into the Past* (1990), 378–383, identify other freestanding temples on the mainland, on the island of Melos, and at Kition in Cyprus.

17. Evans first suggested that the Minoan king was a theocratic ruler. More recently, see Marinatos, 1993 (above, n. 1); and Rodney Castleden, *The Knossos Labyrinth: A New View of the 'Palace of Minos' at Knossos* (1989), and *Minoans: Life in Bronze Age Crete* (1990).

18. On Minoan shrines of various types, see B. Rutkowski, *Cult Places in the Aegean World* (1972). The one freestanding shrine, that at Anemospilia, was destroyed in the earthquake(s) that played a role in destroying the Old Palaces and was not rebuilt in the New Palace period; rather, the shrine form appears to have been incorporated into the New Palaces.

19. As demonstrated by John Cherry, "Generalization and the Archaeology of the State," in D. Green, G. Haselgrove, and M. Spriggs, eds., *Social Organization and Settlement* (1978), vol. 2, 429–430.

20. Plato, *Laws*, 624b.

21. P. M. Halstead, "From Determination to Uncertainty: Social Storage and the Rise of the Minoan Palace," in A. Sheridan and G. F. Bailey, eds., *Economic Archaeology* (1981).

22. This question has inspired enough scholarly debate to produce a symposium on the subject in Hägg and Marinatos, 1987 (above, n. 1); for an interesting discussion of methods of investigating evidence for "colonization," see E. Schofield, "The Minoan Emigrant," in Krzyszkowska and Nixon (above, n. 1), 293–301.

23. See M. H. Wiener, "The Tale of the Conical Cups," in Hägg and Marinatos, 1987 (above, n. 1), 19–20.

24. G. E. Bass, "Oldest Known Shipwreck Reveals Splendors of the Bronze Age," *National Geographic* 172 (1987), 693–733.

25. See J. Chadwick, "The Minoan Origin of the Classical Cypriote Script," in *Acts of the International Archaeological Symposium "The Relations between Cyprus and Crete, ca. 2000–500 B.C."* (1979), 139–143.

26. See Z. A. Stos-Gale, "Lead Isotope Evidence for Trade in Copper from Cyprus during the Late Bronze Age," in E. B. French and K. A. Wardle, eds., *Problems in Greek Prehistory* (1988), 265–282, esp. 275.

27. See K. Thorp-Scholes, "Akrotiri: Genesis, Life and Death," in C. Doumas and H. Puchelt, eds., *Thera and the Aegean World I* (1978), 439, and other articles in that and subsequent volumes.

28. See the references above, n. 27.

29. Nanno Marinatos, whose interpretations focus on cult, suggested that it portrayed a puberty rite; see "A Puberty Rite at Thera: Evidence from New Frescoes," *Journal of Prehistoric Religion* 3–4 (1989–1990), 49–51.

30. Interpretation of these frescoes as cult scenes has been made by N. Marinatos, *Art and Religion in Thera: Reconstructing a Bronze Age Society* (1984); but convincing arguments against this interpretation are given by Sarah Morris, "A Tale of Two Cities: The Miniature Frescoes from Thera and the Origins of Greek Poetry," *American Journal of Archaeology* 93 (1989), 511–535, see esp. 512–515 and nn. 9, 15, 27 for other references.

31. On the Expedition Fresco see P. Warren, "Miniature Frescoes from Thera," *Journal of Hellenic Studies* 79 (1979), 115–129; see also Lyvia Morgan, *The Miniature Wall Paintings of Thera: A Study in Aegean Culture and Iconography* (1988).

32. See W. -D. Niemeier, "Mycenaean Elements in the Miniature Fresco from Thera?" in D. A. Hardy, C. G. Doumas, J. A. Sakellarakis, and P. M. Warren, eds., *Thera and the Aegean World III* (1990), vol. 1, 267–284.

33. But see Morris, above, n. 30.

34. A. E. Hoekstra, *Epic Verse before Homer* (1981); Sarah Morris, above, n. 30; the existence of epic poetry in the fifteen century B.C. is argued by M. L. West, "The Rise of the Greek Epic," *Journal of Hellenic Studies* 108 (1988), 151–172.

35. M. H. Wiener, "Trade and Rule in Palatial Crete," in Hägg and Marinatos, 1987 (above, n. 1), 261–266; "The Isles of Crete? The Minoan Thalassocracy Revisited," in Hardy et al., 1990 (above, n. 32), vol. 1, pp. 128–155; see also P. M. Warren, "The Place of Crete in the Thalassocracy of Minos," in Hägg and Marinatos, 1984 (above, n. 1), 39–44.

36. Similar scenes are found on the Town Mosaic from Knossos, on Minoan materials from the Mycenaean Shaft Graves (see next chapter), on a fragmentary rhyton, and on numerous rings and seals.

37. The Hyksos were foreign princes, probably from the Levant, who gained control of Egypt and ruled for about a century (1648/37–1540/29 B.C.) from their capital in the delta. See Vronwy Hankey, "Egypt, the Aegean, and the Levant," *Egyptian Archaeology* 3 (1993), 27–29.

38. Y. Sakellarakis and E. Sakellaraki, "The Keftiu and the Minoan Thalassocracy," in Hägg and Marinatos, 1984 (above n. 1), 197–203.

39. These dates are adapted from P. Warren and V. Hankey, *Aegean Bronze Age Chronology* (1989), 169. Arguments for a revised date for the eruption on Thera can be found in Stuart Manning, "The Bronze Age Eruption of Thera," *Journal of Mediterranean Archaeology* 1 (1988), 17–82, see esp. Table 10 on p. 56.

40. Suggested New Chronology:

MM III	1800–1775/1725
LM IA	1775/1725–1630/20 (eruption of Thera, 1630–1625)
LM IB	1630/20–1570/40
LM II	1570/40–?/1490/50
LM III A1	1490/50–1420/1380
LM III A2	1420/1380–1360/25
LM IIIB	1360/25–1200 (Trojan War, 1250?)

CHAPTER THREE

Bronze Age Greece

$\mathbb{A}$ s the palace civilization of Minos' Crete flourished, on the mainland of Greece another great mythical antecedent of the Greeks was developing: the Mycenaeans, given enduring fame by the poet Homer in his epic tales of the Trojan War and its aftermath, the *Iliad* and the *Odyssey*. The Mycenaeans also built a great palace civilization, in large part as the conquerors and heirs of the Minoans. Yet Mycenaean civilization was more than just a development of Minoan antecedents; the Mycenaeans were for us quite literally the first Greeks.

As we saw in the first chapter, with the introduction of bronze into the Aegean area, the Greek mainland appears to have developed in much the same way as prepalatial Crete. Settlements increased in number and size, and some buildings could be called monumental. But around 2300 B.C. this picture changed; a series of destructions inaugurated a period of cultural setbacks on the mainland, while in Crete a palace civilization arose. It was not until about 1600 B.C., at the time of the building of the New Palaces on Crete, that signs of a new wealth and sophistication appeared on the Greek mainland in the form of numerous large-scale beehive tomb burials in Messenia (the southwest Peloponnesus), and, even more dramatically, a group of extraordinarily rich Shaft Grave burials in the Argolid at the site of the later palace of Mycenae.

THE ADVENT OF THE MYCENAEANS: SHAFT GRAVES AND THOLOS TOMBS[1]

The Shaft Graves at Mycenae

The **Shaft Graves** at Mycenae were monumental in size and their burials were accompanied by a rich collection of luxury goods that amazed their discoverer, Heinrich Schliemann. The burials were made in rectangular shafts, some as

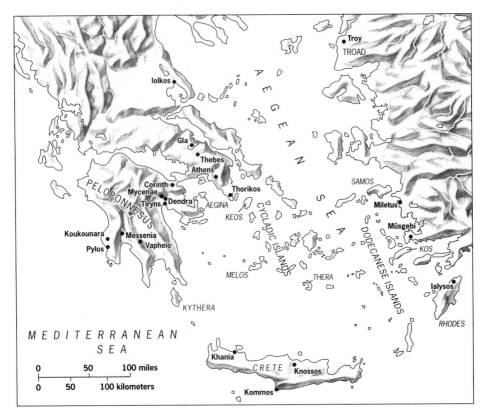

Map 3 Bronze Age: Mycenaean Greece.

deep as 4 meters, some large enough to hold as many as five burials. The floors of the shafts were covered with pebbles, and a wall of stones or bricks was built up the sides of the shaft to a height of about a meter and a half. After the body was laid on the pebble floor and surrounded by its grave gifts, log beams were laid down, resting on the top of the sidewalls. The beams were covered with clay or slate panels to provide a roof for the burial chamber, and then the shaft was filled in with dirt. When the filling reached ground level, a funeral meal was celebrated, and the remains of the meal, including broken wine cups, were scattered on the ground and covered over with a mound of earth. On top of some of the mounds a grave marker, or *stele*, was placed. The graves were used more than once: at each new burial, the shaft was dug out again, the previous occupants and their gifts unceremoniously pushed aside, and the new inhabitant installed.

The Shaft Graves are grouped in two circles, one of which, Circle A, was reconstructed and enclosed by a stone circle later in the Mycenaean period. Circle A contained six deep shafts and many humbler burials, and Circle B held fourteen true shafts, plus other burials. The two circles are now thought to have been in use in the same time period, from about 1600 to 1500 B.C. In Circle A, each shaft contained multiple burials of from two to five people. In all there were nine men, eight women, and two children buried in the shafts of Circle A, while Circle B's fourteen shafts held twenty-four bodies. There were rich burials in both circles, but the graves of Circle A were considerably richer than those of Circle B.

Objects included among the grave gifts in the Shaft Graves were gold jewelry and clothing ornaments (683 gold disks and ornaments in one grave alone), gold death masks (and complete coverings for the bodies of the children), and a silver rhyton (probably imported from Crete) portraying a siege. There were also swords decorated with inlay, knives, arrowheads, boar's tusks (from helmets), ivory, amethyst and Baltic amber beads, a game board, ostrich eggs, rock crystal, lapis lazuli, alabaster, faience, cobalt blue glass, and bronze and clay vessels, including imports or imitations of Cycladic and Minoan vases.

The question of how to analyze such a collection is a fundamental one for the archaeologist, and the answers have shifted over time. One approach has been to investigate the origins of the various objects, their materials, and their motifs. The results of this approach have shown that the objects themselves came from a wide geographical range: Egypt, Crete, Syria, Anatolia, the Adriatic area, and central Europe. Many of the objects display mixtures of motifs, materials, and techniques from various areas, and for many objects, foreign techniques and materials were used to represent interests quite different from those of their sources. The most striking examples of this are to be found in the famous inlaid bronze daggers. The bronze probably came from Bohemia. The **niello technique** used for the inlay came from the Near East: cutout figures of gold, silver, *electron* (a natural mixture of gold and silver), and dark bronze were hammered into cutouts in a bronze blade, details were engraved, and the engraved lines were then filled with black *niello* (a compound of copper, lead, sulfur, and borax) which was burned in to provide a black outline around the figures. The subject matter varies from a scene reminiscent of the Nile River to a lion hunt which reflects mainland interests (Figure 3-1). It is thought that the daggers were produced in Greece, probably by Minoan craftsmen, as were many other objects in the graves. The combination of Minoan and Helladic cultures which many of these objects reveal is called *Mycenaean*, from the site of these graves, and the name has been extended to the whole culture.

Based on information about the origins of the grave goods, archaeologists have created various scenarios to explain the Shaft Graves. One suggestion is that the sudden appearance of so much wealth came from raiding, probably on neighboring Crete, from which much of the workmanship derives. Another possibility is suggested by the Expedition Fresco from Thera. Many close similarities exist between this miniature fresco scene and the objects found in the Shaft Graves. In particular, there is a similarity between the battle scene and the siege scene portrayed on the silver rhyton in the Shaft Grave collection, while the

FIGURE 3-1 Lion Hunt dagger from Mycenaean Grave Circle, niello technique, "painting in metal."

river scene in the fresco resembles the river scene on one of the niello swords. Possibly these similarities can be explained by Mycenaean mercenary service, which could have provided the Mycenaeans with a sudden influx of foreign wealth and knowledge.

Another theory of the origins of the Shaft Grave "princes" has recently been the subject of a lively debate. This is the suggestion made by Martin Bernal in his book *Black Athena*[2] that these princes were part of the *Hyksos,* "foreign princes" of Palestinian and Hurrian origins, who invaded and occupied Egypt during the **Second Intermediate Period** (ca. 1785–1550 B.C.). In Bernal's reconstruction, the Hyksos first established themselves in Crete in the seventeenth century, then went on to take control of Mycenae, and were buried in the Shaft Graves. The thesis serves Bernal's more general claim that scholars in the nineteenth century, who formed the present-day discipline of Classical Studies, created an *Aryan Model* by downplaying the Semitic and Egyptian influences on classical Greek culture. To redress this bias, Bernal creates what he calls the *Ancient Model,* which gives due (some would say excessive) weight to the Egyptian and Near Eastern elements in Greek culture. But convincing evidence for the presence of the Hyksos in Crete or Mycenae is lacking, as Bernal himself admits.[3]

A more recent approach to the interpretation of the Shaft Graves focuses on an analysis of the gifts in the graves for clues about the social structure of the society. For example, Imma Kilian-Dirlmeier, in analyzing the male burials, has identified three phases in which increasingly rich offerings were made.[4] In the earliest phase, the graves with gifts were poor, with only one weapon and no jewelry or precious vessels; there is no pattern of association in the goods, suggesting that burial customs were not yet fixed. In the second phase, those men who were buried with weapons were given a complete set of offensive weapons (sword, dagger, and spear), but no defensive equipment, and their graves included precious vessels, jewelry, and diadems. In the third phase, only swords and daggers were included in the male burials, and gold masks, seals, and necklaces make their appearance (necklaces for the men; women were buried with them even in the earlier phases). Even in the last, richest phase, some burials were accompanied by only a few poor grave gifts or none at all. Yet analysis of the bones has shown all the burials to be of people in very good physical condition, suggesting that all were members of an elite.[5] Kilian-Dirlmeier concludes that access to wealth depended on certain military qualities (perhaps courage displayed as aggression and dominance, since only offensive weapons were included), and not on age groups (since children also were buried with rich offerings). She argues further that only those of highest rank were accorded burial in the shafts in the latest phase, and thus assumes that the archers and spearmen were of lower rank. However, the presence of burials of males without weapons then requires an explanation. Finally, she finds agreement between these signs of rank and prestige with those in Minoan representations—there being no known actual Minoan warrior burials—and concludes that the Mycenaeans, as they developed differentiated status groups, probably adapted these traditional designators from the Minoans.

The Tholos Tombs

For about fifty years after the last Shaft Grave burial, there were still no palaces on the mainland, and we can best trace the development of Mycenaean culture by analyzing another type of monumental burial: large, beehive-shaped *tholos tombs* (Figure 3-2). Tholos tombs first appeared in mainland Greece in Messenia at the time of the Shaft Graves. These tombs were constructed on the principle of a *corbelled arch*. (A corbelled arch is not a true arch: each layer is placed slightly farther in, and there is no keystone to support the resultant dome. Support comes from the weight of the earth piled up on the layers of stone.) A long entryway, or *dromos,* was also constructed. After the interment (in a side chamber, a cist grave in the floor, or simply on the floor of the great domed chamber), the whole structure was filled in again. As in the case of the Shaft Graves, multiple burials in one tomb, and reuse, were the rule.

The tholos tomb now appears to have developed out of a merging of a mainland tradition of burial under or in a tumulus, and a Minoan tradition of large circular tombs with corbelled sidewalls.[6] The district of Pylos in Messenia

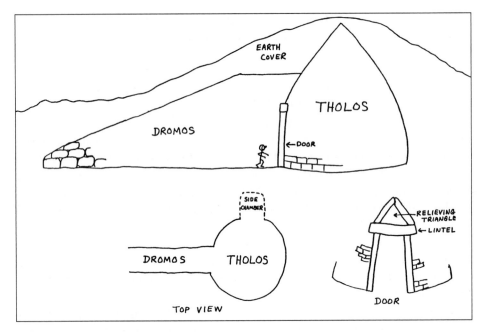

FIGURE 3-2 Tholos tomb diagram.

is especially rich in early examples. At one location, Koukounara, seventeen tholoi have been found. The earliest are rather small (6 meters in diameter) and are built of field stones, but they are still clearly indicative of growing wealth: some of the tombs yielded materials in the same mixed tradition as the Shaft Graves at Mycenae, including a sword inlaid with Minoan argonauts. However, the large number of these tombs associated with one settlement over a relatively short period of time seems to rule out the hypothesis that tholoi burial was restricted to "kings."

Two other unplundered tombs also yielded important finds. One, a tholos tomb at Vapheio in Lakonia, discovered in 1888 and dated after 1500 B.C., contained gold Minoan cups that portray the capture of a bull. The second, a chamber tomb at Dendra in the Argolid just east of Mycenae, discovered in the late 1950s and dated about 1400 B.C., yielded a full set of Mycenaean armor that fits surprisingly well the descriptions of armor in the Homeric poems. These objects confirm that the interconnections between Mycenaean and Minoan cultures, which the Shaft Graves at Mycenae first revealed to archaeologists, were in fact widespread and continuing.

At Mycenae, the nine tholoi have been grouped into three chronological types of increasing size and ever greater quality of workmanship. The earliest are probably early fifteenth century B.C. (LH IIA), the most advanced date around 1250 B.C. Included in the latest group are the so-called tombs of Atreus and Clytemnestra, which are of truly monumental size (14.6 meters and 13.2

meters in diameter, respectively). Unfortunately, all the tholoi at Mycenae were robbed long before modern archaeologists came upon the scene.

THE FALL OF KNOSSOS AND THE RISE OF THE MYCENAEANS

In ca. 1450 B.C. the palaces on Crete were destroyed; only Knossos escaped relatively intact, although increasing evidence from the western port site of Khania suggests that a functioning palace may have continued to exist there as well. Signs of mainland presence appear on Crete: numerous warrior burials; tholos tombs in the mainland tradition; and a new, more stylized and rigid monumental vase type, called *Palace Style*. Somewhat later, a building form typical of the mainland appears, the **megaron** (in its simplest form, a rectangular room with a door and porch on its short side and a central hearth; pl., *megara*). But most important, tablets similar to the Linear A tablets but inscribed in an early form of Greek, called **Linear B**, were reported by Sir Arthur Evans in the excavation level of Knossos dated 1450–1375 B.C. In ca. 1375 B.C., another generalized destruction occurred; after this, the palace at Knossos continued to be used, but in ways that did not respect earlier usage (for example, industrial production was carried on in former ceremonial areas).

According to the traditional view, the archaeological finds show that people from the mainland took over control of Crete after the destruction of 1450 B.C. These people carried on the administration of the Minoan palace system using the Linear B style of writing, and adopting and adapting Minoan motifs in frescoes and vases of the Palace Style. They remained in control until the destructions of 1375 B.C., which ended palatial life on Crete. These people, the Mycenaeans, lived in a culture that was an amalgamation of Minoan and mainland elements. For us, they are the first Greeks, the first Greek speakers, to enter history; of their origins, we can only speculate (see Chapter 1).

THE MYCENAEAN PALACES

The Mycenaeans developed palaces on the mainland only after the final destruction of the Minoan palaces. Mycenaean palaces are known at Mycenae, Tiryns, Pylos, and Thebes; there was also a fortified center with no palace at Gla in Boeotia. Although at first glance the mainland palaces may appear similar to those of the Minoans, in very basic ways they are quite different. This can be seen by comparing the plans of the three major Mycenaean palaces at Tiryns, Mycenae, and Pylos with those of the Minoan palaces (Figures 3-3, 3-4, and 3-5).

The Mycenaean plans, with the exception of Pylos, feature very imposing defensive walls. These fortifications, and the tholoi tombs as well, were built

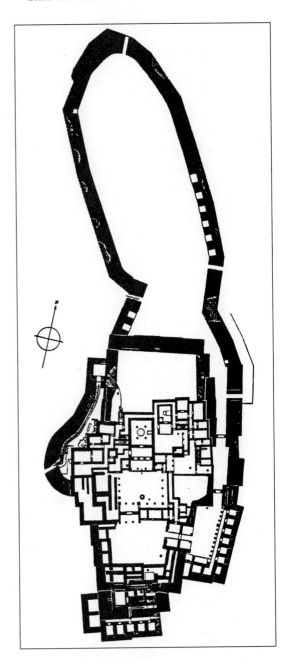

FIGURE 3-3 Site plan of Tiryns.

with huge blocks of stone. For example, the stones in the dromos of the Treasury of Atreus were as large as 18 feet by 14 feet and the lintel weighed 100 tons.
Later Greeks seeing these huge blocks assumed they must have been moved by
superhuman forces and attributed them to the giant Cyclops hence the term
Cyclopean masonry. It is now recognized, however, that similar blocks were

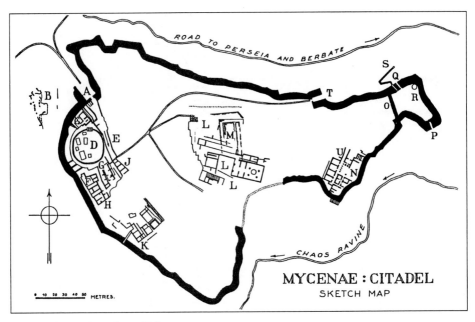

FIGURE 3-4   Site plan of Mycenae.

managed in the building of the pyramids by the use of ramps and sledges, and the Mycenaeans must have employed similar methods. In fact, as the building of a tholos tomb proceeded, earth was piled up to cover and support the courses of stone, and this would have created a natural ramp for the next course. This experience would have shown them the method by which fortified walls could be constructed as well. By the end of the effective life of the palaces, the Mycenaeans had equipped the walls with well-developed systems of defensive postern gates and made provision for safe access to water supplies that were protected from enemy attack by their underground location. Clearly the Mycenaeans, unlike the Minoans, had a great need for physical defense.

The central focus of a Mycenaean palace also differed from that of a Minoan palace. Rather than the large central courtyard that formed the core of the Minoan palace, the focus of the Mycenaean palace was a monumental megaron, or, often, pair of megara, one larger than the other. The megaron, in its fully developed monumental form, usually consisted of a porch with a central column, an anteroom, and an inner room with a large central hearth set within four columns that supported a clerestory and an upper balcony. At Pylos, a place for a "throne," and peg holes in the floor, connected by sunken channels (probably for pouring libations), have been found in the megaron.

The Mycenaean palaces lacked the monumental staircases, light wells, and pillar-and-door construction so characteristic of Minoan palaces. Moreover, al-

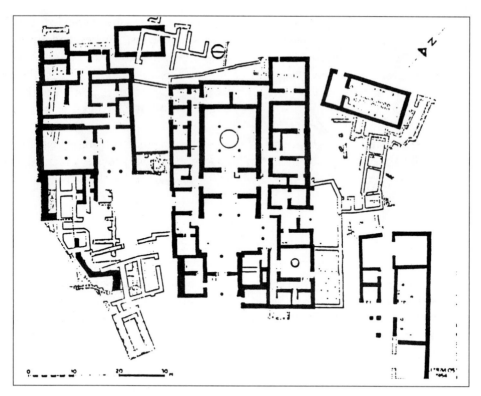

Figure 3-5　Site plan of Pylos.

though Mycenaean palaces possessed bathrooms and a system of drainage for rainwater, there is no evidence of the sort of flushable toilet facilities which existed in Minoan palaces. Obviously, comfort, light, and air were not primary considerations to the Mycenaean rulers.

But, despite these fundamental differences, important similarities existed between Minoan and Mycenaean palaces. A major point of likeness is, of course, the very concept of a palace as an administrative center, as evidenced by the size of the complex, the provision for large-scale storage of commodities, the presence of workrooms for the manufacture of various products, and the Linear B records. Like the Minoan palace, the Mycenaean palace was decorated with frescoes, which often feature the same motifs and clearly copy Minoan work. In Mycenaean frescoes, however, hunting and battle scenes are much more popular, and there is more concern for symmetry and order than is evidenced in the Minoan works.[7] Such similarities and differences suggest that the Minoan palace provided the model, but that, in borrowing that model, the Mycenaeans transformed it to suit their own lifestyle and interests.

Evidence does not exist for the political dominance of one Mycenaean palace over the others, as it does for Knossos in Crete. The two palaces at Mycenae and Tiryns, which were very close neighbors and very well defended, certainly raise questions about palace relationships, but Pylos, Thebes, and a presumed palace at Athens would have dominated well-defined areas, and there is little to suggest that one palace exerted central control over all the others. Perhaps Mycenaean Greece was made up of a number of independent kingdoms sharing a common culture. This picture would be very similar to that presented in Homer.

In the case of the Mycenaean palaces, we are fortunate to have readable records (in the form of tablets inscribed in Linear B) that provide a picture of the internal operation of the palaces and their methods of control over people, commodities, and production.

THE LINEAR B TABLETS

In 1939, in the initial excavation of the Mycenaean palace at Pylos, conducted by Carl Blegen, the first trial trenches passed through an archive room containing over 600 fragments of tablets inscribed in the same Linear B script already known from the tablets that Evans had found at Knossos. The sheer number of inscriptions that this discovery made available, and the systematic storage of the tablets in the archives at Pylos, eventually made possible the decipherment of Linear B. In 1954, Michael Ventris, an architect and amateur linguist, announced to the International Classical Congress at Copenhagen that he had deciphered the language of the tablets and found it to be an early form of Greek.[8] As confirmation, he showed a slide of a tablet containing the recognizable ideogram for a tripod, and the Linear B characters to which he had assigned the values *ti-ri-po-de*. Since that time, most scholars have come to accept Linear B as an early form of Greek.

Like Linear A, Linear B is written in a syllabic rather than an alphabetic script. Signs represent combinations of consonants with vowels rather than individual sounds: for example, there are separate signs for the syllables *pa, pe, pi, po*, and *pu*. As Ventris's reading of the tripod table showed, ideograms depicting the object described were also employed to aid in reading and perhaps to guide illiterates in handling the tablets.

While Linear B is known to be Greek, it is a syllabic system of writing that presents certain intrinsic disadvantages which can make interpretation difficult. For example, Linear B cannot easily express the consonant clusters of Greek: thus, to write *tripod*, the Mycenaean scribes had to write *ti-ri-po-de*. Certain final consonants that are important elements in Greek words (-*n* and -*s*) were also not written. Another problem that impedes interpretation is the fact that a number of symbols represent more than one sound. For example, the sounds representing *p* and *b* and those representing *r* and *l* are not distinguished. Thus, the Greek word **basileus** (king) is written *pa-si-re-u*. When several such ambiguous signs are combined, the possibilities are numerous, and in some cases one brief group of words may have several dramatically different Greek equivalences. Still another source of difficulty is presented by numerous Linear B words that have no apparent equivalents in later Greek. All of these problems make translation and interpretation difficult, but nonetheless the tablets provide the historian with one of the most valuable sources of evidence about Mycenaean Greece.

Most of the Linear B tablets are simply lists: personnel, livestock and agricultural produce, landownership and use, tribute and ritual offerings, textiles, vessels, furniture, metals, military equipment (chariots, wheels, weapons, armor). The accounts are often very detailed: some record broken objects, and in one case the name of a cow is recorded (oddly, the name of a king never appears).[9] Religious offerings were also recorded on the tablets, and these provide interesting information about the divinities worshipped by the Mycenaeans, which will be considered in the next section.

The tablets provide especially valuable information about the political and social hierarchy. The highest status, as indicated by land and other allocations, was that of *wanax,* a word applied in Homer to both men and gods and in later Greek only to the gods ("lord"). The Mycenaean *wanax* is usually interpreted as *king*, but this entity may have been only one of a number of such men with this rank at Pylos.[10] Lower in status than the wanax was the *lawagetas*, a term that in later Greek had the meaning "Leader of the War-Host." The *basileus*, a word that later Greeks used to designate a king, appears to have been only a comparatively minor local official in Mycenaean times. Priests and priestesses also appear as high-ranking individuals on the tablets; they are listed as holders of parcels of land measured in terms of amounts of grain, and others hold land possibly leased from them. People also hold land leased from the *damos* (*demos;* or *people,* in later Greek). Military units *(oka),* with their leaders and dispositions, are also detailed. One interesting but enigmatic tablet assigns rowers to watch on the coast; it is tempting to see this as an emergency provision in a time of danger, since the tablet itself was preserved by the fire that destroyed the palace.

At the bottom of the social pyramid were the workers. Many were skilled specialists; the lists include wheelwrights, furniture makers, workers in gold and lapis-colored glass, and bronze smiths. Other workers were listed only as recipients of rations of figs and grain. Some of these, such as women listed with their working children but without husband or family affiliations, were clearly slaves. Close palatial control over production is attested by allocations of materials; for example, smiths were allocated specific amounts of bronze for the making of items such as arrowheads and spearheads. Inventories of supplies, such as spare parts for chariots, were detailed. Agriculture and animal husbandry were also closely controlled, with numbers and descriptions of animals listed, along with their herdsmen.

A good example of the information about the organization of the palatial economy that can be drawn from the tablets is provided by Cynthia Shelmerdine's analysis of the records of the perfumed-oil industry at Pylos.[11] Since the Pylos tablets list only finished products and supplementary allotments of ingredients to workers, and not the full list of ingredients used, Shelmerdine studied these records in the context of the architectural evidence and information about perfume production in other ancient societies, such as the portrayal of perfume workers on Egyptian tomb paintings, and recipes from Mesopotamian records. Most of these tablets were found not in the archives, but scattered about various other rooms of the palace. By considering their "find-spots," and the archaeological remains of vessels used for preparing, storing, and shipping perfume, Shelmerdine has been able to identify the perfume workshops in the palace as well as to draw conclusions about the organization of the palace scribes and their activities.

Because the Linear B tablets appear to have been used almost exclusively for the purposes of palatial administration, it seems unlikely that literacy was widespread in Mycenaean society. This has been confirmed by an analysis of scribal handwriting: in the kingdom of Pylos, where a population of about 50,000 has been estimated, only 23 scribal hands have been identified out of an estimated total of 32 scribes.[12]

MYCENAEAN RELIGION

In their first contacts, the Mycenaeans were particularly receptive to the much more advanced Minoan culture, and they readily adopted Minoan iconographical forms and conventions, such as the Great Goddess-Mistress of Animals, snakes, bull rhytons, double axes, and Horns of Consecration. As a result, Mycenaean religion viewed from the archaeological point of view tends to look quite Minoan. When the Linear B tablets could be read, however, it became possible to distinguish a truly Mycenaean religion under the Minoan facade. For instance, the tablets contain the names of non-Minoan deities familiar in later Greek religion—Hera, Poseidon, Zeus, Artemis, Ares (?), and Dionysus (?)—as well as other unfamiliar but apparently related gods, such as an intriguing Zeus-ess and a female Poseidon. These divine figures appear on the tablets as recipients of offerings, not only of precious objects but also of men and women, possibly an indication of human sacrifice.

Mycenaean religious rites involved the burnt sacrifice of animals, as in later Greek religious custom. In this they differed fundamentally from the Minoans, who did not make burnt offerings. Another characteristic innovation in Mycenaean religious practice was the use of cult images and the ubiquitous small figurines in *phi* and *psi* shapes (Figure 3-6).

It is, however, in the places of worship that the Mycenaeans differed most clearly from the Minoans. There is no evidence that the Mycenaeans made use of typical Minoan cult sites in the countryside, such as peak, cave, or tree sanctu-

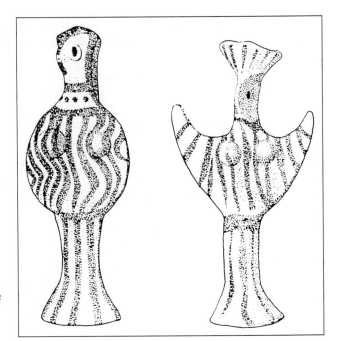

FIGURE 3-6 *Phi* and *psi* figurines (Lord William Taylor).

aries, or that they held ritual celebrations before large groups of people such as are portrayed on Minoan frescoes. Rather, the Mycenaeans seem to have centered their religious rites within the palace, and, in fact, within the megaron at its central hearth. There, sheltered from the general view, they appear to have carried out their most important religious activities. Some shrines have also been found in other buildings within the walls of Mycenae, but there are no indications that palace inhabitants and the common people came together in public rites. There is also no evidence for widespread use of Linear B for dedications. Thus, while the Minoan rulers seem to have used religion as an integrative force within the community, the Mycenaeans appear to have had no such concerns.

THE MYCENAEANS OVERSEAS

That the Mycenaeans were both the heirs of the Minoans in overseas connections and prolific exporters themselves is suggested by the distribution of their pottery, which has been found at sites in the Cyclades, Cyprus, the Levant, Asia Minor, Rhodes, Egypt, Sicily and Italy, and the Balkans, reaching even to central Europe.[13] A number of Mycenaean swords and daggers also traveled. That the Mycenaeans exported other goods is probable—for example, the perfumed oil whose production Shelmerdine has documented at Pylos, and textiles made from the flax and from the wool of the large flocks described by the Linear B tablets—but there are few archaeological traces. Nor do we know what the Mycenaeans received in return, aside from metals (especially copper and tin) and a few luxury items.

Evidence for Mycenaean settlement abroad, which might be related to trade, is increasing in many areas as the result of ongoing excavations. Mycenaean settlement on Rhodes, an important step in the route to the east, is well-attested, as well as at the sites of Miletus and Iasos in Asia Minor. At Miletus, a large megaron building and other evidence of Mycenaean occupation and agriculture date to the fourteenth century B.C.[14] A number of Mycenaean chamber tombs have also been excavated at Müsgebi, near modern Bodrum (later Greek Halicarnassos), but no settlement has yet been found. New finds continue to extend the number of known Mycenaean settlements on sites on the west coast of Anatolia and on the adjacent islands.[15]

Caution against inferring settlement from the finds of even large numbers of Mycenaean pots is suggested, however, by the case of an area in which we expected to find Mycenaean settlement, but did not—the island of Cyprus. The island was probably an important source of copper for the Mycenaeans as well as providing access to tin carried from Afghanistan through Levantine ports. However, although large quantities of Mycenaean pottery have been found on the island, there is little evidence for Mycenaean settlement until the refugee influx at the time of the general collapse of Mediterranean civilization in the twelfth century B.C.

Another puzzle of Mycenaean trade is that, despite the numerous finds of Mycenaean pottery throughout the Mediterranean, the Mycenaeans' production of oils and textiles far in excess of their own apparent needs, and evidence for Mycenaean settlement abroad, firm evidence of their actual involvement in trade is lacking.[16] Mycenaean objects found on overseas sites may have been carried by non-Mycenaeans along the lively trade routes of the Mediterranean, as the evidence from two Bronze Age shipwrecks off the southern coast of Turkey suggests.[17] Only one tablet, from Mycenae, even hints at trade by its record of the dispatch of textiles to Greek Thebes; none record overseas transactions.

This apparent lacuna in the tablets may, however, be only an accident of preservation. It is likely that Mycenaean trade was only an occasional affair: the Cape Gelidonya shipwreck was carrying about a ton of copper, perhaps a year's supply for a Bronze Age kingdom (one of the Pylos tablets records a ton of bronze).[18] Moreover, trade in this period often took the form of the exchange of guest-gifts between rulers. That such gifts in the Bronze Age went far beyond the occasional decorated sword or other ceremonial object can be seen from the "Amarna letters" of Egypt. In these letters to and from the ruler of Egypt, the king of Alasia (probably Cyprus) sends copper to the Pharaoh and requests silver, clothes, golden couches, chariots, and olive oil jars in return, while the Babylonian king sends him lapis lazuli and horses, asking gold in return.[19] If Mycenaean trade followed this pattern of occasional shipments and guest-gifts, there may not have been occasion to document any transactions in the Linear B records, which were temporary and covered only a portion of a year.

There is additional strong but indirect evidence for Mycenaean involvement in Mediterranean trade, as suppliers and recipients, if not as traveling merchants: the palatial economy shared in the general collapse of Mediterranean civilization that occurred in the twelfth century B.C. To be as thoroughly affected as they were by the general state of confusion, much of it caused by sea raiders who disrupted normal shipping routes, the Mycenaeans must have been dependent upon this sea traffic and the trade it involved. This general collapse, and the end which it brought to Mycenaean civilization, is a topic that we must now consider in some detail.

IMPORTANT PLACES IN CHAPTER 3

On Chapter Map: Aegina, Athens, Corinth, Dendra, Gla, Ialysos, Iolkos, Khania, Knossos, Kommos, Koukounara (in the Pylos district), Messenia, Miletus, Müsgebi, Mycenae, Pylos, Rhodes, Thebes, Thorikos, Tiryns, Vapheio

On Other Maps *(Use map index to find these):* Afghanistan, Babylon, Cape Gelidonya, Cyprus, Egypt, the Levant, the Nile River, Mittani, Ulu Burun

SUGGESTIONS FOR FURTHER READING

John Chadwick, *The Mycenaean World* (1976) and *Linear B and Related Scripts* (1987); O. T. P. K. Dickinson, *The Aegean Bronze Age* (1994); G. Bass, "Oldest Known Shipwreck Reveals Splendors of the Bronze Age," *National Geographic* 172 (1987), 693–733.

ENDNOTES

1. On the Mycenaeans in general, see Emily T. Vermeule, *Greece in the Bronze Age* (1972); see also John Chadwick, *The Mycenaean World* (1976).

2. Martin Bernals, *Black Athena*, vol. 2. (1987), chaps. 9 and 10.

3. See Vermeule (above, n. 1), 106–110, for a pre-Bernals discussion of the Egyptian and Near Eastern context of the Shaft Graves.

4. Imma Kilian-Dirlmeier, "Jewellery in Mycenaean and Minoan 'Warrior Graves,' " in E. B. French and K. A. Wardle, eds., *Problems in Greek Prehistory* (1988), 161–171. This and other chronological analyses establishing the gradual development of wealth in the Shaft Graves over time rather than as a sudden and unprecedented influx do much to counter the argument of Robert Drews in *The Coming of the Greeks* (1988) that the occupants of the Mycenaean Shaft Graves were foreign princes who took over power in Mycenae and brought chariot warfare and the Greek language to Greece.

5. J. L. Angel, "Human Skeletons from Grave Circles at Mycenae," in G. E. Mylonas, ed., *O Taphikos Kyklos B ton Mykenon* (1973), 379–397.

6. J. B. Rutter, "Review of Aegean Prehistory II: The Prepalatial Bronze Age of the Southern and Central Mainland," *American Journal of Archaeology* 97 (1993), 745–797, 789.

7. On Mycenaean frescoes, see M. Lang, *The Palace of Nestor at Pylos in Western Messenia*. II: *The Frescoes* (1969).

8. The Linear B tablets: John Chadwick, *Linear B and Related Scripts* (1987) provides an excellent introduction; Chadwick, *The Decipherment of Linear B* (1958), gives the story of the decipherment; Chadwick, (above, n. 1) reconstructs Mycenaean society based on information from the tablets.

9. There is some controversy about this. Chadwick (above, n. 1), 71–72, 116–117, 126, reads the word *Enkhalyawen* as the name of a king, but J. T. Hooker, "The Wanax in Linear B Texts," *Kadmos* 18 (1979), 100–111, rejects this interpretation.

10. Chadwick calls him a king, Hooker disagrees (above, n. 9).

11. Cynthia Shelmerdine, *The Perfume Industry of Mycenaean Pylos* (1985).

12. T. Palaima, "Scribal Organization and Palatial Activity," in C. Shelmerdine and T. Palaima, eds., *Pylos Comes Alive* (1984), 31–39.

13. The exported pottery consists mainly of storage jars and a type of jar used for exporting oil, but it also includes many fine painted vases and cups which must have been exported for their own sake. Vase painting styles were adaptations of Minoan work, but over time the motifs were often rendered almost unrecognizable by the Mycenaean tendency to stylization.

14. M. J. Mellink, "Archaeology in Asia Minor," *American Journal of Archaeology* (1974), 114.

15. See C. Mee, "A Mycenaean Thalassocracy in the Eastern Aegean?" in E. B. French and K. A. Wardle, eds., *Problems in Greek Prehistory* (1988), 301–305.

16. See J. T. Killen, "The Linear B Tablets and the Mycenaean Economy," in A. Morpurgo Davies and Y. Duhoux, eds., *Linear B: A 1984 Survey* (1985), 241–305.

17. G. Bass, "The Gelidonya Wreck," *American Journal of Archaeology* 65 (1961), 267ff.; regarding the Ulu Burun wreck, G. Bass, "Oldest Known Shipwreck Reveals Splendors of the Bronze Age," *National Geographic* 172 (1987), 693–733; also see E. H. Cline and M. J. Cline, "Of Shoes and Ships and Sealing Wax: International Trade and the Late Bronze Age Aegean," *Expedition* 33 (1991), 146–154.

18. Killen, (above, n. 16), 241–305, 266.

19. W. L. Moran, *The Amarna Letters* (1992): Hittites, #34; Alasia, #35–37; Babylon: #7, 9, 10, 11; Mittani, #19.

CHAPTER FOUR

From the Bronze Age to the Iron Age

THE COLLAPSE AND FALL
OF MYCENAEAN CIVILIZATION

I n the thirteenth century B.C., as Mycenaean contacts overseas reached their peak, there was increasing attention to defense at home. Fortification walls were strengthened and extended, and elaborately fortified gates were added, such as the postern gate at Tiryns with its multiple traps to ensnare unwitting intruders. Considerable effort was expended to assure safe access to water sources. On the Acropolis at Athens, a shaft 120 feet deep was constructed leading down to a spring; five flights of stone and wooden steps gave access, making the fetching of water possible even if the palace were under attack (Figure 4-1). A wall was built at the Isthmus of Corinth, and in Gla in Boeotia, where the Mycenaeans had drained the great Copaic Lake for agricultural use, a fortress stronghold was constructed to provide defense against hostile attempts to flood the plain. We do not know if the threats that gave rise to these precautions were from external foes or from neighboring Mycenaeans, but the palace destructions in the twelfth century show that they were real.

Between approximately 1200 and 1100 B.C., both palace buildings and large private houses at numerous sites were attacked and destroyed; in some cases, as at Pylos, one destruction ended occupation at the site, while other sites suffered repeatedly but were rebuilt. For example, recent excavations at Tiryns have shown that the destruction of the palace led to a period of occupation amidst the ruins, followed by repairs to the fortifications, new building activities in the lower citadel, and the removal of people from scattered inland settlements into the protection of the reactivated fortress. These changes imply the exercise of

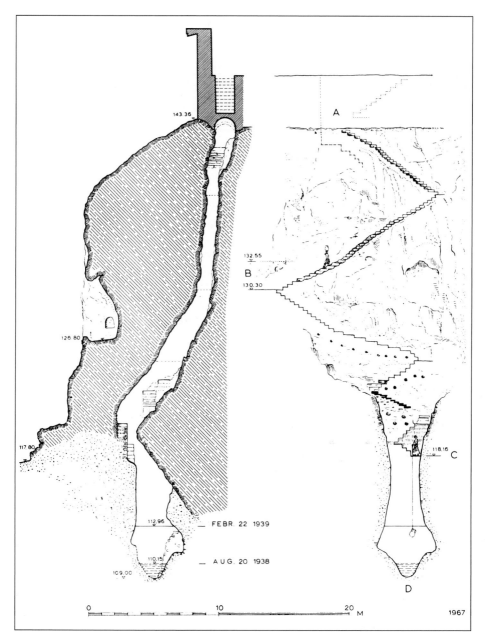

FIGURE 4-1   Athenian Acropolis, Mycenaean well diagram (Travlos).

some sort of central authority that focused upon the interests of the general population. As a result of such evidence of recovery, it has even been suggested that this period (LH IIIC) should be classified as "Late Mycenaean City Life," to contrast it with the earlier palatial period.[1]

S O U R C E   A N A L Y S I S

he evidence of survival and rebuilding is presented graphically in these plans of the succeeding phases in the life of Tiryns as revealed by excavation (Figure 4-2). This example shows how systematic recording of the finds at each level during excavation can provide evidence for the development of a site over time.[2]

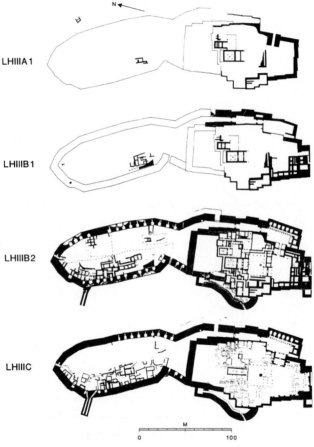

FIGURE 4-2 Development of palace at Tiryns.

Despite rebuildings and apparent reorganizations, in the end the entire Mycenaean system collapsed. Population dropped precipitously, and survivors scattered in various directions as they sought havens. Of the major Mycenaean palace sites, only Athens appears to have survived the destructions without a period of abandonment. According to tradition, it provided a temporary refuge and a port of embarkation for refugees moving east; nevertheless, Athens did not escape the loss of literacy, craft skills, and outside contacts that characterized the Mycenaean collapse throughout Greece.

Greece was not alone in its experience of catastrophe and downfall. The entire eastern Mediterranean was engulfed in turmoil. The Hittite Empire, afflicted by famine, unrest, and outright rebellion in border areas, collapsed shortly after 1200 B.C. Troy suffered extensive destructions. Cyprus and most of the major sites in Palestine and Syria fell under attack; most managed to survive, but Ugarit was destroyed and never rebuilt. Egypt experienced successive waves of invaders, some with families and in search of land to settle; these hordes, made up of many different peoples—the *Sea Peoples*—were finally turned back by Ramses III in 1186 B.C., at least according to his official inscriptions. But the evidence suggests that the Pharaoh may have magnified his victory: Egyptian rulers never admitted failure in their official accounts, and the seriousness of the invasion may be reflected in the Egyptian retreat from areas in Asia in which they had formerly had influence.

The names of the invading Sea Peoples are preserved in the inscriptions of Ramses III, but translating them into the names of known peoples is mainly a matter of guesswork, with the exception of the Peleset, who can be identified as the Philistines. It is unlikely that the Sea Peoples were responsible for the destructions of the Mycenaean palaces; in fact, some Mycenaean refugees were probably among their number. They simply contributed to the general unrest.

Some memory of this time of troubles may be preserved in Homer's *Iliad* and *Odyssey*. Although much in the epics may reflect the poet's own eighth-century B.C. culture, a few elements go back much earlier and may dimly recall Mycenaean times. In fact, it was belief in the historicity of the Homeric poems by Heinrich Schliemann in the late nineteenth century that first brought the era of Bronze Age Greece to the eyes of the world. Convinced that Homer's Trojan War had been a real event, Schliemann used information given in the *Iliad* to identify a site at Hissarlik in Turkey as that of Troy. Excavating the site, he found the remains of at least seven superimposed cities. Later, he had similar success at Mycenae, where he discovered the Shaft Graves. Schliemann, however, had no idea that the finds that he identified as Trojan and Mycenaean—a treasure of gold jewelry in the second level at Troy, and the burial of "Agamemnon" at Mycenae—were centuries older than the Trojan War. Nonetheless, his work put an end to the idea that Greek history began only in 776 B.C., the date of the first recorded Olympic games.

The war over Troy (probably the city of Level VI of the great Trojan mound) fits well into the time of troubles that engulfed the eastern Mediterranean world in the twelfth century B.C. Perhaps it was marauding raiders from Greece, refugees themselves, who sacked Troy, or perhaps the victors of the war went home to find their positions usurped and the battle lines drawn for the internecine warfare that destroyed the palaces (as perhaps reflected in Aeschylus' *Agamemnon*, telling of the returning king's murder by his queen Clytemnestra and her lover Aegisthus, Agamemnon's cousin).

With the collapse of the palaces on the Greek mainland went the downfall of the entire palatial economy and the cultural system it served. Knowledge of the techniques of monumental building in stone, gold working, ivory carving, and other luxury craft skills were all lost. Regular contact with Eastern peoples essentially ceased, as disturbances in the Mediterranean made sea travel risky and the attention of survivors was necessarily devoted to basic subsistence. Even writing ceased in Greece; the limited subject matter of the Linear B texts suggests that it had not been in widespread use, and thus it did not survive the collapse of the palace economy.

Numerous explanations have been given for the fall of Mycenaean civilization. Greek tradition attributed it to an invasion of the ***Dorians***—specifically, the violent return of the Dorian Sons of Heracles (the Heraclids) a century after they had been driven out of the Peloponnesus. The most convincing argument for a Dorian invasion is the distribution of the Greek dialects in the Classical period: while East Greek dialects—such as Aeolic, Attic, and Ionic—were spread across the mid-Aegean region (carried by refugee Mycenaeans), Dorian dialects predominated in the Peloponnesus, the region to which the Dorians "returned," and in areas to which they later migrated (the southern Aegean, Crete).

The hypothesis of a Dorian invasion, while believed by the Greeks themselves, cannot be completely supported for a number of reasons. Perhaps most important is that it does not account for the widespread nature of the collapse. If there were Dorian invaders, they played only a minor role in the overall drama and left no archaeological traces. The iron, swords, fibulae, and cist grave burials that have at one time or another been attributed to them are now all known to have been present in Greece before the destruction of the palaces. A few "barbarian" pots have been found at a number of sites, but their significance and origins are still unclear—were they the customary pottery of a few newcomers, or simply the homemade products of those who could no longer afford professionally made pots?[3] If they do signal newcomers, there were still too few newcomers to account for the many destructions, and they were assimilated quickly into the mainstream Mycenaean culture.

Other hypotheses may account better for the situation. The myth of the return of the Heraclids may have been a later creation to legitimatize Spartan claims to supremacy in the Peloponnesus, for Greeks often shaped mythology to serve contemporary political purposes. The strongest evidence for the invasion is the existence of the Dorian dialect, but J. T. Hooker has provided an explanation that does not depend on an invasion: Dorian was a form of Mycenaean, a dialect spoken by the lower classes who were left behind when the palaces collapsed and the upper classes found refuges elsewhere.[4] If, on the other hand, the Dorians were indeed newcomers on the scene, they did not cause the massive destructions, but must have filtered in during the resulting upheavals and settled amidst the ruins of Mycenaean palace civilization, leaving no traces except their dialect, and perhaps a few pots.

A number of modern alternative hypotheses have been suggested, ranging from climate change,[5] earthquakes (attested in LH IIIB at Tiryns, Mycenae, the Menelaion shrine at Sparta, Pylos, and Troy),[6] the uprising of oppressed workers,[7] or troubles associated with the return of rulers long absent on military expeditions, suggested by the stories of the returns of Agamemnon and Odysseus from the Trojan War. But, to be persuasive, any explanation must take into account not simply the troubles in Mycenaean Greece, but the turmoil in the whole eastern Mediterranean. A number of explanations that meet this criterion focus upon the economic system as a whole. One of these, by the archaeologist Colin Renfrew, involves a sophisticated application of mathematical *systems collapse theory*.[8] Simply put, complex systems are susceptible to collapse as a result of relatively minor dislocations. (Consider the problems that have been caused in the late twentieth century by fluctuations in the price and availability of oil.)

Emily Vermeule offered a nonmathematical version of the systems collapse theory framed in terms of the supply of copper and tin for the production of bronze.[9] We have seen that the Mycenaean leaders depended upon imports of copper and tin. Any disruption in sea trade would have caused a severe crisis, even worse than a direct invasion. This disruption was provided by the activities of the Sea Peoples, and the result was economic collapse. Those with sufficient resources took to their ships, either to raid or to settle elsewhere, while the poor were left behind, as noted earlier.

As candidates for catalysts in the turmoil, the Sea Peoples seem recently to have replaced the Dorians in popularity.[10] They have the advantage of historical documentation in Hittite correspondence and the Ramses III inscription, and at least some of them have archaeological identity in the form of the Philistines. On mainland Greece, fear of sea raiders seems to be reflected in the precautions dictated in the Pylos tablets against invaders from the sea on the eve of the destruction of the palaces. On the other hand, the building of a defensive wall across the Isthmus of Corinth suggests that attack was expected by land, as does the inscription of Ramses. On the whole, however, the Sea Peoples were more likely to have been a contributing factor than a primary cause. What set them in motion remains a question.

Robert Drews has drawn attention to still another factor that he considers crucial to an understanding of the crisis: a radical change in the methods of warfare that occurred around 1200 B.C.[11] While the Bronze Age kingdoms of the Near East had previously relied primarily on chariot warfare, at this time new weapons and defensive armor come into prominence. The principal weapon of the charioteer was the bow, and his armor could sacrifice mobility in favor of coverage; in the twelfth century B.C., however, equipment suited to foot soldiers came into prominence. This included javelins, spears, and a cut-and-slash sword. For protection, there were small, round, easily maneuvered shields; corselets allowing freedom of movement; and greaves to protect the lower legs. Masses of infantry equipped with these weapons proved to be a match for chariots and were able to wreak amazing destruction on Bronze Age cities. The effect must have multiplied, with survivors of the attack on one city themselves becoming the refugee raiders of another. Drews noted the tendency to establish large fortified cities on the coast among the long-range results of the new methods of warfare. Such sites provided lookout points that allowed seaborne attacks to be anticipated, and, if necessary, their own access to the sea would better allow them to survive a siege. Drews also suggested that the change in warfare had a tendency to promote community solidarity, for success in close-order infantry fighting required the cooperation of all, as did the defense of the city.

All of these explanations were devised to account for the same basic body of evidence, and none can be decisively established at present. Thus, an explanation involving multiple causation seems most persuasive at this time. A palatial system that indulged in excessive building and overexploitation of the land and that exercised stringent control over its people; localized environmental problems such as drought or earthquake; interruption of trade routes by pirates and raiders, themselves driven from their homes by economic or environmental problems or by other raiders—all of these factors seem to have contributed to the escalating chaos that ended the Mediterranean Bronze Age.

THE DARK AGE AND MIGRATIONS

The Mycenaean world died gradually. As we saw, many of those who survived the catastrophic fall of the palaces in mainland Greece lived on in reduced circumstances on palace sites for some time; some, such as those at Tiryns, may even have been on the verge of creating a new political form, the city. Perati, the site of a cemetery used in the transition period between the fall of the palaces and the complete collapse of Bronze Age society in Greece, provides an interesting glimpse into a refugee settlement of that time. The site is on a natural harbor on the east coast of Attica, midway between Cape Sounion and Marathon. Although only the cemetery has been discovered, it has been totally excavated. Two hundred nineteen tombs were found in an area of over 13 acres. Of these, 192 were chamber tombs, cut deep into the rock and approached by a dromos; most (150) were family tombs, containing multiple burials made over a period of

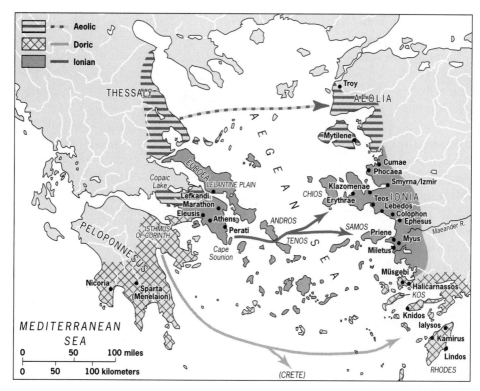

MAP 4A Dark Age Greece and the Aegean.

time. The grave goods included jewelry, clothing ornaments and accessories, amulets, seals, weapons, tools, pottery, and terracotta figurines; the materials used included gold, silver, ivory, bronze, and iron. Numerous items were imported from sites in the Aegean, as well as from Egypt, Syria, and Cyprus. Thus the grave goods attest considerable prosperity and lively contacts with the outside world. But gradually this last effort to regain the prosperity of the Bronze Age world failed; the last burials are dated to about 1075 B.C., and Perati then joined the rest of the mainland Greeks in "an era of withdrawal, depression and mere survival in a reduced and impoverished world."[12]

In this period of abandonment, counts of known settlement sites show a decline from 320 to 40.[13] Numbers of people succeeded in fleeing either to join the Sea Peoples or scattering to places of refuge. Given the small size of ships at the time, refugee groups probably did not number more than 100 or so, if that many. They may not have included women and children, for the tradition about the settlement of Miletus tells of the new arrivals seizing wives from among the native inhabitants.[14]

The earliest emigrants were speakers of the Aeolic dialect from Thessaly and central Greece, who settled the northern coast of Asia Minor. From the standpoint of later Greek history, however, the best-known of these refugees, and those who had the most promising future, were speakers of Ionian Greek, who went east, across the Aegean to the central coast, to establish Greek settlements in what would henceforth be known as *Ionia*.[15] Athens took credit for the leadership of this, the **Ionian Migration.** Somewhat later, Dorian speakers crossed the Aegean to the south, establishing settlements.

The Ionian cities that were most probably established in the initial colonization in the eleventh century B.C. were Miletus, Ephesus, Myus, Priene, Colophon, Lebedos, Teos, and, perhaps, Samos. Chios, Phocaea, Klazomenae, and Erythrae were settled a generation later; Halicarnassos (established near the Mycenaean tombs at Müsgebi) was originally Dorian, and Smyrna (Izmir) originally Aeolian, although both later became Ionian either officially (Smyrna) or in culture (Halicarnassos). Some of these sites—Miletus, Halicarnassos, Ephesus, and Samos—had seen Mycenaean occupation, but the extent of continuity is still being clarified by excavation. Definite breaks in occupation occurred at many sites, but at Miletus both the pottery and the building remains show continuous occupation with no break and only partial destruction—probably as the result of minor earthquakes—and rebuilding.[16] On the other hand, Homer tells us nothing about these sites, which might suggest that the tradition of their Bronze Age existence had been largely lost by the eighth century B.C. (unless he was deliberately suppressing events he knew to have taken place after the time of his story).

Our information about these early developments in Ionia is heavily dependent upon Greek traditions, but these must be examined carefully for signs of later invention. Tradition gave Athens a key role in the migrations as a meeting place for refugees and as a provider of assistance and leadership for the trip across the Aegean to Ionia. But suspicion is cast upon this by the fact that the seventh-century B.C. poet Mimnermus of Colophon seems unaware of Athenian involvement, for he identified the home of the founders of his city as Pylos. It is only in the sixth century B.C. that the Athenian role appears in our sources, and then only indirectly, when Solon calls the Athenians the "eldest of the Ionians."[17] By the fifth century B.C., however, the tradition of Athenian assistance to the Ionian Migration was a well-established part of the historical record: Thucydides (1.12) reports that refugees went first to Athens, and that the Athenians then organized them and sent them on to Ionia.

The tradition of the migration, as well as that of Athenian assistance, clearly was developed and embroidered over time. A major impetus for this was probably the later formation of an **Ionian League** by the twelve cities established by the Ionian-speaking settlers. The members of this league celebrated their ethnic identity in a common festival, the *Panionia*, and they also developed foundation legends that recalled the migration settlements, even though some of the cities were in fact later foundations. An impetus to the development of the tradition of Athenian assistance can also be found in the later ambitions of that city. As we shall see, the Athenians in the fifth century B.C. created an empire, nominally a league, to which many of these Ionian cities (living under Athenian control) paid tribute. The tradition that these members were originally Athenian colonists would have served to justify the power that Athens then exercised over them. Nevertheless, there are hints that Athens did play some role in the actual migrations, even if not the central and formal role attributed to the city by Athenian tradition. These hints include the reference in Solon's poems, which predates fifth-century B.C. Athenian imperialism and cannot have been affected by it, and the fact that some of the Ionian cities, or their colonies, adopted elements of the Athenian calendar, cults, and tribal system.

Those who did not join in the migrations may have abandoned farming for a nomadic or seminomadic existence, complicating the historians' job of estimating population.[18] The Linear B tablets attest extensive Mycenaean animal holdings, and herds of sheep and goats are movable forms of wealth. In unsettled conditions, they would have offered more security than crops, which could not be easily protected from hungry raiders. Archaeological evidence that diet switched from about 11 percent meat in the late Mycenaean period to a high of 40 percent in the ensuing period supports this suggestion.[19] We can also see this change mirrored in the use of livestock rather than landholdings as a measure of wealth in the Homeric poems, which probably reflected Dark Age conditions. The presence of herding groups without permanent settlement sites or regular burial places would easily elude the archaeologist.[20] Nevertheless, even if some of the population is "lost" in this way, the evidence of violent destructions and the drastic change in living conditions suggests that many simply did not survive the destructions. In one way or another, it has been estimated that the population of mainland Greece dropped by three-quarters.[21]

Much of the darkness of this "Dark Age" may be simply the by-product of our own lack of information. In its early days, archaeology focused on monumental buildings and valuable objects deemed fit for museum display, and most of the material from the Dark Age fits neither category. Recent archaeological interest in more mundane evidence, such as the burials at Perati, and the use of survey archaeology have revealed details of everyday life and habitation patterns over time in large areas. These new directions are far more suited to investigations of Dark Age Greece than the more traditional archaeology was. The study of the Dark Age today is a fast-moving field, and no true synthesis of hypothesis and evidence is possible. The rest of this chapter will therefore concentrate on a few of the more promising subjects of current research: metallurgy, the Mycenaean occupation of Cyprus, and the settlement of Lefkandi on Euboea.

METALLURGY AND THE SHIFT TO IRON[22]

Difficulty in obtaining copper and tin was probably responsible for the shift to the use of iron as the basic metal during the Dark Age. In fact, the change was so marked that the name *Iron Age* is used to refer to the period. The adoption of iron, despite its potential superiority to bronze for many uses, did not immediately bring about a significant improvement in lifestyle. In fact, in many ways, the use of iron must have seemed to be a step backward. Iron is not as attractive as bronze, nor does it provide a surface that can be inscribed—both features that made bronze desirable for offerings to the gods. Moreover, many bronze articles had been made by casting, but the Greeks were not able to cast iron. In fact, the readier availability of iron ore seems to have been its only advantage at this period, and bronze made a significant comeback when communications reopened sufficiently to make tin and abundant supplies of copper available again. Even in the late eighth century B.C. the epic poet Hesiod described the Age of Iron as one of unparalleled misery for human beings, and in many ways the less attractive characteristics of the metal seem to reflect the difficult conditions which drove men to its use.

Turning iron ore into a useful product presented many difficulties. If iron is to take a hard edge, it must be subjected to a complex process of carbonization and tempering, developable only by considerable trial and error. The process had already been worked out by the Hittites in Asia Minor, and, by the twelfth century B.C., the Cypriots, with long experience in copper mining and production, were extracting iron ore and producing iron objects. V. Desborough has, in fact, suggested that those who introduced the process to Athens were Cypriots, perhaps Mycenaeans who had taken refuge in Cyprus and then returned to the mainland at the time of the catastrophe that destroyed the cities in Cyprus.[23]

CYPRUS IN THE LATE BRONZE AND EARLY IRON AGE[24]

Cyprus was well known to the Mycenaeans as a source of copper and as a point of access to the markets of the Syro-Palestinian coast, although the Mycenaeans had never established settlements on the island. Thus, it is not surprising that the island attracted Mycenaean refugees. The choice was not a bad one, for, although Cyprus suffered numerous attacks and destructions, there was no generalized collapse of culture: neither writing nor outside contacts were lost. Major centers recovered rapidly even from the widespread destructions.

A number of waves of raiders and refugees reached Cyprus from around 1230 B.C.; they included Mycenaean Greeks, mixed groups of Sea Peoples, and refugees from the Syro-Palestinian coast, especially Ugarit. These repeated waves of newcomers created a mixed population in which Mycenaean Greeks played a central role, and it was from this time that the island became *Hellenized*. Those Cypriots who chose to maintain their ethnic identity (the *Eteocypriots*, or Old Cypriots) concentrated at Amathus, although in some communities, such as Lapethos, Greeks and Cypriots continued to live side by side. The island was

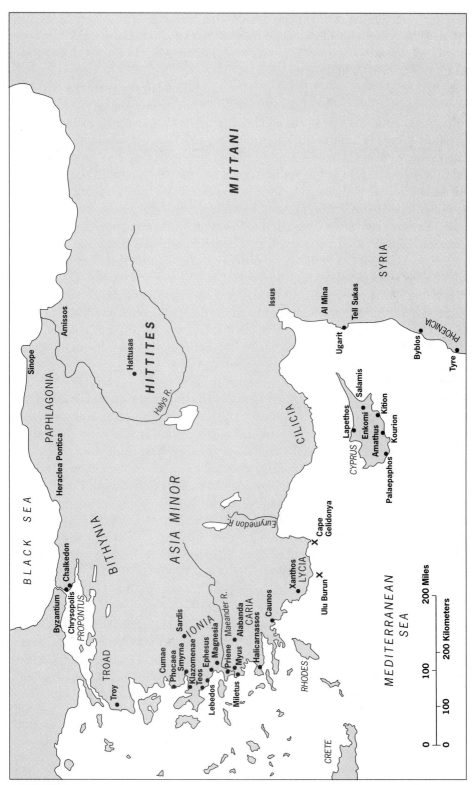

MAP 4B Dark Age Asia Minor, the Levant, and Cyprus.

generally peaceful and maintained contact with both the Aegean and the Near East, and the refugees made valuable contributions to its culture in the form of new techniques in bronze working and fresh artistic ideas in the production of pottery and terracotta figurines.

At some time between 1075 and 1050 B.C., widespread destruction attests to a major disaster on the island, probably caused by an earthquake, which brought Bronze Age culture on Cyprus to an end. Numerous sites were abandoned, but new cities soon replaced them, often on sites near the old abandoned settlements, as at Kourion, Lapethos, and Enkomi near Salamis. The link with the Bronze Age past was never broken in Cyprus, and Mycenaean traditions lived on even as the mixed population gradually coalesced. Writing continued in the Cypriot-Minoan syllabary, as attested by an engraved bronze skewer or spit of middle-eleventh-century B.C. date found in a tomb in Palaepaphos; the language is Arcadian Greek, and the spit provides the earliest evidence of the use of Greek on Cyprus.[25] Copper continued to be produced, and Cypriot metallurgical skills were applied to iron, increasingly the metal of choice for weapons. Politically, the historical form of the Cypriot kingdoms seems to have developed out of Mycenaean aristocracy and kingship to attain at least embryonic form in the eleventh century B.C.[26] Trade with the Near East flourished, and contact was maintained even with the Aegean, where Cypriot imports and influence appear at Lefkandi in Euboea, in Athens, and at sites in Crete.

During the Early Iron Age, the distinction between Eteocypriot and Greek culture faded, and the less sophisticated Cypriot influence gradually came to predominate. By the mid-ninth century B.C., the Phoenicians, who had long had trade relations with the island, created their first colony at Kition on the south coast. It was the first colony of their westward expansion, and they named it *Qarthadast*—"New City"—a name that they later applied to their more famous colony in North Africa, which we know as Carthage. From Kition, Phoenician influence spread: Phoenician material has been found in tombs at Amathus, and there is some evidence for Phoenician involvement in copper mining. Their ships carried copper to the Aegean, and they may have been responsible for spreading the Cypriot decorative motif of concentric circles to potters in Rhodes, Crete, Euboea, and Athens.

The importance of Cyprus to mainland Greece in the Dark Age was twofold. Contact with the island gave Euboean Greeks access to its abundant supplies of copper and to the experience of skilled craftsmen who worked in both iron and bronze. Moreover, the island's location and traditional trading contacts made it an entry point and staging post to the Levant, and its Hellenized, Greek-speaking population made it approachable. Soon Greek traders on Cyprus had used their new contacts to establish connections with the Phoenician capital of Tyre and to trade at sites on the Syrian coast such as Al Mina and Tell Sukas.

LEFKANDI: EARLY RECOVERY IN GREECE[27]

The earliest evidence for the reestablishment of Greek contacts with the East has been found at Lefkandi, a site on the west coast of Euboea. Lefkandi had been the site of a Mycenaean settlement in the Bronze Age and had received a large influx of newcomers in about 1200 B.C., probably refugees from the mainland. By the end of the twelfth century B.C., however, the site was abandoned. Since Herodotus (1.146) says that the Abantes from Euboea took part in the Ionian Migration, we might identify the people who abandoned Lefkandi as the *Abantes*.

The site was too attractive to remain vacant for long, however. Its good anchorage and access to the extensive Lelantine Plain soon attracted settlers, and it was reoccupied in the eleventh century B.C. By the tenth century B.C. the people of Lefkandi had developed a wide range of external contacts, all significantly accessible by sea: Athens, Thessaly, Macedonia, the islands of Andros and Tenos, Crete, and, notably, Cyprus. Cypriot influence appears especially in the casting of bronze tripods, and Near Eastern contacts via Cyprus are evidenced by the appearance of gold in tombs (gold had been missing in Greek burials since the collapse of the Mycenaean kingdoms).

In addition to gold and bronze work, the burials at Lefkandi present other unusual features. There are a few of Athenian type, which suggests the strong probability that some Athenians actually lived in Lefkandi. There are also warrior tombs with unusual inhumation burials in wooden coffins, differing from the usual Lefkandian cremation or cremation-inhumation burials. Most impressive (and puzzling), however, is a multiple shaft grave burial of the early tenth century B.C., with grave goods of a startling richness for this period.[28] One compartment of the shaft contained three or four horses, and the second, a female inhumation and a male cremation. The female burial was accompanied by rich offerings, including gilt hair coils, a gold pendant decorated with granulation, gold and faience beads, bronze and iron pins (the iron ones covered with gold foil), an iron knife with an ivory handle, and an unusual gold "brassiere." The male burial was in a bronze amphora of Cypriot origin, decorated with animals and huntsmen with bows. The ashes were wrapped in a cloak that has been remarkably well preserved: it is made up of two lengths of linen, with flokati-type weaving at the top, reminiscent of a shaggy modern Greek rug. Placed beside the amphora were an iron sword, a spearhead, and a whetstone. A heroic-style funeral is suggested by the remains of the cremation site. But perhaps most remarkable is the fact that the burial site was enclosed in a large apsidal building over 45 meters in length, with an external colonnade (Figure 4-3).

The colonnaded building at Lefkandi is by far the earliest temple-type building of such size found in Greece up to this time. The excavators suggest that it was not a temple to an Olympian god, but a **heroön**, or hero tomb, where

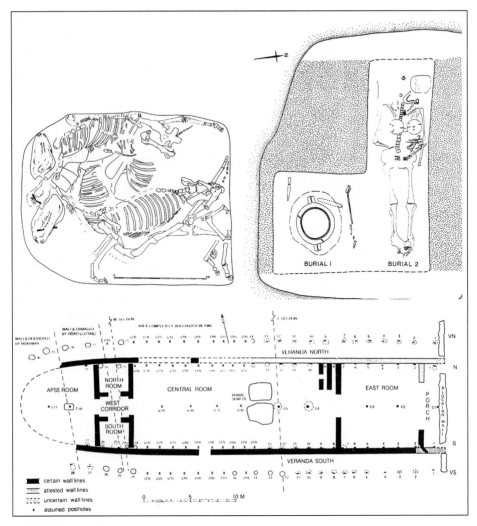

FIGURE 4-3 Site plan of Lefkandi.

honor would have been paid, and sacrifices offered, to a deceased mortal. The hero had been accompanied in death by his consort and his horses; there are parallels for the sacrifice of slaves in contemporary Cypriot burials and for the sacrifice of horses in eighth- and seventh-century B.C. burials in Cyprus.[29] Before 950 B.C., the building had been deliberately dismantled and covered with a great tumulus; the excavators suggest that this may have been done from fear when it was discovered that the heroön had been built over part of a Mycenaean cemetery.

The finds at Lefkandi demonstrate that by the early tenth century B.C. its inhabitants had considerable access to foreign luxury items such as gold, faience, and ivory. This predates by at least a century the rich grave of an Athenian woman found in the Agora at Athens, which attests a noteworthy level of recovery there.[30] The heroic honors paid to the occupant of the heroön show that marked class distinctions existed within the Lefkandi community. Evidence of metalworking at Lefkandi and the presence of Cypriot objects attests to the importance of the Cypriot connection in Greek recovery.

THE DARK AGE SUMMED UP

In Greece, the losses involved in the collapse of Mycenaean civilization led in the long run to cultural development along new and different lines and eventually to the classical patterns of Greek culture. The way was opened by contacts with the older civilizations of the Near East, via Cyprus. The loss of imports of copper and tin pushed the survivors to learn the new skills of ironworking in order to supply their needs for metal, and they found teachers in Cypriot metalworkers. The loss of literacy fostered the highly developed oral tradition that gave rise to the Homeric epic. It also made possible the later adoption of the alphabet from the Phoenicians. Finally, the collapse of the centralized palace system left survivors adrift in small groups under local leaders who could most efficiently direct continuing survival efforts, or lead migrations. These small refugee groups provided the nucleus out of which developed the autonomous city-state, or polis.

S O U R C E   A N A L Y S I S

Protogeometric and Early Geometric Pottery

T he chronology of the Dark Age depends largely upon the gradual changes in pottery decoration found on a series of vases from the Kerameikos cemetery in Athens. After the collapse of the palaces, the survivors made a less skilled version of Mycenaean pottery that is called *Submycenaean*. In the eleventh-century B.C., however, potters in Athens (using a faster potter's wheel and multiple brushes and compass) transformed Submycenaean into the far superior product known as *Protogeometric*. Protogeometric vases are characterized by the use of concentric semicircles and by simple bands that accentuate the

continued

Figure 4-4 Attic Protogeometric amphora.

shape of the pot. An example is a belly-handled amphora from the Kerameikos cemetery, which also portrays a small horse (see Figure 4-4).

By the late tenth century B.C., Protogeometric had developed sufficiently in its shapes and favored motifs to warrant a new name: *Geometric*. Because the geometric style had a long life, it is divided into subclasses: Early, Middle, and Late Geometric (EG, MG, and LG; scholarly publications make even finer distinctions within each of these classes). The EG subclass is characterized not by the circular motifs of Protogeometric, but by rectilinear forms such as the meander pattern that is still an identifying mark of traditional Greek crafts (Figure 4-5). Full concentric circles do appear, but they are framed in characteristic rectangles. Over time, more and more of the vase came to be covered with design, and animals as well as geometric figures played a role in the decorative bands, probably inspired by designs on Eastern textiles. By the eighth century B.C., hu-

FIGURE 4-5 Attic Early Geometric amphora.

man figures appear in funerary scenes and also in scenes that appear to tell a story: a MG skyphos portrays battles on both land and sea (Figure 4-6). LG vases used as grave markers often took on monumental proportions, but these developments will be discussed in the next chapter.

The gradual development of Attic Protogeometric and Geometric pottery provides a valuable chronological tool because the pottery was widely traded and thus is found in most excavations, and because it influenced the pottery of other poleis, making it possible to create parallel series for them in terms of Attic developments. Pottery dates, while they are hardly exact, are still useful to keep in mind, for, as in the case of the Bronze Age, discussions of Dark Age history and

continued

archaeology often indicate chronology in terms of pottery styles. The approximate initial dates for Attic Geometric, according to A. M. Snodgrass, are[31]:

1125/1100	Submycenaean
1050/1040	Protogeometric (PG)
900	Early Geometric (EG)
860/840	Middle Geometric (MG)
770/760–ca. 710 (700)	Late Geometric (LG)

FIGURE 4-6 Middle Geometric *skyphos* (a type of drinking cup) from Eleusis.

IMPORTANT PLACES IN CHAPTER 4

On Map 4-A: *Dark Age Greece and the Aegean:* Andros, Athens, Cape Sounion, Copaic Lake, Eleusis, Euboea, Isthmus of Corinth, Kephallenia island, Lefkandi, Lelantine Plain, Marathon, Menelaion, Nicoria, Perati, Samos, Sparta, Tenos, Troy (Hissarlik)

Asia Minor West Coast and Migration Settlements:

Müsgebi (a Mycenaean cemetery)

Aeolic Migration: Cumae, Smyrna/Izmir (added to Ionian League ca. 700 B.C.)

Ionian Migration and League: Chios, Colophon, Ephesus, Erythrae, Klazomenae, Lebedos, Miletus, Myus, Phocaea, Priene, Samos, Teos

Dorian Migration and Hexapolis: Ialysos, Kamirus on the island of Rhodes, Knidos, Kos, Lindos; Halicarnassos, originally one of six Dorian cities in Dorian Hexapolis, but expelled early

On Map 4-B: *Northern Asia Minor Shore:* Bithynia (Roman name), Halys River, Hattusas, Hittites, Paphlagonia; *Greek colonies:* Byzantium, Chalkedon, Chrysopolis, Heraclea Pontica, Sinope

Southern Asia Minor Shore: Cape Gelidonya (shipwreck), Caunos (Carian city), Cilicia, Eurymedon River, Lycia, Ulu Burun (shipwreck), Xanthos (Lycian city)

Levant: Al Mina, Byblos, Issus, Phoenicia, Syria, Tell Sukas, Tyre, Ugarit

Cyprus: Amathus, Enkomi, Kition (Phoenician Qarthadast), Kourion, Lapethos, Palaepaphos, Salamis

On Other Maps *(use map index to find these):* Carthage, Gla

SUGGESTIONS FOR FURTHER READING

A good overview of the collapse is provided by N. K. Sandars, *The Sea Peoples* (1985, rev. ed.). The two fundamental but specialized works on the Greek Dark Age are A. M. Snodgrass, *The Dark Age of Greece* (1971), and V. R. d'A. Desborough, *The Greek Dark Ages* (1972). On Cyprus, V. Karageorghis, *Cyprus from the Stone Age to the Romans* (1982), and on Lefkandi, M. R. Popham, E. Touloupa, and L. H. Sackett, "The Hero of Lefkandi," *Antiquity* 5 (1982), 169–174.

ENDNOTES

1. K. Kilian, "Mycenaeans up to Date," in E. B. French and K. A. Wardle, *Problems in Greek Prehistory* (1988), 134–135.
2. Kilian, (above, n. 1), fig. 9, 132.

3. See H. W. Catling and E. A. Catling, " 'Barbarian' Pottery from the Mycenaean Settlement at the Menelaion, Sparta," *Annual of the British School at Athens* 76 (1981), 71–82; D. B. Small, " 'Barbarian Ware' and Prehistoric Aegean Economics: An Argument for Indigenous Appearance," *Journal of Mediterranean Archaeology* 3 (1990), 3–25.

4. J. T. Hooker, *Mycenaean Greece* (1976), 171–173.

5. Rhys Carpenter, *Discontinuity in Greek Civilization* (1966).

6. Kilian, (above, n. 1) has collected the evidence for archaeologically proven catastrophic earthquakes in this period, see his note 2 and fig. 10.

7. Hooker (above, n. 4).

8. Colin Renfrew, "Systems Collapse as Social Transformation," in C. Renfrew and K. L. Cooke, eds., *Transformations, Mathematical Approaches to Culture Change* (1979), 481–506.

9. Emily Vermeule, "The Fall of the Mycenaean Empire," *Archaeology* (1960), 66–75. Veremeule also suggests that the importation of grain may have been necessary, for population levels were high and the land was not very productive; she interprets Mycenaean colonial ventures as signs of population pressures on the food supply.

10. For a good discussion of the Sea Peoples, see N. K. Sandars, *The Sea Peoples* (1985, rev. ed.).

11. Robert Drews, *The End of the Bronze Age: Changes in Warfare and the Catastrophe ca. 1200 B.C.* (1993).

12. The site at Perati is described by Spiros Iakovidis, *Excavation of the Necropolis at Perati* (1980), quotation, p. 111.

13. A. Snodgrass, *The Dark Age of Greece* (1971), 561–564.

14. Hdt. 1.146.

15. On the Ionian Migration, see J. M. Cook in I. E. S. Edwards, C. J. Badd, N. G. L. Hammond, and E. Sullivan, eds., *Cambridge Ancient History* 2 (3d ed.), chap. 38.

16. Gödecken, in French and Wardle, (above, n. 1), 313.

17. Aristotle, *Constitution of the Athenians*, 5.2.

18. A suggestion made by A. Snodgrass, *An Archaeology of Greece* (1987), 193–209; see, too, B. Eder, "The Dorian Migration: Religious Consequences in the Argolid," in R. Hägg and G. C. Nordquist, eds., *Celebrations of Death and Divinity in the Bronze Age Argolid* (1990), 207–211. Although there has been considerable criticism [for example, the collection of articles edited by C. R. Whittaker, *Pastoral Economies in Classical Antiquity* (1988), especially the article by John Cherry], much of it centers on a narrow definition of nomadism, and M. H. Jameson, in commenting on Eder's paper (p. 210), suggests that a modified version of the hypothesis "can be fully supported by more careful historical and more modest claims."

19. W. A. MacDonald, W. E. Coulson, and J. Rosser, *Excavations at Nicoria in Southwest Greece. III: Dark Age and Byzantine Occupation* (1983), 323–324.

20. The recent work of Roger Cribb, *Nomads in Archaeology* (1991), may go far to remedy this problem.

21. Snodgrass (above, n. 13), 561–564.

22. On the introduction of iron, see R. Maddin, J. D. Muhly, and T. S. Wheeler, "How the Iron Age Began," *Scientific American* (Oct. 1977), 122–131.

23. V. Desborough, "Mycenaeans in Cyprus in the 11th Century B.C.," in *Acts of the Mycenaean Symposium 'The Mycenaeans in the Eastern Mediterranean'* (1973), 79–87.

24. A good source on the history of Cyprus is V. Karageorghis, *Cyprus from the Stone Age to the Romans* (1982); for more detail on the role played by Cyprus in terms of trading contacts between mainland Greece and the Levant, see J. N. Coldstream, "Early Greek Visitors to Cyprus and the Eastern Mediterranean," in V. Tatton-Brown, ed., *Cyprus and the East Mediterranean in the Iron Age* (1989), 90–94.

25. Karageorghis (above, n. 24), 120 and fig. 93.

26. See Karageorghis (above, n. 24), 90–123.

27. For the excavation reports on Lefkandi, see M. R. Popham, L. H. Sackett, and P. G. Themelis, *Lefkandi I. The Iron Age* (1980).

28. On this burial, which was discovered after the publication of *Lefkandi I*, see M. R. Popham, E. Touloupa, and L. H. Sackett, "The Hero of Lefkandi," *Antiquity* 5 (1982), 169–174.

29. Slaves sacrificed to serve their masters after death were found in three tombs at Lapethos, roughly contemporary with the Lefkandi burials (CG I), in Tombs 412, 417, 420; see Gjerstad, in *The Swedish Cyprus Expedition* IV: 2, 431–433; horses, with their chariots, were found in the eighth or seventh century B.C. necropolis at Salamis in Tombs 1, 2, 3, 10, 47, 50, 79; sacrificed slaves were also found in Tomb 2; asses without vehicles were found in Tombs 19 and 31, which were smaller and less monumental structures than those containing horses and chariots; see V. Karageorghis, *Salamis: Recent Discoveries in Cyprus* (1969).

30. E. L. Smithson, "The Tomb of a Rich Athenian Lady, c.850 B.C.," *Hesperia* 37 (1968), 77–116.

31. These absolute dates are adopted from A. Snodgrass (above, n. 13), 123.

CHAPTER FIVE

Archaic Greece: Renaissance and Revolution

he signs of recovery that we have seen at Lefkandi in the tenth and ninth centuries B.C. accelerated and spread in the Archaic period, from the eighth through the sixth centuries B.C. The early part of the Archaic period has been called both the *Greek Renaissance*—because many of the accomplishments of this period recalled the Mycenaean world as it was then remembered by epic poets—and the *Orientalizing Revolution*, because Eastern influences were prominent, most visibly in the Orientalizing pottery produced in the city of Corinth.[1] These two terms look in two directions in explaining Greek development, one toward internal development, the other toward external influences. But, as was the case when we examined the origins of Minoan civilization, to consider these two possibilities as mutually exclusive creates a dichotomy that fails to do justice to the complexities of the historical situation. We must try to balance the two approaches, neither attributing everything to outside influences, nor insisting that everything that we see as characteristically Greek was indigenous and unique.

The discoveries at Lefkandi have shown that the separation between the Dark Age and the succeeding period is to some extent an artificial one, as in all historical periodization. Nonetheless, giving that period a special name (or names) does serve a useful purpose, for it draws our attention to the far greater scope and degree of change that took place. The Greek world was reviving and the most characteristic elements of classical Greece were taking shape.

HOMER AND EPIC POETRY

The period comprising the eighth century and early seventh century B.C. was the age of epic. The epic poems of Homer, the *Iliad* and the *Odyssey*, date probably to 750 and 720 B.C., respectively, and the poems of Hesiod to the end of the eighth century B.C. The *Iliad* tells the story of the tenth year of the Trojan War and of the coming of age of the great hero Achilles, while the *Odyssey* relates the adventures of Odysseus as he returned home from the war to a household barely clinging to its position of authority. The gods figure prominently in the actions of both poems. Homer's poems have been called the "Bible of the Greeks," for they expressed the values that lay at the heart of Greek culture and were the primary means of transmitting those values to succeeding generations.

Homer's poems depicted the Bronze Age for an Iron Age audience through the transforming medium of an oral poetic tradition that preserved only fragments from the Mycenaean past. Homer's heroes know nothing of the complex bureaucracy of the real Mycenaean palaces as revealed in the Linear B tablets: his princess even does the family laundry. No one remembers how the great palaces were constructed, although their ruins were a familiar part of the Dark Age world, and so the labor of moving the great building blocks, some as much as 2 meters in length, is assigned to the giant Cyclops.

The poems of Hesiod, while also in epic form, are quite different in subject matter from the Homeric epic. Rather than telling stories, they relay information directly. Hesiod's *Theogony* relates the generation and genealogies of the gods and other divine beings, and his *Works and Days* describes and offers advice about the year's work of the farmer. Both are useful as contemporary evidence for aspects of everyday life and for religious beliefs and values in the eighth century B.C., as long as their work is interpreted in the light of what is known about the development and functioning of oral tradition.

The composition of Greek epic poetry was an oral art, and our understanding of it has been greatly enhanced by the study of modern poets who employ similar oral techniques.[2] The oral poet's methods depend upon the poetic language with which he works, which in the case of the classical Greek epic was *dactylic hexameter.* The basic line in dactylic hexameter is made up of six metrical units, or feet (hence *hexameter,* or six meters); each foot has a pattern of short and long syllables in the form "long, short, short" (the dactyl); the syllables can be replaced by metrical equivalents, as at the end of the line ("long, long"). This pattern of long and short syllables, rather than rhyme or accent, is the defining characteristic of Greek epic poetry.

Because he composed in a well-defined rhythmical form, the poet could use formulaic phrases embodying various parts of the dactylic line as his basic units of composition. These formulas consisted of partial lines of specific metrical pattern, often composed of a name and an epithet, such as "fleet-footed Achilles" or "ox-eyed Athena," which could be plugged into a line wherever needed, at the beginning, end, or middle. The poet's formulaic stock also included whole lines, groups of lines, and even entire type scenes (arrivals, departures, meals, sacrifices). He learned all of these by years of apprenticeship, and their mastery allowed him to compose his work extemporaneously as he sang.

The art of such poets did not lie in original creation, but in the skillful handling and faithful transmission of traditional poetic material.

An interesting parallel is often drawn between the formulaic construction of Homeric epic and that of the ornamentation on Late Geometric vases. This is especially noteworthy in the case of the giant vases that are called *Dipylon*, because they were found near the Dipylon Gate. The Dipylon vases, which date from the same period as the epic poems, stand 4 to 5 feet in height and were used as monumental grave markers. Their surface is covered with bands of repeated motifs in a pattern that seems to echo the repeated verbal formulas of the Homeric poet (Figure 5-1).

Although the best-known Greek epic poems are Homer's *Iliad* and *Odyssey* and the poems of Hesiod, in antiquity these were part of a much larger poetic repertoire. It included stories about other parts of the Trojan War not covered by the *Iliad* and *Odyssey*, as well as stories with entirely different casts of characters, such as the voyage of the Argonauts and the labors of Herakles. Most of these other epics are preserved only in fragments or summaries.

Homer's world reflects the increasing Eastern contacts that the Greeks had in his day. The Phoenicians feature prominently in the tales of Odysseus as merchants and pirates, and Odysseus visited Egypt, as did Helen on her way both to and from Troy. But it is Hesiod who especially shows the influence of the Near East. The Hesiodic story of the castration of Uranos by his son Kronos is a version of a succession story that appears in Hittite and Ugaritic mythology in the ancient Near East. Comparative study of the narrative techniques and the literary style of Greek and Near Eastern epic has shown that the similarities are not limited to the simple use of a story motif, but extend to the epic form itself.[3]

THE ALPHABET AND EPIC

The most important by-product of Greek contact with the peoples of the Near East was the alphabet. From about the mid-eighth century B.C., evidence appears that the Greeks were once again writing. The new system that they used, the alphabet, was borrowed from the Phoenicians. The Phoenician system, however, recorded only consonants, and the reader depended upon recognizing an already familiar word by the consonant cluster and the context (for example, *ct* could be read as "cat," "cut," "cot," or even "kite"). The Greeks adapted this system to their own needs—and revolutionized it—by using some of the symbols not needed for Greek in order to express the sounds of the vowels. Using the alphabet, a person could sound out even unfamiliar words. Thus, by the addition of symbols for vowels, the Greeks created a highly flexible and easily learned writing system, a true alphabet.

FIGURE 5-1   Attic Geometric Dipylon amphora.

The Greek alphabet offered another advantage that may provide a clue as to the motive behind its creation. As we saw, epic depended upon the length of vowel sounds in syllables for its rhythms. In contrast to the vowel-less Phoenician writing system and the Cypriot syllabary, the Greek alphabet was able to record the epic meter in a way that preserved and transmitted this metrical information. Thus, when we ask why the Greeks invented vowels for their alphabet, the answer that suggests itself is that they wanted to record epic verse. H. T. Wade-Gery first proposed this,[4] and recently the hypothesis has been argued in detail in a book by Barry Powell.[5] Powell attributes the invention of the alphabet to a Euboean, one of those adventurers who traveled the trade route from Lefkandi-Eretria and Chalkis to Cyprus and on to the Levant, and he puts the date at around 800 B.C. Alan Johnston suggests that the contact took place in Cyprus, where a visiting Greek could have become familiar with both the

Cypriot use of writing (in a syllabic script similar to Linear B) and the much simpler Phoenician system.[6] In keeping with these suggestions, one of the earliest long alphabetic inscriptions was found in Pithekussai, the first Euboean settlement in the west. It reads, "I am the cup of Nestor, a joy to drink from. Whoever drinks this cup, straightway that man the desire of beautiful-crowned Aphrodite will seize."[7]

An alternative hypothesis about the adoption of the alphabet was that it had a commercial origin: Greek traders, most probably in Syria, picked it up in order to keep records and mark goods. This hypothesis is supported by the fact that the particular form of the Phoenician alphabet that the Greeks adopted was the cursive North Semite version used in commerce. Weighing heavily against the hypothesis, however, is the fact that there are no commercial records among the earliest preserved examples of Greek alphabetic writing. In fact, many of the early inscriptions are simply graffiti scratched on pots: names indicating ownership, erotic or obscene remarks, abecedaria for learning, and, significantly, snatches of hexameter poetry. There are no inventories, contracts, mortgages, or land transfers, such as are common in Near Eastern texts. It could be, of course, that business records were made on perishable material, and hence that none have survived. There are also no collections of laws or judicial decisions, such as are found in the Near Eastern texts; this suggests that the origin of alphabetic writing was not closely connected with the origins and early definition of the polis.

The role of women in the transmission of literary was suggested in 1960 by L. H. Jeffery.[8] Jeffery pointed out that alphabetic literacy could not have been passed on through casual contacts, and that the bilingual environments of mixed marriages would have provided a favorable means of transmission. Jeffery's insight about alphabetic literacy has been further supported by J. N. Coldstream's study of mixed marriages in both the eastern and western Greek worlds.[9]

The spread of literacy had far-reaching consequences for Greek civilization. Nevertheless, it must be stressed that the culture remained basically an oral one until the late fifth century B.C.,[10] and even Plato in the fourth century decried the use of writing as a pernicious crutch that would destroy memory. The most revolutionary uses of the new literacy came later as part of political reforms in the Archaic period, when the traditional laws were written down in a form accessible to all. After this, the ordinary citizen would no longer be at the mercy of the (possibly convenient and self-serving) memory of the aristocratic leaders. But this anticipates the full Archaic period; as we have seen, there are no remaining inscriptions or other evidence from the eighth century B.C. to suggest that the Greeks immediately began writing down their customary laws and procedures (*nomoi*) or keeping official records. Nor should we expect them to have done so, for *nomos*, the "way things were done," was still embodied and transmitted through oral tradition.

THE RISE OF THE POLIS

After the collapse of the palace-centered kingdoms of the Mycenaean age, the survivors must have lived in small groups with a fairly rudimentary organization: leaders with bands of followers. The persistence of the Mycenaean title *basileus* suggests either that these officials survived, to become leaders of local groups after the collapse, or that people considered the Mycenaean term (perhaps passed down in oral tradition) as the most appropriate title for the new leaders. When the mists clear in the eighth century B.C., with Homer, however, the Greek polis already exists in a rudimentary form, and this revival of organized political structures is one of the lasting achievements of the Greek Renaissance.

Homer knows the polis well. In the *Iliad*, he describes the cities of peace and of war.[11] The city of peace has an ***agora*** (meeting place and marketplace), a dancing place (later to become the Greek theater), and an orderly distribution of fields, vineyards, and pasture. A sceptered basileus directs the work on his estate, while in the city center a trial is taking place, with heralds to keep order, an arbitrator, elders to make the decisions, and ordinary people as observers. While these institutional beginnings will become more developed and elaborated over time, a protopolis already is in place.

The polis was unlike a modern city in two important respects. The first was autonomy. The polis was self-governing: it was not subject to a larger regional or national state (although it might limit its autonomy by voluntary membership in a league). The second was the possession and control of a territory. While the polis usually consisted of an urban center, or ***astu***, its agriculturally based economy depended upon the possession of a territory, or ***chora***, which might contain dependent villages. In some cases, most notably that of Sparta, there was no urban center, but only a collection of villages. These two main characteristics of a polis explain why it is translated as *city-state*.

Other distinguishing characteristics of the polis are hard to pin down. Because it was not identical with a center city (for it might lack one), it cannot be identified by its urban characteristics, such as a city wall or a certain size urban population. Nor, since it might be relocated, can it be identified with a specific location. The Greeks themselves seem to have identified the polis with its citizens, for, in references to poleis and in inscriptions recording the official acts of the polis, it is "the Athenians" or "the Spartans" who are said to act, not "Athens" or "Sparta."

Although we do not have detailed information about the structure of the early polis, it is clear that rule was by the members of the few "best" families (aristocracy). At this period it is likely that the wealthier men really were the best in a physical as well as a social sense, since they had the most adequate diet, freedom from debilitating heavy physical labor, and an education; their lives were spent in the "noble" pursuits of warfare, games, and feasting. In contrast, the

poor were often stunted in their development by inferior nutrition, heavy physical labor starting at an early age, and harsh working conditions.

Prominent in the early aristocracy was the figure of the basileus. The term,
at least, was a legacy of Mycenaean times. It is usually translated as *king*, but
this is somewhat misleading, since it carries connotations of a royal splendor
and absolute power that were absent in eighth-century B.C. Greece.[12] The
basileus was probably the leader in warfare, as in the *Iliad*, and his authority depended, as in the epic, upon the assent of the ***demos*** (the male citizenry arrayed
for battle) and upon the agreement of other basileis to support him (for example, in the *Iliad*, when Achilles withdraws his support from Agamemnon, it is
considered his right, even though it is detrimental to the Greek cause). From
his earliest appearance, therefore, the basileus had an authority that was
bounded by informal but real limits. Nevertheless, near the end of the century,
the poet Hesiod complains bitterly about the "bribe-eating" basileis who per-
vert the ends of justice.[13]

One of the most interesting puzzles connected with the beginning of the
polis is the question of Near Eastern—specifically, Phoenician—influence. The
Phoenicians lived in organized city-states long before the Greeks had formalized the institutions of the polis, and, by the ninth century B.C., they had established their first overseas colony at Kition on Cyprus. Their Greek Cypriot
neighbors thus had the opportunity to observe the process of city foundation
firsthand, and they could have observed the continuing operation of Kition
over a long period of time. The Phoenicians established other colonies
throughout the western Mediterranean in the ensuing period, just at the time
that the Greeks were beginning to colonize in the same area. The first Greek
colonial settlement—actually, more a trading post or emporium than a
colony—was made by the Euboeans at Pithekussai, on a small island off the
west coast of Italy, early in the eighth century B.C., and evidence shows that
some Phoenicians lived among them. While only a few historians attribute the
origins of the polis to Phoenician influence,[14] the Euboean presence in Cyprus
and their creation of the first Greek colonial settlement at Pithekussai seem unlikely to be mere coincidence.

THE RISE OF THE PANHELLENIC
SANCTUARIES

While many poleis developed to the point of recognition as such in the eighth
century B.C., a number of important cults of Panhellenic nature also began their
rise to prominence, at first sight seeming to belie the tendency toward local autonomy that was inherent in the poleis. These cults were usually situated in re-

mote regions, far from the strongest of the poleis, and it may have been this relative isolation that enabled them to take on a Panhellenic role. The best known of these sanctuaries were the *Oracle of Apollo at Delphi* and the cult of Zeus at Olympia, whose athletic festival has been revived in modern form in our Olympic games. Other important cult centers include the oracular shrine of Zeus at Dodona in Epirus and the shrine of the twin deities Artemis and Apollo on Delos, which served in particular as a center for the Ionian Greeks. Other cults that transcended polis boundaries but served more limited regions included the Panionion on Mount Mykale in Asia Minor, founded as a communal shrine by the twelve members of the Ionian League, and the cult of Apollo Ptoion in Boeotia, which served as the center for a league of Boeotian cities. Sanctuaries situated in powerful poleis also began to draw clientele from other cities, giving them a Panhellenic cast as well; important among these were the shrines of Athena on the Athenian Acropolis, Hera on Samos, and the Perachora near Corinth.

The development of Panhellenic sanctuaries in the eighth century B.C. is attested archaeologically by a sudden upsurge in the number of dedications that were made to their patron divinities. No bronze dedications of the eleventh and tenth centuries B.C. were found at Delphi or Delos, and only ten terracotta figurines were found at Olympia; the ninth century B.C. saw only one bronze dedication at Delphi, one at Delos, and twenty-one at Olympia. In contrast, 152 dedications from the eighth century B.C. have been found at Delphi, 19 at Delos, and 837 at Olympia.[15]

These sanctuaries not only transcended polis boundaries and helped to create a sense of Greek identity, they also played an important role in the definition and enhancement of the individual poleis.[16] Great festivals featuring contests of various sorts were held periodically at these sanctuaries. We are most familiar with the games at Olympia that took place every fourth year, but there were athletic competitions at the other sanctuaries as well, and also literary and musical contests. In these festivals, polis competed with polis for the honors of victory. Poleis also competed with one another in giving gifts to the gods, housing the gifts in elaborate and showy treasuries that advertised their civic achievements to all those who visited the sanctuary. The oracular sanctuaries offered the god's advice to poleis perhaps even more often than to individuals; usually this involved the simple ratification of new cult practices or the clarification of ritual questions, but the oracle might involve itself in substantive political decisions as well. For example, the constitution of Sparta (Greek Rhetra) was traditionally attributed to the Oracle at Delphi, and the Therans established their colony at Cyrene as a result of Delphic advice and prodding. Thus, we can say that the rise in the Panhellenic sanctuaries both fostered a sense of common Greek identity among peoples who lived in politically independent poleis and, through the rivalry of interpolis competition, helped to define and to strengthen these poleis as independent entities.

THE BEGINNING OF GREEK COLONIZATION: ITALY AND SICILY[17]

The First Colony: Pithekussai

One reflection of the development of the polis was the beginning of colonization, a process of urban foundation by which Greek culture was eventually spread throughout the Mediterranean and Black Sea world. As we noted above, this movement was begun by the Euboeans with the settlement of Pithekussai on the island of Ischia off the western coast of Italy ca. 770 B.C.[18] The Euboeans' participation in the metals market in the east via Cyprus provided the background for their new venture in the west. Italy was rich in metal resources, and the Euboeans had made trading voyages there before they decided to establish a settlement, as is shown by the presence in the area of Euboean pottery that predates the foundation of Pithekussai. In using the wealth that they had amassed in the east to exploit the promising situation in the west, the Euboeans were perhaps following the example set by the Phoenicians. And, as was noted above, there is evidence of the presence of Phoenicians among the settlers of Pithekussai itself.

The location chosen for the first western settlement was notable for its distance from Greece; had the settlers been searching only for arable land, they could have stopped long before they reached Ischia. The rocky site, on a defensible headland of an offshore island, offered good security, but it must have been the specific attraction of Etruscan metals that led the Euboeans to bypass nearer, more fertile, and equally secure sites to settle on a rugged island so far from home.

Archaeological finds at Pithekussai provide evidence of a settlement that fits this picture. It was a mixed community: inscriptions include Aramaic-Phoenician as well as Greek, and the preponderance of *fibulae* (safety-pin-type fasteners used especially by women) of Etruscan type produced in Pithekussai suggests that the colonists had not brought their families with them, but found wives locally among the Etruscans.[19] Such marriages would have enabled them to establish useful family ties with the Etruscans, upon whom they depended for access to the metals that had motivated the settlement. The population was made up of traders and craftsmen; there were rich graves, but no princely tombs have been found as yet (although only a small portion of the cemetery has been excavated). The colonists engaged in metalwork, including the making of jewelry, and they traded with the Etruscans as well as with their earlier trading partners—the Phoenicians and Syrians. Historians classify the settlement as more than a trading post (the Greeks at Pithekussai did not form a resident enclave in someone else's city), but not quite a self-sufficient polis (it lacked an adequate chora for agricultural self-sufficiency as well as the full social structure usual in a polis— no obvious aristocratic elite has been found, at least up to this time).

Some time between 760 and 735 B.C., most of the inhabitants of Pithekussai moved to the Italian mainland and founded a settlement at Cumae. This site had better agricultural potential than did Pithekussai, and the settlers apparently felt secure enough to take on the risks of the more exposed mainland site. Some people remained on at Pithekussai but, by 700 B.C., the main phase of settlement on the island was over.

Other Colonial Settlements

The establishment of Pithekussai and Cumae was followed in the last third of the eighth century B.C. by a great wave of colonization in the area: ten poleis were established in southern Italy and Sicily, beginning with the Chalkidian foundation of Naxos in 734 B.C., the first port of call in Sicily from the east. Six years later, the Naxians established two other colonies which gave them control of a rich plain: inland Leontini and Katane on the coast. In 733 B.C., the Corinthians entered the picture, founding Syracuse, which enjoyed access to good farmland and the best harbor on the eastern coast of Sicily. The Megareans also founded a polis, Megara Hyblaea, on the coast north of Syracuse.

In the 720s B.C., settlers from Cumae and Chalkis founded Zancle, which commanded one side of the straits giving access to the western Italian coast. Some ancient sources attribute the first settlement to pirates from Cumae, and the site was especially suited for preying on ships headed for the west coast of Italy. It would also have been useful in controlling passage of Phoenician ships from Carthage headed towards Etruria. But it lacked adequate agricultural land, and a dependent colony was soon established on a small plain at Mylae, about 20 miles west of Zancle. Again, trading (or raiding) interests had to produce their own food supply.

Another early settlement made by the colonists at Zancle was Rhegion, across the straits on the Italian coast, a site which completed their control of the straits. The people of Zancle requested the help of Chalkis in founding the city, but even so, available manpower seems to have run short, for some refugees from the Spartan war against Messenia were invited to join the new colony. Another series of late eighth-century B.C. colonizations in the west was sponsored by Achaeans from the Peloponnesus. They selected sites in the rich farmland in the "instep" of Italy, where they established Sybaris (720 B.C.), Kroton (710 B.C.), and Metapontum (700 B.C.). While these seem to have been predominantly agricultural communities, the later foundation, perhaps by people from Sybaris, of Posidonia on the west coast of Italy (at the end of an overland route from the "instep"), shows the propensity of Greek settlers to exploit the commercial as well as the agricultural possibilities of their sites.

At the end of the eighth century, ca. 706 B.C., a group of Spartans founded Taras, at the "heel" of Italy. This was the result of an unusual situation: during the course of some 20 years of warfare spent in subjugating their neighbors the

MAP 5 Greek Colonies and Tyrants. (Reprinted with the permission of Scribner, a Division of Simon & Schuster Inc., and Weidenfeld & Nicolson, London, from *The Rise of the Greeks* by Michael Grant. Copyright © 1987 Michael Grant.)

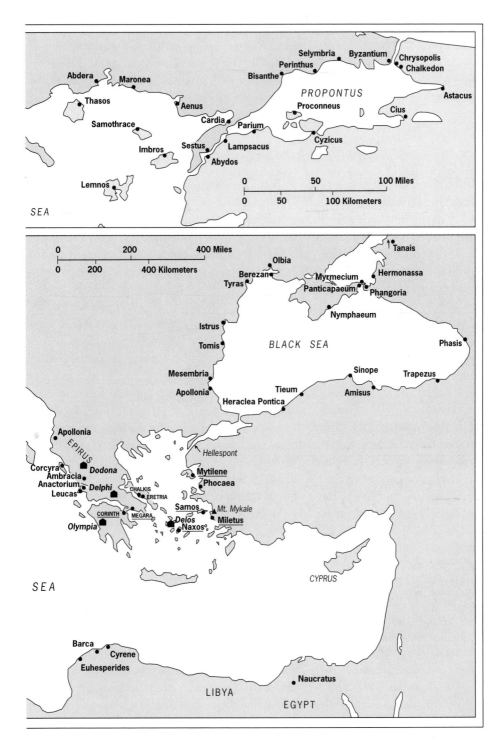

PROPONTUS

Selymbria

Byzantium

Chrysopolis

Perinthus

Chalkedon

Bisanthe

Astacus

Abdera

Maronea

Thasos

Aenus

Proconneus

Cius

Samothrace

Cardia

Parium

Sestus

Lampsacus

Cyzicus

Imbros

Abydos

Lemnos

0   50   100 Miles

0   50   100 Kilometers

SEA

0   200   400 Miles

0   200   400 Kilometers

Tanais

Olbia

Berezan

Myrmecium

Hermonassa

Tyras

Panticapaeum

Phangoria

Istrus

Nymphaeum

Tomis

BLACK SEA

Phasis

Mesembria

Sinope

Trapezus

Apollonia

Tieum

Amisus

Heraclea Pontica

Apollonia

EPIRUS

Hellespont

Corcyra

Dodona

Mytilene

Ambracia

Phocaea

Anactorium

Delphi

CHALKIS

Leucas

ERETRIA

Samos

Mt. Mykale

CORINTH

MEGARA

Olympia

Delos

Miletus

Naxos

CYPRUS

SEA

Barca

Cyrene

Euhesperides

Naucratus

LIBYA

EGYPT

Messenians, the Spartans found that the absence of the men was causing a drop in the population; they remedied the situation by sending the younger men home on leave. But the resultant offspring were never fully accepted in Spartan society, and when they became adults they rose up in protest against their inferior status. A solution was found by allowing them to emigrate, and they settled Taras.

Characteristics of Greek Colonization

Although each case of colonization had its own unique elements, and there were important differences in colonies—depending on the date of their foundation and the area in which they were established—certain characteristics were common to all Greek colonial ventures. Perhaps the most important was the model employed: the self-sufficient polis. This is a major point of difference from the colonies of modern history, which were created as dependencies serving the interests of the founding state. Once successfully established, the Greek colony was a full-fledged polis, independent of its mother city. Nevertheless, it maintained significant ties of cult and kinship with the founding city.[20] It was, for example, considered shameful for a colony to fight against its mother city or against other colonies of the same mother city, for these were seen as its natural allies.[21] Colonies had informal but nonetheless real claims to the assistance of the mother city in times of trouble; and the mother city enjoyed a certain predominance over its colonies, especially in matters of religion. The degree to which the mother city exploited its traditional role varied widely. In general, greater distance made for weaker ties, while tyrannical governments made relatively strong claims to influence and even control colonies, as did Athens in its imperialistic ventures in the fifth century B.C.

The decision to send out a colony seems in most cases to have been an official decision of a polis, rather than an individual venture. Often the mother city was itself a colony; in this circumstance, an invitation to provide a founder (*oikistes*) was usually sent to the mother city of the colonizing polis.

The founder was the key person in the colonization. It was he who made the detailed plans and led the actual colonization; he usually then became the leading citizen of the new polis and received heroic honors after his death. Such a man naturally had to have leadership abilities that would inspire the confidence of his followers. Probably he also needed wealth, in order to assist with the expenses of the expedition. It is therefore not surprising that the little evidence which we have for such men identifies them as aristocrats. Traders probably founded Pithekussai, but, as we have seen, that was an unusual situation; it seems unlikely that such men, with their low social status, would have been acceptable in the role of founder in most poleis, even if they possessed the wealth to make it possible.

Why would an aristocrat from a landed family agree to such an adventure?

Even such men might have been affected by a rise in population and by land hunger. Wealthy families would have been able to exercise more power in the community by keeping larger blocks of land intact, and they may have encouraged surplus sons to join a colony in order to reduce partition by inheritance. Troubles at home—for example, political strife or an accidental (or intentional) killing—might also make emigration desirable. Less dramatic incentives surely were present as well: the prospect of heroic honors and the chance to escape the restrictions of a tradition-bound community. Sheer adventure must also have been a factor: Homer's *Odyssey* preserves many travelers' tales and reflects the general attraction that unknown lands and peoples held for the Greeks.

The approval of the gods was an essential element in colonization. Not only was a new polis to be created, but the colony was probably going to take over land that was already occupied by others (non-Greeks, but still people in whom the gods might take an interest). The participants would have wanted to have a clear title to their land, and this could be provided only by the gods. Greek tradition portrays the Oracle of Apollo at Delphi as the primary source of such religious sanction, although only 14 of the 139 colonies known to have been established between 750 and 500 B.C. are associated with preserved oracular response.[22] Sometimes Delphi is credited with taking the initiative in ordering a colonization, but in most cases the oracle probably merely gave its assent to plans presented to it. Some oracular responses may even have been invented at a later time by poleis tidying up their local histories.

Sites were probably chosen on the basis of information provided by travelers or traders.[23] Such information could have been passed on during the great Panhellenic festivals, when crowds gathered from poleis throughout Greece. Since the Oracle at Delphi was traditionally consulted about colonization, the priests there may have been especially interested in information about the possibilities and problems of potential sites. According to Herodotus, it was Delphi who directed the Therans to found a colony off the coast of North Africa, an area completely unfamiliar to them. As noted earlier, access to good farming land must have been a primary consideration in choosing a site, but locations at strategic points along trade routes were sometimes chosen in apparent disregard of their lack of agricultural potential. Such was the case of Pithekussai, which was conveniently situated where it could safely exploit Etruscan interest in metals, and of Zancle in Sicily, as well, which soon founded Mylae to supply its needs. Native resistance must also have been a factor in choosing a site, but settlers appear to have been willing to fight for their new homes if necessary. Thus, easily defensible sites were naturally favored: most desirable were offshore islands or peninsular sites, from which the initial settlement might spread in later times, or even be relocated, as was Pithekussai to Cumae.

The individual participants must have had many motivations. Some surely were self-selected: landless men or those with poor or insufficient land, men who were driven to emigrate after taking the losing side in a factional struggle, homocides or men who had committed some other offense against their kin or the community, traders who saw opportunities to further their professional interests as well as to increase their status by becoming landowners. Often participants were recruited from other cities, or two or more cities joined in organizing a venture. Compulsion was used in some cases: in the colonization of Cyrene (see below), men were selected by lot and required to join the colonizing party on penalty of death.

There is some question whether women were among the settlers; most of the few who are attested were priestesses whose presence was necessary for ritual purposes, but ordinary women would probably not have been considered worthy of mention. We have seen that some settlers at Pithekussai took Etruscan wives, and Herodotus relates that the settlers of Miletus in the migration period killed all the local men and took the women as wives. These were pioneering ventures, but even later, when colonization was a more established affair, it seems unlikely that many women were taken along. Most male colonists were probably unmarried: as we shall see, those chosen by lot for the colonization of Cyrene were sons still living at home, and the landless and the poor were unlikely to have been able to afford wives.

After the appropriate offerings had been made to the gods, and the cults of the mother city installed (and if no native resistance had to be countered), the first order of business was to lay out the city, setting aside areas for an agora, public buildings, and the temples of the gods, and making the individual allotments of land for houses and farming.

City Planning

The physical planning of the colonial settlements had a great impact upon the development of urban planning in the polis. The use of grid plans was adopted for this purpose, and colonial sites offer some of the earliest and best evidence of both city planning and the systematic distribution of farmland.[24] A fifth-century B.C. citizen of Miletus, Hippodamos, was credited with the creation of such city planning, and the fact that Miletus is said to have established over 90 colonies lends some credence to this claim. We now know, however, that similar methods of land distribution were used much earlier in the western colonies; even in the Bronze Age, the city of Enkomi in Cyprus was laid out in a grid pattern. Nevertheless, the fact that Hippodamos wrote a treatise on planning and incorporated it into political theory probably earned him the credit for its "discovery." In later times, such systematic planning was often adopted by older Greek cities as they expanded: for example, Athens is said to have employed Hippodamos to plan the rebuilding of its port, the Piraeus, and an extension of the city of Olynthus was laid out in an orderly rectilinear fashion. City planning was also widely employed for the many city foundations of the Hellenistic period.

The Colonization Accounts of Cyrene

Herodotus provides an account of the colonization of Cyrene in north Africa (ca. 630 B.C.) that gives life to this schematic picture. It provides a good idea of the type of information about colonization that was available to Herodotus in the fifth century B.C., and the use he made of it. It also gives us the opportunity to compare the evidence of the historian with that of an inscription purporting to be a copy of the original colonization decree.

The second source for the colonization of Cyrene is an inscription from the fourth century B.C. In it a Cyrenian, Demis, seeking to obtain citizenship for recent immigrants from Thera, cites what he claims to be a copy of the original foundation degree for the colony.[25]

COMPARATIVE
SOURCE ANALYSIS

ERODOTUS. 4.145–158.   How well does Herodotus' account fit the general pattern of colonization outlined above, which is a product of modern rationalization? For example, what was the motive for the colonization of Cyrene? What does the story suggest about the role of Delphi? From what sources did the settlers get their practical information about the site?

HE THERAN DECREE   "Resolved by the Assembly. Since Apollo spontaneously told Battos and the Therans to colonize Cyrene, it has been decided by the Therans to send Battos off to Libya, as Archagetes [founder] and as King, with the Therans to sail as his Companions. On equal and fair terms shall they sail according to family (?), with one son to be conscripted [from each household, 100 in number],[26] adults, and from the other Therans those who are freeborn shall sail. If they establish the settlement, kinsmen who sail later to Libya shall be entitled to citizenship and offices and shall be allotted portions of the land which has no owner. But if they do not successfully establish the settlement and the Therans are incapable of giving it assistance, and they are pressed by hardship for five years, from that land shall they depart, without fear, to Thera, to their own property, and they shall be citizens. Any man who, if the city sends him, refuses to sail, will be liable to the death penalty and his property shall be confiscated. The man harboring him or concealing him, whether he be a father [aiding his] son or a brother a brother, is to suffer the same penalty as the man who refuses to sail."

continued

Since it is a fourth-century B.C. inscription purporting to be a copy, this document has naturally been questioned; nevertheless, there are good arguments in favor of its authenticity.[27] One is that Demis' source could not have been Herodotus, since the inscription contains information not in the historian's account. A second argument is the fact that the Cyrenians obviously believed that Demis had an authentic source; since foundation documents recorded important rights, they must have been carefully preserved, and the Cyrenians could well have had a copy of the original agreement. In what ways does this document agree with, or conflict with, the account as given by Herodotus?

The Spread of Greek Colonization

The Greek colonial expansion that began in the eighth century B.C. escalated in the seventh and sixth centuries B.C. New poleis were established in southern Italy and Sicily, and Greeks created settlements in the east on the shores of the Hellespont, Propontus, and the Black Sea. In the Black Sea area, the Milesians led the way, founding over 90 colonies, while the mainland Greeks established Byzantium, today's Istanbul, as well as other cities. On the African continent, a number of Greek poleis were allowed to establish a joint trading center at Naukratis in Egypt, and, as we have seen, the people of Thera, itself settled by the Spartans, founded Cyrene in Libya (see Map 5). The colonial enterprise had far-reaching and long-lasting consequences. It not only spread Greek culture throughout the Mediterranean, but it contributed in vital ways to the development of the polis, the political form that lay at the heart of that culture.

TYRANNY: THE VIEW FROM CORINTH[28]

As populations grew and cities sent out colonies, prosperity increased and spread beyond the traditional wealthy few. But the stresses of living in these changed conditions under a still very restricted aristocracy brought many cities, especially the small seafaring states around the Isthmus of Corinth, to political crises that ultimately led to takeover by a strong-man, or **tyrant.** This was the term used to refer to any ruler who came to power by irregular means, whether he was imposed by an outside authority, as were the rulers of the Ionian states, or seized power for himself in conditions of internal political and economic crisis.

In its archaic usage, the word does not necessarily imply that the ruler was tyrannical in the modern, oppressive sense. Such men were able to break the grip of the aristocrats and pave the way for a reformed and revitalized political structure. In doing this, they made the polis, rather than the aristocratic families, the focus of civic authority, and in the process the people gained a greater share in the life of the polis. However, by giving the people an awareness of their own political potential, the tyrants prepared the way for their own demise, for a people brought to civic consciousness would eventually throw off the tyrant's rule.

The Kypselid Tyrants in Corinth

The city of Corinth is the best documented of these archaic tyrannies. Its location at the Isthmus of the Peloponnesus put it in a position to exact tolls both from land traffic between the Peloponnesus and central Greece and from sea trade, and this, according to Thucydides (1.13), was responsible for its great prosperity. Corinth is well known for its Orientalizing vases, which are found in museums around the world. The vases, often miniatures probably used for perfumed oil, were decorated with friezes of ordinary animals and birds such as deer, dogs, and lions and fantastic hybrid creatures borrowed from Near Eastern art, like the Sphinx (see Figure 5-2).

In the eighth century B.C., Corinth was ruled by a closed aristocracy; the assembly consisted of only 200 members of a single *genos,* or clan, the ***Bacchiads,*** who intermarried only among themselves. The city first began to exploit the potential of its location at this time, for, by the middle of the century, Corinthian pottery appears in the east at the Greek city of Posideion.[29] It was also under the Bacchiads, in 734/33 B.C., that Corinth joined the colonization movement, founding the two great western colonies of Corcyra and Syracuse in a single year.

At the end of the eighth century B.C., Corinth took part in the Lelantine War, which was the first war to draw a number of Greek cities into a general conflict. It was fought between the Euboean cities of Eretria and Chalkis over the possession of the rich Lelantine Plain. (A Corinthian shipbuilder built a new type of warship, the *trireme,* for the Samians in this war.) In the end, Chalkis seems to have been victorious, but the conflict exhausted both primary participants, and the Euboeans, who had formerly been so active in the east and had founded Pithekussai in the west, from this time on no longer played a major role in trade and colonization. Corinth, on the other hand, appears to have profited by the war, and for a time the city was predominant in Greek trade.

In the second quarter of the seventh century B.C., however, the growing power of Argos under the tyrant ***Pheidon*** must have weakened Corinth's position. In 664 B.C. Corinth also fought its colony Corcyra in the first sea battle

FIGURE 5-2 Corinthian Orientalizing vase.

known to Thucydides, a further indication of weakness. These problems undoubtedly contributed to the growing dissatisfaction with Bacchiad rule that
eventually led to their overthrow and the rule of a tyrant, Kypselus.

Another factor that may have contributed to political change was the rise of
a group of men whose economic position was improving but who lacked political rights. The existence of such a group is suggested by archaeological finds
that reveal a significant surge in the number of bronze weapons, especially helmets and shields, that were dedicated at Panhellenic sanctuaries in the eighth
century B.C. While this reflects the increasing popularity of such sanctuaries, as
well as the development of a fashion of dedicating armor, it is also grounds for
the belief that there was a significant rise in the number of men who could afford to equip themselves with such armor and even to sacrifice it in dedications
to the gods, and thus that prosperity had grown more widespread. Since we can
assume that aristocrats had long been outfitting themselves with armor, and
there is no evidence that these aristocrats had lost their monopoly on power, this

means that by the seventh century B.C. there were rising numbers of men who were able to afford heavy armor, but who had no say in the aristocratic government of the polis. It seems likely that this did indeed provide the setting for revolutionary changes in Corinth and elsewhere.

The story of the rise to power of the tyrant in Corinth is told by Herodotus in the source analysis below.

S O U R C E   A N A L Y S I S

ERODOTUS 5.92. The folktale elements in this story reflect the popular nature of oral transmission. In what literary context does the story of Kypselus' rise to power appear, and how might this also have affected the account?

Herodotus' story seems to reflect both popular discontent with the tyrant, and elements that were friendly to him. Another ancient source, the fourth-century B.C. Athenian Ephorus, who is known only through later sources, portrays him as a popular ruler.[30] In this version, Kypselus gained popularity when he held office as *Polemarch* (in Athens, one of the ten archons, who originally served as the commander-in-chief of the army; after the reforms of Kleisthenes there were ten generals, one elected from each tribe). In this office he was required to imprison those who had been fined until the fines were paid, but he refused to do this, accepting security from the debtors instead, or even providing it for them. He then seized power by killing the last Bacchiad king, exiled the Bacchiads and confiscated their property, founded colonies to which he sent his enemies, and ruled mildly without a bodyguard.

The colonies that Kypselus founded in the northwest of Greece, safeguarding the route to Italy and Sicily and also opening up trade with the interior, are his best-attested works. In the early sixth century B.C., his son and successor Periander built new port installations and the *diolkos,* a stone runway across the isthmus that enabled ships to be pulled across to avoid the dangerous sea voyage around the Peloponnesus (today a canal allows passage). These tyrants also founded, or augmented, the popular cult of Demeter and Kore, and may have built fountains and a temple, although the archaeological remains of these cannot be dated precisely.

But if Kypselus was a mild and popular ruler, the case was quite different with his son and successor Periander, who became the archetype of the evil tyrant. The fragments of the lost *Constitution of Corinth* by Aristotle begin with a list of Periander's tyrannical methods; nevertheless, it ends by saying that he was moderate in other ways and did not tax the people, for the state was able to live from its market and harbor dues.[31]

S O U R C E　　A N A L Y S I S

ERODOTUS 3.48–53.   In this selection Herodotus elaborates on the vices of the tyranny. To what extent might such stories be political invective? Can we take them at face value?

Consequences of Tyranny

The tyranny in Corinth is only the best attested of a number of similar regimes that arose during this time. The first recorded tyrant was Pheidon of Argos, and tyrannical rule is also attested for the cities of Megara, Sikyon, Epidaurus, Mytilene, and, somewhat later, Athens. All fit a common pattern that was exemplified by Kypselid Corinth.

Not surprisingly, tyrants were often popular rulers, for more than one segment of society had had reason to be dissatisfied with the narrow and arbitrary government of the old aristocratic regimes. Tyrants also rewarded their supporters, offering citizenship and offices to them, and this gave an opportunity to newly prosperous men who had previously been excluded.[32] Tyrants usually won widespread support by sponsoring useful public works, such as the harbor works and diolkos of Periander; water supply and temple building were other favorite projects. These projects offered employment and enhanced the quality of life in the city. Tyrants also sponsored elaborate and entertaining festivals and games that celebrated the gods of the whole polis rather than the private cults of the aristocratic families, thus encouraging civil consciousness, as the Kypselids did with the cult of Demeter and Kore. And, by their patronage of poets, they advertised their own fame and the glory of their poleis, further increasing civic pride.

The tyrants' emphasis on the polis often led them to conduct their rule within the framework of customary laws and institutions. Such a course was made possible by the widespread popularity that they enjoyed, at least in the early years of their regimes. In most cases, it was only in the second or third generation of a hereditary tyranny that personal rule became arbitrary and oppressive, again, as happened in Corinth.

Most of the written evidence for the archaic tyrants dates from times when the oppressive culmination of tyrannical rule was remembered more vividly than its earlier accomplishments. Moreover, the authors of many of our sources were members of the upper class and thus tended to reflect aristocratic viewpoints. Yet, despite the general antityrannical bias of our sources, the periods of tyranny appear to have been generally beneficial episodes in the development of the Greek poleis. Tyranny tended to foster the values of the polis against aristocratic privilege and to expand the circle of political participation beyond the narrow limits of the aristocracy.

CONCLUSION

The eighth century B.C. was a period of revolutionary change in Greece. Because it was a time when the Homeric epic revived reflections of Bronze Age heroes, it is often called the *Greek Renaissance*. The resumption of foreign contacts brought with it the introduction of the alphabet. This was a writing system that was well suited to the expression of the epic, if not created for that purpose, but its potential for assisting political reform through the recording of traditional laws and the common decisions of the polis was not realized until somewhat later. As prosperity and populations grew and settlements increased in complexity, however, many Greek communities did take on the embryonic form of the classical polis. Some began the dissemination of the polis and Greek culture throughout the Mediterranean world by colonization, a process that probably helped to shape the poleis at home as well. Often these changes created literally revolutionary situations as newly prosperous men chaffed under the rule of closed aristocratic regimes. And often a resolution was achieved only by a tyranny that opened a formerly closed ruling class to a wider range of men and focused loyalty on the polis rather than on the aristocratic families.

Many poleis followed this pattern, but it was not universal. In the following chapters we will consider first an exceptional case, Sparta, a polis that responded quite differently from most Greek poleis to the revolutionary conditions of the Archaic period; next we will look at Archaic Athens, where the process occurred later than usual but is unusually well documented; and, finally, we will consider the development of the poleis of Archaic Ionia, which were more subject than other poleis to direct non-Greek influences and political pressures.

IMPORTANT PLACES IN CHAPTER 5

On Chapter Map:

Cities with tyrants: Acragas, Argos, Athens, Corinth, Epidaurus, Gela, Katane, Megara, Megara Hyblaea, Miletus, Mytilene, Naxos, Samos, Sikyon, Syracuse

Some colonies mentioned in the text (all the cities in small type on the map were colonies): Byzantium, Cumae, Cyrene, Elea, Katane, Kroton, Leontini, Megara Hyblaea, Metapontum, Mylae, Pithekussai/Ischia, Posideion, Rhegion, Sybaris, Taras/Tarentum, Zancle

Sanctuaries: Delos, Delphi, Dodona, Olympia

Other places: Chalkis, Epirus, Eretria, Euboea, Hellespont, Kition, Lelantine Plain, Libya, Messenia, Mt. Mykale, Naucratus, Olynthus, Piraeus, Propontus, Straits of Messina

SUGGESTIONS FOR FURTHER READING

The best overall view of the Archaic period is A. Snodgrass, *Archaic Greece* (1980). On colonization, see John Boardman, *The Greeks Overseas* (1980), and, on tyranny, A. Andrewes, *The Greek Tyrants* (1956). J. B. Salmon's *Wealthy Corinth* (1984) is an interesting in-depth study of a polis notable for colonization, trade, and tyranny in the Archaic period.

ENDNOTES

1. See R. Hägg, *The Greek Renaissance of the Eighth Century B.C.* (Stockholm, 1983), and W. Burkert, *The Orientalizing Revolution: Near Eastern Influence on Greek Culture in the Early Archaic Age* (1992).
2. See the work of A. B. Lord, including *The Singer of Tales* (1960), and his collected essays in *Epic Singers and Oral Tradition* (1991); G. S. Kirk, *Homer and the Oral Tradition* (1976); and John M. Foley, *The Theory of Oral Composition: History and Methodology* (1988), who provides a complete bibliography.
3. See Albin Lesky, *A History of Greek Literature* (1963), 94–95; Burkert (above, n. 1), 4–6.
4. H. T. Wade-Gery, *The Poet of the Iliad* (1952), 11–14.
5. Barry B. Powell, *Homer and the Origin of the Greek Alphabet* (1991).
6. Alan Johnston, "The Extent and Use of Literacy; the Archaeological Evidence," in Hägg (above, n. 1), 63–68.
7. Nestor's cup: Homer, *Iliad* 11.632–637; on the inscription, see D. Ridgway, *The First Western Greeks* (1992), 55–57; Powell (above, n. 5), 163–167, tr. inscription, p. 164.
8. L. H. Jeffery, *The Local Scripts of Archaic Greece* (1990, rev. ed.), 1–2, 4–12.
9. J. N. Coldstream, "Mixed Marriages at the Frontiers of the Early Greek World," *Oxford Journal of Archaeology* 12 (1993), 89–107.
10. See especially Rosalind Thomas, *Literacy and Orality in Ancient Greece* (1992).
11. Homer, *Il.* 18.474–617.
12. On the basileus, see Robert Drews, *Basileus: The Evidence for Kingship in Geometric Greece* (1983).
13. Hesiod, *Works and Days*, 38–39 (this is my translation of the Greek, but it is literal).
14. English-language historians who adopt this position include A. Snodgrass, *Archaic Greece* (1980); R. Drews, "Phoenicians, Carthage and the Spartan *Eunomia*," *American Journal of*

Philology 100 (1979), 45–58; Sarah Morris, *Daedalos and the Origins of Greek Art* (1992); and Martin Bernal, "Phoenician Politics and Egyptian Justice in Ancient Greece," in Kurt Raaflaub, ed., *Anfänge politischen Denkens in der Antike* (1993), 241–261.

15. Snodgrass (above, n. 14), 53.

16. C. Morgan, *Athletes and Oracles: The Transformation of Olympia and Delphi in the Eighth Century B.C.* (1990).

17. On the eighth-century B.C. colonization of the west, J. N. Coldstream, *Geometric Greece*, chap. 8; on Greek colonization in general, John Boardman, *The Greeks Overseas* (1980).

18. The most recent discussion of Pithekussai is Ridgway (above, n. 7).

19. Coldstream (above, n. 9).

20. On the relations between colonies and mother cities, see A. J. Graham, *Colony and Mother City in Ancient Greece* (1983).

21. Graham (above, n. 20), 10, 86, 214.

22. P. Londey, "Greek Colonists and Delphi," in J.-P. Descoeudres, *Greek Colonists and Native Populations* (1990), 117–127, 119. This article in general provides a useful discussion of the role of Delphi in colonization.

23. See A. J. Graham, "Pre-Colonial Contacts: Questions and Problems," in Descoeudres (above, n. 22), 45–60.

24. See A. Di Vita, "Town Planning in the Greek Colonies of Sicily from the Time of the Foundations to the Punic Wars," in Descoeudres (above, n. 22), 343–371; J. C. Carter, "Metapontum—Land, Wealth, and Population," in the same volume, 405–441.

25. Charles W. Fornara, *Archaic Times to the End of the Peloponnesian War* (1983), #18, lines 24–41, adapted.

26. This is the conjecture of L. H. Jeffery, "The Pact of the First Settlers at Cyrene," *Historia* 10 (1961), 139–147, cited by Fornara (above, n. 25).

27. See Jeffery (above, n. 26).

28. On Greek tyranny, see A. Andrewes, *The Greek Tyrants* (1956); on Corinth, J. B. Salmon, *Wealthy Corinth* (1984), especially chaps. 5–11 on trade and chap. 15 on the tyranny.

29. M. Robertson, "The Excavations at Al Mina, Sueidia. IV. The Early Greek Vases," *Journal of Hellenic Studies* 40 (1940), 2–21, 16–21.

30. Ephorus' information on the tyranny survived only because a later historian cited his work, and it is available today only in Greek; see the fragments of Nicholas of Damascus in F. Jacoby, *Fragmente der griechschen Historiker* (1922–), no. 90, Frags. 57–60.

31. Aristotle, fr. 611.20.

32. While tyrants depended on men whom their opponents called mercenaries, many of these were probably previously unenfranchised inhabitants of the city itself rather than foreign recruits.

CHAPTER SIX

Sparta: An Alternative
to Tyranny

n the Classical period, Sparta was universally acknowledged by the Greeks to be the preeminent military power in Greece. Even today, the name *Sparta* calls up images of military strength and prowess, of a way of life devoted single-mindedly to patriotic duty. The image, in fact, has become part of our everyday vocabulary; *Webster's* defines *spartan* as "warlike, brave, hardy, stoical, severe, frugal, highly disciplined."[1] How Sparta reached this state is, however, an unusual story.

Sparta, like many other communities in the southern parts of Greece and Crete, such as Corinth, Argos, and Knossos, was a Dorian city; that is, its people spoke a Dorian dialect of Greek (similarly, the Athenians spoke Attic, a form of Ionic Greek, and the inhabitants of cities to the north spoke an Aeolic dialect). Dorian speakers shared some institutions, such as a division of their citizens into the same three tribes, but by the Classical period they had diverged widely in the way they developed those institutions. For example, Corinth, which lay at a crossroads on the Isthmus of Corinth with convenient access to ports on both sides and control of the route from the Peloponnesus to central Greece, had developed into a trading center, sent out many colonies, and undergone a relatively early period of tyranny. In contrast, Sparta, which neither colonized in the usual manner nor solved its problems by tyranny, lay inland, 46 kilometers from Gytheion (the nearest port), but with a commanding position over the best land in the valley of the Eurotas River and in the center of a naturally defined region, *Lakonia,* or *Lakedaimonia* (the territory of Sparta). The position was one of natural security and relative isolation: Lakonia was protected from its nearest neighbors to the east by mountains that hemmed in the valley, and to the west by the peaks of Mount Taygetus, which separated Spartan territory from the

FIGURE 6-1 Modern Sparta with Mount Taygetus in background.

much more extensive, fertile plains of Messenia (Figure 6-1). To the north, hill country and sheer distance provided a natural boundary with Tegea, although not an impassable or even difficult barrier. The most valuable land in Lakonia lay in the plain of the Eurotas River, but other habitable niches existed in outlying areas, some occupying plains as small as 1 square kilometer, some with small harbors, most isolated by natural barriers that made travel to and from the center difficult. Although this geographical situation did not determine Spartan development (as we shall see, the Spartans made certain quite definite choices as they developed their state), it contributed greatly to the distinct contrast between classical Sparta and Corinth, even though both were Dorian-speaking poleis.

Sparta's earliest history is hidden in the period of chaos and unrest following the collapse of the Mycenaean palace system. In the Bronze Age Lakonia was well populated, the site of roughly fifty settlements including Sparta, home of the mythical *Menelaus* (Mycenaean king and husband of Helen) and *Helen* (whose seduction by Paris, son of Priam of Troy, was the cause of the Trojan War). Although no palace has been located at Sparta, a large megaron complex found at the site of the shrine of Menelaus was perhaps one of the forerunners of such palaces.[2] At the end of the Bronze Age Lakonia seems to have shared in the depopulation that is evidenced throughout Greece, for there is a gap of about a century in the archaeological evidence for habitation. Nevertheless, there is good reason to suspect that some people survived, probably leading a simple pastoral life that has left no archaeological traces. For example, some Bronze Age cults in the area were carried over into historical times. Moreover, the Greek language also survived, and although it could have been reintroduced, the later structure of the population suggests a more complex picture.

According to Spartan tradition, around 950 B.C., groups of Dorian speakers, the *Sons of Herakles,* returned to Lakonia from the northeast after a period of exile of about a hundred years. They were a simple, but aggressive and warlike, people who reduced the existing non-Dorian inhabitants to a subservient status, helotry.

Over time the status of the *helots* developed and become more formalized. By the Classical period, which is the earliest time for which we have evidence, helots were in a situation somewhere between slave and free; they were tied to the land and could not be sold, but they were not the slaves of any individual. Rather, they belonged to the Spartan state. And, unlike chattel slaves, they were able to form stable families without fear that individual family members would be sold away. Their main function in the Spartan state was as agricultural laborers: they lived and worked allotments of land that were assigned to Spartan citizens to provide these citizens with a livelihood. Male helots also accompanied Spartan *hoplites* (Greek infantrymen who used a round shield called a *hoplon*) in battle as servers, and on occasion helots were even freed to be drafted into the hoplite corps (after this they still held an inferior status, that of *neodamodes*). The large numbers of helot workers, Sparta's absolute dependence upon them, and the fear of a helot rebellion led to extremely harsh measures being employed in their control, including a perpetual state of war that allowed helots to be killed without penalty. Such a status was not unique in the Greek world; similar subjected peoples are known to have existed in other areas, such as Thessaly and the Black Sea colonies, but none seem to have lived under as brutal conditions as the Spartan helots did in the fully developed Spartan state.

The question is, who were these helots? They were non-Dorians, but because of their servile condition, they left no records behind to clarify their situation. Nor is there pertinent evidence from the early Spartans about the development of their state. As a result, we can only speculate, based on the evidence we do have from classical times. But before we attempt this, we should consider another group in Lakonia that had status inferior to the Spartans by the Classical period. These were the inhabitants of the smaller towns in Lakonia, beyond the five towns that made up Sparta itself, whom the Spartans called *perioikoi* ("dwellers round about"). The perioikoi were Dorians. In fact, in historical times they seem not to have been differentiated from the Spartans ethnically, linguistically, or culturally. At that time, perioikoi were allowed local self-government, but in matters of military service and foreign policy they were under Spartan control, and they were permitted no voice in the conduct of the Spartan polis. One of their important functions was to fight alongside the Spartans and at their command. Their status has thus been described as "semiallies" (full allies had a veto over joint military actions that the perioikoi lacked). Not only were the perioikoi of military value, but a number of the perioikoi settlements, which commanded important land routes into Lakonia, possessed great strategic value. These settlements also played a role in the control of the helots, although the perioikoi themselves used chattel slaves, not helot workers.

The origins of perioikoi status are unclear, just as are those of the helots. Most perioikoi towns seem to have dated back to the original Dorian settlement. Perhaps the Spartans' hold on the rich Eurotas Valley allowed them to gain control over these neighboring settlements in various ways over time. Some settlements may have voluntarily subjected themselves because they were too small to maintain an independent existence, others may have been coerced, and a few seem to have been purposely settled by Sparta. The type and degree of control may have been dictated in part by the geographical isolation of many of the perioikoi settlements, which would have made their active participation in government—and hence, a truly unified political system like that in Attica—difficult, if not impossible.[3] However, there are reasons to believe that more was involved than geographical determinism. For instance, the inequality inherent in the perioikoi system was marked even in nomenclature. Unlike most poleis, Sparta did not share its name with the outlying territory: while its citizens were called *Spartiates* or *Spartans*, its territory was called *Lakonia* or *Lakedaimonia*. Moreover, the rigid control that the Spartans exerted over the helots and even over their own citizens suggests that a system of shared rule with neighboring towns would have had little intrinsic appeal to the Spartans.

In the Classical period, although the perioikoi settlements occupied only small patches of marginal land, many commanded important nonagricultural resources and played a vital role in the Spartan economy. In particular, some perioikoi towns had access to iron ore, and it appears to have been perioikoi who manufactured and repaired the arms and equipment of the Spartan army. Lead was another perioikoi mineral resource that found a ready use: small lead votive figurines, the product of perioikoi craft skills, have been found in the thousands at Spartan shrines, as well as abroad. Perioikoi harbor settlements produced fish and murex shells, the source of the purple dye so valued in antiquity. Among the

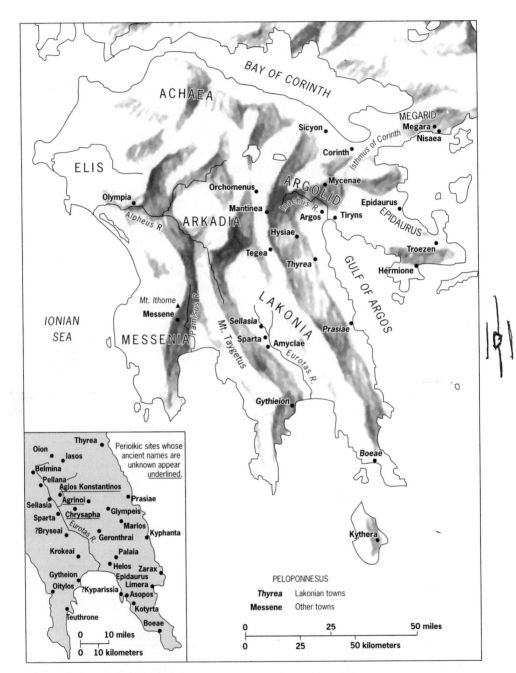

MAP 6 The Peloponnesus; inset map of Lakonia and perioikoi towns. (*Source:* Inset map from *Philolakon: Lakonian Studies in Honour of Hector Catling*, edited by Jan Motyka Sanders. London: The British School at Athens. Copyright © The Managing Committee, British School at Athens, 1992. Used by permission.)

Greeks, the Lakonians and the Spartan colony of Taras in southern Italy were the primary producers of this dye, which was used to color the famous crimson cloaks worn by Spartan hoplite warriors. Perioikoi harbors also provided for importation of whatever foreign items were necessary; Lakonia was relatively self-sufficient in supplying the needs of the simple Spartan lifestyle, but tin and copper were essential imports for the production of bronze military equipment. Craft production in general was probably relegated to perioikoi, at least by the Classical period, since in Sparta, as in most of the Greek world, handwork did not bring high status.[4]

If we consider the Greek tradition of a "Dorian invasion," we could account for the advent of Dorians into Lakonia. Returning to their ancestral lands, they would have subjected the small surviving local population—as helots. As the society developed, the superior position of those Dorians who had occupied the best sites could have become formalized as Spartan citizenship, while the inhabitants of less favored sites fell into a somewhat inferior position, as perioikoi. But, as we have seen, there is great difficulty with the hypothesis of a Dorian invasion as the cause of the collapse of Mycenaean civilization. If the Dorians were newcomers, or newly returned, they must have infiltrated the area gradually, taking advantage of the vacuum left by the collapse. Or perhaps they were there all along, in the form of the lower classes of Mycenaeans who could not manage to emigrate, and their identifying feature, the Dorian dialect of Greek, was only a form of sub-Mycenaean. Who, then, were the helots? Perhaps they were the remnants of a non-Dorian, pre-Mycenaean population that had originally been subjected by the Mycenaeans, and simply continued to occupy a servile position as agricultural workers as the Spartan state developed.

The Spartan system of landownership, labor, and semialliance that made use of these two subservient populations had radical consequences for the development of the Spartan state when it was extended to meet problems that emerged in the eighth and seventh centuries B.C. At that time, when other Greek poleis were sending out colonies in response to overpopulation pressures and finding solutions to social and political stresses by establishing tyrannies, the Spartans followed the path that they had already developed in these early status relationships.

THE CONQUEST OF MESSENIA AND ITS CONSEQUENCES

When the population of Sparta began to press upon its resources, the Spartans, rather than turning to overseas colonization, looked instead with envy to the fertile land of the Messenians on the other side of Mount Taygetus. Probably the two peoples both used summer pastures in the mountains. This would have given the Spartans knowledge of the resources of the Messenians and familiarity with routes between the two areas, despite the formidable mountain barrier.

Such contacts could also have engendered long-lived border grievances, providing additional motives for a Spartan attack on Messenia.

The *First Messenian War* is only faintly visible in the historical sources.[5] It lasted for about twenty years in the mid-eighth century, from 740 to 720 B.C., and the Spartans were the ultimate victors. Some of the conquered fled to mountainous areas of Arkadia, or to havens overseas, as in the case of those who joined the Cumaeans in the colony of Rhegion in southern Italy (probably shortly after its establishment in 720 B.C.). Messenians who failed to escape met mixed fates. Those who lived in outlying towns received perioikoi status, while those who lived in the fertile plain were incorporated into the Spartan system as helots. The poet **Tyrtaeus**, who fought in the Second Messenian War, describes them:

> Like asses exhausted under great loads: under painful
> necessity to bring their masters full half the fruit their
> ploughed land produced.

Tyrtaeus, Frag. 6 (tr. Cartledge)

The conquest of Messenia made Sparta wealthy. The first temple of Artemis Orthia is dated to ca. 700 B.C., and to it came a flood of exotic votive offerings from many areas of the Greek world and the Near East, as Sparta entered the Orientalizing world of trade and exchange. The export of Messenian grain was unlikely as a source of this wealth, since Messenian grain now had to feed both the Messenians and their new overlords. A more likely source was booty from the war and a continuing trade in slaves. Certainly the enslavement of Messenians not needed for agricultural labor would have been a practical expedient, and one fully in keeping with Greek traditions of the treatment of defeated enemies at that time.

Among the consequences of the First Messenian War was the founding of the Spartan colony of Taras in southern Italy, established by the men born as a result of a compassionate leave granted during the prolonged war (see Chapter 5). But the most far-reaching result of the war for the Spartans lay in the extension of the helot system to Messenia, a land that was both distant and difficult of access. Spartans traditionally lived and fought together, taking their identity and status in both war and peace from participation in "men's messes," or common meals. There is no evidence that they occupied Messenia in the usual colonization pattern, establishing homes there for themselves in poleis. Rather, the land with its helot workers was allotted to individual Spartans, probably mainly to the wealthiest men; the Spartan overlords exacted half the crops produced by the helots, but they themselves lived across the mountains in Sparta. While a number of other Greek poleis were able to prosper by a system of absentee landownership, none of these were so far removed, or separated by such difficult terrain, from the land and the workers who provided their sustenance.

Problems of transport and of control were inevitable. The former seems to have been solved by requiring the helots to undertake the hardships of the delivery of the produce themselves. The enforcement of such a requirement was another matter, however, and the new helots lived in constant hope of regaining their lost freedom.[6]

After their success in the conquest of Messenia, the Spartans continued their aggressive expansion, aiming next at their northern neighbors. In 669 B.C., however, they met a signal defeat at the hands of the tyrant **Pheidon** of Argos in the **battle of Hysiae.** Such a defeat could set back a small Archaic state for a generation while it made up its manpower losses. Pheidon, in fact, was able to seize control of the Olympic festival of 668 B.C. and was for a time effectively master of the northwest Peloponnesus.[7] The Messenians seized the opportunity provided by Spartan weakness and rose in revolt. The result was a second, even longer war, the *Second Messenian War,* from 650 B.C. to 620 B.C., which brought Sparta very close to defeat. The perilous situation caused a hardening of attitude and a more rigorous pursuit of security and control on the part of the Spartans from that time forward, even after their final victory.

It was perhaps at this point that the Spartans made the decision to use institutionalized terror as a means to control the helot population. Modifying the traditional male initiation rites, they periodically selected the strongest of their young men (up to the age of thirty) for service in the **Krypteia,** or "secret service." These men, taking only knives and a supply of food, went out into the countryside, hiding by day and attacking and killing by night any helots whom they observed to be particularly strong or who otherwise showed dangerous leadership potential. Another element in this strategy of "control by terror" consisted in the annual declaration of formal war on the helots; as a consequence, any Spartan could kill helots with impunity, for the declaration of war absolved him from legal penalties and even from the religious pollution that normally resulted from the shedding of blood.

The last line of defense in the event of an open helot rebellion was the Spartan army. The possibility of a need for such a deployment was never far from the minds of the Spartans, and they devoted themselves to military readiness with a single-mindedness that became proverbial. The result was the creation of the fabled Spartan way of life that eventually made Sparta the strongest hoplite power in Greece.

THE AVOIDANCE OF TYRANNY: INTERNAL PROBLEMS AND REFORMS

The Second Messenian War not only brought danger to Sparta from external sources, it aroused internal discord as well. The poet Tyrtaeus, a veteran of the war, spoke of demands for the redistribution of land on the part of men ruined by the war.[8] If, as seems likely, the land acquired in the First Messenian War had gone mainly to the wealthiest men, the expectation that this second extended war was also to be fought for the benefit of the few, while ordinary men's farms lay neglected in their long absence, would have been an explosive issue. This is the period—the second half of the seventh century B.C.—when tyrants were seizing power in other Peloponnesian cities in response to similar dissatisfactions over the aristocratic monopoly of land and civic status. But just as the helot system had led the Spartans in a different direction in solving the problem of population pressure, so too it prodded them to solve the problems of internal discord without the open split between citizen factions that was involved in tyranny. Any division in their ranks would have created an opening for helot revolt, and this was their greatest fear.

It seems that the Spartans did bow to the demands for redistribution of land, using the newly acquired territory in Messenia. This at least is a likely origin for the tradition that each male Spartan was allotted a parcel of land at birth, a practice that provided the basis for their considering themselves *homoioi* (equals, peers, or similars).[9] Since we know that there were great inequalities of wealth in Sparta,[10] there can be no question of their attaining absolute equality of land-holdings by this reform. But the provision of a basic minimum allotment, which would allow the individual to make the required contributions to his mess, may well have been the reform that satisfied the discontented in the seventh century B.C.

But land was only half the issue: lack of political status also seems to have rankled many who had fought and suffered in the war, as reflected in constitutional reforms that appear to be dated to this period. These reforms are outlined in an enigmatic document, the ***Great Rhetra,*** purportedly an oracle of Apollo that tradition held had been given to the reformer ***Lykurgus.*** Thucydides (1.82) dates Lykurgus to the ninth century and Herodotus (1.66) dates him to the sixth. In fact, it was unclear even in antiquity whether the reformer was a real historical figure, and the reforms attributed to him seem to have been enacted at various times.

S O U R C E   A N A L Y S I S

T he Great Rhetra is reported in two ancient sources. Plutarch appears to quote the exact wording (unfortunately, the ending of the passage is corrupt in the manuscript of Plutarch's work). But Plutarch wrote nearly a millennium after the probable date of the reform; a more contemporaneous reference also exists in a poem by Tyrtaeus, who lived during, and perhaps participated in, the Second Messenian War.

According to Plutarch[11]:

> Having established a cult of Syllanian Zeus and Athena, having done the "tribing and obing," and having established a Gerousia of thirty members, including the kings, season in, season out, they are to hold Apellai between Babyka and Knakion; the Gerousia is both to introduce proposals and to stand aloof; the damos is to have power to [in Plutarch's gloss on a badly garbled Doric phrase] "give a decisive verdict"; but if the **damos** (Dorian form of *demos*, "people") speaks crookedly, the Gerousia and kings are to be removers.

The translation of the Rhetra reported by Plutarch is uncertain not only because of the manuscript corruption, but also because its language is archaic. *"Tribing and obing"* refers to organizing the citizens in political groups; the tribes were perhaps like the tribes of Kleisthenes in Athens (see Chapter 7) and the **obai** (political divisions) perhaps like the Attic **phratries** (a term itself not well understood, perhaps fictive "brotherhoods"). The document establishes the meeting place of the Assembly (Apellai) and lays down procedures for decision making: the *Gerousia* (board of elders) is to introduce measures to the damos. The assembled people are then to approve or disapprove them. But (and this seems to have been an amendment), if the people make a crooked decision, the kings and the Gerousia are to "straighten" it.[12]

According to Tyrtaeus:

> Lord of the silver bow, far-striking Apollo
>   from his wealthy temple commanded
> the kings, caretakers of lovely Sparta, honored
>   by the gods, and the noblest elders
> to direct the council [*boule*]. On common men he enjoined
>   obedience to the covenants undistorted,
> noble speech, justice in all their deeds,
>   and adopting no crooked counsel.

In what ways does Tyrtaeus' version differ from that given by Plutarch?

There is great dispute over the dating of both the Great Rhetra and the amendment. The Rhetra itself clearly existed by the time of the poet Tyrtaeus, since he refers to it. It is possible that it instituted procedures and institutions to resolve the unrest at that time; but, whenever these procedures were established, the amendment suggests that the experiment in broadening the sphere of political power was soon judged to have gone too far and was curtailed to reassert oligarchic control. Whether Tyrtaeus knew of the amendment is unclear, but it seems probable that he did.

THE SPARTAN CONSTITUTION
IN THE CLASSICAL PERIOD

The primitive and somewhat enigmatic Great Rhetra formed the essential basis for the Spartan constitution. From it, by the Classical period the Spartans had developed a sophisticated political system that combined elements of both democracy and oligarchy in a "mixed constitution" that was considered by many, including Plato and Aristotle, to be a model for other poleis.

The Spartan constitution, or *rhetra,* in its developed form had three parts that were common to most poleis: the kingship (Sparta's was unique in being dual); the council of elders, or Gerousia; and the Assembly. Unlike other states, it also had the *Ephorate*, an annually elected body of five that was apparently instituted after the establishment of the Great Rhetra.

The two hereditary kings came from two separate lines, the Agiad and Eurypontid families; they had equal powers and held office for life. Unlike most Greek kings, those in Sparta did not develop over time into merely ceremonial figures, but retained a significant role in the Classical period both in the government and as active commanders of the army. As commanders of the army they had the right of making war upon whatever country they chose, and in the field they exercised unlimited right of life and death, and had a bodyguard of 100 men. Their powers were, however, restricted by a reform that allowed only one of them, chosen by the people, to lead the army in a given campaign, and held him responsible to the community for his conduct of the campaign.[13] The kings held certain important priesthoods, but they did not have judicial power over criminal cases. They were given perquisites at public sacrifices, but their main source of income was from royal land that they held in the territory of the perioikoi. They were ceremonially honored with the first seat at banquets, were served first, and received a double portion.

The power of the kings was intrinsically limited by its dual nature, but as time went on it was further limited by a number of reforms. Perhaps the most important of these reforms was the creation of an institution unique to Sparta, the annually elected board of five *ephors.* Although a variety of duties came to be assigned to the ephors in classical times, the most basic of their duties reveals the primary function of the office. This was the monthly exchange of oaths between the ephors and the kings: the ephors swore to uphold the rule of the kings as long as the kings kept their oath, while the kings swore to govern in accordance with the laws. Thus they provided a check on the power of the two kings. We have no sure date for this reform, although the failure of the Great Rhetra to mention the Ephorate suggests that it was instituted after that time, probably at some time in the century after Tyrtaeus.

The *Gerousia* consisted of thirty members, including the two kings. The other twenty-eight members had to be over sixty years of age, and thus they constituted a true council of elders, such as we see in Homer. They were elected by acclamation by the Assembly and held their office for life, but only men from noble families were eligible for election. The Gerousia thus constituted an oligarchic element in the constitution. They served as a court of justice for criminal cases, and, as the Great Rhetra indicates, they prepared measures for consideration by the Assembly, and, if the decision of the Assembly was "crooked," the Gerousia had the power to overturn it.

The Assembly was made up of Spartan male citizens over the age of thirty. Citizenship depended upon successful completion of the course of training and education which was provided by the state, and upon election to, and continuing membership in, a mess. (We will discuss these institutions in detail below.) The Assembly elected the Gerousia, the Ephorate, and the other magistrates, decided disputed successions to the kingships, and determined matters of war and peace and foreign policy. Debate was not allowed, only assent or dissent by acclamation to measures presented by the Gerousia. Thus, theoretically Sparta was a democracy, but the power of the people in the Assembly was strictly limited, and the Assembly's decisions were subject to overturn by the Gerousia.

By the Classical period, these constitutional reforms had resulted in a mixed constitution that combined the merits of both democracy and oligarchy. The ability to compromise and to bring into harmony the interests of competing groups had enabled the Spartans to avoid the phase of tyranny through which many other Greek poleis passed in order to achieve similar reforms. Sparta became proverbial for its orderly conduct of government *(eunomia)*, as well as for its disciplined military might. But the final key to Spartan eunomia, as well as to its military success, lay in the Spartan way of life.

THE SPARTAN WAY OF LIFE: AGOGE, COMMON MEALS, AUSTERITY

With the conquest of Messenia and its incorporation into the helot system, the Spartans committed themselves to a life of constant vigilance in the task of keeping the helot population under control. Over time, the need for this shaped the Spartan lifestyle into one of extreme militarism focused entirely on the maintenance of an effective fighting force. We see the results of this only in its final form, and even then only as later admirers and critics portrayed it, for the Spartans left no written records of what they thought and why they chose the course they did. Scholars have rightfully called the picture that we have the "Spartan mirage"—an illusion, not a reality. The Spartan mirage was the public image of Spartan austerity and military prowess that the Spartans created to intimidate their enemies, but with the help of those writers who are our ancient sources—

Xenophon, Plato, Aristotle, and Plutarch—it gained a life of its own as an ideal of authoritarian government that has persisted even until modern times.[14]

In the Spartan system, the polis and its welfare was all in all. Individual and family interests and ambitions were to be put aside to create a society focused on the common good. To this end, the polis oversaw the upbringing of children from infancy. At birth, it was the Gerousia—not the child's father, as in most Greek poleis—who decided whether or not the infant was to be raised. Boys from the age of seven lived in "herds" in a system of training called the *agoge* (the Greek word comes from the verb *ago*, "to lead," and denoted a system of training and a way of life). The agoge was carefully planned to weaken ties to family and to strengthen collective identity: the boys were taking the first steps in becoming homoioi. All adults were responsible for the behavior of all children, with the right (and obligation) to discipline not only their own offspring, but any Spartan child.

When they entered the agoge, boys were divided into age groups and lived under the immediate supervision of older boys. Although they were taught the rudiments of reading and writing, the focus of the agoge was on rigorous physical training to develop hardiness and endurance and on music—patriotic choral poetry embodying Spartan traditions and values. When boys reached the age of twelve the agoge became increasingly more military in form and more demanding: according to Plutarch, the boys were allowed only a single cloak for winter and summer, required to sleep in beds that they made themselves from rushes picked from the Eurotas River, and fed meager rations that they were expected to supplement by stealing (if caught, they were whipped for their failure to escape detection). On occasion they attended the men's messes, perhaps in a form of "rushing," in preparation for their later election to one of these groups. To further their acculturation, they were expected to develop homosexual "mentor" relationships with one of the *hebontes*, men between the ages of twenty and thirty who played a quasi-parental role in socializing their young charges.[15]

For those who successfully completed the agoge, the next step was to gain acceptance in the fundamental institution of adult Spartan male life, the *mess*, or *sysitia*. A mess consisted of a group of about fifteen men of mixed ages who ate and fought together throughout their lives, and who lived together until the age of thirty, when they were allowed to set up their own households. Entry into a mess required a unanimous vote by its members. It was a crucial vote, for full citizenship depended upon membership. Those who failed to be elected were relegated to an inferior status, possibly to be identified with the *hypomeiones*, literally "inferiors."[16] Continuing membership in the mess (and, so, citizenship) was dependent upon one's contribution of food and wine, which was supplied by the allotment of land worked by helots. Should a man fail to provide his contribution, he would be expelled from the mess and lose the status of full citizenship. Thus he had a strong incentive to keep his helots working effectively.

Upon election to a mess, the young men, now classed as hebontes, were still not in possession of full citizenship rights. While they could probably attend the Assembly and vote, they remained under the close supervision and control of the **paidonomos** (the official in charge of all males between the ages of seven and thirty). The hebontes were encouraged to marry, but they were not permitted to live with their wives until they reached the age of thirty. As a result, they spent far more time and developed closer emotional ties with their young male charges, whose every stage of development and behavior they were expected to oversee, than with their wives. This was the period in which they were most active in military service, and, as we saw above, they were also subject to serve in the Krypteia.

At the age of thirty, the Spartan became a full citizen and was expected to move out of the barracks and set up his own household. He also became eligible to hold office. But he continued to take his main meal in his mess, and his military obligations continued until the age of sixty. At that time he became eligible for the Gerousia and no longer had military obligations. He still ate in his mess, however, and was expected to participate actively in the training and disciplining of the younger men and boys.

SPARTAN WOMEN AND THE DOWNFALL OF THE SPARTAN STATE

The woman whom the Spartan married had also been raised under a system developed with the polis's need for citizen warriors as the paramount concern. Spartan girls received formal exercise and other physical training, often unencumbered by clothing, so that they would develop healthy and strong bodies that would produce vigorous offspring. They were allowed to move freely about the city, rather than being secluded in the home, and regularly took part in religious festivals and processions where they were seen by, and saw, young boys and men. As children, they were fed as much as boys were. Nor did the Spartans follow the customary practice of most poleis of marrying girls at puberty; in Sparta marriage and childbearing were put off until girls reached physical maturity (at eighteen to twenty years old), again in order to ensure the best reproductive outcome.[17]

Marriage was by "capture": the girl was carried off, her hair was cut, and she was dressed as a boy by her "bridesmaids"; she was then left in a dark room where her husband-to-be would visit her. If pregnancy resulted, the marriage was valid, but the husband continued in his mess until he reached the age of thirty, visiting his wife only at night and by stealth. The ancient sources report that this regime was adopted to heighten sexual attraction and increase the vigor of any resulting infants. Another view is that it would ensure that the couple would see each other primarily as sexual partners and that the husband would not invest himself emotionally in the welfare of his wife and family to the detriment of his military duties.[18]

The limitation of affective ties between husband and wife, and the strength of such ties between men, that resulted from, or were reflected in, Spartan marital customs, can be seen in the openness of Spartan men to the sharing of women. In Spartan law and practice, it was acceptable for a husband to loan his wife to his friends if he wanted no more children himself, or to borrow the wife of another man for reproductive purposes. Old men with young wives were expected to provide a young man as a sexual partner for their wives. Such practices of course fostered reproduction: the potential of female fertility was fully exploited even when the luck of the marriage draw did not favor it. Other Greeks looked askance at these practices and at the "freedom" allowed to Spartan women and viewed Spartan women as licentious.[19] But it was not the women who were in control; in each case, it was the husband who arranged for and sanctioned such extramarital relationships. These relationships can be looked upon as a logical extension of the general Greek conception of women as property, in the context of the Spartan practice of sharing resources.[20]

S O U R C E   A N A L Y S I S

D ifferent views of Spartan women are expressed by the philosophers Plato and Aristotle—teacher and pupil, respectively—in fourth-century B.C. Athens. In reading these passages, keep in mind the historical context and also the biases of their authors. Despite these biases, what can be learned from these passages about the life of Spartan women?

Plato, who grew up during the final years of the Peloponnesian War, which Athens lost to Sparta, contrasted the Spartans' practices with regard to women with those of Athenians, who " 'pack' all our belongings . . . 'into one' house, and make over to our women the control of the store closet and the superintendence of the spinning and woolwork at large."[21] Plato saw the Spartans' treatment of women as quite different, but in fact he complains that the Spartans did not go far enough[22]:

> Your women are expected in their girlhood to take their share in physical training and music. When they have grown up, they have no woolwork to occupy them, but you expect them to contrive a composite sort of life, one that calls for training and is far from being unworthy or frivolous, and to go halfway with the work of medicine chest, store chamber, and nursery, but to take no share in the business of war. The

consequence is that if circumstances should ever force them to a fight for their city and their children, they would prove quite unequal to playing an expert's part with the bow, like Amazons, or any other missile weapon. They could not, could they, even copy our goddess by taking up spear and shield with the mien of doughty protectors of a harried motherland, and so strike an invader with alarm, if nothing more, by their appearance in martial formation? . . . A legislator should be thorough, not halfhearted; he must not, after making regulations for the male sex, leave the other to the enjoyment of an existence of uncontrolled luxury and expense, and so endow his society with a mere half of a thoroughly felicitous life in place of the whole.

Our other source, the philosopher Aristotle, wrote after the Greek world was shocked by the defeat of the Spartan army by the Thebans at the **battle of Leuktra** in 371 B.C. and the subsequent loss of Messenia. He discusses seven reasons for Sparta's downfall, prominent among which is their treatment of women[23]:

The licence of the Lacedaemonian women defeats the intention of the Spartan constitution, and is adverse to the happiness of the state. For, a husband and a wife being each a part of every family, the state may be considered as about equally divided into men and women; and, therefore, in those states in which the condition of the women is bad, half the city may be regarded as having no laws. And this is what has actually happened at Sparta; the legislator wanted to make the whole state hardy and temperate, and he has carried out his intention in the case of the men, but he has neglected the women, who live in every sort of intemperance and luxury. The consequence is that in such a state wealth is too highly valued, especially if the citizens fall under the dominion of their wives, after the manner of most warlike races, except the Celts and a few others who openly approve of male loves. The old mythologer would seem to have been right in uniting Ares and Aphrodite, for all warlike races are prone to the love either of men or of women. This was exemplified among the Spartans in the days of their greatness; many things were managed by their women. But what difference does it make whether women rule, or the rulers are ruled by women? The result is the same. Even in regard to courage, which is of no use in daily life, and is needed only in war, the influence of the Lacedaemonian women has been most mischievous. The evil showed itself in the Theban invasion, when, unlike the women in other cities, they were utterly useless and caused more confusion than the enemy. This licence of the Lacedaemonian women existed from the earliest times, and was only what might be expected. For, during the wars of the Lacedaemonians, first against the Argives, and afterwards against the Arkadians and Messenians, the men were long away from home, and on the return of peace, they gave themselves into the legislator's hand, already prepared by the discipline of a soldier's

continued on next page

life (in which there are many elements of virtue), to receive his enactments. But, when Lycurgus, as tradition says, wanted to bring the women under his laws, they resisted, and he gave up the attempt. These then are the causes of what then happened, and this defect in the constitution is clearly to be attributed to them. We are not, however, considering what is or is not to be excused, but what is right or wrong, and the disorder of the women, as I have already said, not only gives an air of indecorum to the constitution considered in itself, but tends in a measure to foster avarice.

The mention of avarice naturally suggests a criticism on the inequality of property. While some of the Spartan citizens have quite small properties, others have very large ones; hence the land has passed into the hands of a few. And this is due also to faulty laws; for, although the legislator rightly holds up to shame the sale or purchase of an inheritance, he allows anybody who likes to give or bequeath it. Yet both practices lead to the same result. And nearly two-fifths of the whole country are held by women; this is owing to the number of heiresses and to the large dowries which are customary. It would surely have been better to have given no dowries at all, or, if any, but small or moderate ones. As the law now stands, a man may bestow his heiress on any one whom he pleases, and, if he die intestate, the privilege of giving her away descends to his heir. Hence, although the country is able to maintain 1500 cavalry and 30,000 hoplites, the whole number of Spartan citizens fell below 1000.
. . . Again, the law which relates to the procreation of children is adverse to the correction of this inequality. For the legislator, wanting to have as many Spartans as he could, encouraged the citizens to have large families; and there is a law at Sparta that the father of three sons shall be exempt from military service, and he who has four from all the burdens of the state. Yet it is obvious that, if there were many children, the land being distributed as it is, many of them must necessarily fall into poverty.

Contributing Demographic Factors

In addition to the problems cited by Aristotle, a number of other factors may have contributed to Sparta's demographic difficulties. Intermarriage within a closed group and a preference for first-cousin marriages that was exercised more frequently in the closed society of Sparta than in other, more open poleis would have resulted in increased birth defects and would have raised infant mortality rates even higher than those normal in ancient times.[24] Even the effects of a severe earthquake in the mid-fifth century B.C. must have contributed to the problem; although demographic losses are normally made up fairly quickly, the Spartan population was already at risk from other factors. One should also consider whether the Spartan system in general might have favored the survival rate of females in contrast to that of males. Exercise and sufficient nourishment in childhood, and delayed childbearing, worked to the advantage of females, while males were subjected to a continuous process of testing and culling that began at birth as the midwife administered a wine bath intended to weed out weaklings— a procedure that would have resulted in a preponderance of female infants. The rigorous Spartan agoge must have had its young male victims as well as its successful graduates. In adulthood war took its toll of males, even though the Spartans were very conservative in exposing their men to the risks of battle; moreover, the warrior was always subject to loss of citizenship status if he failed to meet community norms of behavior in battle or if he failed to make the required contributions to the common mess. On the other hand, the main threat to women's lives once they reached adulthood was, of course, childbearing.[25] In antiquity all childbearing was hazardous, but Spartan interest in successful reproduction, and the measures they consequently took in the upbringing of girls, probably gave Spartan women some slight edge over other Greek women in surviving childbirth. On the other hand, as we saw above, Aristotle reports that the Spartans favored large families and offered military and political exemptions to fathers of three or four sons. In order to produce three male infants, women would have had to bear, on the average, six children; in order to produce three grown sons for the Spartan army in an age in which only half the infants born survived to adulthood, they would have had to bear twelve infants. Since each successive pregnancy after the third increases the likelihood of maternal death, any edge that the Spartan woman had as a result of her upbringing would probably have been compensated for by the risks of frequent childbearing (this makes it all the harder to understand the declining population of Sparta, and perhaps should lead us to question the accuracy of Aristotle's report on Spartan family size).

Many Spartan practices appear to have been forms of primitive customs known elsewhere, both in the ancient Greek world and among modern third-world and indigenous peoples. Thus the men's messes and a less rigorous agoge were institutions found also in Dorian Crete, while a parallel to the messes can be found in the Men's Houses of some Native American tribes. Homosexuality as a factor in upper-class male acculturation was also practiced in Athens, and the Thebans had an elite corps of warriors made up of pairs of lovers. Transvestism that was somewhat similar to Spartan marriage rituals also marked marriage in Dorian Argos: the girls there wore false beards. The sharing of women in polyandry is well known from a number of cultures, and has a pale reflection in the relative ease of divorce in Athens, where a husband might also arrange for the remarriage of his wife, as did Pericles. The Krypteia was very similar to widely practiced initiation rites noted by modern anthropologists in which the young withdraw from the community to the wilderness, and are often expected to prove their manhood by the killing of an enemy.[26] But in Sparta all these customs had been developed from their primitive forms into instruments that would serve the single-minded purpose of maintaining Spartan control over their subject population.

The Cost of Security

In terms of the values of Athens and other, more liberal societies, the Spartans paid a high price for their security. Their way of life was marked by extreme austerity. They were notorious for the simplicity of their meals; mess contributions consisted of barley, cheese, figs, and wine, which were supplemented by occasional bits of meat provided by one of the wealthier men or a successful hunter. They were prohibited from possessing gold and silver and allowed to use only iron spits for coinage (hard to conceal, inconvenient to carry, and without monetary value outside Sparta). In contrast to the Athenian fascination with the poetry of tragedy and comedy and the love of rhetorical display, the Spartans took pride in *laconic* (terse) habits of speech and confined their literary and music appreciation to patriotic songs, such as those of Tyrtaeus. By the Classical period the earlier achievements in the crafts (probably mostly the work of perioikoi) had disappeared; even monumental public building had ceased. Thucydides (1.10) says that no one, on seeing the ruins of Sparta in future days, would realize that it had once been the most powerful city in Greece, for the Spartans lived scattered in five villages that had no notable buildings.

The Spartans, however, did not see the austere features of their society as drawbacks but as virtues, and many other Greeks agreed. In antiquity the Spartans were widely admired for their courage and military prowess, and many Greeks—and later, Romans—had a romantic fascination with the Spartan way of life. This was especially the case among conservative oligarchs and aristocrats, who often adopted Spartan fashions in dress and the long hair that was Spartan custom. Among these admirers were some of our most important sources—Xenophon, Plato, Aristotle, and Plutarch—and of course this cannot have failed to affect their descriptions of Spartan life.

There were, however, definite weaknesses in the Spartan way of life viewed from the standpoint of its compatibility with their own aims. The agoge, with its emphasis on strict control and obedience, did not foster the development of individual judgment, and we shall see in later Greek history many instances of Spartans at a loss to handle unusual situations. Nor were the Spartans immune to the temptations of luxury or power when they were away from home and the watchful eyes of their fellow Spartans. Moreover, by the fourth century B.C., Aristotle attests that the Spartans were self-indulgent even at home: the Spartan system of external controls did not build self-control. Moreover, although the concept of homoioi—as well as the whole system of the agoge—was directed toward the weakening or elimination of family ties, this seems not to have been successful, at least in the case of the aristocratic families. Again, as at-

Figure 6-2   Statue of Spartan in modern Sparta.

tested by Aristotle, by the fourth century B.C. there were great differences in wealth among the Spartans, and much was determined by family and patronage. This meant that the most able were not always in positions of authority; this was even the case in the army, where ineffectual generals with powerful connections were often reappointed to command. The system of inheritance also tended over time to concentrate wealth more and more into a few hands—and, unusually for Greece, these hands were often those of women.[27] Finally, there was the crucial problem of declining numbers of Spartans, which no measures seem to have been able to reverse. As we consider the events of the fifth and fourth centuries B.C., we will have an opportunity to assess these weaknesses, and this will allow us to better judge whether the Spartan alternative was as successful in the long run as many classical Greeks and modern admirers have thought it to be.

IMPORTANT PLACES IN CHAPTER 6

On Chapter Map: Peloponnesus: Achaea, Argolid, Arkadia, Elis, Epidaurus, Isthmus of Corinth; *poleis:* Argos, Corinth, Epidaurus, Hysiae, Mantinea, Olympia, Sikyon, Tegea; *Lakonia-Messenia:* Amyclae, Eurotas River, Kythera, Sparta, Messene, Messenia, Mount Ithome, Mount Taygetus

On Inset Map of Lakonia: *Perioikoi towns:* Boeae, Gytheion, Prasiae, Sellasia, Thyrea

On Other Maps (*use map index to find these*): Leuktra, Rhegion

SUGGESTIONS FOR FURTHER READING

L. F. Fitzhardinge, *The Spartans* (1980); J. T. Hooker, *The Ancient Spartans* (1980); E. Fantham, H. P. Foley, N. B. Kampen, S. B. Pomeroy, and H. A. Shapiro, *Women in the Classical World: Image and Text* (1994), chap. 2: "Spartan Women: Women in a Warrior Society."

ENDNOTES

1. *Webster's New World Dictionary* (1955).
2. See R. N. L. Barber, "The Origins of the Mycenaean Palace," in *Philolakon*, J. M. Sanders, ed. (1992), 11–23.
3. L. F. Fitzhardinge, *The Spartans* (1980), 21.
4. See Fitzhardinge (above, n. 3), chap. 3 and the distribution map of Lakonian fine pottery in fig. 14. A kiln found in Sparta itself may suggest that some Spartans were still involved in the production of pottery around 600 B.C.
5. The chronology of the Messenian Wars and the reforms associated with them is very unclear, and various books on Sparta may provide different dates than those given here. In general, I have followed the chronology of Paul Cartledge, *Sparta and Laconia* (1979), which is a rather specialized treatment. There are many books on Sparta that are aimed at a more general audience; two interesting books that are oriented more towards topics of social history rather than political history are Fitzhardinge (above, n. 3), and J. T. Hooker, *The Ancient Spartans* (1980).
6. Arist., *Pol.* 1269a37–8.
7. Hdt. 6.127.
8. Arist., *Pol.* 1306b38–1307a3 = Tyr. Frag. 3 (Edmunds).
9. This is the interpretation of Cartledge (above, n. 5), 160–175.
10. Arist., *Pol.* 1270a15–1270b6.
11. Plut., *Lyc.* 6, Cartledge, tr.
12. Tyr., Frag. 2, Mulroy, tr.; in the Loeb edition, *Greek Elegy*, it appears in vol. 1 as Frag. 4.
13. C. G. Thomas, "On the Role of the Spartan Kings," *Historia* 23 (1974), 257–270.
14. The term *mirage* was introduced by P. Ollier, *Le Mirage Spartiate*, 2 vols. (1933–1943); for the later development of the Spartan tradition in antiquity, see E. N. Tigerstedt, *The*

Legend of Sparta in Classical Antiquity, 2 vols. (1965–1974); and in modern times, Elizabeth Rawson, *The Spartan Tradition in European Thought* (1969).

15. Xen., *Constitution of the Lacedaemonian* 2.12–14, claims that these relationships were "Platonic," but adds, "Who would believe this?" In fact, Aristotle seems to have believed it, as suggested in the passage above (*Pol.* 1269b). Anton Powell views the conflicting ancient evidence and says that we must look at the detail; he finds that "references to particular homosexual attachments of Spartans are conspicuous even by Greek standards," *Athens and Sparta* (1988), 223–224.

16. This term is only used once of Spartans, by Xenophon, Hell. 3.3.6; there it refers to some sort of second-class membership in the Spartan community, but it is not clear exactly what. Other terms denoting less than full Spartiate status were *neodamodeis*, helots freed for army service; *tressantes*, or "tremblers"—those who exhibited fear in battle (Hdt. 7.231, Plut., *Ages.* 30.2–4); and *mothakes*, boys of unclear but inferior status brought up as companions to the sons of wealthy patrons.

17. On Spartan women, see P. Cartledge, "Spartan wives; liberation or licence?" *Classical Quarterly* 31 (1981), 84–109; Redfield, "The women of Sparta," *Classical Journal* 73 (1977–1978), 146–161; M. B. Skinner, "Family dynamics and female power in ancient Sparta," in *Rescuing Creusa: New Methodological Approaches to Women in Antiquity*, M. B. Skinner, ed., *Helios* n.s. 13, no. 2 (1987), 31–48; S. Hodkinson, "Land Tenure and Inheritance in Classical Sparta," *Classical Quarterly* 36 (1986), 378–406; S. Hodkinson, "Inheritance, Marriage and Demography: Perspectives upon the Success and Decline of Classical Sparta," in A. Powell, *Classical Sparta* (1989).

18. Anton Powell, *Athens and Sparta* (1988), 223–224.

19. Plato, *Laws* 637c.

20. Xen., *Constitution of the Lacedaemonians* 6.3.

21. Plato, *Laws* 805e, Taylor, tr.

22. Plato, *Laws* 806a–c, A. E. Taylor, tr. (Hamilton and Cairns).

23. Arist., *Pol.* 1269b, 13–1270b6, B. Jowett, tr.

24. Athenians and other Greeks favored first-cousin marriages, but probably practiced them less than was the case in the more closed citizen group at Sparta. The deleterious effects of such marriages depend upon the presence of adverse recessive genes in both parents. Not all couples would have problems, and not all offspring would necessarily be affected; moreover, a higher *rate* of defect and mortality would probably have escaped notice or been otherwise explained in a society that was not aware of modern statistical analysis.

25. See N. Demand, *Birth, Death and Motherhood in Classical Greece* (1994).

26. See the classic article by H. Jeanmaire, "La cryptie lacédémonienne," *Revue des Etudes Grecques* 26 (1913), 12–50.

27. See above, n. 10.

CHAPTER SEVEN

Archaic Athens: Crisis and Reform

The territory of Attica, which covers approximately 1000 square miles, is divided by mountains into three plains: Pedia (containing Athens), the central Mesogeia, and Thriasia (with Eleusis as its chief town).[1] It was thus even less of a "natural" unity than were the Boeotian or Arkadian plains, which in the historical period were shared by a number of independent city-states in loose and often contested confederations. Yet by the fifth century B.C. the large territory of Attica with its natural divisions was politically unified. All its citizens, regardless of their place of residence, enjoyed equal status as citizens. Outlying towns were not restive under Athenian control, as were the Plataeans under the leadership of Thebes, nor did they have an inferior status, as did the perioikoi towns of Lakonia. This unity was a remarkable achievement. Its story spans the Archaic period and is closely interwoven with the transition from aristocratic rule to the self-rule of the Athenian demos (democracy).

By classical times this political unification, or *synoikism,* was viewed as an event of the distant, mythical past. It was attributed to the Bronze Age Athenian hero Theseus, who was also credited with killing the Minoan Minotaur. Thucydides relates the tradition as it was known in his time.

S O U R C E   A N A L Y S I S

THUCYDIDES 2.15–16.   Here, Thucydides combines an accurate picture of the effects of the synoikism with the attribution to Theseus. What evidence does Thucydides offer for the synoikism? In many Greek poleis, synoikism involved the physical relocation of the people; what evidence does Thucydides offer that this was not the case in Attica?

Few scholars today share Thucydides' belief in a Bronze Age unification that survived into the Dark Age.² Some date the unification to the early ninth century B.C.,³ a period of prosperity—as attested by the Attic graves—that supporters of this dating argue was associated with the synoikism. A shift in the balance of the economy from pastoralism to arable farming may have laid the basis for this rise in prosperity, as suggested by the miniature granaries buried with a woman who has been dubbed the "Rich Athenian Lady" by the excavators of her tomb (Figure 7-1).⁴ Arable farming would have put an emphasis upon landownership and common action in defense of the fields, both of which were closely associated with the concept of citizenship in classical times. A ninth-century B.C. unification would also have been early enough to have been thoroughly forgotten by the Classical period, as it must have been to have escaped even the careful investigations of Thucydides. Yet whether the synoikism of Attica, which was a political union of towns, if not of fully formed poleis, could have so far preceded the date at which the formation of the polis is usually set, the eighth century B.C., is a problem that lends some weight to arguments for a later date.⁵

Several arguments focus on the period around 700 B.C. for the synoikism. For example, J. N. Coldstream interpreted as such evidence the cessation of burials in the Agora, which occurred around 700.⁶ In Coldstream's interpretation, this was the point at which the area was marked out as a formal civic center as a result of the synoikism, in keeping with Thucydides' statement that the city center moved at that time from the Acropolis to the area below (that is, the site of the Agora).⁷ An early seventh-century B.C. date is also suggested by those who date the Athenian conquest of Eleusis to ca. 675 B.C., since that would have been the last step in unification; however, this date for the conquest is contested.⁸

Only a little is known about the political structure of Athens in the early days of Attic unification, but nothing suggests that it deviated in any significant way from that of other early poleis. At the head of an aristocratic society there was the usual basileus (king); at some early time he was joined by, or replaced by, an official called an *archon*. The first twelve archons ruled for life, then a series each held office for ten years; somewhat later the office became an annual one, perhaps in 682/1 B.C., when the list of annual archons begins. Later two more senior archons were added, making a total of three: the Archon Basileus, the Chief Archon, and the Polemarch. The Archon Basileus had mainly ritual functions inherited from the early office of Basileus; the Chief Archon, or **Archon Eponymous,** gave his name to the year and was the effective head of state; and the Polemarch served as commander of the army. A council, the *Areopagus Council,* had broad but ill-defined powers. Only members of an exclusive group of aristocratic families, called the **Eupatrids** ("sons of good fathers"), were eligible for the archonships or the Council. In this early period the Eupatrids were also the repositories of the law, which was unwritten and customary. (Somewhat later, six junior archons were added, the **thesmothetes;** their duty in classical

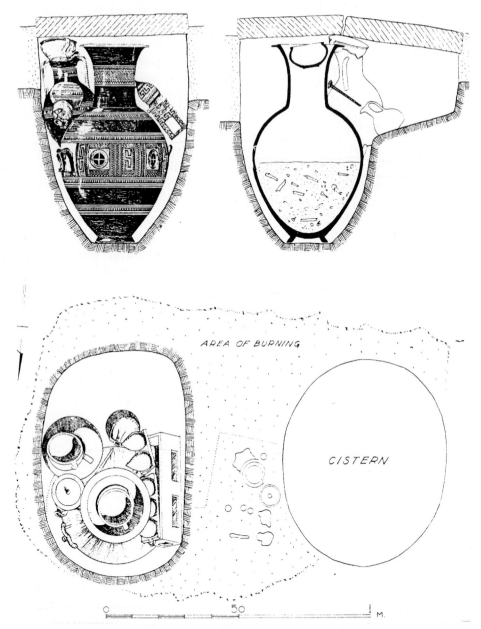

FIGURE 7-1 Tomb of the "Rich Athenian Lady."

times was to act as recorders of judicial decisions and as court officials.) The citizenry was distributed among the four traditional Ionian tribes; they may have had some right to express their opinion in an assembly, but political decisions were essentially in the hands of the Eupatrid families.

THE FIRST ATTEMPT AT TYRANNY: KYLON

In the mid-seventh century (some time between 640 and 621 B.C.), an Athenian aristocrat and Olympic victor, Kylon, attempted to establish a tyranny. Kylon was assisted by his father-in-law, the tyrant of nearby Megara, one of Athens' perennial enemies. The conspirators managed to seize the Acropolis, but the Athenian people rose up against them, foiling the attempt. Kylon himself escaped, but a number of his followers were cornered and took refuge in a temple as suppliants of the god. The archons induced them to give themselves up by the promise that, as suppliants, they would not suffer punishment, but as the suppliants left the temple they were cut down. This ruthless killing of suppliants, in violation of the most sacred laws, had long-lasting consequences for the offenders and their descendants and shadowed Athenian history for a long time to come.

The concept of blood pollution became especially strong during the course of the seventh century B.C. Any shedding of blood was held to pollute and to require purification, even that which was accidental or innocent (as in the purely physiological functions of menstruation and childbirth). Deliberate and unjustified killing, of course, incurred the most serious pollution, especially when it was associated with sacrilege, as was the Kylonian incident. For a city, the result could be civic disorder and epidemic; for a family, an inherited stain, or *miasma,* that inflicted calamities on successive generations as well.⁹ In the case of the Kylonian killings, a trial was held and the archons, including the Archon Eponymous Megacles and his entire genos (clan), the Alkmeonidai, were adjudged guilty. The bodies of Alkmeonids who had died were ordered removed from Attica and the living went into exile. Soon after, when a plague afflicted the city, it was seen as a consequence of the pollution and a special purifier, Epimenides of Crete,¹⁰ was brought in to cleanse the city. The city was saved from the plague, but the pollution remained permanently upon the Alkmeonids and their descendants. As a consequence, members of the genos, many of whom played important roles in Athenian politics, often had checkered careers, now suffering exile, now received back into the city. This became especially significant when political exploitation of the curse affected such central figures in Athenian political life as Kleisthenes, Pericles, and Alkibiades, all Alkmeonids.

The fact that Kylon made an attempt at tyranny suggests some level of popular discontent in Athens at the time; aversion to the involvement of Megara may have been the major factor in Athenian resistance to the attempt. After the failure of the coup, the first sign of possible accommodation of the discontents was the decision to have the traditional laws set down in writing (but not changed or reformed). This was done, according to tradition, by a man named *Drakon* (literally, "Snake"). It was a significant step forward, for publication in writing gave the aristocratic keepers of the law less chance to "remember" the laws to their own advantage. Little is known about the content of Drakon's laws, for they were superseded, with the exception of those dealing with homicide, about a generation later by the "Laws of Solon" (see below). Tradition held that Drakon's laws were extremely harsh—"written in blood" (hence our term, draconian). Nevertheless, those dealing with homicide, which were republished in 409/8 B.C., made the important distinction between premeditated and unpremeditated homicide.

SOURCE ANALYSIS

rakon's law of homicide (brackets indicate conjectures made by the editor to fill gaps in the surviving inscription)[11]:

> Even if without premeditation [someone kills someone, he shall be exiled]. Judgment shall be passed by the Kings as guilty of homicide either . . . or the man who plotted [the death]. The Ephetai shall give the verdict. [Pardon may be granted, if the father] is alive, or brothers, or sons, by all of them, or the one [opposing it shall prevail: if none] of these exists, and the killing was involuntary, and judgment is passed by the Fifty-One, the Ephetai, that it was involuntary homicide, he may be admitted [into the country] by [members of his phratry, ten in number, if they wish. These] the Fifty-one [shall elect] according to their rank. [And those also who] prior [to this time] committed homicide [shall be bound by this ordinance. Proclamation shall be made] against the homicide [in the] agora [by relatives as far as the degree of cousin's son and cousin. Prosecution shall be made jointly] by cousins, [sons of cousins, sons-in-law, father-in-law] and member of the phratry responsible for homicide . . . If anyone [kills the homicide or is responsible for his murder when he has kept away from the market] on the frontier and [from the games and from the Amphictyonic rites, just as one by whom an] Athenian is killed, [just so shall he be treated. The verdict shall be brought in by the] Ephetai . . . And [if a man unjustly carrying away one's property by force is immediately] repelled and killed, there shall be no recompense [for his death].

What reflections are there in this passage of the early stage of kin self-help, and what indications of the development of restrictions on this? What rights did a man accused of homicide have?

THE REFORMS OF SOLON

Drakon's publication of the laws did not solve the problems that were afflicting Athens. Unrest threatened the city, and in 594/3 B.C. it was agreed that a special legislator should be appointed with full powers to restructure the political and economic system as he saw fit. Similar situations had given rise to tyranny in many cities, and the aristocrats probably felt that agreement to what they expected would be a moderate reform might spare them a harsher fate under a tyranny. The man chosen was Solon, a member of an aristocratic family but of middling wealth himself.

S O U R C E   A N A L Y S I S

 he best description of the situation that led to Solon's appointment comes from his own words, expressed in the traditional form of poetry[12]:

Our city will never perish by decree of Zeus
    or whim of the immortals; such
is the great-hearted protector, child of thunder, who holds
    her hands over us: Athena.
But by thoughtless devotion to money, the citizens are
    willing to destroy our great city.
Our leaders' minds are unjust; soon they will suffer
    the pangs of great arrogance.
They cannot control their greed and enjoy the cheerful
    feast at hand in peace.
. . . .
Their wealth depends on crime.
. . . .
    They seize and steal at random
without regard for the holy, the public good,
    or the sacred foundations of Justice,
who is silent but knows present and past, and comes
    for full retribution in time.
The deadly infection spreads throughout the city,
    rushing it into slavery,
which wakens internal strife and war that kills
    so many beautiful youths.
Malicious conspiracies easily ruin a city,
    though the people love it dearly.
These are the evils stalking the people: many
    impoverished leave for foreign
soil, bound and sold in chains of disgrace.

What were the main problems leading up to the crisis, according to this poem? More information comes from a second poem in which Solon described his work[13]:

She who bore the gods of Olympus,
    Earth, greatest and best, whom I cleansed

continued on next page

of [*horoi*], planted everywhere,
shall testify for me in the court of Time.
Then she was slave, now she is free.
I restored to Athens, their god-built home,
many who were sold abroad, sometimes
by crooked judgments, or voluntarily fled
a crushing burden of debt and wandered
so far they lost their Attic accents.
Others I freed from the shame of slavery
in the heart of Athens, where once they trembled
at a master's whim. And though I gained
my ends by force, I melded Power
with Justice and did what I promised to do.
The laws I wrote were the same for lowborn
and noble; both were straightened by Justice.

How do these actions fit the picture of the crisis in the first poem?

Aristotle, in his *Constitution of Athens*, adds that many who were **hektemoroi, or "one-sixth partners"** working the land of others for a one-sixth rent, fell into slavery when they failed to pay.[14] (The status of hektemoros was probably itself not a result of debt, but a remnant from the Dark Age, when poor men voluntarily gave themselves over for protection to the more affluent and powerful.[15])

Causative Factors of the Crisis

Solon's picture of aristocratic greed and oppression, enslavement and civil discord, leaves many questions unanswered. Solon's audience did not need to be told in detail about the conditions that led to the crisis, but the modern historian cannot fill these gaps. As a result, the exact mechanisms that brought about the crisis cannot be determined, and the historian is reduced to speculation.[16] Some relevant factors are the following:

Debt: As in much of Greece, farming in Attica was marginal at best; a bad year could bring disaster (see Chapter 1). A century earlier, in more fertile Boeotia, Hesiod warned repeatedly that the least lapse in diligence would result in the farmer being forced to borrow. But in Hesiod's Boeotia the worst consequence seems to have been social stigma and hunger; Hesiod never suggests that slavery awaited the debtor, as it did in seventh-century B.C. Attica.

Greed: In the late eighth century B.C. Hesiod already complains about the "bribe-swallowing" basileis. By the late seventh century B.C. in Athens the costs of maintaining an aristocratic lifestyle had risen as prosperity grew; new "needs" appeared in the form of imported luxury goods, which the Athenians could observe in the possession of their wealthier neighbors on the nearby island of Aegina, whose economy was based almost entirely on trade.[17] Silver was in use as a medium of exchange, but Athens did not yet mint coins. An important clue to the effects of greed on the aristocracy is the law of Solon prohibiting the export of every agricultural product except olive oil; certainly in bad years, and perhaps even in good, selling grain to the highest bidder overseas would have been more profitable than selling it to the poor at home.

Horoi: The term ***horoi*** means "border marker"; in the fourth century B.C. it was applied to stones marking mortgaged land, but it is unlikely that the sophisticated concept of a mortgage was applicable to conditions of land tenure in the late seventh century B.C. Solon's poetry tells us only that the horoi marked land that was somehow encumbered. They may have indicated the owner's hektemoros status, land on which other debts were owed, or perhaps even land seized (legally or illegally) for debt. These issues are complicated by uncertainty about whether land was *alienable* (could be sold or otherwise transferred).

Solon's Remedies

As evidenced by his poetry, Solon resolved the immediate crisis by freeing the unjustly enslaved, even seeking out and redeeming those who had been sold abroad, and he abolished debt-slavery for the future. He freed the land from its enslavement by the horoi, thus wiping out the debts owed by the poor, and the status of hektemoros was abolished. These reforms were called the ***Seisachtheia,*** or "shaking off of burdens."[18] Solon was willing to cancel debt, but rejected the radical step of redistributing the land, nor did he abolish rent, loans, or indebtedness itself for the future.

Solon instituted a number of important constitutional changes as well. The most fundamental was a new classification of the citizens that substituted wealth for birth as the criterion for holding office. This gives a clue to another aspect of the problem: there must have been men who had achieved some degree of affluence but who lacked political input. The citizens were divided into property classes according to the fruits of their land in measures of both wet (oil, wine) and dry (grain) produce. (It is noteworthy that this classification was still based on landed wealth: any man enriched by trade would have had to acquire land in order to qualify.) The four Solonian property classes were:

Pentecosiomedimi ("500-bushel men"), eligible to be treasurer and archon

Hippeis ("300- to 500-bushel men," perhaps men who could support horses), eligible for lesser offices and possibly also for archonship

Zeugitae ("200- to 300-bushel men," either those with a yoke of oxen, or hoplites),[19] possibly eligible for minor offices

Thetes (all others, including those without land), eligible to attend the Assembly, which now functioned as a court of appeal (see below).

One of the most important of Solon's reforms in terms of the later development of democracy was his institution of the right of appeal. Judicial decisions, which had formerly been in the hands of the archons, without the right of appeal, could now be appealed to the Assembly meeting as a court of appeal (in that role it was called the **Heliaia**). Solon also added a second council, made up of 400 men, 100 from each of the traditional four tribes. The new council perhaps provided a check on the power of the Areopagus Council.[20]

Solon also rewrote the laws, retaining only the murder code of Drakon. Since the Athenians in later times attributed all their laws to Solon, just as the Spartans attributed theirs to Lykurgus, we cannot tell which of the many laws that were later called *Laws of Solon* were actually his. Some that are often cited by historians as genuinely Solonian are the right of a third party to take action on behalf of a victim who had been wronged (formerly only victims or their families could take action, as is clear from the rules of kinship outlined in the homicide law of Drakon); the prohibition of all exports except olive oil; the law that required all fathers to teach their sons a craft if they were to lay claim to their support in old age; and the law allowing and encouraging immigrant families (presumably craftsmen) to settle as citizens in Athens.

Solon's solution was a work of moderation. He rejected a tyrant's role,[21] and favored neither side in the dispute[22]:

> I gave the people the rights they needed without
>   stealing or adding honor.
> Thanks to my precautions, the powerful and wealthy
>   suffered no disgrace.
> I lent both sides my shield's protection, conceding
>   to neither an unjust victory.

But such moderation did not make Solon popular with either side in the conflict[23]:

> So keeping my guard in every direction,
> I whirled like a wolf circled by dogs.

When his legislation was complete, tradition says that Solon left Athens for ten years in order to avoid being pressured into revising his work. But moderation and restraint did not succeed in resolving the problems: the Athenians continued to act like a "pack of dogs," and eventually a tyrant did seize power. Nevertheless, Solon's work set the institutional framework for the future Athenian state, guaranteeing personal freedom and establishing rights that were vital to the later development of democracy, especially the right of appeal. His work also greatly affected the character of the tyranny that was to follow, for our sources agree that it was conducted within the framework of existing laws and institutions.[24]

THE TYRANNY OF PEISISTRATUS

The immediate result of Solon's reforms was a state of chaos. The reforms had brought both financial and political losses to the aristocrats and yet had left the poor still discontented. But perhaps the greatest problem was Solon's failure to create effective means of enforcing compliance with his reforms. It is therefore not surprising that a period of literal anarchy followed: in some years no archon could be elected, and one archon made an attempt at tyranny, overstaying his term of office by two years until he was forcibly removed. In 580/79 B.C. a solution was sought in the appointment of a board of ten to serve jointly as archon, including five Eupatrids, three *Agroikoi* (probably farmers of less than noble status), and two *demiourgoi* (craftsmen, perhaps among them men attracted to Athens by Solon's legislation permitting immigration).

While institution of the board of ten at least temporarily solved the problem of anarchy, factionalism persisted. The names of the three factions suggest that geographical interests formed the basis of the division, and Aristotle says they took their names from the regions in which their leaders farmed their land: the Plain, the Shore, and "Beyond the Hills." *The Plain* refers fairly clearly to Pedia, the central plain of Attica where the best land was located, and among these men must have been the wealthiest landowners, and therefore a force for conservatism. *The Shore* is also not hard to identify as referring to the coastal regions; the men associated with it probably included traders and fishermen as well as farmers; moreover, the silver mines of Laurion were also located near the coast, and men with interests in them probably also formed part of this group. Such men included both the owners of the surface land (the polis owned the resources beneath the surface) and others—for example, those who leased the right to work the deposits or rented slaves or equipment to do so. Those able to exploit the mines were probably wealthy: silver was the single most important Athenian resource and the only significant export. Both the traders and those with mining interests were probably revisionary rather than conservative forces, and Aristotle identified the Shore as taking a middle position. Finally, the group called *Beyond the Hills* is the most puzzling of all. It may have referred to the land beyond the Parnes-Pentelikon, Hymettos ring, and it surely included both Marathon and Brauron. Peisistratus, the leader of the faction, was from Brauron, but Herodotus says that many of Peisistratus' supporters came from the city, and Aristotle identified them as made up of three elements: the common people, those who had lost through the cancellation of debts, and those not of pure Attic descent (perhaps craftsmen attracted by Solon's laws). None of these would have been connected with a specific region, but all stood to gain by change and were ready to support a revolution that would bring in a tyranny.

Despite the support of varied groups, including the demos (which, however, had no official power at this time), the accession of the Athenian Peisistratus as tyrant was not smooth or rapid. In fact, it was only after many years and on his third attempt that he was finally successful. Herodotus' description of his various attempts is instructive about aristocratic political strategies and tyrannical methods of gaining power; the dates of the three attempts are probably 561/0 B.C., an attempt lasting five years; 556 B.C., lasting six years; and 546 B.C., the successful attempt.[25]

S O U R C E   A N A L Y S I S

ERODOTUS 1.59–64. What types of support did Peisistratus rely on in each attempt? An interesting reflection of these events may be provided by a number of Attic black-figure vases that portray Athena (Phye?) ready to lead Herakles (Peisistratus?) into Athens on a cart (Figure 7-2). These suggest that the tyrant made use of propaganda associating himself with the popular hero and the patron goddess of the city.[26]

Life under Tyranny

Once established, the tyranny provided Athens with nearly twenty years of peace and order. Peisistratus ruled in accordance with the constitution and the Laws of Solon, but the archon lists show that he maintained ultimate control by making sure that he himself, or one of his relatives or followers, always held the Chief Archonship, and he used appointment to the other, lesser archonships to reward support from aristocratic families (from whom he also took hostages for good measure). Since the archons at the end of their office passed automatically into the Council of the Areopagus, where they had life tenure, the supporters of Peisistratus gradually filled that powerful body. His strongest enemies, the Alkmeonids, at first went into exile, but later in the tyranny one of them is recorded as holding an archonship, demonstrating that Peisistratus had successfully co-opted them. Nevertheless, they eventually played a central role in ending the tyranny.

Peisistratus gained the support of the poor by economic and other reforms, all of which also tended to cut back the powers of the aristocratic families. For example, he instituted a tax of one-twentieth of produce to provide for public works. This was considerably less oppressive than the one-sixth required of the hektemoroi before the reforms of Solon, and was probably welcomed by them as

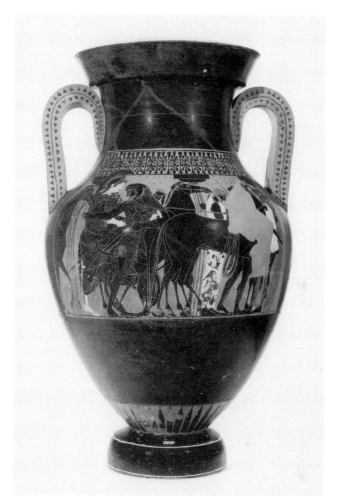

FIGURE 7-2   Attic black-figure vase (Peisistratus and Phye?).

a replacement for the random exactions from local aristocrats to which the farmers had formerly been subject. Loans at good rates for farmers also reduced their dependence on aristocratic neighbors, as did the replacement of local aristocratic judges by traveling judges sent out from Athens. Peisistratus himself also toured the countryside to check on the administration of justice.

In a pattern of activity typical of Archaic tyrants, Peisistratus, and later his sons, undertook extensive building projects and sponsored various cults. While such activities were self-aggrandizing, they also fostered civic consciousness and were important factors in shifting the balance of political power away from the aristocratic families and toward the polis. The earliest of these projects, however—the apparently contemporaneous building of the first large stone temple of Athena on the Acropolis and the institution of the ***Greater Panathenaia***, the festival of Athena which was celebrated with additional pomp every fourth year—present a problem. Because they fit so well the pattern of activities associ-

FIGURE 7-3   Panathenaic prize amphora portraying wrestlers.

ated elsewhere with Archaic tyrants, as well as the later known activities of Peisistratus and his sons, it is tempting to attribute them to Peisistratus as well. One piece of ancient evidence, however, gives a date of 566 B.C. for the institution of the Greater Panathenaia,[27] five years before the date of Peisistratus' first period of tyranny. An attractive solution is to identify the reorganization of the festival as an early effort to resolve the problems afflicting Athens—an attempt made by Peisistratus as a private citizen, probably while holding civic office. But whether Peisistratus inaugurated the Greater Panathenaia or not, he and his sons endowed it with special significance and added to the traditional athletic contests new competitions in the recitation of Homeric poems. Among the prizes for the athletic contests were large black-figure vases (called *Panathenaic vases*) filled with olive oil;[28] as the victors carried them home to their various cities, they spread the reputation of Athenian potters and advertised the high quality of Athenian olive oil (Figure 7-3).

Another traditional festival that was given new life and direction during the

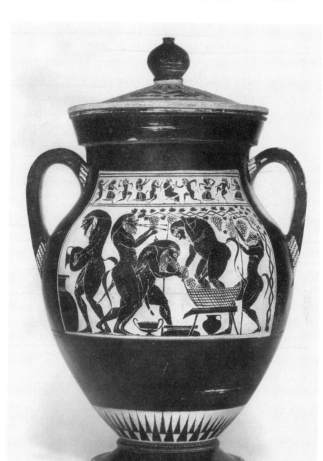

FIGURE 7-4   Dionysiac scene on Attic black-figure amphora.

tyranny was that of <u>Dionysus.</u> Originally a rural celebration of the fertility of the vine and all wild growing things, it took on a new form in the city as the *City Dionysia*, and began a gradual process of transformation that culminated in Classical Attic tragedy and comedy, among the greatest of the achievements of ancient Greece. Tradition puts the first performance of tragedy, by the poet Thespis, who both acted and produced a play for a competition offering a goat as prize, in 534/3 B.C., during the rule of Peisistratus. A marked increase in scenes of Dionysus on Attic vases also has been noted at this time, reflecting increased interest in the festival (see Figure 7-4).[29]

Whether the first monumental Athena temple can also be attributed to Peisistratus' political maneuverings in the period before the tyranny is uncertain. Other buildings on the Acropolis are, however, more securely associated with the tyrant.[30] These include the Archaic phases of the sanctuary of Athena Nike, and the establishment of a shrine for Artemis Brauron, an offshoot of the goddess's shrine at Brauron, Peisistratus' home territory.

Firm evidence also links Peisistratus with the reorganization of the Athenian Agora. During his reign the Agora was cleared of private houses, as evidenced by the closing of wells, and transformed into a monumental civic center. Peisistratus provided a system of drainage that still functions today and improved the water supply by constructing an aqueduct and building an ornamental fountain house called the *Enneakrounos* ("nine spouts"). He also built the "Altar of the Twelve Gods," which served as the official center of the city.[31] It seems likely that Peisistratus himself lived in the Agora.[32]

These building activities, which required the services of architects, engineers, and sculptors, as well as ordinary workmen, created a situation in which the traditional barter economy was no longer satisfactory. Another factor operating in this same direction was the tyrant's reliance on mercenary troops. Thus it is not surprising that coinage was first introduced into Athens during Peisistratus' reign. Peisistratus himself may at first have provided the silver from his holdings in the mining area of Thrace, where he had spent much of his time in exile. These earliest Athenian coins are called *Wappenmünzen* ("heraldic coins," German name given to these coins by coinage experts), because they bear a variety of emblems that were once thought to be heraldic crests. A more recent explanation of the "crests," however, looks to models of coinage from Asia Minor. Both the Lydians under their king, Croesus, and later the Persians attacked the Greek cities of Ionia and reduced them to tribute status (see Chapter 8), and some refugees from these events must have found shelter on the mainland. Among them may have been silversmiths who took advantage of Solon's legislation to exercise their craft in Athens, using a type of design with which they were familiar.[33] The denominations of the Wappenmünzen were too large to be used for retail trade, but they were suitable for lump-sum payments to mercenaries and for payments of long-term contracts with workers in the building trades.

Athenian Leadership under Tyranny

Looking beyond Athens, Peisistratus also focused on civic power, increasing Athenian influence in three areas: the Hellespont, the Aegean, and the Greek mainland. In the Hellespont, Sigeum, which could provide a port of call near the entrance of the waterway, was reconquered (it had been settled forty years earlier, but had subsequently been lost), and Peisistratus installed one of his sons as governor. The colonization of the Chersonese by Miltiades, one of Peisistratus' supporters, ensured that both shores of the Hellespont were occupied by Athenian colonists. In the Aegean, Peisistratus conquered the island of Naxos and installed the tyrant Lygdamis (who had himself helped the Samian tyrant Polykrates to gain power). He purified the island of Delos, site of the pan-Ionian sanctuary of Apollo, by removing all the old burials and forbidding deaths and childbirths on the island in the future;[34] this gave Athenians a strong claim to leadership over the Ionians. On the mainland, Peisistratus continued to foster the connections that had been useful to him in gaining power: at Thebes (where he made dedications to the nearby shrine of the Ptoion Apollo), Eretria, Argos (from which he had taken a wife), Thessaly (he named one of his sons "Thessalos"), and Sparta.

Peisistratus died of natural causes in 527 B.C. and was succeeded by his son Hippias. Hippias' policies and methods, at least in the beginning, seem to have been a continuation of those of his father; in fact, it is sometimes difficult to differentiate the activities of the tyrant and those of his sons Hippias and Hipparchus, since the sons participated actively in rule during the lifetime of their father. Tradition, however, attributed to Hipparchus a special interest in the arts and made him responsible for inviting the poets Anacreon and Simonides to Athens, while Hippias was seen as the successor to his father as political leader.

The sons continued their father's building activities—notably, work on the most ambitious Peisistratid building, the giant temple of the Olympian Zeus, at a site in the lower city.[35] The temple was left unfinished at the fall of the tyranny and was only completed by the emperor Hadrian in the second century A.D. While the extant ruins are those of the Roman period, they attest to the ambitious Peisistratid plan, which rivaled the giant temple of the tyrant Polykrates of Samos, the largest of its time.

An interesting and important change that can be dated securely to the rule of Hippias was the introduction, in ca. 525 B.C., of a new coinage that featured explicit Athenian symbolism: the head of Athena, her owl, and, to make matters absolutely clear, the abbreviated name of the polis. These coins were soon nicknamed *"Owls"* (Figure 7-5). The Owls were twice the value of the Wappen-

FIGURE 7-5   Athenian "Owl" coin, *tetrachm*, head of Athena-owl (ca. 460–450 B.C.).

münzen, and thus they too were far too large for retail trade. Since, unlike the Wappenmünzen, the Owls are found abroad in large numbers, it is likely that silver was exported as a commodity in this form, and that Athens was by this time producing more silver than it needed in the mines of Laurion. The Owl remained the basic Athenian coin until the second century B.C., and it became the standard coin throughout the Greek world.[36]

In 514 B.C. the character of the Peisistratid tyranny changed dramatically as a result of the assassination of Hipparchus. According to Thucydides, his death resulted not from a political plot but from a lovers' quarrel. Both Herodotus and Thucydides tell the story.

SOURCE ANALYSIS AND COMPARISON

HERODOTUS 5.55–57, 62–65; THUCYDIDES 1.20, 6.53 (last sentence)–59. Why does each historian tell the story? How do the accounts differ and in what do they agree? What political significance might the story have had in their day?

After the assassination, the rule of Hippias became increasingly suspicious and harsh, truly tyrannical in the modern sense. Relief from the oppression came by way of the Alkmeonids, who hoped to restore aristocratic power by overthrowing a tyranny grown unpopular. Unable to achieve their goal by force, they undertook to subvert the Oracle at Delphi. Gaining the gratitude of the priests by their generosity in building the temple of Apollo, they convinced them (according to Herodotus, by a bribe) to reply to whatever request the Spartans might make that they should free Athens. After repeated messages to this effect, the Spartans decided to comply, despite their earlier friendship with the Peisistratids.

The first Spartan attempt, by a small force, was defeated by Hippias with the help of Thessaly. In the second attempt, the Spartans arrived with a larger force under their king, but they were successful only when the Peisistratid children fell into their hands. In order to retrieve the children, Hippias agreed to withdraw, taking refuge in Persian territory in Asia Minor. He did not abandon his hope of return, however: during the Persian Wars it was the aged former tyrant who guided the Persians across the Aegean with the expectation that they would reinstate him as ruler of Athens after their victory. The involvement of the Alkmeonids in the fall of Hippias demonstrates that the power of the aristocratic families and their propensity for factional strife had not died out during the rule of the tyrants, although the difficulty encountered by those trying to overthrow the regime also attests to the strength of the new order in Athens.

The Peisistratid tyranny made important contributions to the development of Athens by enhancing the polis and its power and reducing the power of the aristocratic families. Peisistratus and his sons managed this by astute diplomacy and clever manipulation of the archonships, by real reforms in the countryside, by building useful and impressive public monuments in the city, and by providing festivals that celebrated gods popular with the people while fostering civic consciousness and pride. They maintained the framework of Solon's constitution, and Herodotus and Thucydides both call Peisistratus' rule fair and unoppressive.[37]

The final years of the tyranny demonstrated, however, that too much had depended upon the personal management of the Peisistratids, and that safeguards to prevent the misuse of power were lacking. Nor had the tyranny provided any permanent and institutional solution to the regionally based factionalism of aristocratic politics. The need was for constitutional reforms that would eliminate the undue power of these factions and their aristocratic leaders.

THE REFORMS OF KLEISTHENES[38]

Among the first measures taken after the expulsion of Hippias were the reenactment of an old law outlawing any person attempting or aiding in the establishment of a tyranny and a revision of the citizen rolls to exclude "those of impure descent." These "new citizens" included not only the supporters and mercenaries of the tyrants, but also the craftsmen admitted to the city by the Laws of Solon and their descendants. To the discontent of those excluded was added the renewal of political strife between rival aristocratic families. These political struggles focused on two candidates for the Chief Archonship in 508/7 B.C.: the Alkmeonid Kleisthenes, who had experienced both exile and service as an archon under the Peisistratids and had joined the Spartans in expelling them, and a certain Isagoras, who seems to have come to terms with the tyranny, remaining in Athens throughout its duration. Isagoras at first held the upper hand, winning the election for the Chief Archonship. Kleisthenes then took a revolutionary step that was to lead eventually to the establishment of democracy in Athens: he took the people into partnership as his *hetairoi*, a term traditionally applied to the small circle of aristocratic friends who provided each other with political support. In appealing to the people, Kleisthenes promised a comprehensive program of reform. Isagoras retaliated in aristocratic fashion by appealing for assistance to his guest-friend, the Spartan king Kleomenes (who had just recently been instrumental in expelling the tyrants). (**Guest-friendship,** or **xenia,** was a relationship of mutual hospitality and privilege between two men in different poleis.)

Kleomenes came to the aid of Isagoras first by calling for the expulsion of the accursed Alkmeonids, and Kleisthenes at once went into exile. Soon after, Kleomenes himself arrived with a contingent of Spartan troops to see to the expulsion of the 700 other Alkmeonids; he demanded the dissolution of the Council and entrusted the government to a group of 300 of Isagoras's supporters. But the Council resisted, and the people joined them, besieging Isagoras and the Spartans on the Acropolis. On the third day, the Spartans were allowed to leave Athens; all of Isagoras's followers were arrested and executed, but he escaped, fleeing from Attica.

With the expulsion of the Spartans and the flight of Isagoras, the way was open for the reforms that Kleisthenes had proposed. These created an entirely new political structure, in which ten new tribes replaced the traditional four Ionian tribes. The old tribes had been based on the aristocratic gene, which had great local influence stemming from their wealth, ownership of land, and control of many ancient cults. By forming alliances among themselves, these families had monopolized the highest offices in Athens. But their exclusivity and rivalries had been largely responsible for bringing on the tyranny, and after its fall these factors again threatened the stability of the Athenian state. In contrast to the old Ionian tribes, the new Kleisthenic tribes were constituted not on a basis of ancestry but on residence; membership was determined by the **deme,** or village, where a man resided at the time of the reorganization (deme membership thereafter was hereditary). Probably part of Kleisthenes' appeal to the demos was the inclusion of those who had been excluded by the post-Peisistratid revision of the citizenship rolls, even the descendants of craftsmen whom Solon had admitted (as noted earlier). All citizens, new and old, would start as equals under the new system.

SOURCE ANALYSIS

 ERODOTUS 5.66, 69–76. What were Kleisthenes' motives in putting forward his reforms, according to Herodotus?

The ten tribes were constructed from the demes in such a way as to break up the regional power blocs of the aristocracy. In order to achieve this, a complex arrangement was set up. The 139(?) demes were arranged in thirty groups, or *trittyes* ("thirds"; sing., *trittys*); there were ten trittyes in each of three regions: the city, the coast, and inland. Each tribe was constructed of one trittys from each of the three regions (hence a trittys was a third of a tribe). The actual regional divisions and the trittyes, insofar as they are known, are shown on the map (Map 7).

The result of Kleisthenes' reform was a system in which no tribe had a regional basis: each tribe had residents from each region (city, plain, and coast), and each tribe had residents in Athens itself. Thus no tribe could be predominant by virtue of having more members resident in the city, where they could easily attend the Assembly, and men from all parts of Attica would be brought together in the administration of the affairs of the polis.

Post-Reform Government

After Kleisthenes' reforms, the basic political units were no longer the aristocratic families, but the demes. These now became the guarantors of citizenship and the official basis of citizen identity: a man could only be a citizen if he was accepted as a member of a deme, and his official name designated not the name of his father, as formerly, but the name of his deme. Thus the historian Thucydides, formerly identified as "Thucydides son of Sophillus," became officially "Thucydides of Halimus" (although most Athenians continued to refer to themselves informally in the old way).

In the decades following the reforms, the ten tribes provided the structural basis for the other organs of government. The army was marshalled by the tribes, and from this time on men from various parts of Attica fought side by side. Each tribal contingent was led by a general, and thus there were ten generals. A new Council of 500, which replaced the Solonian Council of 400, was composed of 50 members from each tribe. A *prytany*, or executive body, was created from the Council: each tribe held the prytany for one month of the ten-month Attic year. The months themselves were divided into five periods of seven days, and ten men served for a seven-day period; of these men, one was chosen each day to be the president. Popular courts were also established on the basis of the tribes: 6000 jurors were chosen by lot, and, from these, 5000 were selected each day that the courts sat. The 5000 were divided among smaller courts composed of hundreds, and even thousands, of jurors (such large juries were thought to be a safeguard against bribery). Whereas Solon had constituted the Assembly (acting as the *Heliaia*) as an appeals court, now the people

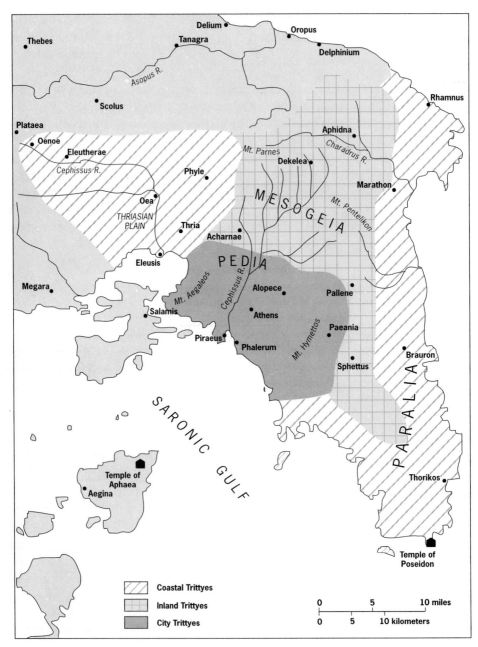

MAP 7   Attica and the Kleisthenic reorganization.

served on primary, independent courts as well, although the Council of the Areopagus continued to judge cases involving religious violations, such as homicide.

A practice known as ***ostracism*** was probably also introduced as a part of Kleisthenes' reforms, although it was first used in 487 B.C. This was a sort of reverse popularity contest: the man who received the most votes had to leave Athens for ten years. It was an honorable exile, however, and the ostracized man retained his citizenship and property. Each year a preliminary vote was taken to determine if an ostracism was to be held; if there was a majority in favor, the second, actual ostracism vote was taken. Voters wrote the name of the person they wanted to banish on broken pieces of pottery, or *ostraca;* hence the term *ostracism.* The purpose was to prevent any one man from gaining too much power—in other words, to prevent a return to tyranny—but in time it became a political tool. Ostracism was last used in 417 B.C., when the two "candidates" managed to gang up and throw the vote to a third man.

Kleisthenes' reforms ended the monopoly on political power by the aristocratic families as well as the regional factionalism that had plagued Athens for so long. They gave every citizen a share in government by membership in a deme: not only could he attend the Assembly, he could also serve in the courts, and in any case he would be judged by his peers if he came before the court himself; he might serve on the Council and on a prytany; he might even be "president for a day." Thus the reforms gave the people more power and rights. Nevertheless, the result was not a democracy, for the highest offices were still restricted by law to the upper Solonian property classes. The name applied to the new system of government seems to have been *isonomia,* "equality before the laws." But even though Athens was not yet a democracy, Kleisthenes' reforms laid the basis for it by the creation of a deme-based structure of government and by two new institutions—the board of ten generals and the popular courts. These turned out (perhaps unexpectedly) to be the key factors in the development of the radical democracy of the fifth century B.C.

IMPORTANT PLACES IN CHAPTER 7

On Chapter Map: *Regions of Attica:* Laurion, Mesogeia, Paralia, Pedia; polis of Athens

Attic towns: Acharnae, Alopece, Brauron, Dekelea, Eleusis, Marathon, Phalerum, Salamis, Thorikos

Non-Attic poleis: Aegina, Delium, Megara, Plataea, Tanagra, Thebes

Other geographical features: Mount Aegaleos, Mount Hymettos, Mount Parnes, Mount Pentelikon, Saronic Gulf

SUGGESTIONS FOR FURTHER READING

A. Andrewes, *The Greek Tyrants* (1956), has useful chapters on Solon and Peisistratus; on Kleisthenes, see D. M. Lewis, "Cleisthenes and Attica," *Historia* 12 (1963), 22–40. More detailed discussions, with bibliography, can be found in the *Cambridge Ancient History (CAH)*, III 3 and IV.

ENDNOTES

1. Michael Grant, *Rise of the Greeks* (1988), 34.
2. This is argued by R. A. Padgug, "Eleusis and the Union of Attica," *GRBS* 13 (1972), 135–150.
3. A. Andrewes, *CAH* III 3, 363; S. Diamant, "Theseus and the Unification of Attica," *Hesperia* Suppl. 19 (1982), 38–47; A. Snodgrass, *CAH* III 1, 668–669, 676–678, 687.
4. E. L. Smithson, "The Tomb of a Rich Athenian Lady, c. 850 B.C.," *Hesperia* 37 (1968), 77–116.
5. Or perhaps to an earlier date for the polis, as suggested by K. Raaflaub, mainly on the basis of Homer, "Homer to Solon: The Rise of the Polis. The Written Sources," in M. H. Hansen, ed., *The Ancient Greek City-State* (1993), 41–105, 75–80.
6. J. N. Coldstream, *The Formation of the Greek Polis: Aristotle and Archaeology* (1974).
7. On the other hand, E. T. H. Brann, in the publication of the excavations of the Agora, suggested that the area ceased to be used for burials because an increasing population needed the space for housing. E. T. H. Brann, *The Athenian Agora* VIII: *Late Geometric and Classical Pottery* (1962), 113.
8. See N. J. Richardson, *The Homeric Hymn to Demeter* (1974), 5–11. A still later date, in the sixth century B.C., was suggested by W. R. Connor, who viewed the attribution to Theseus as an invention of political propaganda by the Athenian tyrant Peisistratus; see "Theseus in Classical Athens," in A. G. Ward, *The Quest for Theseus* (1970), 143–174, based on the report of Plutarch (*Them.* 20) that Peisistratus had a verse dishonoring Theseus deleted from the *Homeric Hymns* and one favorable to him added to the *Odyssey*. But it is difficult to see how this could have been forgotten already in Thucydides' day.
9. See Robert Parker, *Miasma: Pollution and Purification in Early Greek Religion* (1983).
10. Arist., *Ath. Pol.* 1; Plut., *Solon* 12; Diogenes Laertes 1.111.
11. Charles W. Fornara, *Archaic Times to the End of the Peloponnesian War* (1983), no. 15, adapted.
12. Solon, Frag. 4, cited by the fourth-century B.C. orator Demosthenes; the numbering of the fragments is that of J. M. Edmonds, *Elegy and Iambus* (1931), vol. 1; translations are taken from David Mulroy, *Early Greek Lyric Poetry* (1992), 68–69.
13. Solon, Frag. 36, Mulroy, tr.
14. Arist., *Ath. Pol.* 2.2.

15. P. J. Rhodes, *Aristotle. The Athenian Constitution* (1984), commentary on 2.2; Andrewes (above, n. 3), 180.

16. For example, Andrewes (above, n. 3), 380–381.

17. On Archaic Aegina, see L. H. Jeffery, *CAH* IV, 364–365.

18. Arist., *Ath. Pol.* 6.1.

19. Plut., *Pelopidas* 23.4, applies the term to hoplites.

20. Plut., *Solon* 19.2; Andrewes (above, n. 3), 387–388.

21. Solon, Frag. 32.

22. Solon, Frag. 5, Mulroy, tr.

23. Solon, Frag. 36, Mulroy, tr.

24. Hdt. 1.59.6; Thuc. 6.54.6.

25. The evidence for the dates is conflicting; see Andrewes (above, n. 3), 398–401.

26. J. Boardman, "Herakles, Peisistratos and sons," *Revue Archéologique* (1972), 57–72; arguments against this interpretation are offered by J. M. Cook, "Pots and Pisistratan Propaganda," *Journal of Hellenic Studies* 107 (1987), 167–169.

27. The ancient, but late, sources disagree about the establishment of this festival in its enhanced form as the Greater Panathenaia. Some form of celebration of the festival of Athena surely existed before the sixth century B.C.; what is in question is the introduction of the expanded form called the *Greater Panathenaia*. The two sources appear to disagree. Eusebius (third or fourth century A.D.) for the year 566/5 writes that gymnastic contests were conducted at the Panathenaia; this was six years before Peisistratus' first period of tyranny, but it does not specifically call the festival the "Greater Panathenaia." A second source, Marcellinus (late third century A.D.), says that the Panathenaia were instituted in the archonship of Hippokleides, but we have no idea when this was. The third source is a scholiast (ancient commentator) on Aelius Aristides, and he specifically assigns the origins of the Greater Panathenaia to Peisistratus. (Aelius Aristides lived in the second century A.D.; the scholiast no earlier than the fourth century A.D., and probably later.) The enhancement of the festival by the addition of new contests was undoubtedly carried out gradually by the tyrant and his sons, and they could have received the credit even had Peisistratus not instituted the special observances every fourth year. Nonetheless, the civic difficulties that gave rise to the tyranny in the first place seem unlikely to have provided the positive leadership and spirit of innovation associated with the institution of a new festival.

28. J. Neils, ed., *Goddess and Polis: The Panathenaic Festival in Ancient Athens* (1992), gives a fully illustrated discussion of the vases and their use as prizes.

29. H. A. Shapiro, *Art and Cult under the Tyrants in Athens* (1989), chap. 5.

30. The identification and dating of building activities on the Acropolis at this early date are heavily contested. For various opinions, see John Travlos, *Pictorial Dictionary of Ancient Athens* (1971); Shapiro (above, n. 29), chap. 2; and T. L. Shear, "Tyrants and Buildings in Archaic Athens," in *Athens Comes of Age: From Solon to Salamis* (1978), whose interpretation is followed here.

31. Pausanias 1.14.1; Thuc. 2.15.5, 6.54.6.

32. Shear (above, n. 30), 6–7.

33. C. M. Kraay, *Archaic and Classical Greek Coins* (1976), 25–26; Andrewes (above, n. 3), 409.

34. Hdt. 1.64.2; Thuc. 3.104.1.

35. Begun by Peisistratus according to Vitr. 7.15.

36. On Athenian coinage, see Kraay (n. 33, above).

37. Hdt. 1.59; Thuc. 6.54.

38. For the scholarly reconstruction of Kleisthenes' reforms, see D. M. Lewis, "Cleisthenes and Attica," *Historia* 12 (1963), 22–40.

CHAPTER EIGHT

Archaic Ionia:
Greeks and Persians

ome of the earliest developments in Greek culture took place in the cities of Ionia on the coast of Asia Minor. These cities, according to tradition, had been settled by refugees fleeing the mainland in the Ionian Migration at the close of the Bronze Age (see Chapter 4). By the fifth century B.C., the Athenians laid claim to sponsorship of the migration and hence to the status of mother city of the Ionians. We do not know to what extent this claim was justified, but the dialect spoken by the Athenians, Attic Greek, was a form of Ionic Greek, and many of their institutions were similar.

During the Archaic period the Ionian Greeks also had close ties with their non-Greek neighbors, the Lydians, and, later, the Persians, who were heirs to the ancient civilizations of the Near East. Despite difficulties, especially with the Persians, the expanded horizons that these contacts brought contributed greatly to the flourishing of Greek culture in what has been termed the *Ionian Enlightenment*. Expressions of this cultural and intellectual ferment appeared in the development of geography and history, and especially in the crucial shift on the part of the pre-Socratic philosophers from mythological to natural explanations for the cosmos. In a political sense, the climax of these interactions was the Persian Wars, in which the Greeks of the mainland successfully defended themselves against attempts by the Persian kings to extend their empire. However, even after this Greek victory, the Persians remained important factors in Greek history until Alexander the Great conquered the "Great King" of Persia and took the crown of the empire for himself. They served as the "Other" in terms of which the Greeks could better define themselves, but they also sometimes played a more active role, providing the Greeks with their own version of a Cold War. Just as we could not understand the history of the United States in the late twentieth century without considering the Soviet Union, so we cannot understand Greek history of the Archaic and Classical periods without keeping in mind the Persians.

For much of the history of this period, including the history of Persia, we are dependent upon the fifth-century B.C. Greek historian Herodotus, a citizen of Halicarnassos in Asia Minor and himself a product of the Ionian Enlightenment. While the subject of Herodotus' history was the Persian Wars of the fifth century B.C., he traced the great confrontation back to the origins of the Persian Empire, and investigated in detail many of the peoples encompassed by that empire, from the Scythians to the Egyptians (see Map 8). It is true that Herodotus saw events from a Greek point of view and that his sources were sometimes less than ideal from the standpoint of the modern historian (for example, we do not know to what extent Herodotus could understand the language of some of the places that he visited, and local guides and interpreters, even today, may not always provide the most accurate information). Nonetheless, Herodotus provides the only cohesive account of these events. Two points are important to keep in mind in evaluating his work as history, however. First, when they exist, we must also consider and compare primary sources, such as inscriptions and official records, even though they are sometimes problematic (official inscriptions tell the official side of the story, and even official records provide only bare-bones facts that require interpretation).[1] Second, we must keep in mind the cultural and intellectual context in which the historian himself worked and how this may have affected his work.

HISTORIOGRAPHICAL ANALYSIS

Herodotus as a Historian

erodotus was a native of the East Greek city of Halicarnassos, whose population was heavily intermixed with native Carians. In Herodotus' time the city was ruled by a Carian dynast who served as *satrap*, or governor, for the Persian overlords. Herodotus' family was exiled from the city at some point early in his life—probably, as was not unusual for the Greeks, for political reasons—and they found refuge on the nearby Greek island of Samos. The historian recounts at some length, and as a matter of pride, a number of the achievements of the tyrant of Samos.

Herodotus did not live out his life on Samos, but spent much of his time traveling, visiting lands ranging from Egypt and Libya to Babylon and Scythia.

continued

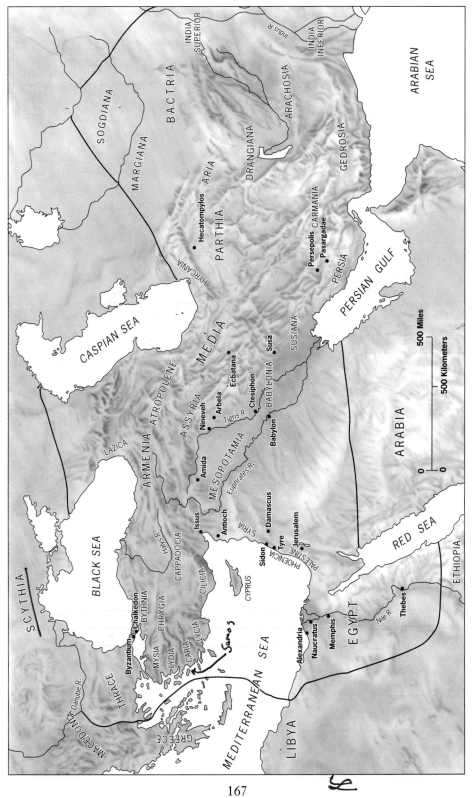

MAP 8   The Persian Empire at its greatest extent.

SCYTHIA

MACEDONIA

Danube R.

THRACE

BLACK SEA

Byzantium
Chalkedon
BITHYNIA
MYSIA
PHRYGIA
LYDIA
CARIA
Samos
LYCIA
CILICIA
CYPRUS
CAPPADOCIA

Halys R.

MEDITERRANEAN SEA

GREECE

LIBYA

Alexandria
Naucratus
Memphis
EGYPT
Thebes
Nile R.
ETHIOPIA

RED SEA

Sidon
PHOENICIA
Tyre
PALESTINE
Jerusalem
Damascus
SYRIA
Antioch
Issus

Amida
MESOPOTAMIA
Euphrates R.

ARMENIA

LAZICA

ATROPOLENE

Nineveh
ASSYRIA
Arbela
Tigris R.
Ctesiphon
Ecbatana
Babylon
BABYLONIA
Susa
SUSIANA

MEDIA

CASPIAN SEA

HYRCANIA

PARTHIA

Hecatompylos

ARIA

MARGIANA

SOGDIANA

BACTRIA

INDIA
SUPERIOR

INDIA
INFERIOR

Indus R.

DRANGIANA

ARACHOSIA

CARMANIA
Persepolis
Pasargadae
PERSIA

GEDROSIA

PERSIAN GULF

ARABIA

ARABIAN SEA

500 Miles
500 Kilometers

167

He apparently lived for a time in Athens, and in 444 B.C. he participated in the Athenian foundation of the Panhellenic colony of Thurii in southern Italy, where he settled (although some believe that he returned to Athens at the end of his life).[2] His work must have been widely known, for he is reported to have given readings at the Olympic games, as he probably also did in Athens.

Given his personal history, we can fairly assume that Herodotus' experiences under Persian rule would have lent a negative cast to his view of the rise of that imperial power, and especially to his account of the attempted Persian conquest of Greece. Moreover, another aspect of Herodotus' life that may have shaped his history was his relationship to Athens. His work exhibits a heavily Athenian focus, and he may have regarded Athens (then, of course, the center of Greek intellectual life) as his adopted home.

In the opening passage of his *Histories*, Herodotus reports his motive in composing the work: so that the great deeds of men, the great and marvellous works produced by both the Greeks and the Barbarians, and the reasons why they fought each other, might not be forgotten. In this he was following in the epic tradition of Homer, and that tradition colors his vision throughout his work. Perhaps most important for us to keep in mind is the oral nature of that tradition and the fact that the methods by which oral cultures preserve and transmit knowledge are fundamentally different from those of literate cultures.[3] Interesting stories are easier to remember than bare facts, and, in the telling, even more interesting details are often added. Thus in Herodotus' work stories tend to shift into familiar patterns and to incorporate moral and ethical lessons. Folktales, animal fables, myths, and family histories all form part of the stuff of oral tradition, and oral tradition was Herodotus' primary source. Thus many of the stories that he tells would today not be classified as history, but as folktales, and the modern historian must assess each of his accounts in order to discover the nucleus of "facts" (in the modern sense) that underlies these often fascinating stories.

Nevertheless, in many vital ways Herodotus reflects an intellectual environment that was in the process of becoming a literate culture. Although he gave oral performances of his work, it was essentially a written work, and it was a work in prose. Perhaps most important, Herodotus, unlike the epic poets, did not rely on the Muses to reveal the truth about the past, but investigated it himself. For this purpose he employed *historie* (inquiry), traveling widely in both Greek and barbarian lands, listening to the stories of veterans, merchants, priests, and tour guides (among others), always weighing and assessing the information that he obtained. When he heard conflicting accounts, he usually in-

continued

cluded them all, often without giving his own opinion about their comparative worth, leaving it to his audience to decide for themselves. It was above all this spirit of inquiry that led to his being awarded the title "Father of History."

THE LYDIANS AND THE GREEKS

In the sixth century B.C., as the kingdom of the Lydians rose to prominence in Anatolia, the Greeks in the Anatolian coastal cities suffered frequently from Lydian attacks. One of these raids, the sack and destruction of the Greek city of Smyrna by the Lydian king Alyattes, is well attested by archaeological evidence, although it is mentioned only briefly by Herodotus (1.16).⁴ Smyrna was surrounded by formidable walls. The attackers built a massive siege mound, beginning some distance from the walls, in order to create a height from which they could fire arrows down into the city and which would also protect their men from the return fire of the defenders as they filled in the gap between the peak of the mound and the wall, thereby creating a path of entry into the city. For a time the two sides raced to gain the advantage of height; the ultimate success of the Lydians is attested by the height of the mound, which, even today, after centuries of erosion, still reaches over 21 meters above sea level, while the city walls at their highest reached only 10 meters. To create their mound, the Lydians used materials from houses built outside the walls, and the fill contains construction materials such as mud brick, worked stones, and roof timbers that reveal construction methods, as well as household items that give clues about daily life. The remains of arrowheads provide information about the weapons used by both sides and suggest that both sides employed foreign mercenaries.

After the death of King Alyattes, Croesus, his son, continued intermittent attacks on the Greeks. He also introduced a significant innovation in dealings with the Ionians: instead of demanding "gifts" on an arbitrary and irregular basis, he instituted the payment of a regular tribute. While this was an infringement on Greek independence, it had its compensations, for it allowed the Ionians to live in peace and to benefit from economic and cultural interchange with their Barbarian neighbors.

The Lydians were a wealthy and sophisticated people with extensive resources of gold, silver, and electrum. They invented the use of coins, probably initially for the payment of mercenaries rather than for trade or everyday purchases. The Greeks adopted the use of coinage from them, and the first Greek coins, which were found in the foundation deposit of the temple of Artemis that Croesus built in Greek Ephesus, show the evolution of the technique in Greek hands. These earliest Greek coins are dated to ca. 600 B.C.; in comparison, the earliest Athenian coinage, the Wappenmünzen, began only in the 550s, and the widely used Athenian coins called "Owls" (see Chapter 7), ca. 525 B.C.

As the foundation deposit of the temple of Artemis at Ephesus suggests, the wealth of the Lydian kings was often employed in seeking the favor of the gods, including the gods of the Greeks. Croesus was the primary contributor to the building of the temple at Ephesus, which was the largest building in the Greek world at that time (about 55 by 115 meters), and the first monumental structure to be built of marble. Croesus also outdid all the earlier Lydian kings in his gifts to the oracular shrines on the Greek mainland. Herodotus describes some such gifts that Croesus sent to Delphi: the figure of a lion of pure gold that originally weighed 10 talents (about 820 pounds); a figure of a woman in gold 3 cubits (about 5 feet) high, said to have been a portrayal of the Persian king Cyrus' baker; and a silver mixing bowl that held 600 amphoras of wine (about 3600 gallons), said to have been the work of Theodoros of Samos, a Greek. The Lydian king also sent a shield and spear of solid gold to the oracular shrine of the god Amphiaraos in Boeotia, which were kept in the shrine of Apollo in Thebes in Herodotus' day. We can assume that the historian himself saw all these treasures on visits to these shrines and that he heard about Theodoros' accomplishments in Samos.

For the modern historian, Herodotus' descriptions of the wealth of the Lydian kings provide valuable economic evidence. In the background we can see Greek craftsmen—Theodoros of Samos and other workers skilled in goldwork and silverwork, as well as the countless anonymous workers who helped to build the great temple at Ephesus. The period was clearly one of economic prosperity for the Ionian Greeks. In addition to their contacts with the riches of Lydia, the cities of the coast and the nearby islands were particularly well positioned to carry on trade by sea. It was a ship's captain from Samos who was the first to reach the silver-rich land of Tartessos in Spain, and traders from the Ionian cities were prominent among those that the Egyptian Pharaoh allowed to establish a trading post, Naucratus, in Egypt.

Evidence, on a more personal level, of Greek prosperity and the close relationships that developed between Lydians and Ionian Greeks is provided by the poet Sappho, who lived on the offshore island of Lesbos around the end of the seventh century B.C. For her, Lydia was a source of the latest luxury fashions and a place to which her young friends sometimes went as brides. Her poems give us some insight into the way in which Greek women (admittedly, the privileged among them) viewed their own lives; thus they provide a counterbalance to the overwhelmingly male-oriented picture of women which we find in our major sources (such as Herodotus). In this fragmentary poem, Sappho consoles a girl whose friend is now a wife in Sardis[5]:

. . . . Sardis . . . .
. . . . with her mind often here . . . .
. . . . you, like a familiar goddess . . . .
She delighted in your dancing.

But now she stands out among Lydian women
As, when the rosy-fingered sun sets, the moon
    surpasses all the stars.
Light spreads over the salty sea
Like fields full of flowers,
The dew is scattered in beauty,
Roses bloom, and the delicate wild parsley and the flowering clover.
She wanders about, remembering gentle Atthis.
Her delicate heart is consumed with longing for your heart.

Herodotus tells us that Sappho's brother, Charaxus, bought a well-known prostitute at Naucratus for a large sum of money, and freed her, for which the poet strongly criticized him.⁶ His presence at Naucratus, whether on a trading mission or for adventure, reflects the mobility and the foreign connections that formed the basis of Ionian prosperity.

THE COMING OF THE PERSIANS

The Fragmentation of the Near East

Meanwhile, farther east, a new and more expansive barbarian power was developing that would soon dramatically affect the course of Near Eastern and even Greek history. In 612 B.C., the Medes, an Indo-European people living in what is now called Iran, joined the Neo-Babylonians in sacking Nineveh, the capital of the Assyrian Empire. This caused the collapse of that empire, and for more than a half century control of the Near East was fragmented, divided among the Medes, Neo-Babylonians, Egyptians, and Lydians.

From 590 to 585 B.C. the Medes fought the Lydians. In 585 B.C., the war was brought to an unexpected end by a solar eclipse whose prediction tradition attributed to the philosopher Thales of the Ionian Greek city of Miletus. The two sides concluded a treaty of peace, sealed with a marriage alliance, and the boundary between the kingdoms was set at the Halys River.

In 550 B.C., Cyrus, the king of the Persians, an Indo-European tribe related to the Medes, conquered the Medes. He forged the two peoples into a single political entity, sharing positions of responsibility and authority with the Medes. This provides the first illustration of the Persian practice of incorporating conquered peoples into the administration of newly acquired territory. The system proved overwhelmingly successful in the long run, as "the Medes and the Persians" went on to establish the first effective working empire.

Opposition soon arose to the early expansion of the Persians, however. In 547 B.C. King Croesus of Lydia, which had been an ally of the Medes since the pact of 585 B.C., now sought to avenge the Lydian defeat by the Persians. As the story is told by Herodotus (1.46–49), he first asked the advice of the Oracle of

Apollo at Delphi. Yet, despite the rich gifts that he had lavished upon the god in the past, he received an ambiguous and essentially deceptive reply: If he crossed the river Halys, a great kingdom would fall. Misled by pride, he interpreted this in the way he wished to hear it, and, confident of victory, he led his army across the river. But the kingdom that fell was his own.

Cyrus, Cambyses, and the Persian Expansion

The victory of the Persian king Cyrus over Croesus had far-reaching consequences for the Greeks in Anatolia. The city of Miletus, which had had the most favorable terms with the Lydians, quickly made terms with the Persians, but the other Greek cities resisted, and one after another they were conquered. Herodotus relates stories of heroic resistance. In Lydia the people of Xanthos committed mass suicide rather than submit (Hdt. 1.176). Two Ionian cities were able to escape by flight: the people of Phocaea sailed away to the west and eventually founded Elea in southern Italy; the Teians also established a new city, Abdera, on the north shore of the Aegean (Hdt. 1.164–167). The people of Knidos tried to make their land into an island by cutting through the peninsula on which their city stood, but repeated injuries to the workmen finally caused them to seek the advice of Delphi. The god replied that, had Zeus wanted their land to be an island, he would have made it one. The Knidians then abandoned their efforts and surrendered to the Persians (Hdt. 1.174). In a later chapter, we will see how this resistance eventually escalated into a full-scale confrontation between the Persians and the Greeks of the mainland.

After the conquest of Lydia and the Ionian Greeks, Cyrus continued his imperial expansion, subduing Babylonia, Syria, Phoenicia, and Palestine. His conquest of Babylonia illustrates one of the reasons for Persian success. The city of Babylon had long been chaffing under the rule of Narbonidus, a Chaldean from the south. Narbonidus, a fanatical devotee of a foreign god, neglected the gods of Babylon and left uncelebrated their principal festivals. When the Persians arrived and began assiduously to revive traditional Babylonian religious practices, they were overwhelmingly welcomed by the people. (Similarly, in the Bible the Persians are lauded for allowing the Hebrews to return from the Babylonian Captivity and to rebuild their temple).[7]

With the conquest of Phoenicia, the previously land-based Persians obtained a fleet and the potential to threaten the Greek islands. But, according to Herodotus, Cyrus turned first to Scythia in the north, probably in an effort to secure the land route to Greece and the west. The historian relates that Cyrus died there in 530 B.C., fighting against the queen of the nomadic Massagetae, Tomyris. Failing to show respect for the queen, he suffered the consequences of his hubris when she wreaked barbarian vengeance upon him for the death of her son by immersing his decapitated head in a skin filled with blood, giving him what he had sought, "his fill of blood" (Hdt. 1.215). The historian notes that there were many accounts of Cyrus' death, but that he had chosen the one he thought most likely to be true. Unfortunately other ancient sources are silent about the last eight years of Cyrus' reign and the manner of his death. It seems likely that he devoted much of his attention to organizing his conquests, since the traditional tribal organization of the Persians would not have sufficed for the vastly increased territories that they now ruled. We do know that he appointed governors over Sardis and Babylon, thus laying the foundations for the provincial system that was later notable not only for its efficiency, but also for its tolerance of the ethnic, religious, and political identities of its subject peoples. This makes it unlikely that Cyrus acted as Herodotus reports in the account of his death, although he may well have died on a campaign against the Scythians.

Cyrus was succeeded by his son Cambyses. In the fourth year of his rule, Cambyses set out on a successful campaign to extend Persian rule to Egypt. The main source for this is again Herodotus. The historian portrays Cambyses as a madman whose invasion of Egypt was motivated by uncontrolled anger, and who continued on the same dangerous course after the conquest, going so far in his disrespect for Egyptian customs and religious beliefs as to kill the sacred Egyptian Apis bull. In Herodotus' account, the king suffered divine retribution for this last grave violation of the divine: in 522 B.C. he died from an infection in an accidentally self-inflicted stab wound to his thigh,[8] and Herodotus notes that his wound was just like the one with which he had killed the sacred Apis bull.

In fact, however, other evidence appears to contradict Herodotus' lurid picture of Cambyses' activities. Inscriptions attest his many actions to propitiate the Egyptian gods and to follow Egyptian royal customs. Moreover, the coffin of the Apis bull bears an inscription that says that Cambyses ordered it made in honor of his father, Apis-Osiris (as Pharoah, Cambyses was considered to be the son of a god), and a stele represents the king in native costume kneeling before the bull, and records that he ordered all due honors for the bull.[9] Such official inscriptions would, of course, put the best light on the king's activities, portraying them in keeping with traditional Persian policy; if in fact he had been mad, his irrational acts might well not have been recorded.

Darius and the Development of the Empire

It seems likely, however, that the historian, in his portrayal of Cambyses, fell victim to the propaganda of Cambyses' successor, Darius. We have two principal sources for the events of the succession: the account of Herodotus and that of Darius himself. Neither is an entirely reliable source. Darius' account, which survives in the form of an inscription on a cliff at Bisitun in Media, is a primary source, but it is also a piece of propaganda intended to justify his rule in an irregular succession.[10] It was widely disseminated in various copies throughout the empire, and the report of one of these by Ionian Greeks may have been the source of Herodotus' fascinating moralizing tale. Thus, while Herodotus and the Bisitun inscription agree on a number of points, they may not be independent and thus cannot be used to confirm each other.

Both Herodotus and the Bisitun inscription relate that Cambyses secretly had his full brother Bardiya (Smerdis in Herodotus) killed, and that a usurper, a Mede posing as Bardiya, then appeared. After the death of Cambyses, which both sources agree was somehow by his own hand, Darius, who was a member of a collateral branch of the royal family, took part in a conspiracy in which he killed the false Bardiya. He then succeeded in gaining power—according to his own account because he was chosen by the Persian god Ahura Mazda, according to Herodotus, by rigging a horse race that the conspirators had agreed would decide the issue. The horse trick may, however, have been a confused reflection of the use of horses in Persian divination;[11] in that case, the two accounts would agree in essence in attributing the choice of Darius to the god.

Bardiya, whether as impostor, usurper, or legitimate heir,[12] had ruled with much support as a popular king for seven months before he was killed by Darius, and the new claimant to the throne was challenged by more than fifteen rebellions in various parts of the empire before his control was assured.

In solidifying his hold over the empire, Darius established the detailed workings of a system of government that would enable him to govern successfully the many peoples who were his subjects. He expanded the provincial system begun by Cyrus, dividing the empire into twenty satrapies. This system provided for the regular collection of taxes and for the rigorous accounting for these taxes as well. A network of roads with way stations for the provisioning of travelers was created to serve both the swift communication of official business (many provincial problems, even minor ones, were referred to the king for judgment) and commercial purposes. The king involved himself not only in the collection of taxes but also in the economic health of his territories through the stimulation of agriculture and trade. Vast water regulation projects are described by Herodotus (3.117), and state involvement in industries such as cloth or rug making seems to be reflected in the official accounts of rations given to workforces consisting mainly of women, girls, and boys.[13] Trade was fostered by the development of ports along the Persian Gulf and the construction of a canal linking the Nile with the Red Sea.

A letter of Darius to Gadatas, a Persian official living at Magnesia-on-the-Maeander in Ionia, reflects a number of Darius' concerns as king:

S O U R C E   A N A L Y S I S [14]

T he King of Kings Dareios son of Hystaspes to Gadatas, his slave, thus speaks: I find that as to my injunctions you are not completely obedient. Because you are cultivating my land, transplanting from [the province] beyond the Euphrates fruit trees to the western Asian regions, I praise your purpose and in consequence there will be laid up in store for you great favor in the Royal House. But because my religious dispositions

continued

are being nullified by you, I shall give you, unless you make a change, a proof of a wronged [King's] anger. For the gardeners sacred to Apollo have been made to pay tribute to you; and land which is profane they have dug up at your command. You are ignorant of my ancestors' attitude to the god, who told the Persians all of the truth. . . .

This letter, a Greek translation of a letter that was probably written in Persian (for Gadatas was a Persian), reveals by the forms of its letters that it was inscribed in the second century A.D., to be displayed on the temple of Apollo. The purpose of the inscription, which was probably a copy of an earlier inscription, was to document the great age of the temple and the honor it received from the Persian king. It does seem odd that a letter of reproach should have been made public by its recipient, and this has led to some question of the letter's authenticity.[15] Yet one might argue that a forger would have been unlikely to have created a letter with such personal details, and that the letter seems authentic in these details. It begins with an expression of Darius' interest in the improvement of agriculture, as he notes favorably the introduction of a new species of fruit tree. The king then asserts absolute personal power over Gadatas, and threatens him; this is not done arbitrarily, however, but in terms of holding him to contemporary standards of moral behavior and the proper honoring of foreign gods. Gadatas had used his position to exact money illegally from a local official, an offense in any culture; moreover, he had ordered the cultivation of unconsecrated land, thereby violating local religious laws. The letter shows Darius' concern that his officials treat his subjects fairly and honor local divinities. Finally, the letter strikes an authentic note in its concern for the oracular Apollo, who always spoke the truth; this was of particular interest to Darius as a Zoroastrian, for Zoroaster's teachings laid great stress on truth telling.

In the time of Darius, Persian religion was in a state of transition from the early Indo-European and pre-Indo-European polytheistic faith to the religion revealed by the prophet Zoroaster.[16] In its fully developed form, *Zoroastrianism* is a dualistic religion, in which the forces of Justice and Truth, in the person of the god Ahura Mazda, battle against the forces of Evil and the Lie, led by Ahriman. Zoroaster emphasized the purity and value of fire, which he made central to ritual practices. The only altars were fire altars, which were often portrayed on official Persian reliefs. In the time of Darius, however, the religion was still in a state of flux, with some older practices still in effect (thus in some respects Herodotus' description of Persian religious practices and beliefs differs from Zoroastrianism in its fully developed form).[17] But the essential ethical core of the Zoroastrian faith was fully in force, as we see in the letter of Darius to Gadatas.

The absolute power asserted by Darius over Gadatas, expressed by the term *slave*, was an integral aspect of the Persian form of government, in which one man held supreme power in a sharply defined hierarchical system characterized by clear indicators of status. This stood at the opposite extreme to the type of government favored by the Greeks, in which each man (at least those considered worthy of account) held himself to be the equal of his peers and entitled to share in the making of decisions. The conflict of these two extremes, carried out on the fields of battle and dramatically memorialized in the work of Herodotus, has, however, tended to obscure the benefits of the Persian system. The Persians did successfully govern widely diverse peoples in a huge empire with a remarkable degree of religious, ethnic, and political tolerance for over 200 years. As long as the power at the center was strong, the system worked well, and much imperial pomp and circumstance was devoted to maintaining that center. Godatas may have turned pale with fear as he read the king's threat, but he did not feel himself to be an unnoticed cog in a vast imperial machine, nor were the victims of his injustice entirely without recourse.

It was not until 514 B.C., three years after he had won power, that Darius turned to plans for the further extension of the empire by an expedition to Scythia. According to Herodotus,[18] the king was accompanied by Ionian Greek forces, and he left behind a number of Ionian tyrants to guard the bridge over the Danube for the return of his army. The Scythian strategy was to refuse to meet the Persians in pitched battle. Instead, the Scythians withdrew as the enemy advanced, drawing the Persians further and further into land which the Scythians made useless by choking the springs and destroying the forage. At the same time the Scythians made surprise raids on the Persians when the latter sought provisions and were encamped for the night. Herodotus reports that the most effective weapon the Persians had was an accidental one: their donkeys and mules frightened the Scythian horses and thus hindered the effectiveness of their raids.

As Darius futilely chased the retreating Scythians, Herodotus portrays the waiting Ionian tyrants as being tempted by the Scythians to destroy the bridge and strand the king. Finally, however, Histiaeus, tyrant of Miletus, persuaded the others to stay at their post, pointing out that their rule depended upon the continuing power of Darius. As a result, Darius, unlike Cyrus, was at least able to escape with his life from his Scythian adventure. Nevertheless, playing on his audience's emotions, Herodotus reports that the Persian withdrawal was accomplished only at the cost of the heartless abandonment of the injured and sick, as well as of the pack animals, creatures that had done the most to help the Persian cause.

THE IONIAN ENLIGHTENMENT

As a part of the vast Persian Empire, which stretched from Egypt to India, the Ionians had an expanded view of the world. Under Persian rule, the Ionian Greeks moved about more than ever before, and over a greater area, some as travelers and some perhaps as traders, as Sappho's brother did. The Persian road system facilitated travel and had a considerable impact on the dissemination of geographical knowledge. Some people may have traveled under compulsion as workers, being deported for rebellion; these, however, were few in number compared with those deported by the Assyrians. They did, however, include Greeks such as the Milesians and the Eretrians who were punished for involvement in revolt, and this made a considerable impression on Herodotus. Most, however, were free workers, and such free workers could be seen as participating in an early version of a Common Market. The skilled Greeks from Ionia who helped to build Cyrus' palace complex at Pasargadae included workers of every level, from stonemasons to architects engaged in planning, and they are judged to have been free laborers attracted by good pay and working conditions.[19]

In this expanded world, travelers' tales were a popular form of entertainment, and we see a reflection of this in Herodotus' works. One of his predecessors was a man from Miletus, Hecataeus, whose work described the lands and peoples he encountered during his travels in the Mediterranean and the Black Sea areas. Thus Herodotus was following in a local tradition when he set out on his investigations. His interest in foreign peoples was so great that he devoted the second book of his *Histories* to an extended account of his researches in Egypt, and many other passages, such as his descriptions of the Scythians and of the peoples of India, are ethnographic in nature.

One of the most important intellectual achievements of Archaic Ionia was the development of natural philosophy.[20] The first man to be given the title of philosopher was a Milesian named Thales, who is traditionally dated to ca. 640–546 B.C.[21] A number of the practical activities attributed to him reflect experience with the learning of the Near East. Thus Herodotus (1.75) reports the common opinion among the Greeks that Thales enabled Croesus' army to cross the Halys River by diverting its flow; manipulation of rivers for irrigation had a long history in the Near East, and awareness of these methods may be reflected in this achievement (although Herodotus himself believed that the army used the bridges that were there in his own day). More definitive evidence of intellectual contact is Herodotus' report that Thales predicted the year of the eclipse of May 28, 585 B.C., a phenomenon that brought the battle between Lydians and Persians to an end (Hdt. 1.74). Traditionally the Greeks had viewed eclipses as omens sent to men by the gods. If Thales could have even framed the problem of how to predict an eclipse, he must have considered the phenomenon not as a message from the gods, but as a natural occurrence. To have been successful in his prediction, he must have had access at least to records of previous eclipses, probably Babylonian records accessible in Sardis, and to have been lucky besides, for even these records would not have allowed him to predict that the eclipse would be visible in Ionia.[22]

In cosmology, Thales is said to have held that the earth floats on water, a Near Eastern concept that contrasts with the traditional Greek mythological picture of an earth that is surrounded by the waters of Ocean.[23] He is also reported by Aristotle (Frags. 86, 87 KRS) to have identified water as the basic substance of the cosmos, that material out of which all other things are created and into which they pass away. The idea of a single basic substance was a startling innovation. Thales could have come to this idea from reflecting on the various forms that water can take, from airy mist to solid ice, or on the fact that the fetus begins its life in water. Unfortunately, we cannot be sure, for we do not have Thales' own words, and Aristotle tended to read his own concepts in the work of his predecessors.

On the other hand, there is good evidence that Thales's successors took the momentous step of explaining the cosmos in terms of changes in a basic natural substance. Thus the Milesian philosopher Anaximander, by tradition a pupil of Thales, and thus dated to 610/9–547/6 B.C., postulated that all things arose out of and passed away into the *Apeiron,* a boundless and undefined substance. He described this process in terms of the human values of justice and reparation: ". . . for they pay penalty and retribution to each other for their injustice according to the assessment of Time" (Frag. 143 KRS). He also postulated an evolutionary theory about the origin of animals and men: "Living creatures came into being from moisture evaporated by the sun. Man was originally similar to another creature—that is, to a fish" (Frag. 139 KRS). In describing the workings of the heavenly bodies, he postulated not gods but a mechanical system of fiery wheels with apertures through which the fire appeared as stars, the moon, and, in the outer ring, the sun (Frags. 125–128 KRS). M. L. West drew attention to the parallel with the heavenly wheels that Ezekiel saw near Babylon in 593–592 B.C., and to the fact that the order of the heavenly bodies in Anaximander's theory was the same as that held by the Persians.[24]

The third Milesian philosopher, Anaximenes, by tradition the pupil of Anaximander, and thus dated to 585–525 B.C., held that the basic substance was *Aer* (something like air), which became fire by rarefaction, then water, and finally, earth by compression (Frag. 143 KRS). This was a theory that proved very long-lived: in the fifth century B.C. it was adopted by the philosopher Diogenes of Apollonia, and the comic poet Aristophanes attributed it to Socrates in his play *The Clouds*; it appears in the sophistic treatise *Breaths* in the Hippocratic Corpus of medical texts, and a fourth-century historian of medicine attributed it to Hippocrates himself.

In neighboring Ephesus the philosopher Heraclitus, whose floruit (period of flourishing) was fixed at 504–501 B.C., taught that at the basis of all things was the *Logos,* a word that probably meant "measure" or "proportion" (the same word is, of course, used in the Gospel according to John). He seems to have meant that all things, though apparently plural and discrete, are really part of an ordered arrangement. Heraclitus made use of a number of metaphors for the cosmic process, and his deliberately obscure and oracular style makes consistent interpretation difficult. Prominent among the metaphors was strife—"It is necessary to know that war is common and right is strife and that all things happen by strife and necessity" (Frag. 214 KRS). Another metaphor was fire: "All things are an equal exchange for fire and fire for all things, as goods are for gold and gold for goods" (Frag. 222 KRS). Fire is sometimes identified as Heraclitus' basic substance, like Aer and the Apeiron of the Milesians; however, fire for him seems to be a process rather than an originative substance, and so the parallels are not exact.

However it was expressed, for Heraclitus the world was in a constant state of flux. This made self-identity a puzzle: "Heraclitus somewhere says that all things are in process and nothing stays still, and likening existing things to the stream of a river he says that you would not step twice into the same river" (Frag. 217 KRS). A similar insecurity affects human knowledge in general. Heraclitus recognized the joint roles of perception and reason in knowledge, but saw them as problematic: "Evil witnesses are eyes and ears for men, if they have souls that do not understand their language" (Frag. 201 KRS). The result is relativism—"Sea is the most pure and the most polluted water; for fishes it is drinkable and salutary, but for men it is undrinkable and deleterious" (Frag. 202 KRS). Nor was certainty to be found in traditional religion, for Heraclitus was scornful of the ways in which the Greeks worshipped the gods: "They vainly purify themselves of blood-guilt by defiling themselves with blood, as though one who had stepped into mud were to wash with mud; he would seem to be mad, if any of men noticed him doing this. Further, they pray to these statues, as if one were to carry on a conversation with houses, not recognizing the true nature of gods or demigods" (Frag. 244 KRS).

The possible debt of the role played by fire in Heraclitus' system to the role fire plays in the Persian religion of Zoroaster has been considered since antiquity.[25] It is true that fire plays a central role in both, and Heraclitus may well have been influenced in his choice of the metaphor by his awareness of its role in Zoroastrianism. Nevertheless, the parallel is too general in itself to be very significant, and many discussions are not rigorous enough in their treatment of the sources to proceed beyond speculation and conjecture. M. L. West has, however, recently made some persuasive suggestions not only about possible Persian influence, but also about the influence of Indian philosophy.[26] Although India was far distant from Ephesus, both were part of the Persian Empire, and Indians came to mainland Greece with Xerxes' army in 480 B.C.

Whatever its debt to the Near East for specific ideas and information, Ionian natural philosophy constituted a definitive break with traditional anthropomorphic ways of explaining the cosmos in both the Near East and Greece. The Ionian search for natural, rather than mythological, explanations prepared the way for Hippocratic medicine in the fifth century B.C. and for the further achievements of ancient philosophy by Plato and Aristotle in the fourth century B.C. Ultimately it laid the basis for the development of science in the modern world.

IMPORTANT PLACES IN CHAPTER 8

On Chapter Map: *Persian Empire:* Babylon, Black Sea, Caria, Caspian Sea, Cilicia, Danube, Danube River, Egypt, Euphrates River, Halys River, Indus River, Libya, Lycia, Lydia, Media (Bisitun), Mediterranean Sea, Naucratus, Nineveh, Palestine, Pasargadae, Persian Gulf, Phoenicia, Red Sea, Scythia, Syria, Tigris River

On Other Maps *(use map index to find these):* Abdera, Elea, Ephesus, Eretria, Halicarnassos, Knidos, Lesbos, Magnesia-on-the-Maeander, Miletus, Phocaea, Tartessos, Teos, Thurii, Samos, Sardis, Smyrna, Xanthos.

SUGGESTIONS FOR FURTHER READING

For the history of Persia, see J. M. Cook, *The Persian Empire* (1983); on Ionia, see Carl Roebuck, *Ionian Trade and Colonization* (1959), and C. J. Emlyn-Jones, *The Ionians and Hellenism* (1980); on Ionian philosophy, see G. S. Kirk, J. E. Raven, and M. Scholfield, *The Presocratic Philosophers* (1984, abbreviated as *KRS*), and M. L. West, *Early Greek Philosophy and the Orient* (1971); in general, relevant sections of *The Cambridge Ancient History* IV: *Persia, Greece and the Western Mediterranean c. 525–479* (1988) are useful and provide extensive bibliography.

ENDNOTES

1. Scholars disagree on the possibility of reconciling Herodotus' account with the primary sources; most skeptical is P. R. Helm, "Herodotus' Mêdikos Logos and Median History," *Iran* 19 (1981), 85–90, who argues that Herodotus' source was nonhistoric, a "saga of national liberation"; for a discussion, see Stuart C. Brown, "The Mêdikos Logos of Herodotus and the Evolution of the Median State," in A. Kuhrt and H. Sancisi-Weerdenburg, *Achaemenid History* III: *Method and Theory* (1988), 71–86.

2. Podlecki, "Herodotus in Athens?" in K. H. Kinzl, *Greece and the Eastern Mediterranean in Ancient History and Prehistory* (1977), 246–265, questions whether Herodotus was ever in Athens, although he does not appear to question his other travels. The ancient evidence that he did visit Athens is not strong, except for the evidence of his own descriptions of the city (which seem proof enough), but given the central role of Athens in Herodotus' *Histories*, and his visits to nearby Greek sites as well as to far more distant and exotic sites, a failure to visit Athens would seem to require far more proof than a visit there.

3. The recognition of the basically oral nature of classical Greek culture is fairly recent; some important contributions to the question include Rosalind Thomas, *Literacy and Orality in Ancient Greece* (1992), and W. V. Harris, *Ancient Literacy*; on Herodotus' use of oral sources, see Mabel Lang, *Herodotean Narrative and Discourse* (1984).

4. J. M. Cook, and R. V. Nicholls, "Old Smyrna," *Annual of the British School at Athens* 53/54 (1958–59), 1–137.

5. Sappho, Frag. 96, David A. Campbell, *Greek Lyric Poetry* (1967).

6. Hdt. 2.135; her Frag. 5 mentions the brother, but in an affectionate manner.

7. A Biblical reference, Isaiah 45:1–3 and 13.

8. That the wound was self-inflicted is also stated by Darius' inscription at Bisitun, his own account of his accession to power; see Jack Balcer, *Herodotus and Bisitun* (Stuttgart, 1987), chap. 1, with illustrations; whether it was an accident or a matter of suicide—or even whether Darius might have been involved—is not clear.

9. G. Posener, *La première domination perse en Égypte* (1936), nos. 3 and 4, and pp. 171–175.

10. See Rüdiger Schmitt, *The Bisitun Inscriptions of Darius the Great: Old Persian Text*, vol. 1 (1991).

11. Suggested by G. Widengren, "La Royauté de l'Iran Antique," *Acta Iranica* 1 (1974), 84–100, 85.

12. See Mabel Lang, "Prexaspes and Usurper Smerdis," *Journal of Eastern Studies* 51 (1992), 201–207.

13. R. T. Hallock, *Persepolis Fortification Tables* (1969), nos. 919–920.

14. Charles W. Fornara, *Archaic Times to the End of the Peloponnesian War* (1983), no. 35.

15. M. van den Hout, "Studies in Early Greek Letter-Writing II," *Mnemosyne* n.s. 2 (1949), 144–152.

16. For a brief discussion of Persian religion, with references to further reading, see T. C. Young, Jr., *CAH²/IV*, 99–103.

17. Hdt. 1.131–132.

18. Hdt. 4.1, 83–98, 102, 118–144.

19. See Carl Nylander, *Ionians in Pasargadae: Studies in Old Persian Architecture* (1970).

20. The best introduction to early Greek philosophy is G. S. Kirk, J. E. Raven, and M. Scholfield, *The Presocratic Philosophers* (1984) (abbreviated as *KRS*), which also gives the fragments in translation; the Greek texts can be found in H. Diels and W. Kranz, *Fragmente der Vorsokratiker* (1968, 6th ed.). Here the fragments are identified by the numbering system used in KRS, and all translations are from that work.

21. Little is known about the actual dates of these men, with the exception of Thales, who is roughly datable by his prediction of the solar eclipse of 585 B.C. In the ancient tradition, men were assumed to have been 40 at the peak of their careers (their floruit, abbreviated *fl.*), which is the date often given; without other information, their death was assumed at age 60. The ancient sources also calculate dates for the philosophers after Thales by assuming teacher-pupil relationships, which may or may not have been the case. Thus Anaximander is said to have been the pupil of Thales, and Anaximenes of Anaximander, and both are dated accordingly.

22. KRS 82; A. A. Mosshammer, "Thales' Eclipse," *Transactions and Proceedings of the American Philological Association* 111 (1981), 145–155, argues that the prediction and eclipse could not have occurred as Herodotus says; he suggests that the story was a literary conflation of two outstanding events, on the principle that one marvel deserves another, and that famous men must be connected with famous events that occur in their day.

23. KRS 90–93.

24. A Biblical reference, Ezekiel 1:15–19, 3:13, 10:9–22, cited in M. L. West, *Early Greek Philosophy and the Orient* (1971), 88–89.

25. See West (above, n. 24), chap. 6, for discussion.

26. West (above, n. 24), esp. chap. 6.

CHAPTER NINE

The Persian Wars and the History of Herodotus

The Eastern connections that had been so fruitful for the Greeks in the Archaic period became problematic with the Persians' more vigorous assertion of imperialistic ambitions. The Greeks had grown relatively comfortable with tributary status under their Lydian neighbors, but the Persians interfered in the internal affairs of the cities, establishing one-man rule by Greek collaborators. Resistance grew among the Ionians, culminating in the Ionian Revolt of 499–494 B.C. Ionian appeals for assistance to mainland Greece led to the involvement of both the Athenians and the Eretrians, and the small contingents sent by these mainland cities took part in a daring attack on Sardis, the Lydian capital. The revolt was unsuccessful, but Persian annoyance at Greek interference ultimately resulted in a full-scale confrontation of East and West, the Persian Wars (see Map 9).[1]

The Persian Wars were of fundamental importance in Western history, not only because the victory of the Greeks assured the survival of their culture, but also because it actively contributed to the forging of that culture. From the unexpected victory of a small people over the incursion of a mighty empire arose a new consciousness of Greek identity and an increased self-confidence that fostered the flourishing of the Greek spirit in the century that followed.[2]

THE IONIAN REVOLT

It might seem that Persian-imposed tyrants, and Persian tribute, would have weighed heavily upon the Ionians. Yet, at least according to Herodotus, when revolt came in Ionia, it was not as a result of widespread dissatisfaction with Persian rule, but rather because of the personal machinations of individuals. The key players were Histiaeus, the Persian-supported ruler, or tyrant, of Miletus,

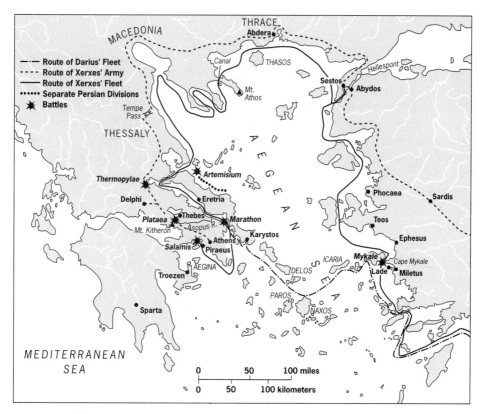

MAP 9 The Persian Wars.

and his son-in-law Aristagoras, actually in control of Miletus at the time. It was Histiaeus who had earlier convinced his fellow tyrants to safeguard the bridge over the Danube and thus assure Darius a means of escape from the Scythians. As a reward for his loyalty, Histiaeus asked for an estate in Thrace, but this roused Darius' suspicions. Thrace was a strategic area on the route to Greece, and it also had rich gold resources. Concerned, yet unable to prove Histiaeus's disloyalty, Darius removed him to an honorable exile in Susa, ostensibly as an adviser. Aristagoras was left in control of Miletus.

But Histiaeus soon grew tired of his sheltered life in Susa and devised a complex plot to have himself recalled to Miletus. His plan involved sending a secret message to foment revolt among the Ionian Greeks, for he believed that the king would send him back to quell the disturbance. He tattooed the message on the shaven head of his most trusted slave; then, when the man's hair had grown back, he sent him off, telling him only to ask Aristagoras to shave off his hair and look at his head (Hdt. 5.35). The arrival of the message coincided with Aristagoras's own decision to instigate a revolt to save himself from the consequences of some local misadventures of his own. The plan worked to the extent that Darius did send Histiaeus back to help quell the rebellion. However, when Histiaeus reached Sardis, the Persian satrap of that city realized his real plans and Histiaeus was forced to flee, leaving Aristagoras in charge of the revolt.

Faced with the threat of Persian military power, Aristagoras sought assistance from mainland Greece. While he was unsuccessful in his appeal to the Spartans, he managed to convince the Athenians to send twenty ships. As Herodotus comments (5.97), many people (the Athenian Assembly) are easier to fool than one man (the Spartan king). The people of Eretria, a city in Euboea, also sent a small force. What began as a relatively minor involvement in the revolt became more serious when the Athenian and Eretrian forces aided in a surprise attack on Sardis, during which the city was set afire. The attackers were driven off, pursued, and suffered a clear-cut defeat near Ephesus. Nevertheless, according to Herodotus, this attack inspired an obsession for revenge in the Persian king: Darius ordered his servants to remind him three times a day that he must punish the Athenians.

The revolt itself was crushed by the defeat of the Ionians in a sea battle at Lade, near Miletus. Aristagoras fled to Thrace, where he was killed by the Thracians. Histiaeus, rejected by the Milesians in his bid to return to the tyranny, led a series of private campaigns so complex that it is unclear whether he was aiding the Greeks, or the Persians, or both. He was eventually captured and executed by the satrap of Sardis, who sent his embalmed head to the king. Darius, at least, still believed that Histiaeus had been loyal to the Persian cause, for he provided the head with an honorable burial.

HISTORIOGRAPHICAL ANALYSIS

W hat can we make of Herodotus' account of the causes of the Ionian Revolt (5.30–38)? The story of the secret message sent on the scalp of the slave stands out as a particularly memorable element in the account, and typical of Herodotus' interest in what modern scholars would classify as folktale motifs. Such motifs were useful in keeping alive the oral transmission of stories about the past; their frequent occurrence in Herodotus' work is one mark of his strong reliance upon oral tradition. But even Herodotus' account does not put the whole causal weight upon the scheming of Histiaeus: he recognizes that Aristagoras's own intrigues had brought him to the point of revolt when he received his father-in-law's message. Moreover, other Ionian Greek cities joined in the revolt, as did Greeks as far away as Cyprus. Even the Persians had second thoughts about the policy of imposing pro-Persian tyrants on the Greeks once the revolt had been put down. A more modern view would posit economic pressures and political unrest as causes for the revolt, causes that the Persians themselves recognized when they later made changes in their relationship with the defeated subjects.

After punishing the rebels with various deportations and civic destructions, the Persians attempted to remedy the conditions that had led to the revolt. They abandoned the support of despotic rulers in the subject cities and set up democracies in their stead; they also instituted new and more equitable methods of assessing the tribute.

THE EXPEDITIONS OF DARIUS AND THE FIRST PERSIAN WAR

The Ionian Revolt was the first step in the series of events that led to the great Persian expeditions against Greece itself. As Herodotus saw it, the revolt engendered in Darius a spirit of revenge against the hubristic mainland Greeks who had participated in the burning of Sardis. But in Herodotus' view the Persian kings Darius and Xerxes did not act alone; the gods conspired to lead them astray. Modern scholars view the cause in more pragmatic terms. For example, Peter Green posits economic causes: the Persian king's need for gold to maintain an economy that focused on the stockpiling of wealth, and the pressures put upon the Athenian food supply by Persian control of the Hellespont.[3] He also suggests religious motivations: the Zoroastrian doctrine that "all men must work for the establishment of God's Righteous Order on earth, a clarion-call for would-be imperialists in any age, and especially attractive to Darius."[4]

The first Persian approach to Greece was by sea. In 492 B.C. Darius sent his son-in-law Mardonius on an expedition against Macedonia and the Greek island of Thasos. The area, which was rich in both gold and timber for ships, had provided Peisistratus with the resources to establish his tyranny in Athens. Peisistratus's son and successor, Hippias, who had escaped from Athens and found refuge with the Persians, could have provided Darius with specific information about the area (although it is clear from the story of Histiaeus that Darius was already aware of the area's strategic potential). In fact, the region was probably already under some degree of Persian control as a result of the Scythian campaign, and Mardonius' expedition was intended to extend and consolidate this control. Mardonius' fleet came to a disastrous end, however, when a violent storm off Mount Athos destroyed most of the ships.

According to Herodotus, the loss of the fleet was simply one more factor pushing Darius irrevocably toward an attack on Greece: A desire for revenge against Athens; the advice of the Peisistratid Hippias, who was eager to regain his lost position as tyrant in Athens; and the nagging of his queen, Atossa, instigated by her Greek doctor who saw his own role in a reconnaisance trip as a means of getting back to his homeland were other factors. This type of multiple motivation embodied the historian's own belief in the inevitability of fate: many factors conspired to goad Darius into his ill-fated attack on Greece.

In 490 B.C. Darius sent a fleet directly across the Aegean, moving from island to island. He thus avoided the dangerous route around the cape of Mount Athos, but modern strategists point out that one of his aims was to also gain control of the Cycladic Islands. Hippias was on board to lead the way, expecting his supporters at Athens to welcome his return. The Persians, as planned, easily subdued the islands as they went. When they reached Eretria, which was betrayed to them after a fierce resistance of six days, they plundered and burned the city and deported its population. But when they reached the Greek mainland, they met unexpected resistance at the hands of the Athenians on the plain of Marathon.

The Battle of Marathon

The battle of Marathon is one of the most famous battles of Western warfare. From antiquity it has embodied a cluster of ideas central to Western culture and Western self-definition: the victory of a small contingent of men fighting heroically to defend their homeland and their freedom against a foreign invader whose vastly superior force marched under the lash of political servitude—in brief, Western freedom versus Eastern slavery.

When the Athenians realized that a Persian attack was imminent, they sent off a long-distance runner to ask the Spartans for assistance. But the Spartans replied that they were celebrating a religious festival and that sacred law forbade them to leave the city until the full moon, which would occur in six days (Hdt. 96.105–106). Only a contingent of the Plataeans, historic allies of the Athenians, joined the Athenian forces. The Greek forces took up a stand at a strong position commanding the main road into the plain. Herodotus reports that disagreement about the wisdom of resistance arose among the ten generals, each of whom held command for one day at a time. In the debate, the opinion of Miltiades to fight finally won out, but Herodotus says that Miltiades postponed the attack until his day of command (Hdt. 6.109–110). Herodotus was surely mistaken about the rotating command, for at this time the commander in chief was the Polemarch;[5] the source of his confusion was perhaps the fact that the Polemarch gave Miltiades a free hand in carrying out the plan that he had advocated. Mardonius' delay is not hard to explain in other terms: the Greeks could only have gained by delay—perhaps the Spartans would arrive—while it was in the Persians' interest to fight as soon as possible. What motivated the Greeks to attack when they did is not known. A report that "the horses are away" seems to have been the deciding factor, but scholars are not agreed as to whether this meant that the Persians had begun to reembark their horses to head for Athens, or that the horses were away being pastured.[6] Miltiades led the charge in an unusual running attack over the kilometer and a half that separated the two armies. As they fought, the Persians broke through the center of the Greek line, but the Greeks were victorious on the wings and were then able to turn back upon the Persians who had broken through the center. Routed and in confusion, the Persians rushed to the sea and their boats, where many were killed as they tried to reembark. Herodotus put the Greek losses at 192, the Persian at 6400.

S O U R C E   A N A L Y S I S

HERODOTUS 6.102–124.   Herodotus' description drew upon the memories of veterans of the battle, aging men who had come to play an almost legendary role in Athenian consciousness. He provided very few details of the battle, and the facts that he did choose to relate differ in many respects from those that a modern historian would choose. Nevertheless, these differences provide us with considerable insight into Greek culture and values. For example, what do the facts that Herodotus chose to relate about Miltiades reveal about the importance of participation in the Olympian and other Panhellenic games as a factor in Greek politics? What role did visions and dreams play in Herodotus' account? Finally, what cracks in Athenian unity intruded almost immediately into the picture of heroic action?

The Athenian victory at Marathon was a setback for the Persians, but not an overwhelming defeat. They immediately set off by sea for Athens while the Athenians raced at top speed by land to reach the city first. The Greeks arrived to see the Persian fleet approaching the city, but suddenly it turned and then withdrew. Possibly the Persians saw that the Athenian forces had arrived in time, possibly they had received word that the Spartans were on their way to offer assistance. Whatever the reason, they abandoned their attempt to conquer Greece and returned home. The Spartans did arrive; they were too late for the battle, but they visited the battle site and inspected the abandoned Persian equipment, congratulated the Athenians on a job well done, and returned home.

Today the burial mound of the Greeks who fell at Marathon remains as a monument to the Greek victory. It is some 45 meters in diameter and stands at the spot where most casualties occurred, over the cremated remains of the Athenian dead; many Persian arrowheads have been discovered in the soil of the mound (Figure 9-1).[7] Another mound, that of the Plataeans and the slaves, has been excavated nearby,[8] but the Persian burials have never been found. Another

FIGURE 9-1   Burial mound of the Greeks at Marathon.

contemporary memorial, a painting portraying three scenes of the battle, is described by Pausanias.[9] We, of course, recall the victory in our marathon race.[10]

THE SECOND PERSIAN WAR

When the Persians sailed back home again after their defeat at Marathon, the relief at Athens must have been immense. Nevertheless, some recognized that the respite might be only temporary. Miltiades was the hero of the hour. At the height of his popularity he proposed sending out a fleet to punish the Cycladic states that had gone over to the Persians, thus also securing the route of a possible Persian return attack (Hdt. 6.132–136). The fleet was sent out and had some successes before it turned to the island of Paros. Herodotus' sources were hostile to Miltiades, and the historian portrayed Miltiades' attack and siege of Paros as motivated by personal interests. Moreover, he reported that, during the siege, the commander committed an act of impiety that was responsible for the failure of the attack: a priestess, instigated by the god Apollo, tempted Miltiades into entering the precinct of Demeter Thesmophoros, a sacred area restricted to women. As he jumped over the precinct wall, the hero injured his leg. The wound caused him to withdraw his forces from the siege, and by the time he reached Athens he was near death from infection. He was tried and found guilty of "deceiving the People," a form of treason for which the penalty was death by being hurled into a pit; the Assembly, however, allowed him to pay only a fine, although a huge one of 50 talents. He died soon after of gangrene, and his son paid the fine.

The danger of one man gaining excessive power through too much success was exemplified by the fate of Miltiades. It is thus not surprising that the political instrument of ostracism was first used at this time. By this "negative popularity poll," which Aristotle explicitly included in his account of the reforms of Kleisthenes, any person receiving a majority in an ostracism vote of at least 6000 was required to go into exile for ten years. Ostracism was not a punishment, but a safety valve against excessive popularity. The ostracized man retained control of his property and its revenues and was permitted to maintain contact with his family from outside the borders of Attica. In the period after Marathon, three advocates of accommodation with Persia were ostracized—all leading members of the Peisistratid and Alkmeonid families. During this time another route to political preeminence was also closed with the change from direct election of the archons to a mixed process of election and allotment (the lot was used to select from 500 candidates elected by the deme assemblies). This safeguard was not effective for long, however, for it left open the way for holders of the generalship (the remaining high elective office) to amass political power.

Not all the Greek cities chose to oppose the Persians. Many of them capitulated (*medized*). Some, such as Thebes, did so because of their exposed geographical position; others, such as Argos, because of rivalry with other Greek cities. Moreover, most cities had some Persian sympathizers, who posed a threat of treachery from within, as had happened at Eretria.

The Greeks gained some respite from fears of a renewed Persian attack when the Persians became involved in a revolt in Egypt in 486 B.C. Darius died late in that year, and Xerxes, his son and successor, crushed the Egyptian revolt and imposed a harsh regime on the country, but made no move toward Greece. It was not until 483 B.C. that the signs again turned menacing for the Greeks: Xerxes began the work of digging a canal through the neck of the Athos peninsula, the site of the earlier, disastrous loss of Mardonius' fleet.

In the meantime, bickering with neighboring Aegina occupied the Athenians. At this point, a new figure came to the fore at Athens, Themistocles, a strong supporter of naval power who had already advocated fortification of the Piraeus. He now persuaded the Assembly to use a rich deposit of silver newly discovered at the mines at Laurion to finance the construction of a fleet, ostensibly for the war against Aegina, rather than, as was their custom, to distribute it to the people (Hdt. 7.144). They agreed, and turned to the building of the fleet that was to be the key to their victory over the Persians in the Second Persian War.

According to Herodotus, Xerxes did not inherit his father's zeal for war against the Greeks. This lack of enthusiasm on Xerxes' part gave the historian another opportunity to credit Fate with driving the Persians on in their misguided efforts to add the Greeks to their empire. The story, while it is enhanced by folktale elements, is important in providing an insight into Herodotus' conception of the moral universe in which great wars occurred.

S O U R C E   A N A L Y S I S

EROTODUS 7.5–19.   How does this account compare with Herodotus' earlier account of Darius's decision to send out the first expeditions against Greece? Note especially the role of Artabanos, who plays the part of a type-character frequently found in Herodotus, the Tragic Warner. How might recognition of such type-characters be used in the assessment of the historicity of Herodotus' account?

Herodotus recounted Xerxes' preparations for the expedition in great detail, stressing the magnitude of the undertaking. The bridging of the Hellespont in particular provided the historian with an opportunity to portray the hubris of the Persian king. A pair of bridges was constructed at Abydos utilizing the principles of both suspension and pontoon construction and making use of 674 warships. The first pair of bridges was destroyed by a storm, however, and the angry king, in a dramatic act of hubris, ordered the engineer to be executed and the waters of the Hellespont to be punished by lashing. The scale of the undertaking, from the digging of the canal at Athos and the bridging of the Hellespont to the marshalling and provisioning of the vast expeditionary force, was remarkable. While Herodotus' estimate of the total force at 5,283,220 seems to be an exaggeration, both Simonides' estimate of "300 myriad" (3 million) and Aeschylus's estimate ("the entire strength of Asia's sons") attest to the Greek belief in the huge size of the expedition and to the vast areas of empire from which it was drawn.[11]

The Battles of Thermopylae and Artemisium

The expedition of Xerxes, unlike those of Darius, was a combined action by both land and sea. The first land battle of the war, Thermopylae, was again one of the famous battles of history, although for quite different reasons than Marathon. As the Persian expedition made its way across northern Greece, "drinking rivers dry and consuming the entire food supply of small cities in a single meal" (Hdt. 7.118–120, 127), the Greeks of the mainland debated their chances for defense. There was a narrows at Tempe (in Thessaly) at which they might hope to stop the much larger force, but in the end it was determined to be less defensible than the narrow pass between the mountains and the sea at Thermopylae. Led by the Spartans under their general Leonides, the Greeks took up their stand here. For a time they succeeded in holding off the attacking Persians, but eventually a path over the mountain was betrayed to the enemy. With full recognition of the hopelessness of their position, the Spartans sent away the other Greeks and prepared to stand and fight to the last man. While the battle of Marathon had been a great, even legendary, victory for the Athenians, demonstrating the strength of free men fighting for their homeland, the battle of Thermopylae became part of the Spartan mystique. It exemplified the traditional virtues of the Spartan warrior: to come home with his shield or on it.

The heroic sacrificial stand of the Spartans at Thermopylae cannot, however, be considered in isolation from the nearly simultaneous victory that the Greeks won against the Persian fleet in the sea battle of Artemisium. The Persian fleet, which was following along in support of the land army, had its first engagement with the Greeks in the narrow straits just off the coast at Thermopylae. Herodotus attributed the Greek decision to meet them there to Themistocles: the historian's anti-Themistoclean sources reported that the Euboeans bribed him to delay the Persian advance by a sea battle so that they could evacuate their homes, and that Themistocles himself used bribery to achieve this end (and made money from it as well).

The Persian fleet at first avoided battle; it was late in the day and they feared that the Greeks, defeated, would slip away in the dark. To prevent this, they split their forces, sending 200 ships round Euboea to block any Greek attempt to retreat south. The first engagement, begun by the Greeks, was inconclusive. Then in the night a great storm arose; as Herodotus says, the god was protecting the Greeks, for the main body of the Persian fleet suffered great losses, and the 200 ships sent round Euboea were also lost. On the next day, emboldened by the arrival of reinforcements from Athens and by word of the Persian losses, the Greeks attacked and destroyed a small contingent of Persian ships. This so annoyed the Persians that they decided to launch a full-scale battle.

The ensuing encounter was nearly a draw: the Persian fleet, despite its losses, was still larger than the Greek fleet, but its very size caused it to fall into confusion in the narrow passage, and many ships and men were lost. Herodotus noted that this battle occurred on the same day as the battle of Thermopylae, the former at a sea pass, the latter at a land pass. Despite Herodotus' story of the role played by Themistoclean bribery in the Greek decision to fight at Artemisium, the coincidence must have been deliberate. Not only was it strategically sound to coordinate the land and sea forces, but Herodotus reports that the Greeks had made plans for each arm of their forces to notify the other of the results of each engagement.

The Persians' victory at Thermopylae opened the way for their unimpeded march south. Athens was the first city in the Persians' path, and the immediate issue for the Athenians became the fate of their city. Led by Themistocles' interpretation of the Oracle of Delphi's response—that they would find safety behind wooden walls—the Athenians, with a few exceptions (according to Herodotus, the treasurers of Athena's temple on the Acropolis and a few of the poor), decided to commit themselves to the sea, evacuating the city and taking to the wooden walls of their ships.

S O U R C E   A N A L Y S I S

I n addition to the account of Herodotus (8.40–41, 51), an inscription found at Troezen and published in 1960 may be a fourth-century B.C. copy of the decree of evacuation, although its authenticity is in dispute.[12] It is interesting to compare these two sources, which differ in some significant details. Some points of difference to consider are the identification of those left behind in the Acropolis and dating of the evacuation. If genuine, the inscription gives important details about the marshalling of forces in the rapid expansion of the Athenian fleet.

Note on epigraphic conventions: In the inscription, square brackets enclose conjectured restorations, or numbers indicating the number of missing letters when no restoration can be made. A single line | indicates the end of a line; a double line | | indicates the beginning of each fifth line in the inscription.

[Gods] Resolved by the Boule and the People, | Themis[tokl]es son of Neokles of
5   Phrearrhioi made the motion. | The *city* shall be *entrusted* to Athena, Athen | |s' [Protectress, and to the] *other* gods, all of them, for protectio | n *and* [defense against the] *Barbarian* on behalf of the country. The Athenian |s [in their entirety and the aliens] who live in Athens | shall place [their children and their women] *in* Troezen | [-21-]
10   the Founder of the land. [T | |he elderly and (movable)] property shall (for safety) be deposited at Salamis. | [The Treasurers and] the Priestesses are [to remain] on the Akropoli |s [and guard the possessions of the] gods. The rest of the Athe | [nians in their entirety and those] *aliens* who have reached young manhood shall em | bark [on
15   the readied] two hundred ships and they *shall* repu | |lse *the* [Barbarian for the sake of] liberty, both their | own [and that of the other Hellenes,] in common with the Lacedaemonians, Co | rin[thians, Aeginetans] and the others who wis |h *to have a share* [in the danger.] Appointment will also be made of *trie | rarchs* [two hundred in num-
20   ber, one for] each ship, by the g | |enerals, [beginning] tomorrow, from among those who are *own | ers* [of both land and home] in Athens and who have children | who are *legitimate*. [They shall not be more] than fifty years old *and t | he lot shall determine each man's ship*. (The generals) shall also enlist mar | ines, *ten* [for each] ship, from men
25   over twenty years o | |f age [up to] *thirty*, and archers, fou |r (in number). [They shall also by lot appoint] the specialist officers for each ship wh | en they appoint [the] *trierarchs* by lot. A list shall be mad | e *also* [of the rest, ship by] ship, by the generals, on
30   n | otice *boards*, [with the] Athenians (to be selected) from the lexiarchic re | |gisters, [the] *aliens* from the list of names (registered) *wi | th* the *Polemarch*. They shall write them up, assigning them by div | isions, up to two hundred (divisions, each) [of up to] one hundred (men), and they shall appen | d *to each division* the name of the trireme
35   and the tri | erarch and the specialist officers, so that they may know on w | |hat

continued

trireme each division shall embark. When assign | ment of all the divisions has been made and they have been allotted to the tri | remes, all the two hundred shall be manned by (order of) the Boule | and the generals, after they have *sacrificed* to ap-
40 pease Zeus the | All-powerful and Athena and Nike and Posei | | don the Securer. *vv* When they have completed the manning of | the ships, with one hundred of them they shall bring assistance to the Artemis | ium in Euboea, while with the other hundred they shall, all round Salam | is and the rest of Attica, lie at anchor and guard | the
45 country. To ensure that in a spirit of concord all Athenians | | will ward off the Barbarian, those banished for the [t | en-]year span shall leave for Salamis and they are to remain [ther | e until the People] decide about them. Those [-6-] | [. . .]

The Peloponnesians opposed making a stand in defense of Athens, favoring instead a retreat to the narrow isthmus to the Peloponnesus, from which they thought they would adequately protect their own cities. To them, the Persian army was the most obvious threat, far more obvious than their fleet. Yet, as the Athenians argued, continued Persian control of the sea would make a military victory at the isthmus meaningless: Persian ships could carry their infantry beyond any blockade of the isthmus to a landing anywhere along the coast of the Peloponnesus. In the end, Themistocles won out by threatening that, should the Greeks decide to retreat to the isthmus, the Athenians would withdraw their forces, put their families on board their ships, and move their city to Siris in Italy.

Battle of Salamis

As a result of Themistocles' persuasion and threat, the Greeks decided to meet the Persian fleet in the narrow bay of Salamis, off the coast of the Piraeus. Again a ruse of Themistocles' played a central role in events: he sent a pretended informer to tell the Persians that the Greeks intended to slip away by night. Believing the "informer," the Persians manned their ships and sailed around all night, while the Greeks slept. In the morning the refreshed Greeks met the weary Persians in battle. They drew them into the narrows by pretending to escape north, and, as at Artemisium, the Persians found themselves unable to keep their formation in the restricted space. In their confusion many fell victim to the more skilled Greek crews.

Eight years after the battle, the tragic poet Aeschylus presented an eyewitness account of the events in his play *The Persians*. In the following scene, a messenger describes the disaster to the Persian queen, Atossa.[13]

S O U R C E   A N A L Y S I S

ompare Aeschylus' account with that of Herodotus (8.56–103).[14] What has Aeschylus omitted, and how trustworthy is a drama? The passage about Artemisia provides evidence about the historian's treatment of women; what may have been his motivation in focusing on her actions?

> . . . Some fury, some malignant Power,
> Appeared, and set in train the whole disastrous rout.
> A Hellene from the Athenian army came and told
> Your son Xerxes this tale: that, once the shades of night
> Set in, the Hellenes would not stay, but leap on board,
> And, by whatever secret route offered escape,
> Row for their lives. When Xerxes heard this, with no thought
> Of the man's guile, or of the jealousy of the gods,
> He sent this word to all his captains: "When the sun
> No longer flames to warm the earth, and darkness holds
> The court of heaven, range the main body of our fleet
> Threefold, to guard the outlets and the choppy straits."
> Then he sent other ships to row right round the isle,
> Threatening that if the Hellene ships found a way through
> To save themselves from death, he would cut off the head
> Of every Persian captain. By these words he showed
> How ignorance of the gods' intent had dazed his mind.
>   Our crews, then, in good order and obediently,
> Were getting supper; then each oarsman looped his oar
> To the smooth rowing-pin; and when the sun went down
> And night came on, the rowers all embarked, and all
> The heavy-armed soldiers; and from line to line they called,
> Cheering each other on, rowing and keeping course
> As they were ordered. All night long the captains kept
> Their whole force cruising to and fro across the strait.
> Now night was fading; still the Hellenes showed no sign
> Of trying to sail out unnoticed; till at last
> Over the earth shone the white horses of the day,
> Filling the air with beauty. Then from the Hellene ships
> Rose like a song of joy the piercing battle-cry,
> And from the island crags echoed an answering shout.
>   The Persians knew their error; fear gripped every man,
> They were no fugitives who sang that terrifying
> Paean, but Hellenes charging with courageous heart

to battle. The loud trumpet flamed along their ranks.
At once their frothy oars moved with a single pulse,
Beating the salt waves to the bo'suns' chant; and soon
Their whole fleet hove clear into view; their right wing first,
In precise order, next their whole array came on,
And at that instant a great shout beat on our ears;
"Forward, you sons of Hellas! Set your country free!
And temples of your gods. All is at stake: now fight!"
Then from our side in answer rose the manifold
Clamour of Persian voices; and the hour had come.
    At once ship into ship battered its brazen beak.
A Hellene ship charged first, and chopped off the whole stern
Of a Phoenician galley. Then charge followed charge
On every side. At first by its huge impetus
Our fleet withstood them. But soon, in that narrow space,
Our ships were jammed in hundreds; none could help another.
They rammed each other with their prows of bronze; and some
Were stripped of every oar. Meanwhile the enemy
Came round us in a ring and charged. Our vessels heeled
Over; the sea was hidden, carpeted with wrecks
And dead men; all the shores and reefs were full of dead.
    Then every ship we had broke rank and rowed for life.
The Hellenes seized fragments of wrecks and broken oars
And hacked and stabbed at our men swimming in the sea
As fishermen kill tunnies or some netted haul.
The whole sea was one din of shrieks and dying groans,
Till night and darkness hid the scene.

The Battle of Plataea

The Greek victory at Salamis turned the tide of the war in their favor. Faced with the defeat of his fleet (and again tricked by Themistocles), Xerxes decided to make good his own escape before the Greeks destroyed the bridge at the Hellespont, leaving behind a part of the army under Mardonius to continue the war. After wintering in Thessaly, Mardonius resumed the offensive, marching first to Athens, which he sacked again. The Peloponnesians were for the moment secure behind their defenses at the isthmus, although vulnerable to attack should the Persian fleet return from Samos, where it lay idle, but the Athenians remained in refugee camps on Salamis and on their ships. There could be no peace or return to normal life as long as Mardonius remained. In Athens, voices of accommodation began to be raised, and at least two of those elected to the generalship in 479 B.C. were possible advocates of reconciliation. Soon Mardonius made his offer to Athens through King Alexander of Macedonia: amnesty, local autonomy, recovery of territory, and Persian aid in rebuilding the temples destroyed in the war. It was a tempting offer. The Athenians asked time to consider, and it was perhaps they who circulated a prophecy to the effect that the Dorians would one day be driven from the Peloponnesus by the Athenians and the Persians (Hdt. 8.141). In consternation the Spartans sent representatives to Athens while Alexander was still present, and both sides put their arguments to the Athenians. In the end Herodotus portrays the Athenians as patriotically declaring their intention to resist and calling upon the Spartans to march north to meet the inevitable Persian attack (modern opinion suggests that the Athenians would not in fact have been so quick to give up the last card they held and opt for making a possibly suicidal stand).[15]

When the Athenians rejected his terms, Mardonius marched south, reaching Attica and reoccupying the city. He repeated his offer, but the Athenians were in no mood to accept it: when a citizen proposed that it be put to the vote, he was lynched, together with his wife and children. The Athenians, however, sent an urgent message to the Spartans, telling them that they would be compelled to accept the offer unless the Spartans came to their assistance at once. The Spartans, who were once again celebrating a festival and felt secure behind the defenses at the isthmus, delayed their reply for two weeks. Finally they secretly sent a force of 5000 hoplites with 35,000 helots in attendance under the command of Pausanias by a roundabout route north, telling the Athenians only after the fact. The ruse was intended to prevent their local enemies, the Argives, from sending word to Mardonius, in whose pay they were. The effort was not successful, however, for an Argive messenger succeeded in getting word to Mardonius. The Persian general once more sacked Athens and then headed north to Boeotia, where Thebes was friendly and the terrain would favor the Persian cavalry. He took up a position and constructed a fortification near the Asopus River, which formed the boundary between Plataean and Theban territory. In this way he would fight with Thebes behind him. His strategy was to do as little as possible, waiting for dissension to develop among the Greek forces and trying to lure them into battle on terrain unfavorable to their hoplite forces.

Meanwhile the Athenians sent a force of 8000 to join the Spartans under Pausanias, and other Greek cities sent contingents as well. The Greek forces took up a position across the river from Mardonius, in the foothills of Mount Kitheron, in territory that gave maximum scope to their hoplite strength. As the Persian cavalry harassed them, new contingents of men and supplies continued to flow to the Greeks. Finally Mardonius occupied the pass over Kitheron, cutting off further reinforcements and supplies, and, for good measure, choked the

FIGURE 9-2 Serpent column with list of Greek states that fought against the Persians, in Istanbul (Constantinople).

spring that the Greeks depended on for water. They decided to withdraw to a better position that would provide access to water and relief from the cavalry attacks, but the planned nighttime withdrawal somehow went amiss and was delayed until daybreak. With daylight Mardonius could see that the Greeks had deserted their position, and he decided to attack. He caught the Spartans and Tegeans as they marched and compelled them to give battle. Both sides fought furiously, but the Persians, without the heavy armor or the long spears of the Greeks, proved no match for the hoplite forces. When Mardonius himself fell, the battle was decided. The surviving Persians rushed back to their fortified camp, pursued by the Greeks, who stormed the camp, seizing a vast treasure of gold and silver furnishings, inlaid couches, concubines, horses and camels, and hoards of coined money.

A tithe of the plunder from Plataea was dedicated to Apollo at Delphi; from it a golden tripod was made, supported by a bronze pillar in the form of intertwined serpents. The tripod was melted down in one of the Sacred Wars of the fourth century B.C., but the serpent column survived, although headless, to be transported by the Roman Emperor Constantine to his newly refounded capital of Constantinople (Figure 9-2). It can still be seen in the Hippodrome in Istanbul, and on it can be read the inscribed names of the thirty-one states that fought against the Persians at Salamis or Plataea.[16]

Victory at Mykale

As in the case of the battle of Salamis, Greek tradition assigned another great victory to the same day as the battle of Plataea: the victory of their fleet at Mykale off the coast of Ionia. The Persian fleet lay at Samos, the Greek fleet at Delos, when the Samians begged the Greeks for help against the Persians. The Greeks responded, sailing to the island. As they approached, the Persian fleet withdrew to the shelter of Cape Mykale, where their army was stationed. The Greeks landed, attacking and burning the camp. Their victory was decided by the desertion of the Ionians who had been serving the Persians, and by this victory the Ionian Greeks gained their freedom. In his account of this battle, Herodotus (9.104) rounds out his story by returning to its beginning: "for the second time Ionia revolted from the Persians," but this time with success.

The expansionist ambitions of the Persians may have extended even beyond the mainland of Greece. When the Athenians realized that they faced an invasion, they sent a delegation to the powerful tyrant of Syracuse, Gelon, whose fleet was second only to their own. According to Herodotus (7.157–163), Gelon agreed to send forces on the condition that he be made commander of the Greek forces, an offer sharply rejected by the Athenian ambassadors. In fact, however, the Greeks of Sicily soon found themselves faced with an invasion by the Carthaginians, whom they defeated in the battle of Himera, assigned by tradition to the same day as the battle of Salamis (Hdt. 7.166). While Herodotus treats this as sheer coincidence, another source, the fourth-century B.C. historian Ephorus, believed the Carthaginian attack had been carried out in cooperation with the Persians. Ephorus' interpretation has some credibility, since Carthage was a Phoenician colony, and the Phoenicians were Persian subjects.[17]

After the Greek victory at Plataea, the remaining Persian forces under the Persian general Artabazus headed for the Hellespont, and Greece was soon free of the invaders. After the battles of Salamis and Plataea turned the tide, the Persians were never again to return as invaders of mainland Greece. Nevertheless, their presence as a wealthy superpower in the eastern Mediterranean would continue to affect the actions and policies of the Greek cities until Alexander the Great defeated another Darius and took on the mantle of Great King himself.

IMPORTANT PLACES IN CHAPTER 9

On Chapter Map: Abdera, Abydos, Aegina, Artemisium, Asopus River, Athens, Cape Mykale, Delos, Delphi, Ephesus, Eretria, Hellespont, Icaria, Karystos, Lade, Macedonia, Marathon, Miletus, Mount Athos, Mount Kitheron, Naxos, Paros, Phocaea, Piraeus, Plataea, Salamis, Sardis, Sestos, Sparta, Susa, Tempe Pass, Teos, Thasos, Thebes, Thermopylae, Thessaly, Thrace, Troezen

On Other Maps *(use map index to find these):* Constantinople (later name for Byzantium, now called Istanbul), Cyprus, Himera (Italy), Siris (Italy), Susa (Persia)

SUGGESTIONS FOR FURTHER READING

Basic works on the Persian Wars include G. B. Grundy, *The Great Persian War* (1901), A. R. Burn, *Persia and the Greeks* (1962), and Peter Green, *The Year of Salamis, 480–478* (1970). Useful material can also be found in the *Cambridge Ancient History*, Vol. 4. Gore Vidal's *Creation* tells the story of the Greeks and Persians from the Persian point of view in an entertaining historical fiction.

ENDNOTES

1. See G. B. Grundy, *The Great Persian War* (1901); A. R. Burn, *Persia and the Greeks* (1962), and Peter Green, *The Year of Salamis, 480–478* (1970).
2. S. Hornblower, *The Greek World, 479–323 B.C.* (1983), 9–14.
3. Green (above, n. 1), 14–15.
4. Green (above, n. 1), 10.
5. Arist., *Constitution of Athens*, 22.
6. Ancient evidence: Suidas, *"Khoris Hippeis."* Pasturing: N. G. L. Hammond, *Cambridge Ancient History* IV, 511; embarking: W. W. How and J. Wells, *A Commentary on Herodotus* I, 362; Green (above, n. 1), 34–35.
7. Pausanias 1.29.4.
8. At Vrana, reported by S. Marinatos in *Athens Annals of Archaeology* 3 (1970), 357ff.
9. Pausanias 1.15.3.
10. But see the skeptical account by Frank Frost, "The Dubious Origins of the 'Marathon,' " with comments on the Pheidippides-Philippides issue by the journal's editor, Ernst Badian, in *American Journal of Ancient History* 4 (1979), 159–165.
11. Simonides, quoted by Hdt. 7.228; Aesch., *Persians* 12.

12. Charles W. Fornara, *Archaic Times to the End of the Peloponnesian War* (1983), 53, with bibliography; discussion by Hammond (see n. 6), 558–563.

13. Aesch., *Persians*, 353–392, tr. Philip Vellacott, in *Aeschylus, Prometheus and Other Plays* (1961).

14. Grundy (above, n. 1), 369–373, compares the accounts of Aeschylus and Herodotus.

15. J. P. Barron, in *Cambridge Ancient History* IV, 596.

16. See *Cambridge Ancient History* IV, 618, Fig. 51.

17. The information from Ephorus is found in the universal history of Diodorus Siculus 11.1.4. The war in the West is discussed by T. J. Dunbabin, *The Western Greeks* (1948), chap. 14.

CHAPTER TEN

Athens: The Development of Empire and Democracy

I n the half-century following the Persian Wars, Athens turned its naval strength into imperialistic naval power and the isonomia of the Kleisthenic reforms into democracy. These changes were interconnected and grew out of the situation at the end of the war. At that time the league of Greek states that had fought against Persia chose the Athenians to lead a campaign to take vengeance against the Persians for their invasion of Greece. Gradually Athens transformed its leadership in this league into imperial control, while in Athens itself the commitment to sea power that league leadership involved led to the extension of significant political rights to the lowest class, the *thetes,* who supplied most of the rowers for the fleet, and thus to the development of Athenian democracy. Despite the importance of these years, no full-scale treatment of them by a Greek historian survives. Our main source is an abbreviated account by the historian Thucydides, the *Pentecontaetia,* or "Fifty-Years," which forms part of the preliminaries to his history of the Peloponnesian War.

Thucydides, who was born ca. 460 B.C., was about twenty-five years younger than Herodotus. He was a member of an aristocratic Athenian family that possessed a considerable fortune, including interests in the gold mines of Thrace. In 424 B.C., when the Athenians were at war with Sparta during the Peloponnesian War, he was elected general and stationed in the Chalkidike; when he failed to arrive in time to prevent the surrender of the Athenian colony of Amphipolis to the Spartans, he was sentenced to exile (Thuc. 4.103–106; 5.26). He spent the next twenty years in exile until he was recalled during the final siege of Athens, probably spending much of that time on his family holdings in Thrace. His exile gave him the opportunity to consult with both sides in the war, but, of course, he was denied firsthand knowledge of events in Athens during this time.

Thucydides was a scant generation younger than Herodotus, yet in many ways he seems to have belonged to a wholly different age. Although Herodotus was also well versed in the intellectual issues of his day, Thucydides reflects the full flowering of contemporary rhetoric, philosophy, and medicine in the late fifth century B.C. He is said to have studied with the orator Antiphon and to have been an associate of the philosopher Anaxagoras, and he spent his exile in the same area in which Hippocratic doctors were practicing at that time. While Herodotus had described an earlier war that had ended in Greek victory and was perceived as a glorious episode in Athens' past, Thucydides' topic was a contemporary war that Athens was to lose and that he saw as corrupting the most fundamental values of the Athenian state. In keeping with the gravity of the situation, Thucydides' aim was entirely serious. It was not his intention to entertain his audience by recounting intriguing tales or to create an encomium for Athens, as Herodotus had done. Rather, he was intent on making an accurate determination of events and investigating the psychological factors that drove men and states to pursue power. He knew that men, including the Athenians, were not always noble and did not always reveal their true motives. In fact, it was his portrayal of the corrosive effects of power on those who wield it that was perhaps his greatest achievement. He himself said that he had written his work "not to win the applause of the moment but to be a possession for all time" (Thuc. 1.22).

Other contemporary sources for this period include Aeschylus' tragic trilogy, the *Oresteia*, which employed a story set in the post–Trojan War period in an effort to reconcile violent opposition to a present-day reform; an account of Athenian political development by an unknown writer known as *Pseudo-Aristotle*; and the ***Athenian Tribute Lists (ATL)***, fragments of the records of the annual payments made by the Athenians to the temple of the goddess Athena, which were inscribed on stone. These payments were gleaned from the tribute paid to Athens by member states in the league (of which Athena received one-sixtieth); therefore the ATL records can be used to reconstruct the tribute payments in the various years for which they are preserved. As interpreted by specialists in epigraphy, they provide valuable information about the ups and downs of Athenian control.[1] Finally, the work of Plutarch is a frequently used later source. It is easily accessible and entertaining, but not entirely reliable. Plutarch was a Greek who lived in the time of the Roman Empire (ca. A.D. 46–120). He wrote biographies, not history, and he wrote for a Roman audience with the aim of improving his readers morally while entertaining them. His choice of genre and audience naturally shaped his treatment of the material. He included much that Thucydides, if he knew of it, must have considered unsuitable for serious history, but he does at times preserve sound information that does not appear elsewhere. Before using any information from Plutarch, the historian must consider Plutarch's possible source and his purpose in using it, and weigh its historical value accordingly.[2]

ATHENIAN RECOVERY

At the end of the war, Athens, twice sacked by the Persians, lay in ruins. An immediate need was to provide shelter for the inhabitants, but to the Athenians the rebuilding of the walls seemed to be even more vital to the defense of the polis. The Spartans, disturbed by the Athenians' display of initiative and vigor in the war, opposed the reconstruction of the walls, suggesting instead that all the cities of Greece tear down their walls (Sparta itself had no walls). Not willing to follow this advice, but also unwilling to escalate the matter into a direct confrontation, the Athenians, under the leadership of Themistocles, resorted to clever scheming to achieve their purpose.

SOURCE ANALYSIS

The story of this scheme, and of Themistocles' continuing role in turning Athens into a sea power, is told by Thucydides (1.89–93). The passage provides a good introduction to the historian's work. In it he comes close to the style of Herodotus in telling an interesting story in order to make a point: how the Athenians attained the position that in time enabled them to develop their empire. Some scholars discount the story because it fits so well into the pattern of stories illustrating Themistoclean trickery,[3] but that in itself is not cause for rejecting the evidence that Sparta and its allies were ambivalent toward the matter and that neither side was willing to risk a direct confrontation.

FROM DELIAN LEAGUE TO ATHENIAN EMPIRE

After their final victory, the Greek states of the Hellenic League that had fought against the Persians did not immediately disband, but determined to maintain their forces in the Aegean. Sparta continued as leader of the coalition, but difficulties soon arose. The Spartan leader Pausanias began to affect Persian ways and became increasingly distant and arrogant.[4] The other Greeks found his behavior intolerable and appealed to the Athenians to take over the League's leadership. When Athens accepted, a new league was constituted, which is called the *Delian League* by modern historians because the site of its headquarters was on the island of Delos. Each state agreed to furnish ships and men or a monetary contribution; all were to be autonomous and to have equal votes in the meetings of the League, which were to be held in Delos. Athens, as by far the strongest sea power, was to be *hegemon*, with supreme command in military operations and executive authority in the other dealings of the League. The Athenian Aristides (known as "The Just") determined the initial payments of each state, and the Athenians were to serve as treasurers of the funds, which were to be kept on Delos. The League eventually included most of the poleis on the Aegean islands and along its northern and eastern coasts, as well as those on the shores of the Hellespont, the Propontus, and the Black Sea and along the southern coast of Anatolia. Sparta and its Peloponnesian allies did not join, and the old Hellenic League continued to exist until 462 B.C., when Athens and Sparta openly broke off relations, but the Delian League at its inception was in no sense anti-Spartan.

The original purpose of the Delian League was, according to Thucydides (1.96), to join together in ravaging the Persian king's lands to avenge the sufferings that the Persians had inflicted on the Greeks. Another purpose probably also was to free those Greeks still living under Persian domination, but this is not stated in our sources. Still another motivation not mentioned by Thucydides may seem obvious to the modern reader: fear of another Persian invasion. In fact, it was not until 468 B.C., when Cimon won a victory over the Persian fleet at the battle of the Eurymedon (see below), that Greece could feel altogether relieved of the threat that the Persians might return. However, Thucydides' perception of Greek self-confidence at the time may be accurate: he portrays the Greeks as setting out to *punish* the Persians, rather than to protect themselves.

Even before the first joint action of the League, in 487 B.C., the first of a series of moves was taken in Athens that would lead to the development of full democracy. The first step was the introduction of the lot in the selection of archons. Although this lottery was still limited to a group of 500 men chosen by election, who were all members of the two highest property classes, the office lost much of its prestige as a result of this change.[5]

It was probably at about the same time that a politician named Pericles introduced pay for jury duty.[6] Since Athenian juries were large (their numbers could range from 200 to over 1000), and the jury-roll included 6000 men, this was a move that appealed to large numbers of people. It meant that many men could now engage in civic activity without fearing financial loss. In fact, for the poor and the elderly, jury service became an important source of income. It also gave the demos more political weight. The various courts not only tried civil and criminal cases, which were often politically motivated, but also presided over the audit that every Athenian official had to undergo at the end of his term of office and in which the entire conduct of his office was examined. Moreover, as the empire developed, the Athenian courts were given jurisdiction over the more serious cases of the allies, who were required to go to Athens for trials. Thus participation on juries brought a substantial increase in the political influence of the poorer class.[7]

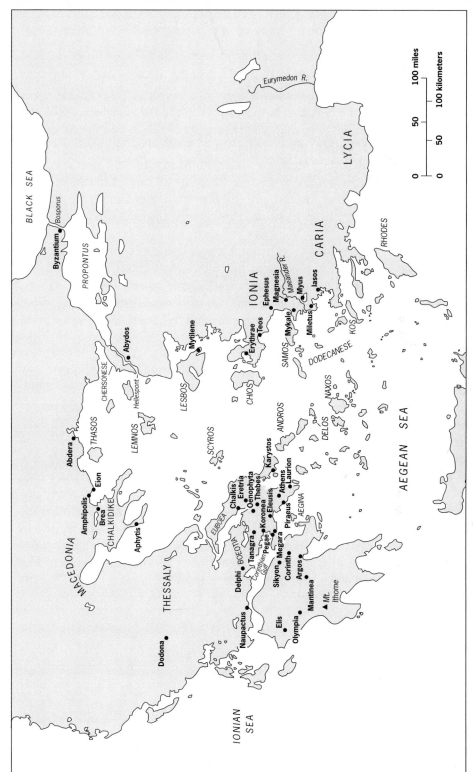

MAP 10   Greece before the Peloponnesian War and the Athenian Empire.

Early Military Actions of the League

The League's first military action occurred in 476 B.C. when it seized control of Eion, a fortress on the north Aegean coast at the mouth of the Strymon River that was still held by the Persians. In the same year, the League's forces took the island of Skyros, a pirates' lair: they sold the pirates as slaves, and the Athenians occupied the island. Both of these actions were important in securing Greek control of the Aegean and its northern coast. A third action in the next few years was an expedition against Karystos, a Greek city in southern Euboea that had medized after the battle of Artemisium; the Karystians were compelled to join the League. All these actions were in keeping with the professed aim of the League.

Not every League member was happy with the required contributions to the League, however. In 470 B.C. the Naxians decided to withdraw from the League. The Athenians, probably with the approval of the other League members, viewed the secession as a violation of the oath of permanent alliance to which they had all sworn, and the "revolt" was promptly crushed. Naxos was denied autonomy (a guarantee of the original League) and henceforward was to be subject to Athens.

One of the signal achievements of the League occurred in the next year, when the Greeks won a decisive victory over the Persian fleet at the battle of the Eurymedon River on the southern coast of Asia Minor. Two hundred Phoenician ships, serving as the Persian navy, were destroyed in the victory. This secured the Greek cities of Caria and Lycia for the League and effectively removed the threat that the Persians might attempt another invasion of Greece.

In 465 B.C. the island of Thasos, which was one of the most powerful members of the League, became disturbed by Athenian activities on the mainland opposite the island, the site of lucrative gold mines; they saw these activities as infringements on their rightful sphere of influence. Unsatisfied with the Athenian response to their concerns, they revolted. The Thasian fleet was quickly defeated, but a blockade of two years was required to put down the revolt. The city's walls were torn down, and its fleet given to the Athenians. The Thasians relinquished all claims to the gold mines on the mainland, and the city became a tributary subject of Athens.

In all of these early League actions the League forces were led by Cimon, an Athenian aristocrat who played an important role in the direction of Athenian policy in the postwar period. He pursued a course of action that was both aggressively anti-Persian and pro-Spartan (even to naming one of his sons "Lakedaimonios"). In seeking good relations with Sparta, Cimon may have simply been avoiding the risk of military action on two fronts. Nonetheless, pro-Spartanism was a perennially popular attitude among Athenian aristocrats, often rooted in a hereditary relationship of guest-friendship between aristocratic families in the two cities. Even in the later fifth century B.C., when Athens was at war with Sparta, the comic poet Aristophanes portrays the aristocratic son in *The Wasps* as dressing his father in Spartan shoes for an elite dinner party, reflecting the tendency of young Athenians of wealth to affect Spartan dress and hairstyles. In the fourth century B.C., another Athenian aristocrat and general, Xenophon, had his sons educated in Sparta and took up residence there himself while he was in exile, and the philosopher Plato created his utopian state after the Spartan model. To such men, conservatives at heart, Spartan self-discipline and military prowess compared favorably with what they viewed as the undisciplined and licentious behavior of the Athenian demos.

In 464 B.C. Sparta suffered a severe earthquake. According to later sources, 20,000 died, including all the **ephebes** (men between the ages of eighteen and twenty), and all but five houses were destroyed.[8] The Messenian helots seized the opportunity to revolt, and Sparta was once again faced with a Messenian war. Help was sent by Aegina and Mantinea in Boeotia. By 462 B.C. the Messenian rebels had been confined to Mount Ithome, and the Spartans sought the help of the Athenians, who were reputed to be expert in siege warfare.[9] Encouraged to act by the pro-Spartan Cimon, the Athenians sent 4000 hoplites to Sparta under his command.[10] But the Spartans suffered a change of heart when their traditional rivals, whom they viewed as both too enterprising and dangerously revolutionary, appeared in their own territory, and they sent them back home.

Reform of the Areopagus Council

The Athenian demos, angered by the ignominious end of an expedition that had been advocated by Cimon, ostracized him. With the conservative Cimon out of the way, his rivals were free to carry out reforms that increased the political power of their own base of support, the demos. In fact, in 462 B.C., even before Cimon's ostracism and while he was absent from the city on the expedition to Lakonia, Ephialtes had carried through the first in this series of revolutionary changes, stripping the ancient and conservative Council of the Areopagus of most of its powers. (See Source Analysis on p. 208.)

The Areopagus Council retained only its ancient religious functions, of which the most important was its role in trying murder cases. In 458 B.C., four years after the reform, the poet Aeschylus presented a tragic trilogy, the *Oresteia*, which apparently sought to conciliate the opposition by celebrating the importance of the powers still remaining with the Areopagus Council. It dramatized the civilizing and beneficial role of the Council as a formal homicide court, one which replaced the unending chain of violence entailed by the primitive system of blood vengeance with a system of justice.

Despite Aeschylus' appeal for the acceptance of the reforms, Ephialtes was assassinated shortly after his reform was instituted. His role as the foremost spokesman of the demos was taken over by a new advocate, Pericles (he had ear-

S O U R C E   A N A L Y S I S

The stages by which Athenian democracy developed are known to us primarily through a work called the *Athenian Constitution*, which has been attributed to Aristotle; some scholars accept it as a genuine work of the philosopher, but it seems most probable that it was the work of one of his pupils, who were assigned the task of collecting accounts of the constitutions of the various cities.[11] This unknown pupil is usually referred to as *Pseudo-Aristotle* (Ps.-Aristotle).

The philosopher Aristotle's approach to the past was to see it as a continuous progression toward the present, and to view the institutions and ideas of his predecessors as early steps toward this goal. Ps.-Aristotle followed the same approach, portraying the early history of the Athenian democracy in terms of the ideological debates of his own day. Thus he saw the early fifth-century B.C. political scene in Athens in terms of a rivalry between an aristocratic faction (headed by Cimon) and a democratic faction (led by Ephialtes and Pericles). Although we find this schematization to be too neat, and we cannot accept its ideological aspects as historical (the concept of democracy was not yet formulated when Ephialtes and Pericles opposed Cimon), the evolution in the Athenian Constitution that Ps.-Aristotle recorded did take place, and he provides our only continuous account of it. Therefore we must follow him, bearing in mind that we cannot trust his account of the ideological motives that lay behind these changes.

PS.-ARISTOTLE, *CONSTITUTION OF ATHENS* (ON THE REFORM OF THE AREOPAGUS COUNCIL)[12]:

> For seventeen years following the Persian Wars, the political order remained essentially the same under the supervision of the Areopagus, although it was slowly degenerating. But as the common people grew in strength, Ephialtes, the son of Sophonides, who had a reputation for incorruptibility and loyalty to the constitution, became leader of the people and made an attack upon that Council [the Areopagus]. First he eliminated many of its members by bringing suits against them on the ground of administrative misconduct. Then, in the archonship of Conon, he deprived the Council of all its added [recently acquired?] powers [prerogatives?] through which it was the guardian of the state, and gave them [back?], some to the Council of Five Hundred and some to the people [Assembly], and some to the law courts.

lier been the one to introduce jury pay, see above). Pericles was well suited by birth and ability to play an important role in affairs of state. He was a member of a powerful and influential aristocratic family and an Alkmeonid through his mother's line. His father had been a general at the battle of Mykale and was prominent politically. He himself was an intellectual and included among his close associates the philosopher Anaxagoras, the sculptor Phidias, and the Milesian hetaira (concubine) Aspasia. She became his mistress and was said to have made considerable contributions to his policies.[13]

Athenian Ambitions Grow

Following the Spartan rejection of the relief force led by Cimon, the Athenians became openly hostile to Sparta. They formally dropped out of the old Hellenic League, and allied themselves with Sparta's enemy, Argos. In 461/60 B.C. Athens assisted Megara in a revolt against the Lakedaimonian League arising out of a border dispute between that city and Corinth. By this assistance, Athens gained the alliance of both Megara and Pegae, a port on the Corinthian Gulf, as well as the lasting enmity of Corinth. In order to protect Megara, the Athenians built the "Long Walls" safeguarding the vital access to the sea and connecting that city to its harbor at Nisaea, fortifications which they themselves garrisoned. Megara, strengthened by its long walls, served to block a possible Spartan invasion of Attica. Moreover, the alliance with Pegae both threatened Corinth and gave Athens easier access to Naupactus, which the Athenians had recently seized from the Ozolian Locrians for use as a base to control the gulf. After the Messenian rebels capitulated under terms that allowed them to leave the Peloponnesus, the Athenians settled them at Naupactus.

From 460 to 445 B.C., with the exception of one five-year truce, the Athenians fought against Sparta and its allies, the Peloponnesian League, in what is often called the *First Peloponnesian War*. Early in the war they built the "Long Walls" connecting Athens to its harbor at the Piraeus and protecting the vital access to the sea (perhaps completed in 457). In the midst of this war, Athens also undertook a major overseas involvement in Egypt from 459 to 454 B.C., assisting the Egyptians in their revolt against their Persian rulers. Athens contributed a large fleet of 200 ships that had been on an expedition to Cyprus, where Greeks still lived under Persian control.

In 457 B.C., the Spartans marched north to help Thebes revive its position of leadership in the Boeotian League, hoping to establish that city as a check on Athenian expansion northward. On their return home they were met by the Athenians at Tanagra, in Boeotian territory. In the ensuing battle, the Spartans defeated the Athenians, but heavy losses led the Spartans to withdraw. Shortly after this, the Athenians gained control over Boeotia by a victory at the battle of Oenophyta. They held power in Boeotia for ten years, until their defeat in the battle of Coronea in 447 B.C. A natural sea empire, the Athenians had failed in their attempt to add a land empire to their domain.

It was also in 457 B.C. that the process of democratization was taken a step further, with the opening of the lottery for the archonship to the zeugitai, the next to the lowest property class. The use of the lot was gradually extended to fill other offices, with the exception of those (such as the generalship, financial offices, and the office of architect) that were considered to entail specific skill requirements, and the direct lot replaced the use of sortition after a preliminary election had narrowed the field of candidates. Payment for offices other than that of juror was only gradually introduced, and we do not always know the exact dates. Payment for attending the Assembly came only in the fourth century B.C.

In 454 B.C., the Egyptian venture also ended in failure, and with great losses. The sources do not agree, but the Athenians and their allies may have lost as many as 250 ships and 50,000 men.[14] The disaster threatened the Delian League's control of the Aegean, and therefore the security of the island of Delos and the League treasury. The Athenians, as noted earlier, consequently transferred the treasury to Athens; this was an important move that gave them physical control over the assets of the League, but Thucydides does not mention it. As we shall see, the Athenians soon exploited this new advantage, for they utilized League funds for the building of the Parthenon and other Periclean building projects.[15] The transfer of League funds to Athens also gave us the Athenian Tribute Lists, an important additional source of historical evidence about the empire that makes possible the reconstruction of the tribute payments from 453 B.C. on (see above).

In about 450 B.C. peace was concluded with Persia. Late ancient sources report an official treaty, the Peace of Callias, which granted autonomy to the Greeks in Asia Minor, excluded Persian satraps from Aegean coastal areas, and barred Persian ships from Aegean waters. Many historians doubt the existence of a formal treaty, however. Thucydides does not mention it, and Plutarch dates the peace to the period after the victory of the Eurymedon and mentions that doubts about genuineness of the treaty had been raised as early as the fourth century B.C. But whether by a formal treaty or by an informal understanding, major hostilities between the League and the Persians ceased about 450 B.C. We will refer to this situation as the *Peace of Callias*, without making any judgment as to its exact form.

A summary of the events of this poorly documented period shows Athenian ambitions extending in several directions. The alliance with Argos secured an important ally against Sparta in the northeast Peloponnesus. The assistance to Megara, the building of the Long Walls from Megara to Nisaea, and the alliance with Pegae secured much of the isthmus; this clearly threatened Corinth, while it gave Athens access to the Corinthian Gulf and allowed an Athenian station at Naupactus, where the Athenians resettled Messenians in revolt against Sparta.

In 459 the Athenians went to the assistance of the Egyptians in their revolt against Persia, using a fleet that had been on an expedition to Cyprus. In 458/7, Athens built its own Long Walls to the Piraeus, assuring its access to the sea, even as it worked to extend its territory on land. Battles against Sparta in Boeotian territory in 457, at Tanagra and Oenophyta, gave Athens control over Boeotia. In 454, however, the Egyptian expedition came to disaster, and in ca. 450 peace was arrived at with the Persians. By 447, defeat at the battle of Coronea had ended Athenian control in Boeotia. It seemed that Athenian expansionism had been checked on both land and sea, and that Athens no longer had justification for enforcing participation in the Delian League.

THE ATHENIAN EMPIRE

The Peace of Callias had indeed removed the justification for the Delian League, and the allies soon objected to the League's continuation and to the continuation of tribute payments. There was much unrest, and some members of the League defected. The Athenians agreed to concessions in order to gain a new thirty-year peace treaty with the Peloponnesians and thus to be able to concentrate on these problems with their allies. In the end the Athenians prevailed because the instruments of empire were already strong. Tribute was continued, and new and more stringent regulations were imposed on its collection. Documents began to refer openly to the allies as "those whom Athens controls," and the Athenians introduced new forms of control. These changes, in effect, transformed the Delian League into an Athenian Empire (Map 10).

One type of control involved the protection of Athenians abroad and their sympathizers, who were naturally unpopular in cities that resented their ties to Athens. Trials involving allies and Athenian citizens were already required to be held in Athenian courts for this reason. To further protect Athenian citizens, the Athenians ruled that any city in which an Athenian, or an Athenian *proxenos* (local person serving as a representative of Athens), was killed was subject to a collective fine of 5 talents, an amount that was more than the annual tribute of many of the cities. Moreover, any individual who killed a proxenos was liable to the same penalty as one who killed an Athenian.[16]

The Athenians also took steps to control silver currency with a decree, the Currency Decree, that required every League member to convert its silver coinage into Athenian coinage, and thereafter to use only Athenian coins, weights, and measures.[17] The tone of the decree was peremptory, and penalties were established for failure to comply, suggesting that the Athenians anticipated resistance. The decree served Athenian imperialistic interests in more than one way. It smoothed the workings of the administrative machinery of the empire by facilitating the handling of tribute, by assuring that distributions and collections, such as fines, would be uniform in every city, and by providing a uniform basis

S O U R C E   A N A L Y S I S

|T| HUCYDIDES 1.89–117.   Thucydides provides a condensed account of the development of the Delian League from its beginnings until it appears transformed into an Athenian empire. The format of a bare listing tends to emphasize Athens' escalating oppression of its allies. In tracing this development, it is helpful to utilize the list format, noting the chronological order of these actions, locating their sites on the map, and considering the justification that Thucydides gives for each.

for payments in support of Athenian administrators and military forces abroad. It also graphically impressed the fact of Athenian power upon cities that had long expressed their civic autonomy by the distinctive designs of their coinage.

Athens at this time also began a policy of establishing Athenian settlements, or *cleruchies,* in allied cities.[18] The cleruchies were citizen colonies in which the settlers, Athenian citizens of the zeugitai and thete classes, received allotments of land that had been taken over from local landowners. Unlike colonists in most Greek colonies, however, the cleruchs retained their Athenian citizenship.[19] The establishment of cleruchies provided an Athenian presence to keep an eye on the local population, as well as a safety valve for the growing population of the poor in Athens. Pericles himself led a cleruchy to the Chersonese, and other cleruchies are known to have been established in Euboea, Naxos, Andros, and Brea (in Thrace). The existence of still others can be inferred from, but are not specifically attested to, by the ancient evidence.

The cleruchies were naturally resented by the allies upon whom they were imposed, even though the tribute of cities with cleruchies was lowered. Not surprisingly, they were popular with the Athenian demos, which benefitted from them. It was not a coincidence that in 451 B.C. Pericles carried a proposal to limit the citizenship, which at this time had significant benefits—eligibility for cleruchies, as well as payment for offices—to offspring of both a citizen father and a citizen mother; earlier the mother's citizenship had not been required.

ATTIC DRAMA AND POLITICS

Attic drama, both comedy and tragedy, provides another perspective on Greek history. Comedy was often frankly and openly political, subjecting public leaders to the most personal of attacks. Tragedy, at times, also openly addressed current political issues, as was done in Aeschylus' play *The Persians*, or his *Oresteia*, which tried to put the best light upon the controversial reform of the Areopagus Council. The tragic poet Phrynichus' portrayal of the fall of Miletus in 494 B.C. (a work now lost) so powerfully affected the Athenian public that the playwright was fined. At other times, however, the political allusions in tragedy are so subtle that to some they seem to exist only in the ingenuity of modern scholars.

Both tragedies and comedies were quite different from modern theatrical performances and also quite different from each other. Both were essentially religious performances, part of the annual festivals held in honor of Dionysus, the god of wine and fertility, but they developed out of different elements of early performance. Tragedy grew out of a type of choral poetry called *dithyrambic* (from its characteristic meter); gradually, solo parts emerged, until the form developed into a performance by three actors and a chorus. The subjects of tragedy were serious and elevated. Aristotle defines tragedy as[20]:

> . . . the imitation of an action that is serious and also, as having magnitude, complete in itself . . . in a dramatic, not a narrative form; with incidents arousing pity and fear, wherewith to accomplish its catharsis of such emotions . . . some portions are worked out with verse only, and others in turn with song.

Comedy grew out of phallic songs in honor of Dionysus, sung at such celebrations, and the Dionysiac spirit of the new wine, fertility, and revelry was an essential element in comic performances. In these annual festivals, as in the Carnival celebrated today in many Catholic countries just before the restrictions of the Lenten season begin, license was allowed to all, and neither the gods nor human politicians escaped the barbs of comic satire. The festival's origins in fertility rites are reflected in the language of the plays, which overflows with double meanings and obscenity, much of which is often lost (or suppressed) in translation. Comic choruses often have fantastic identities, sometimes as animals (in *The Clouds* the chorus is clouds, and in *The Wasps* the character of the chorus is that of jurors—portrayed as wasps, ready to sting the defendants). Choral episodes alternate with scenes in a traditional pattern: a prologue sets the scene, and then the chorus enters; this is followed by a series of episodes, punctuated by choral passages. Some of the episodes have traditional formats: an ***agon*** or contest, which often begins with a physical fight and ends with a verbal contest; and the ***parabasis,*** in which the chorus steps outside the framework of dramatic illusion, dropping the robes of their costumes as well as their specific characters, and addresses the audience on behalf of the playwright. The plays usually end with a celebration of the powers of life—a wedding or even a rejuvenation—and the exodus of the chorus.

Even the conditions of performance make Greek drama a thing apart from the modern theater. Dramatic performances were held only during the annual festivals. They took place outdoors during the day, with several plays being presented each day of the festival; the playwrights competed for the first prize, which was determined by a panel drawn from the spectators. There was little in the way of stage sets or props, but imagination set the scene for the audience. There was a limit of three actors in each play (for speaking parts), and thus the same actor often played more than one role. The problems that multiple roles involved were overcome by the use of masks, which also served to make the characters more visible in the large theaters and to amplify the actors' voices. The chorus was an integral part of the play (in fact, to provide and train a chorus was in essence to present a play and was an expensive civic duty, or *liturgy,* that fell to wealthy citizens).

S O U R C E　　A N A L Y S I S

The Wasps *of Aristophanes*

The political aspects of Attic comedy come out well in Aristophanes' play *The Wasps.* We see the jury system as it operated to empower the demos—and, as Aristophanes thinks, as venal politicians corrupted it in order to exploit the demos. Aristophanes portrays the jury system in operation under Kleon, a demogogic successor of Pericles. Aristophanes had a personal grudge against Kleon, who had brought charges against him for an earlier comic attack, but his objections to the leader were shared by Thucydides. What criticisms of the jury system does Aristophanes make? Are they aimed at the jurymen, or at their exploiter?

THE PERICLEAN BUILDING PROGRAM

Following the Peace of Callias, Pericles proposed the rebuilding of the temples that had been left in ruins after the war as a reminder of the hubris of the Persians. When his call for a Panhellenic conference on the issue failed to win support, however, the Athenians proceeded alone with a building program that he devised. This not only signaled the new state of peace with Persia, it also gave the Athenians the opportunity to advertise their imperial might and cultural splendor to their subjects as they came to participate in the Panathenaic festival or to have their cases tried in Athenian courts. Again, this is an element of imperialism that we do not read about in the history of Thucydides. The main sources are the remains of the buildings themselves, fragments of building accounts, and the late account in Plutarch's *Pericles*.

The Panathenaic festival, which had been reorganized by Peisistratus as a civic celebration, was now transformed into a celebration of the empire of the Athenians. Each subject state was required to play the role of a colony by sending an official delegation to the festival and making an offering of a cow and a *panoply* (a full set of armor). The tribute assessments for the next four years were announced during the festival.

The focus of the Panathenaic festival was on the Acropolis, to which the procession, bearing a new robe for the cult statue of Athena, made its way from the lower city. The focus of Pericles' building program was also on the Acropolis. A new temple to Athena and a new gateway to the Acropolis were built there, as well as a temple to Athena Nike (Victory), while the **Odeon,** site of musical performances, was constructed on the lower slopes of the hill.[21] A significant portion of the funds used in the building appears to have come from the League treasury, as noted earlier[22] (Figure 10-1).

The Parthenon was the centerpiece of the Periclean plan. After the first Persian War a new temple to Athena (the "Old Parthenon") had been started to the south of the Peisistratid temple of Athena, but it had progressed only to the foundation and the surrounding colonnade at the time of the second Persian attack. The Persians set fire to the scaffolding used in the building of this temple, calcining the column drums of the colonnade. Twenty-six of these drums were incorporated into the rebuilt wall of the Acropolis in the 470s as reminders of Persian aggression. In 447/6 B.C. work on a new Parthenon was begun; the tem-

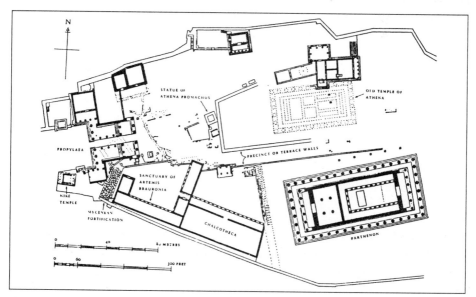

FIGURE 10-1   Plan of the Athenian Acropolis (Travlos).

ple was built upon the foundations of the earlier unfinished building and utilized its salvageable materials. In the Periclean scheme, however, the plan of this new temple was changed in order to provide an impressive setting for a colossal *chryselephantine* (gold and ivory) statue of Athena by the sculptor Phidias. Accommodating the statue required changes in the traditional standard plan of the Doric temple, the most obvious of which was an increase in the width of the temple from the traditional six columns to eight (Figure 10-2). The added width, which necessitated the enlargement of the existing foundation, created a more striking interior setting for the statue, and the interior *cella* (the home of the statue) was provided with an unusual three-sided colonnade that formed a frame for it.[23] In front of the statue a large pool reflected its image and added humidity to help preserve the ivory (see Figure 10-1).

The Parthenon was highly decorated with sculptured reliefs expressing in a variety of ways the glory of Athena's city and the triumph of the Greeks over the Barbarians (Figure 10-3). On the **entablature** the Doric triglyph and metope frieze portrayed mythological combats of **centaurs** (mythical creatures with the head and upper torso of a man and the body of a horse) against **Lapiths** (legendary Thessalian people), **Amazons** against Greeks, gods against giants, and Greeks against Trojans, each celebrating the victory of civilized Greece over the barbarous East. The sculptures on the **pediment** portrayed the birth of Athena on the east and the contest between Athena and Poseidon for the possession of Athens on the west. An especially novel feature was introduced on the exterior cella walls: a running **frieze**, typical of Ionic architecture, represented a human event, the Panathenaic procession. The use of a running frieze, typical of the **Ionic order,** was in itself an innovation in a **Doric** temple, but the more striking departure from tradition was the fact that, even though the gods are portrayed as waiting to receive the procession, essentially the frieze portrayed a human, rather than a divine or mythological, event.[24]

The Peisistratid gateway to the Acropolis, the **Propylaea,** was next reoriented and reconstructed on a monumental scale and plan; work began in 437/6 B.C. Since it replaced the defensive works that formerly guarded the entryway to the Acropolis, the new Propylaea graphically illustrated the new nature of Athenian power: with the Long Walls securing Athenian access to the sea, a formidable defensive system was no longer necessary to protect the Acropolis. The Periclean Propylaea was designed to impress those approaching the Acropolis, not to ward off attackers.

The Periclean building program celebrated the might and intellectual achievements of an imperial Athens as well as its patron goddess Athena: human activities were given a place beside the divine. Symbolic of this was not only the Parthenon frieze, but also the fact that the Parthenon was built to house a cult statue that was created by one of the most celebrated sculptors in the Greek world at that time.

The building program was not without its critics, however. A celebration of

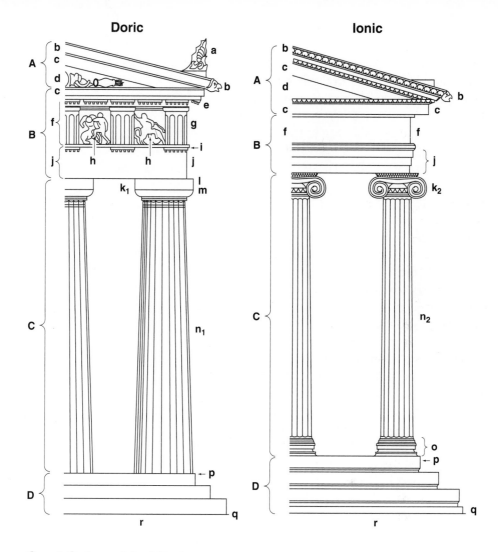

Greek Orders of Architecture

A. Pediment	a. Acroterion	k_1. Capital (Doric)
B. Entablature	b. Sima	k_2. Capital (Ionic) with Volutes
C. Column	c. Geison or Cornice	l. Abacus
D. Crepidoma	d. Tympanum	m. Echinus
	e. Mutule & Guttae	n_1. Shaft with flutes
	f. Frieze	separated by sharp arrises
	g. Triglyphs	n_2. Shaft with flutes
	h. Metopes	separated by blunt fillets
	i. Regulae & Guttae	o. Bases
	j. Architrave or Epistyle	p. Stylobate
		q. Euthynteria
		r. Stereobate

FIGURE 10-2 Doric and Ionic architectural orders.

FIGURE 10-3   The Parthenon on the Acropolis of Athens.

Athenian naval imperialism, which focused on defending overseas possessions rather than Attic farms and estates, a creation of the demos rather than of aristocratic patronage, and a project in which the wealth of the League was distributed to the workers of the demos, the program had little appeal for the wealthy. Some critics turned to the courts, the traditional forum for Athenian political attack. Phidias was accused of embezzling gold intended for use in the statue, and when this charge was defeated (he had made the gold portions of the statue removable, and they could be weighed and checked against the accounts), he was accused of portraying himself and Pericles on the shield of Athena. According to Plutarch, he was put into prison, where he fell sick and died; however, according to the third-century B.C. historian Philochorus, he fled to Elis, where he made the great statue of Zeus at Olympia for the Eleans and was afterwards put to death by them.[25] (The report of death at the hands of the state, in whichever form, is suspicious as a repeated motif.) The comic poets also attacked the building program: Cratinus satirized Pericles as a "new Zeus" who went about wearing the Odeon on his head as a crown. Conservatives criticized the use of League funds for Athenian buildings, and the leading conservative after the death of Cimon,

Thucydides, the son of Melesias (not the historian Thucydides), attacked the buildings as extravagant. But the building program was popular with the demos, for whom it provided employment: it is estimated that about 1000 men worked on the project from 447 to 432 B.C.[26] When the issue came to an ostracism vote, it was Thucydides, son of Melesias, whom the people chose to ostracize, not Pericles.

THE ATHENIAN ENLIGHTENMENT

The spirit of humanism and rationalism that was embodied by the Periclean buildings also found expression in many other forms in Greece in the second half of the fifth century B.C. In Athens the philosopher Socrates turned men's attention to questions of human values, history was born as an investigation of human responses and choices, and tragic poets created dramas that expressed the dilemmas of the human condition and provided lasting models for the understanding of human behavior and development. Greek doctors sought the rational bases of medicine in a tradition that culminated in the work of the near-legendary Father of Medicine, Hippocrates of Cos, and Hippocratic doctors traveled throughout the Aegean with their message that human illness was caused not by demons and the anger of the gods but by natural processes. In all these senses, the latter half of the fifth century B.C. in Greece was the first *Age of Enlightenment*, an age in which traditional values were reexamined and new grounds for these values were sought within the context of human concerns and social interactions.

The Sophists and Their Influence

Perhaps most important for defining both the spirit of the age and the tenor of the Athenian political scene were the professional teachers of rhetoric, the *Sophists*.[27] It was these men who offered the expensive education that provided the skills in public speaking (for example, addressing the Assembly) vital to politically ambitious men. Interest in public speaking was not a concern of only the wealthy, however. While for the most part it was the wealthy who involved themselves in politics and spoke in the Assembly, less affluent men needed public-speaking skills when they used the courts to attack their enemies or to defend themselves (these men often hired the services of speechwriters). There is even a speech preserved in which a man defends his right to the state pension that was given to the disabled poor.[28]

The Sophists found a ready audience in many Greek poleis, but most eventually made their way to Athens, attracted by its growing wealth and lively, congenial intellectual scene. It is there that we meet them, especially in the dialogues of Plato. In addition to their teaching of rhetoric, the Sophists also offered a broad intellectual education, including such subjects as general management of one's affairs, grammar, music, poetry, medicine, and natural philosophy. With their teaching they contributed in large measure to the creation of the intellectual ferment that we call the *Athenian Enlightenment.*

Among the earliest Sophists to visit Athens was Protagoras of Abdera (a Greek city in Thrace), who appears, together with the Sophists Hippias and Prodicus, in the Platonic dialogue *Protagoras.* He associated with the leading intellectuals and political leaders of the time, including Pericles, the tragedian Euripides, and Socrates. He was especially interested in methods of argumentation, but he also taught a humanism and relativism that reflected the best in Sophistic thought. His interest and expertise in politics is confirmed by Pericles' decision to invite him to draw up the laws for the new colony of Thurii in southern Italy in 444 B.C.

Another Sophist who appears in *Protagoras* is Prodicus; he was especially interested in the philosophy of language, specializing in the drawing of minute distinctions between almost synonymous terms. Thucydides sometimes makes distinctions that are credited to Prodicus: between *complaint* and *accusation, fear* and *terror, courage* and *boldness, revolt* and *defection, hegemony* and *empire.* Still another Sophist, Gorgias of Leontini in Sicily, who appears in the Platonic dialogue *Gorgias,* first visited Athens in 427 B.C. as an envoy from his native city. He was noted for the powers of his poetic style, in which he played with final sounds and rhymes, balanced numbers of syllables, and used terms that are parallel in form, sound, or meter. He wrote a tribute to the powers of speech in his *Helen,* and Thucydides made use of many of these Gorgian stylistic devices in writing his history.

The practical nature of Sophistic training is reflected in a technical device that has strong moral overtones, the ***antilogy,*** or a set of paired speeches arguing opposite sides of a given thesis. The invention of the antilogy is attributed to Protagoras by the ancient historian of philosophy Diogenes Laertes, but in fact, it was a legacy of the law courts and appeared in the works of the tragedian Sophocles before the Sophists had become popular. The use of antilogies was well suited to the Sophists and became especially associated with them, for it supported the claim of some of these men of being able to teach methods of arguing effectively on both sides of a question. An anonymous treatise called *The Double Arguments* provided model arguments of this type, and *The Tetralogy* of Antiphon contains sets of speeches for both sides of questions such as who is responsible if a boy is accidentally killed running in the path of the javelin throwers in the gymnasium. Three display speeches of Gorgias survive that argue controversial theses: a defense of Helen against criticism for running away with Paris and causing the Trojan War; a defense of the Homeric hero Palamedes on a charge of treason; and a parody of the philosopher Parmenides that argues that nothing exists, and if it did, it could not be known, and if it were known, it could not be communicated. The use—and misuse—of such antilogies figures largely

SOURCE ANALYSIS

The Clouds *of Aristophanes*

T he 423 B.C. presentation of *The Clouds* is the second version of the play. The first, which has not been preserved, failed to win the prize, and the poet was so stung by the rebuke of the demos that he rewrote the ending, apparently to better reflect public opinion about the Sophists. How do you think the original version ended?

in *The Clouds* of Aristophanes, in which the character Strepsiades seeks to have his son taught the "twofold argument" and how to make the weaker argument prevail so that he can evade his creditors. (See Source Analysis above.)

Despite different approaches and specialties, the Sophists shared a basic core of ideas. They placed the locus of human values firmly in human society. Protagoras sounded the keynote in his famous relativistic dictum: "Man is the measure of all things, of those which are, that they are; of those which are not, that they are not." Protagoras also denied that the existence of the gods could be known, a statement of agnosticism, not of atheism, but nonetheless providing grounds for turning away from debates about the divine nature of such fundamental virtues as justice and seeking the grounds of such values in human life and society. However, if man is the measure, and success in political life is the goal, the way is also open to challenge as well as to support traditional values.

Such "new thinking" was extremely popular in some quarters, especially with the young, but many saw it as a threat to traditional morality. Criticism reached such a pitch that Protagoras was condemned to death for impiety and forced to flee Athens for his life (although, according to Plutarch, the attack was politically motivated and aimed at his friend Pericles). We see a reflection of this opposition to the new ideas in *The Clouds* of Aristophanes, presented in 423 B.C., three years after the arrival in Athens of the famous sophist Gorgias.

The works of the Sophists themselves have survived only in fragments, and for the most part we know them only through reports by their enemies, of whom Plato was by far the most effective in molding later opinion. The result has been a highly biased and negative picture, although a number of modern scholars have worked recently to present a fairer assessment of these men whose contributions often anticipate modern views. One of the most persuasive of these is J. de Romilly.[29] She argues that the immorality often attributed to the

Sophists represented not so much their own teachings as the popular reaction that carried the argument far beyond what these teachers advocated. Thus, in *The Clouds*, it is Strepsiades who plots to use the teachings of the "Sophist" Socrates for unethical purposes, not the philosopher himself. In fact, de Romilly argues that the Sophists' "destruction of traditional values" was really a reconstruction of values resting not on questionable myths, but on a rational foundation, and that to provide this foundation they adopted notions that are familiar from the classic liberalism of early modern Europe: utility and contract. Human beings cannot survive outside society, and they therefore *contract* to exchange the fulfillment of some immediate selfish desires for the long-term protections offered by a cooperative life in society. *Utility* provided the basis for Sophistic arguments of probability that were frequently used in Athenian courts; for example, a defendant might argue, "Would I have been likely to have killed the victim, considering that I am a 100-pound arthritic and he was a 300-pound wrestler?" As a result, a realistic, even pessimistic, conception of psychology emerged. We can see this exemplified in Thucydides' work, where people (despite the altruistic appearance of their motives) are frequently revealed as pursuing their own interests.

THE DEVELOPMENT OF DEMOCRACY IN ATHENS

As the empire developed and the fleet grew in importance, so too did the political voice of the men of the lowest property class who provided its crews. As we have seen, as the demos grew in strength, reforms increasingly limited the traditional political and social predominance of the wealthier Athenians. To a great extent, Athenian reliance upon sea power determined the course of its political destiny. The nature of the trireme, the Greek warship in the fifth century B.C., almost dictated an extension of political rights and powers to the lowest class, the thetes. The ship was propelled by three banks of rowers, 170 in all, and their cramped seating arrangements made exact coordination necessary at all times if the ship was not to founder in a tangle of oars.[30] Since one malcontented rower could disrupt the complex maneuvers of a sea battle and bring on defeat, slaves were used as rowers only in the most extreme emergencies, and even then they were freed. On the other hand, rowing was an arduous and often unpleasant occupation, and it certainly did not appeal to the upper classes. The nucleus of the crews was drawn from the poorer Athenians, and the number of such men was not negligible: during wartime, Athens maintained a standing fleet of 100 triremes, each with a total crew of 200, which amounted to 20,000 men (some of these would, however, have been supplied by the allies). A total of 200 triremes were also kept in reserve, and often more than 100 ships were in commission. In addition, many thetes found a livelihood in building and repairing ships and in providing necessary materials and supplies. As a result of the vital role that the lower classes thus played in the defense of the city and the maintenance of empire, they came to have an increasing say in the affairs of the polis.

The Athenian democracy was a great experiment in self-government whose tradition we continue in our own democracy. Because the Assembly lay at the heart of the democracy, an understanding of the way in which it functioned will be important as we read the works of those contemporaries who were its implicit—and sometimes explicit—critics. First among these was Thucydides himself, but even more outspoken were the comic poet Aristophanes and the philosopher Plato.

Participation in the Assembly

Every male citizen over eighteen was eligible to attend and vote in the Assembly, which made all the important decisions of government in Athens in the fifth century B.C., including declarations of war, decisions about military strategy, and the election of generals, financial officials, and architects (in the fourth century B.C. decision-making processes were divided among the Assembly, *nomothetes,* or legislative commissions of citizens chosen for one day's service, and the courts).[31] In the fifth century B.C. the Assembly had one obligatory meeting in each of the ten prytanies (months) of the year, but in the fourth century B.C. the number was increased to three and then four meetings in a prytany; in both periods there were other meetings in addition to the mandatory ones. The meetings began at sunrise, and probably lasted only until midday.[32]

All matters to be discussed or put to the vote had to be first presented to the Council, which set the agenda for each Assembly meeting. Debate on proposals took the form of speeches by orators. These men, who were almost always wealthy and well educated in rhetoric, voluntarily undertook to address the Assembly; they were not elected or appointed. The politically minded citizen's need to address and to persuade the Assembly was what gave the Sophists their great popularity. There was no formal discussion of the proposals by the ordinary Assembly members, but citizens attending certainly talked among themselves, and they also expressed their opinions of the various speakers by applause, heckling, and even interjecting comments and questions (all technically illegal, but tolerated). Voting was by a show of hands. However, these were not counted: the majority was determined by the officials in charge of the meeting. Anyone who contested the decision could lodge a sworn objection, and the show of hands would be repeated. To protect the people against being misled by persuasive but irresponsible speakers, any man who introduced a measure that was later judged to be unconstitutional was liable to severe penalties. Moreover, any decision of the Assembly could be reversed in the next session after a new debate and vote (as we will see in a later chapter, Thucydides describes just such a case involving the Assembly's decision to punish the people of Mytilene for their revolt).

Men came to the Assembly not only from the city of Athens, but from all over Attica, often walking several hours each way in order to attend.[33] Although in the fourth century B.C. pay for attendance was instituted (the sum amounted to about a day's pay), it is clear that participation in the democracy required a serious commitment of time and energy, quite apart from the duties of any offices to which a man might be called by the lot. Without the firm basis of the noncitizen substructure of society—the work of women, slaves, and metics (resident aliens)—the Athenian democracy could not have functioned.

Even at the height of the Athenian democracy in 431 B.C. it is estimated that, of the total population of about 315,500, approximately one-third, or 115,000, were slaves. Another 28,500 were metics; only 43,000, or 13.6 percent, were adult male citizens between the ages of eighteen and fifty-nine; those over the age of thirty eligible to hold office and hence to participate as full citizens would have been an even smaller percentage.[34] The noncitizen groups rarely appear in the pages of traditional histories, but they formed the indispensable foundation that made the political activities of Greek male citizens possible. In assessing Greek democracy, it is vital to consider the conditions of noncitizens' lives as well as to understand the political activities of the male citizen minority, and it is to this that we turn next.

IMPORTANT PLACES IN CHAPTER 10

On Chapter Map: Abdera, Aegina, Amphipolis, Anatolia, Andros, Aphytis, Argos, Black Sea, Boeotia, Brea (Thrace), Caria, Chalkidike, Chersonese, Corinth, Corinthian Gulf, Coronea, Delos, Elis, Euboea, Eurymedon River, Hellespont, Leontini, Lycia, Macedonia, Mantinea, Megara, Mount Ithome, Mykale, Mytilene, Naupactus, Naxos, Oenophyta, Pegae, Propontus, Skyros, Tanagra, Thasos, Thebes

On Other Maps (use map index to find these): Cyprus, Egypt, Naucratus

SUGGESTIONS FOR FURTHER READING

The fundamental modern discussion of this period in R. Meiggs, *The Athenian Empire* (1972); on the building program, see Alison Burford, "The Builders of the Parthenon," *Parthenos and Parthenon: Greece and Rome*, Supplement vol. 10 (1963), 23–35, and other articles in the same volume; on Greek theater and comedy, see Cedric Whitman, *Aristophanes and the Comic Hero* (1964); on the workings of the Athenian democracy, a good place to start is M. H. Hansen, *The Athenian Assembly in the Age of Demosthenes* (1987).

ENDNOTES

1. B. D. Meritt, H. T. Wade-Gery, M. F. McGregor, *The Athenian Tribute Lists* (1939–1953), 4 vols., contains the lists with translation and commentary.
2. The best in-depth modern work on the empire is R. Meiggs, *The Athenian Empire* (1972).
3. For example, S. Hornblower, *The Greek World, 479–323 B.C.* (1983), 21–26; on the other hand, F. Fine, *The Ancient Greeks* (1983), sees no reason to reject it.
4. Thuc. 1.95, 128–134. Pausanias was recalled to Sparta and tried for Medism, but acquitted; nonetheless, he continued to raise suspicions and finally was driven to take sanctuary in a temple, where he was starved to death.
5. This is questioned by E. Badian, "Archons and *Strategoi*," *Antichthon* 5 (1971), 1–34. Badian finds the number of 500 for those in the elected pool too large to have been practicable, given the probable number of men in the upper two classes, and suggests that 50 would have been a more reasonable number. He also analyzes the lists of known archons both before and after the introduction of the lot and finds no significant drop in the prestige of the archons; however, this seems less than conclusive, since too little is known about individuals in this period, with the exception of a very few outstanding figures, for us to compare relative importance of archons before and after the change.
6. The date is uncertain. Plutarch's story that it was a countermove to Cimon's opening his orchards to the public suggests that it occurred while Cimon was still in Athens (before his ostracism), but Ps.-Aristotle's statement that Pericles only came to the fore after the death of Ephialtes suggests that it should be later. Rhodes (*CAH* V, 76) therefore reads Plutarch as only implying that it happened during Cimon's lifetime, and dates it shortly after the reform of Ephialtes, the position that is taken here.
7. See the oligarchic pamphlet called the *Constitution of Athens*, attributed to Xenophon, 1.16–18; and Antiphon 5.47, with the note in the Loeb edition of Antiphon (*Minor Attic Orators* 1, 192), which gives further references to inscriptions attesting to this requirement.
8. Plut., *Cimon* 16.4–5; Diod., Sic. 11.63.1.
9. Thuc. 1.100–103.
10. The number is provided by Aristophanes, *Lysistrata* 1138–44.
11. The work, which includes both a historical account of the development of the constitution and an account of its fourth-century B.C. workings, is available in full in A. W. H. Adkins and Peter White, *The Greek Polis* (1986); it is printed in a Penguin paperback edition, *Aristotle. The Athenian Constitution* (1984), translated with commentary by P. J. Rhodes, who considers it to be the work of a pupil; a translation and commentary is also offered by J. M. Moore, *Aristotle and Xenophon on Democracy and Oligarchy* (1975), who holds that the author was Aristotle, as does J. J. Keaney, *The Composition of Aristotle's Athenaion Politeia: Observation and Explanation* (1992). But, whoever its author, the same cautious approach is necessary in determining its historical value.
12. Ps.-Arist., *Ath. Pol.* 25.1–2, tr. J. Fine.
13. Plut., *Per.* 24, 25.1, 32.1, 5.
14. Diod., Sic. 11.77.1–5, in a highly rhetorical account, gives these figures, which agree roughly with Thucydides' account, in which an original Athenian fleet of 200 and a relief force of 50 ships were all lost, with most of their crews. The Athenian orator Isocrates (8.86) says that 200 ships and their crews were lost. Since Thucydides' account

of the period following the disaster does not show the effects one might expect from such a great loss, some historians doubt these figures, preferring those of the Greek doctor Ktesias, a resident of Persia, who says that 40 ships and their crews (6000 Greeks) surrendered on condition that they return home (Ktesias 32–34); to these we could add the 50 ships sent in relief, giving a total of about 100 ships lost, with a large part of the crews presumably surviving.

15. The funding of the Parthenon is discussed in detail by T. Shear, *Studies in the Early Projects of the Periklean Building Program* (1983), 249–259; the use of League funds is questioned by L. Kallet-Marx, "Did Tribute Fund the Parthenon?" *Classical Antiquity* 8 (1989), 252–266.

16. See Meiggs (above, n. 2), 171–172.

17. There is considerable debate about the date of this decree; a date in the 420s B.C., once widely accepted, has regained support from the find of a large hoard of coinage in southern Asia Minor, which contains coins from the third quarter of the fifth century B.C. from cities that would have been affected by the decree. In particular, it contains local coins from the small city of Aphytis, one of the sites at which a fragment of the Coinage Decree has also been found. See Meiggs (above, n. 2), 171–172, and the articles by M. J. Price, D. M. Lewis, and H. B. Mattingly in Ian Carradice, *Coinage and Administration in the Athenian and Persian Empires* (1987). Until numismaticists have reached a clearer consensus on the hoard's implications for the dating of the decree, we will continue to favor the earlier, mid-fifth century B.C.

18. On the Athenian use of cleruchies, see Meiggs (above, n. 2), 121–123.

19. It is not known if all cleruchs actually took up residence in their new allotment, as cleruchs later did, or whether some were absentee landlords, simply collecting rent. It seems likely, however, that the usual pattern was for cleruchs to become residents, and that absentee control was exceptional, for inscriptions attest the organization of communities with councils and archons (for example, *IG* i.² 40–42).

20. Arist. *Poetics* 1449b24–31, tr. Ingram Bywater.

21. "Location of Odeon of Pericles on Acropolis Slope," John Travlos, *Pictorial Dictionary of Athens* (1971), 387–391. The Odeon in the Agora indicated on many maps in a later building.

22. See above, n. 2.

23. Rhys Carpenter, *The Architects of the Parthenon* (1970).

24. A recent interpretation of the frieze by Joan Breton Connelly suggests that it represents a mythical story from early Athenian history—the sacrifice of the daughters of King Erechtheus in order to assure Athenian victory. According to this interpretation, the central scene shows the king, Queen Praxithea, and the three daughters preparing for the sacrifice, watched by an assembly of the gods. The cloth is interpreted not as the sacred *peplos* of Athena, but as the shrouds of the daughters. See *American Journal of Archaeology* 97 (1993), 309–310, for a brief summary of Connelly's paper.

25. See A. Powell, *Athens and Sparta* (1988), 59–67, for a defense of Plutarch's reports about the building program.

26. See Alison Burford, "The Builders of the Parthenon," *Parthenos and Parthenon: Greece and Rome*, Supplement vol. 10 (1963), 23–35, 34.

27. The fragments of the Sophists' works are collected in the Diels-Kranz edition, *Fragmente der Vorsokratiker* (many editions and revisions; consult the latest). English translations by R. K. Sprague, *The Older Sophists* (1972), and K. Freeman, *Ancilla to the Pre-Socratic*

Philosophers (1948); excellent discussions are to be found in J. de Romilly, *The Great Sophists in Periclean Athens* (1992), and W. K. C. Guthrie, *The Sophists* (1971).

28. Lysias IV, *On the Invalid.*

29. See above, n. 27.

30. Recently a trireme has been constructed and tested in sea trials; see J. S. Morrison and F. J. F. Coates, *The Athenian Trireme* (1986).

31. This summary is based on M. H. Hansen, *The Athenian Assembly in the Age of Demosthenes* (1987).

32. This is Hansen's view (above, n. 31), 32–34, 126; others believe that the meetings took up a full day, and one such case is attested, the trial of the eight victorious generals who failed to pick up the bodies of the dead after the battle of Arginusae (Xen., *Hell.* 1.7.7).

33. See Hansen (above, n. 31), 8–12.

34. These population figures are based on A. W. Gomme, *The Population of Athens in the Fifth and Fourth Centuries B.C.* (1933), Table 1. This careful review of the ancient evidence remains the fundamental work on the subject of population. Gomme's figure of 43,000 for the adult male citizen population in 431 B.C. is supported by the more recent estimates of M. H. Hansen of at least 40,000 and possibly as many as 50,000, *Journal of Ancient History* 7 (1982), 173–174. Given the nature of the evidence, any estimates can only be educated guesses.

CHAPTER ELEVEN

The Other Greeks:
Women, Metics, Slaves

WOMEN AND THE POLIS

The world of the classical polis was a man's world. Only men could attend the Assembly, vote, hold office, serve on juries, appear in court in their own right, or even own property. In Athens, about which we know most, the legal position of free women of citizen parentage was that of perpetual minors. They could not manage property or handle money beyond the amount necessary to take care of household expenses for a few days. In any economic or legal transaction, they were always represented by a guardian—before marriage by a father, after marriage by a husband, and, if they survived as a widow, by a male relative or a grown son. In their role as mothers, women of citizen parentage served as transmitters of citizen status, but to what extent they were considered to be citizens themselves is not clear.[1]

Androcentric Sources

In trying to reconstruct the world of Greek women, we are severely hampered by the nature of our sources, almost all of which were the work of upper-class males—not only the historical texts, but also such sources as epitaphs, vase paintings, speeches in the law courts, and medical texts. They convey male views of women and male expectations of women, but not necessarily the realities of women's lives. In the Classical period, women do not speak to us in their own voices, and, to find them, we often need to look for clues in nontraditional ways.

Of our admittedly androcentric sources, perhaps the most useful are the speeches from private cases in the law courts.[2] These often provide information about daily life almost inadvertently, and, written by men hoping to appeal to an audience of citizen males, they reflect common (male) opinion. For example, a Greek male's view of the various classes of women is made clear in the following excerpt from a speech[3]:

> We have prostitutes [*hetairai*] for the sake of pleasure, concubines for daily care of the body, and wives for the purpose of begetting legitimate children and having a reliable guardian of the contents of the house.

The term **hetaira,** rendered in this translation as "prostitute," literally means "female companion." It was usually used to refer to women who entertained men in both a social and a sexual sense (perhaps "high-class call girl" would be the best translation), although it can also be used euphemistically of common prostitutes (more usually called **pornai**) (Figure 11-1). Prostitutes and hetairai might be either slaves, free, or freed. The sexual use of slaves employed in domestic service was also common. With luck, a household slave or a hetaira might become a favorite and take on the role of concubine, perhaps for a young, still unmarried son of her master (men did not ordinarily marry until about the age of thirty). Some slave women brought in wages for their masters by going out to work as prostitutes, or as singers, dancers, or flute girls.[4] An Attic vase even depicts a woman decorating a vase in a pottery (or perhaps metalworking) work-

FIGURE 11-1 Attic red-figure vase with scene of hetairai partying.

FIGURE 11-2 Attic red-figure vase with scene of workshop workers receiving prize wreaths from goddesses. The worker on the far right is a woman.

shop (Figure 11-2).[5] Such skills might have given female slaves some protection from unwanted male attentions, since the women were valuable as income producers, but in many cases it seems likely that the line between entertainer and prostitute was a blurred one. If such a woman succeeded in buying her freedom, she would then be a metic, but, without family connections, she would probably have to continue to use these same skills to make her own living.

The speech from which the quotation above was taken was one in which the citizen status of a woman was being challenged. Her name was Neaera, and it was charged that the male defendant had passed her off as his wife—which was illegal if she were not of citizen status—and that he had given her daughters in marriage as his own offspring and as citizens (that is, as children of a legitimate marriage between two people of citizen status). The charges were serious, for the penalties were loss of citizenship for the man and slavery for the woman. The case illustrates the propensity of Athenians to use legal challenges to citizen status as weapons in personal or political attack, and, consequently, how important it was for a male citizen to be sure about the citizen status of the mother of his children. Anxiety about possible challenges to the legitimacy of heirs was probably the basis of many of the restrictions upon women in the Classical period. From puberty until she passed the age of childbearing, a woman was seen as a potential threat to the honor and status of the *oikos* (household or family, including property, animals, and slaves). It was not that women were necessarily suspected of wishing to harm the oikos; they were simply believed to be weak and easily persuadable, and men knew that men from competing oikoi were always on the lookout for ways to damage their neighbors. The legitimacy of a child, even one born within a marriage, would be questioned if there were any shadow of scandal about the mother. Therefore, women had to be continually guarded and watched.

Exposure of Infants

When a child was born, its father had the right to accept and raise or to expose, but not to kill, the child. Exposed infants might be picked up and raised by anyone who found them, either as free or as slave. The birth father, however, retained a right to the child if he ever wished to claim it, and in Greek comedy in the fourth century B.C. many plots hinge upon the discovery of the true free status of young women who had been exposed as infants with tokens that allowed their identification as freeborn after they had been raised as slaves.

There is continuing debate about the extent to which Greeks actually exposed newborns.[6] It is generally agreed that abnormal or sickly infants were routinely exposed, and some suspect that female infants were also likely candidates for exposure because the few statistics that we have often show boys outnumbering girls. However, it is known that daughters were often simply not counted among offspring, and so there is no firm evidence for a statistical sexual imbalance.

The motives for exposure are usually taken to have been a desire to limit the male heirs in a system of partible inheritance and/or a desire to limit the expense of dowries for daughters. However, the high infant and child mortality in Greece—probably at best only half of all infants born survived to adulthood—and the high risk of losing even adult sons and daughters to the hazards of war and childbearing suggest that the best strategy for all but the poorest parents would have been to raise all the children born to them in order to insure the survival of a son to carry on the oikos and care for the parents in old age. (Even a daughter would do; in the event of the death of her father without male heirs, she became an *epikleros,* heiress, and her nearest agnatic male relative, father's brother or his son, was obliged to marry her and produce a son as heir for the deceased.)

FIGURE 11-3   Attic red-figure *pyxis* for cosmetics, portraying a wedding procession. The bride rides on a carriage, and participants carry gifts, including household goods and a box, which probably contained the bride's trousseau of jewelry and fine clothing.

Marriage and Childbirth

After their birth and acceptance into the family, girls were carefully sheltered throughout childhood to preserve their honor. For the same reason, they were married at puberty, conventionally set at fourteen.[7] The husband was usually about thirty, in a position to take over his familial oikos or to establish one of his own. Marriage was arranged by men: the girl's father or guardian and the potential groom and his male relatives. Marriages between cousins were favored, and in such cases the girl may have seen her prospective husband at a family occasion such as a wedding or a funeral, but otherwise girls had no opportunity to meet potential husbands (Figure 11-3). Even second marriages of fully adult women were arranged. Sometimes a man even chose his wife's next husband in his will,

FIGURE 11-3 *(continued)*

or arranged for her remarriage before divorcing her (as Pericles did, with his wife's agreement, when he divorced her to live with Aspasia). Theoretically a bride had a veto over a proposed match if the prospective candidate was morally objectionable, but probably few were in a position to object on those grounds.

Dowry was an important consideration in the choice of marriage partners and very important in assuring the security of the woman.[8] Dowry was legally attached to the woman, but managed by her guardian. When she married, her husband became her guardian, and the dowry became his to manage; he was required to use part of the proceeds to support her. In the event of a divorce, he had to return the dowry to the woman's new guardian, her father or nearest male relative. If a woman with a son was divorced, the dowry still followed her, going

FIGURE 11-4   Funeral stele of Plangon and Tolmides (a childbirth scene).

to her new guardian; her male offspring by the dissolved marriage had no more
claim to it.[9] The need for the husband to return the dowry provided the wife
some protection against hasty divorce and also allowed her new guardian to
dower her in another marriage. In the event she was widowed without sons, the

dowry returned, with her, to her family, who would probably remarry her; if she had a son, he became her guardian, and the dowry, as well as the duty of maintaining her in her old age, was his. Upon the death of a married woman, the dowry became part of her husband's estate and was eventually inherited by the sons on his death.

After marriage the woman's primary role was to produce an heir for the oikos. Everyone was anxious to discover if she would be able to conceive and bear a child successfully; failure would in most cases mean divorce, and there would be difficulty in arranging a remarriage, for the Greeks put the responsibility for sterility solely upon the woman. Testing for fertility and treatment for sterility were the province of midwives, although by the fourth century B.C. some Hippocratic doctors were recording midwives' recipes and treating these problems in their own practices.[10] Normal births were handled by midwives, with the assistance of female kin and neighbors. Doctors were sometimes called in for complications following delivery, but there was little they could do without antibiotics, blood transfusions, or methods of surgical intervention.[11] As in all premodern societies, maternal mortality rates were high; it was only in the 1930s with the advent of antibiotics that the low mortality rates that the United States now enjoys were reached. Puerperal fever and the complications of malaria and tuberculosis took many lives (Figure 11-4).[12] In the Classical period, pregnancy in the early teens did much to contribute to the dangers of childbearing, and the practice of close-kin marriages (first cousins were favored) must also have contributed to the number of birth defects and to the mortality rate of newborns. If both mother and child survived, the mother's status was much enhanced within her new family, especially if the child was a boy (but even a pregnancy resulting in the loss of the infant enhanced a woman's status by proving her fertility).

An interesting defense against a charge of murder provides a great deal of information about attitudes toward childbearing, living arrangements, and relationships within a marriage and household, as well as the law dealing with adultery. In the following Source Analysis, the defendant, Euphiletus, is on trial for murder, having killed an adulterer "caught in the act."[13]

S O U R C E   A N A L Y S I S

YSIAS 1. When I, Athenians, decided to marry, and brought a wife into my house, for some time I was disposed neither to vex her nor to leave her too free to do just as she pleased; I kept a watch on her as far as possible, with such observation of her as was reasonable. But when a child was born to me, thenceforward I began to trust her, and placed all my affairs in her hands, presuming that we were now in perfect intimacy. It is true that in the early days, Athenians, she was the most excellent of wives; she

continued

was a clever, frugal housekeeper, and kept everything in the nicest order. But as soon as I lost my mother, her death became the cause of all my troubles. For it was in attending her funeral that my wife was seen by this man, who in time corrupted her. He looked out for the servant-girl who went to market, and so paid addresses to her mistress by which he wrought her ruin. Now . . . my dwelling is on two floors, the upper being equal in space to the lower, with the women's quarters above and the men's below. When the child was born to us, its mother suckled it; and in order that, each time that it had to be washed, she might avoid the risk of descending by the stairs, I used to live above and the women below. By this time it had become such an habitual thing that my wife would often leave me and go down to sleep with the child, so as to be able to give it the breast and stop its crying. Things went on in this way for a long time, and I never suspected, but was simple-minded enough to suppose that my own was the chastest wife in the city. Time went on, sirs; I came home unexpectedly from the country, and after dinner the child started crying in a peevish way, as the servant-girl was annoying it on purpose to make it so behave; for the man was in the house,—I learnt it all later. So I bade my wife go and give the child her breast, to stop its howling. At first she refused, as though delighted to see me home again after so long; but when I began to be angry and bade her go,—"Yes, so that you," she said, "may have a try here at the little maid. Once before, too, when you were drunk, you pulled her about." At that I laughed, while she got up, went out of the room, and closed the door, feigning to make fun, and she turned the key in the lock. I, without giving a thought to the matter, or having any suspicion, went to sleep in all content after my return from the country. Towards daytime she came and opened the door. I asked why the doors made a noise in the night; she told me that the child's lamp had gone out, and she had lit it again at our neighbour's. I was silent and believed it was so. But it struck me, sirs, that she had powdered her face, though her brother had died not thirty days before; even so, however, I made no remark on the fact, but left the house in silence. After this, sirs, an interval occurred in which I was left quite unaware of my own injuries; I was then accosted by a certain old female, who was secretly sent by a woman with whom that man was having an intrigue, as I heard later. This woman was angry with him and felt herself wronged, because he no longer visited her so regularly, and she kept a close watch on him until she discovered what was the cause. So the old creature accosted me where she was on the lookout, near my house, and said, "Euphiletus, do not think it is from any meddlesomeness that I have approached you; for the man who is working both your and your wife's dishonour happens to be our enemy. If, therefore, you take the servant-girl who goes to market and waits on you, and torture her [slaves could give evidence only under torture], you will learn all. It is," she said, "Eratosthenes of Oë who is doing this; he has debauched not only your wife, but many others besides, he makes an art of it."

Euphiletus threatened the slave-girl with torture, and she told him the whole story—how the man had approached her after the funeral and at last persuaded her to be his messenger, how the wife herself had at last been persuaded, how they arranged for the man's visits, and how the wife had gone to the women's festival of the Thesmophoria with the man's mother while her husband was in the country. They set a trap for the man so that the husband could see for himself. After four or five days Euphiletus came home from the country and had dinner with a close friend upstairs in his rooms; the friend left and Euphiletus went to bed. According to Euphiletus:

> Eratosthenes, sirs, entered, and the main-servant roused me at once, and told me that he was in the house. Bidding her look after the door, I descended and went out in silence; I called on one friend and another, and found some of them at home, while others were out of town. I took with me as many as I could among those who were there, and so came along. Then we got torches from the nearest shop, and went in; the door was open, as the girl had it in readiness. We pushed open the door of the bedroom, and the first of us to enter were in time to see him lying down by my wife; those who followed saw him standing naked on the bed. I gave him a blow, sirs, which knocked him down, and pulling round his two hands behind his back, and tying them, I asked him why he had the insolence to enter my house. He admitted his guilt; then he besought and implored me not to kill him, but to exact a sum of money. To this I replied, "It is not I who am going to kill you, but our city's law, which you have transgressed and regarded as of less account than your pleasures, choosing rather to commit this foul offence against my wife and my children than to obey the laws like a decent person." Thus it was, sirs, that this man incurred the fate that the laws ordain for those who do such things.

Later Euphiletus had the law pertaining to adulterers read out; the law itself is not included in the speech, but Euphiletus paraphrased it:

> The Court of the Areopagus itself, to which has been assigned . . . the trial of suits for murder, has expressly stated that whoever takes this vengeance on an adulterer caught in the act with his spouse shall not be convicted of murder. And so strongly was the lawgiver convinced of the justice of this in the case of wedded wives, that he even applied the same penalty in the case of mistresses, who are of less account.

The issue is, whether Euphiletus actually caught the man in the act, or, as the prosecutors charge, dragged him in off the street and framed him. Note the care Euphiletus took in providing witnesses; these were necessary, yet his having gone out to look for them takes away somewhat from the spontaneity of the act; in order to prevent the situation from appearing to have been arranged beforehand, as the prosecutor claimed, he emphasizes that many of the friends he looked for were out of town.

Women's Daily Lives

The place of a citizen wife was within the household, not in the public life of the city or in its social life. The wives of citizens did not join their husbands at the dinner parties and symposia that were the central focus of male social and political life. As we saw, Euphiletus entertained his male guest quite separately from his wife. The women who did provide female companionship at male parties were hetairai (see Figure 11-1 on page 229); in fact, the very presence of a woman at a *symposium* was enough to mark her as a hetaira.[14]

The fact that women were expected to live their lives within the oikos does not mean that they literally never went out, or that they had no influence on the running of the oikos. It was the job of the housewife to care for the oikos and its possessions, and to oversee the working of wool and other tasks carried out by younger women and slaves (Figure 11-5). They also nursed sick slaves, and assisted the midwife at childbirths of neighbors and friends. As the plays of Aristophanes show, women also left the house to borrow household items and to visit with female friends and relatives. Within the home, women, especially older women, often had considerable informal influence (Figure 11-6). Despite the pessimistic judgment that, at most, 5 percent of Greek women were literate,[15] in Xenophon's discussion of the running of an oikos, the young wife is expected to be able to read lists of household items,[16] and in some of the speeches preserved from the law courts women are portrayed as well informed about the financial matters of the oikos, knowledgeable about wills, and able to consult family records to prove their point.[17] Some of the best evidence for literacy is pictorial, however, for scenes of women on fifth-century Attic vases often portray them reading (Figure 11-7).

The only role that citizen women could properly play publicly outside the confines of the oikos, however, was in religious rituals and ceremonies. As Euphiletus's story illustrates, funerals were a particular female domain. It was female relatives who prepared the body for burial, and they were also allowed to participate in the mourning and the funeral itself. In service to the gods, a few women, usually from elite families, served as priestesses or in other ritual roles, but all women had some cult duties. All girls were obliged to serve the goddess Artemis in coming-of-age ceremonies before marriage, and after marriage women joined in the annual celebration of Demeter Thesmophorios, the ***Thesmophoria*** (to which Euphiletus's wife went with the mother of her lover!). At the Thesmophoria, women left their homes for three days and camped out together in a polis of women from which men were rigidly excluded. The women celebrated the fertility of the soil and their own bodies, and enjoyed a release from the pressures of their day-to-day life, but within the confines of religious ritual.[19]

Such was the norm for life as a citizen woman. The poorest citizen families were not able to live up to this ideal of female confinement to the oikos, however, for their women were often obliged to go outside the home to help support the family. Such women might work as venders of food or small items in the Agora, or in extensions of their household duties—as wet nurses, midwives (if they were past childbearing age), or wool workers—but such activities were always a threat to their reputation and that of their families.[20]

FIGURE 11-5   Attic black-figure *lekythos* by the Amasis painter. Women weaving and spinning.

Women in metic (resident alien) families probably lived lives of much the same pattern as those of citizen women, with their fate depending on the affluence of their families. Some, without families, worked as hetairai or prostitutes: Pericles' mistress Aspasia was a metic hetaira from Miletus.

Women Who Do Appear in Ancient Sources

We will not find many women active in the events of political history or figuring in the works of historians in the city-states of the Classical period. When they do appear, one must immediately be suspicious. Why has the ancient writer brought them in? In some cases, as in Herodotus' story of Queen Artemisia of Halicarnassos, who fought with the forces of Xerxes and served as an adviser to the king,[21] the women are foreigners who actually did play a role in history (one nonetheless suspects an ulterior motive here; did Herodotus play up her role as the bravest commander in the Persian fleet in order to disparage the courage of the Persians—if a woman was the bravest, how brave could the men have been?). Often the information given is intended as slander, meant to attack a man

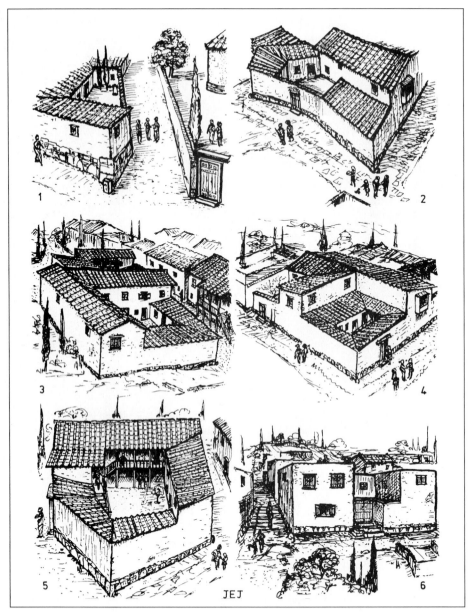

FIGURE 11-6 Private houses of Athens, as reconstructed by J. E. Jones.

through his women. For example, our information about the relation between Aspasia and Pericles comes not from Thucydides, but ultimately from gossip, criticism, and parody. Plato, in *The Menexenus* (a parody of a state funeral oration), portrays Aspasia as writing Pericles' speeches, a claim aimed obviously at the statesman himself.[22] She was said to have operated a brothel,[23] and Aristophanes blames the Peloponnesian War on Pericles' efforts to help some of her "girls" (compare these claims to the criticisms of the activities of some American

FIGURE 11-7 Attic red-figure vase portraying a seated woman reading from a scroll; another woman holds a chest that may contain jewelry or other valuables. Perhaps they are taking inventory of the woman's trousseau, or of the possessions of the oikos, as Xenophon advised.

presidents' wives, such as Hillary Clinton and Eleanor Roosevelt).[24] Similarly, information about another notable woman, this time from a citizen family, comes down to us mainly in slander. This was Elpinike, the daughter of Milti-ades (the victor of Marathon) and half sister of Cimon. She was said to have lived with her brother as a wife (not illegal in Athens since they had different mothers) and to have been the mistress of the famous painter Polygnotus, who was said to have rendered her likeness in a portrayal of Trojan women on a wall painting in a public building (the "Painted Stoa").[25] It was claimed that she was active politically, negotiating with Pericles for Cimon's recall from exile, and earlier, in 463 B.C., pleading with Pericles, who was one of the ten public prosecutors, when Cimon was charged with treason.[26] The picture of Elpinike that emerges, nonetheless, appears to be that of a woman of noble family who took an active part in the culture and politics of Athens; the veil of slander and innuendo through which she is seen reflects not so much the truth about her actions as male disapproval of such activity. Other evidence for the disapproval of female involvement in male affairs appears in the Athenian law that allows a will to be set aside if it was made "under the influence of a woman." Thucydides' advice to the widows of the war dead in the funeral oration for the casualties of the first year of the Peloponnesian War is most typical of the Greek (or at least Athenian) attitude toward women: "To a woman not to show more weakness than is natural to her sex is a great glory, and not to be talked about for good or for evil among men."[27]

Signs of Change

Nevertheless, there are hints in the sources that by the late fifth century B.C. the traditional role of women was being questioned in at least some Athenian circles. The literary sources on Aspasia seem to reflect such a situation, and a number of the plays of Euripides also raise similar questions about the role and treatment of women.[28] Plato, in *The Republic*, sketched an ideal state in which children would be raised communally and women would share the work of the state; even though he maintained that women were inferior to men,[29] he condemned the waste of their talents when they were allowed to live out their lives in the seclusion of the oikos. In Aristophanes' comedy *Ecclesiazusae*, women take over the polis and create a new order that bears a remarkable resemblance to that outlined by the ideas in Plato's *Republic*. Since the comedy was earlier than Plato's work, and it is unlikely that the philosopher borrowed his ideal family structure from comedy, the explanation must be that both reflect an ongoing and widespread debate about traditional family roles. Nevertheless, Greek women did not achieve significantly more rights and freedoms until after the demise of the polis in the Hellenistic period. This, together with the fact that restrictions on women grew as the polis developed, suggests that the search for an explanation for the disparity between the roles allotted to males and females in classical Greece might well focus on the polis itself.[30]

METICS

Another marginalized group that was vital to the maintenance of the good life for Greek citizens consisted of the ***metics,*** or resident aliens. These men and women included immigrants—Greeks from other poleis and non-Greeks—freed slaves, and the descendants of metics. In fifth-century B.C. Athens any non-Athenian who remained in the city for more than a short period of time (probably a month) was obliged to register as a metic and to obtain an Athenian sponsor. Metics could not vote in the Assembly, serve as jurors, hold civic offices, or marry Athenian citizens. They were also excluded from the ownership of land, either for agricultural or for residential purposes. Nevertheless, they were obliged to pay the metic and other taxes and to perform military service. These restrictions obviously limited the ways in which metics could earn a living, and most male metics worked as craftsmen or traders, where they worked beside, and competed on an equal basis with, citizens and slaves. Despite the disadvantages and restrictions of metic status, the economic vitality of Athens continued to attract resident aliens in large numbers, and some metics became men and women of wealth (among these was Kephalos, the father of the orator Lysias, who appears in Plato's *Republic*) or fame (as Pericles's mistress Aspasia). Most metics, however, were probably men and women of modest means.

SLAVES AND SLAVERY

Slaves also played an essential role in the polis without enjoying the rights of citizenship. The polis, and in fact, ancient Greek civilization itself, rested firmly upon a basis of slavery. Ancient philosophers stress that the use of slaves provided male citizens with the leisure necessary for participation in public affairs and government. In fact, however, most Athenian citizens, being small landowners,[31] probably worked the land, often alongside their slaves; and some citizens worked, also alongside their slaves, as craftsmen—for example, Socrates is said to have been a stonemason. Only the upper classes, a tiny portion of the citizen body—and a disproportionately high percentage of the characters who appear in history—were totally free of the need to work, but the ideal nonetheless remained: a free man should not work, or should work only for himself and preferably as a farmer on his own land.

In most Greek cities, slaves were chattel, or property. In others, such as Sparta, they were tied to the land and are better described as serfs. Slaves could be bought and sold at the will of their masters, who could do what they liked with them short of killing them arbitrarily. Slaves could not themselves own property or contract legal marriages. In fact, however, many masters allowed skilled slaves to amass savings, and some slave unions were tolerated, especially when the breeding of slaves was deemed profitable. Usually this was not the case, however, for pregnancy restricted the work capacity of the female slave, and the investment was risky since mortality was high for both mothers and infants.

Although some slaves were home-born and -raised, most were purchased from slave traders. The main sources for slaves were Greece's non-Greek neighbors, "Barbarians" not of Greek speech or culture. Some Greeks, however, did fall into slavery to other Greeks as a result of war or piracy. The reforms of Solon in the sixth century B.C. forbade Athenian citizens from legally enslaving other Athenian citizens, but there were some exceptions: a daughter who committed adultery, a man who was ransomed and failed to repay his ransomer, or an infant that had been exposed and picked up by a stranger to raise. Moreover, Greeks from other states were fair game. In the fifth century B.C., during the Peloponnesian War when Athenian democracy was at its height, the Athenians, on numerous occasions, sold the women and children of a rebellious subject city into slavery.

Slavery was practiced in Greece in all periods from the Bronze Age on, but it became increasingly common as the polis grew and developed in complexity. By the fifth century B.C., probably most Athenian landowners had one or two slaves to work in the house and fields and to carry their armor and equipment during military campaigns.[32] Wealthy men might own dozens—a number to serve in the household and others who brought in income by working outside as craftsmen or entertainers. Such skilled slaves probably lived reasonably comfortable lives, for one criticism made of the Athenian democracy was that you could not tell a slave from a free citizen when you met one on the street.[33]

The polis itself also owned considerable numbers of slaves; they were used as clerical workers and as policemen (the Scythian archers in Athens). Slaves were not used as rowers, however; as noted earlier, the cooperation necessary ruled out the use of potentially recalcitrant labor. In the private economy slaves also worked as business agents and bankers. Probably the worst—and shortest—life for a slave was as a worker in the mines: the Athenians relied on thousands of slaves to operate the vital silver mines at Laurion (in southern Attica), where working conditions were both difficult and dangerous.

It was sometimes possible for slaves to buy their freedom. Skilled slaves who earned money for their masters were often allowed to keep part of their earnings with the hope of eventually buying their own freedom. Even as freedmen, however, former slaves still owed service to their former masters and could not aspire to citizenship, either for themselves or for their descendants. They could live in the city only as metics. Thus the prospects of Greek slaves differed radically from those of Roman slaves, whose offspring, if born after the parents were freed, were legally both freeborn and citizens.

These three groups, all permanently without citizenship rights, provided the foundation upon which the achievements of the classical Greeks rested. They rarely appear in the pages of traditional history, yet it was their work that made possible the male political life that dominates these pages. In assessing the Greek achievement, we must therefore always keep in mind the conditions of the lives of these others, as well as the political activities and achievements of the male citizen minority.

SUGGESTIONS FOR FURTHER READING

On women and the family, see S. Pomeroy, *Goddesses, Whores, Wives, and Slaves: Women in Classical Antiquity* (1975); and E. Fantham, H. P. Foley, N. B. Kampen, S. B. Pomeroy, and H. A. Shapiro, *Women in the Classical World* (1994); on childbirth, N. Demand, *Birth, Death and Motherhod in Classical Greece* (1994); on Greek slavery, Y. Garlan, *Slavery in Ancient Greece* (1988); on metics, D. Whitehead, *The Ideology of the Athenian Metic* (1977).

ENDNOTES

1. For example, Cynthia Patterson, "Hai Attikai: The Other Athenians," *Helios* 13 (1986), 49–67, holds that they were citizens, but not in the same sense that men were: they could not vote or hold office, were restricted in their rights to hold property and carry out legal actions, and were not registered on the citizen rolls of their deme. Whether they *were* citizens in some essential way is a modern question; what was at issue in classical Athens after Pericles' citizenship law of 451 B.C., which required both parents to be citizens in order to pass on citizen status, was whether they qualified in certain defined ways so as to be able to transmit citizenship to male offspring. The lack of registration of "citizen" girls meant that this could be determined only by rather indirect means: by appealing to the fact that they had been married with a dowry, or by appealing to witnesses to a formal marriage, or to evidence that the family treated them as rightful members of the oikos.

    This issue of *Helios* also has other interesting articles about women in antiquity.

2. The speeches of Isaeus dealing with inheritance (for example, "On the Estate of Ciron") and the private orations of Demosthenes (for example, "Against Onetor I" and "Against Neaera") are especially useful. They can be found in English translation in the Loeb Library series.

3. [Dem.] 59.122, Loeb translation.

4. An interesting article about these women is C. Starr, "An Evening with the Flute-girls," *La Parola del Passato* 183 (1978), 401–410.

5. See S. M. Venit, "The Caputi Hydria and Working Women in Classical Athens," *Classical World* 81 (1988), 265–272.

6. D. Engels, "The Problem of Female Infanticide in the Graeco-Roman World," *Classical Philology* 75 (1980), 112–120; Mark Golden, "Demography and the Exposure of Girls at Athens," *Phoenix* 35 (1981), 316–331; W. V. Harris, "The Theoretical Possibility of Extensive Infanticide in the Graeco-Roman World," *Classical Quarterly* 32 (1982), 114–116; D. Engels, "The Use of Historical Demography in Ancient History," *Classical Philology* 34 (1984), 386–393.

7. On marriage in Athens generally, see Cynthia Patterson, "Marriage and the Married Woman in Athenian Law," in S. B. Pomeroy, *Women's History and Ancient History* (1991), 48–72.

8. On dowry, which varied in matters of detail in different poleis, see David M. Schaps, *Economic Rights of Women in Ancient Greece* (1979). The text describes the Athenian situation.

9. Schaps (above, n. 8), Appendix IV.

10. These can be found in the Hippocratic gynecological treatises, *Diseases of Women* and *Na-*

ture of Women; the Greek text with a French translation exists in the edition of Littré (1839), and an English translation of *Diseases of Women* I and II, by Ann Hanson, "Continuity and Change: Three Case Studies in Hippocratic Gynecological Therapy and Theory," in S. B. Pomeroy, *Women's History and Ancient History* (1991), 73–110.

11. On the problems of pregnancy and childbirth, see N. Demand, *Birth, Death, and Motherhood in Classical Greece* (1994).

12. See Demand (above, n. 11).

13. Lysias 1, 6–31, Loeb translation, W. R. M. Lamb.

14. An argument used against Neaera, Dem. 59.

15. William V. Harris, *Ancient Literacy* (1989), 106–107; S. Cole, "Could Greek Women Read and Write?" in *Reflections of Women in Antiquity*, Helene P. Foley, ed. (1981), 219–244.

16. Xen., *Oec.* 9.10.

17. Lys. 32.11–18; Dem. 41; Aesch. 1.170 refers to wealthy young men whose property is managed by their widowed mothers.

18. Harris (above, n. 15), 107, presents the evidence, although here too he is pessimistic, suggesting that these female figures are often meant to portray the Muses, or Sappho, or at least hetairai.

19. Froma I. Zeitlin, "Cultic Models of the Female: Rites of Dionysus and Demeter," *Arethusa* 15 (1982), 129–157.

20. See Dem. 57, esp. 30–31, 35.

21. Hdt. 7.99; 8.68–69, 87–88, 93, 101, 103, 107.

22. The *Menexenus* may not be a genuine work of Plato's. Other evidence about Aspasia comes from Plutarch, *Pericles*, who relates some of the gossip and comic attacks of the day; Aeschines, the Socratic philosopher who wrote a dialogue, *The Aspasia* (incompletely preserved), in which Aspasia criticizes the manners and training of the women of her time; and Xenophon, who mentions her favorably in *Oecon.* 52.14.

23. By the comic poet Hermippus, cited by Plut., *Per.* 31.

24. Ar., *Acharnians* 524ff.; Plut., *Per.* 25, 30.

25. Plut., *Cimon* 4; similarly, Phidias was said to have portrayed the likenesses of himself and Pericles on the shield of the great statue of Athena in the Parthenon, Plut., *Per.* 31.

26. Plut., *Per* 10.

27. Thuc. 2.45, Jowett, tr.

28. See esp. Euripides, *Medea.*

29. Plato, *Rep.* 455d, *Laws* 781b, *Tim.* 42b.

30. On this, see Demand (above, n. 11).

31. See Plato, *Rep.* 565a.

32. For a discussion of the evidence for the extent of slave owning, see V. D. Hanson, "Thucydides and the Desertion of Attic Slaves during the Decelean War," *Classical Antiquity* 11 (1992), 210–228.

33. Pseudo-Xenophon, *Constitution of the Athenians* (also known as the "Old Oligarch").

CHAPTER TWELVE

Thucydides and the Peloponnesian War

he development of Athens into an imperial power, enforcing its will upon its allies turned subjects and openly appropriating the funds of the League for the creation of monuments of imperial splendor, naturally provided a focal point for the fears and jealousies of the other Greek poleis. Sparta and Corinth felt especially threatened by Athenian infringements on their spheres of influence (discussed below), and they had as allies many of the other cities of the Peloponnesus. Thus the scene was set for a major conflict between the poleis of the Peloponnesus, whose greatest strength lay in their hoplite infantry forces, and Athens, whose advantage lay in its naval power.

PRELIMINARIES TO WAR

Even though the scene was set, actual war was slow to develop. Thucydides deals at some length with two events that stood out as precursors of war. In 434/3 B.C. the Athenians came into conflict with Corinth when they accepted an alliance with that city's colony, Corcyra, joining the Corcyreans in a sea battle against their mother city. This breach with Corinth then caused the Athenians to reconsider the stability of their situation in the Chalkidic peninsula to the north, where their principal ally, Potidaea, was another Corinthian foundation. The Athenians demanded evidence of Potidaea's loyalty: the Potidaeans were to pull down their south-facing walls, which were not needed for protection against Macedonia, to give hostages, and to reject the magistrates that the Corinthians annually sent to them. The Potidaeans refused these conditions and appealed to the Spartans for help. Bolstered by a Spartan promise of assistance if the Athenians should attack, the Potidaeans rose in revolt against the Athenians.

While Thucydides describes these political and military events in considerable detail, he gives little attention to another, basically economic, action taken by the Athenians. It was probably in 433/2 B.C. that the city passed the Megarian Decree, by whose terms Megara was forbidden access to Athenian markets and to all harbors in the Athenian Empire. Ancient sources saw the decree as a cause of severe economic difficulties in Megara and as *the* cause of the war.[1] Even Thucydides (1.139) attributed to the Spartans the repeated claim that the lifting of the decree would prevent war. Nevertheless, Thucydides (1.23) saw the true cause of the conflict not in any immediate and specific occasion for complaint, military or economic, but in a deep underlying fear of the growing power of Athens.

In contrast to Thucydides, modern historians attribute considerable importance to economic factors in analyzing the causes and course of the war.[2] Challenges to Athenian power were challenges to its empire, and Athens was dependent for much of its prosperity upon the continuation of that empire. Tribute payments were used for direct military expenditures—such as the building and outfitting of ships, the payment of wages to rowers, and the provision of other military forces—as well as for financing the Periclean building program.[3] A stream of well-to-do visitors from the subject states came to Athens to pursue their cases in the Athenian courts. They spent money on temporary housing, food, and other necessities, and their cases were heard by Athenian juries, who were paid for their services; both visitor spending and jury pay contributed considerably to the income of ordinary people. Aristophanes' outline of the balance sheet of empire in *The Wasps* leaves little doubt that the people were aware of the importance of empire to the Athenian economy.

But payments of tribute and spending by visitors would not suffice to maintain the empire if certain vital imports could not be maintained, and a desire to secure the provision of these goes far to explain Athenian actions during the war. First in importance was grain. By the late fifth century B.C. the city was dependent upon imports of grain to feed its population, and much of this grain came from the Black Sea area. Thus control of key points along the route to the Black Sea—the north Aegean coast and the Hellespont—was crucial for Athens. Second, timber was a vital import. The building of ships required timber, which Attica could not supply. The main source for timber was in the north, in Thrace and Macedonia. There were also vast resources of silver and gold in that area; these had provided the financial basis for Peisistratus' successful bid for tyranny, and Thucydides was probably supported in his exile in the north by family interests in the mines. Athens thus had several important economic reasons to maintain control in the north Aegean, and in 436 B.C. the city established Amphipolis on the river Strymon at a vital crossing point for east-west land travelers. The foundation was made after a long and bloody struggle with a hostile local population. Throughout the course of the Peloponnesian War it is often possible to identify similar economic factors behind incidents that Thucydides saw in politico-military terms. For example, the fact that Sicily was a potential alternative source of grain helps to explain the major expedition that the Athenians mounted there in 416 B.C., ostensibly in support of a small ally in a local dispute.

THE WAR UNDER PERICLES

The First Year of the War

The spark of war was provided by a series of relatively minor military clashes in 431 B.C. involving the small city of Plataea and Athens. Plataea had long been an Athenian ally, but the city lay within Boeotian territory, and the Thebans considered it to be within their sphere of influence and properly a member of the Boeotian League. (A study of Map 12 will show why this was a reasonable position.) In 431 B.C. the Thebans tried to seize the city. The Plataeans successfully drove out the attackers, but in the aftermath they violated the norms of Greek warfare by massacring 180 Thebans whom they had taken prisoner. The Plataeans anticipated retaliation by Thebes and appealed to Athens; the Athenians responded by sending a garrison to reinforce their ally and evacuate the noncombatants. Sparta similarly became involved in the conflict by virtue of its alliance with Thebes. Both sides prepared for full-scale war, seeking support from uncommitted states, and even from Persia.

Enthusiasm for war was high. As Thucydides notes, on both sides there were large numbers of young men with no experience of war who saw it as an adventure. The general feeling among the Greeks was heavily in favor of the Spartans, who were viewed as the liberators of a Greece enslaved by Athenian power. In Athens itself, Pericles persuaded the Athenians to trust their fate to their sea power. The people living in the country villages, following his advice, moved into the city and abandoned the countryside to devastation by the Spartans. The Long Walls, which connected the city with the port at Piraeus, and Athenian control of the sea, would assure that the city's needs could be supplied by imports, even under wartime conditions. Pericles also warned against attempts to extend the empire, advising the Athenians to limit themselves to preserving what they had.

The first year of the war brought a Peloponnesian invasion that sorely tested the self-control of the Athenians cooped up in the city. But Pericles bolstered popular resolve by a number of positive actions: Athenians raided the coast of the Peloponnesus, laid waste to the territory of Megara, and expelled the inhabitants of the island of Aegina, replacing them with Athenians from the crowded city. In the northern Aegean Pericles scored diplomatic advances by securing the alliance of the kings of Thrace and Macedonia (Thuc. 2.23–32). As morale fell in the polis, he refused to call the Assembly, thus preventing the discouraged people from acting on the basis of their immediate frustrations. He also shared in their sacrifices, donating his country properties to the state,

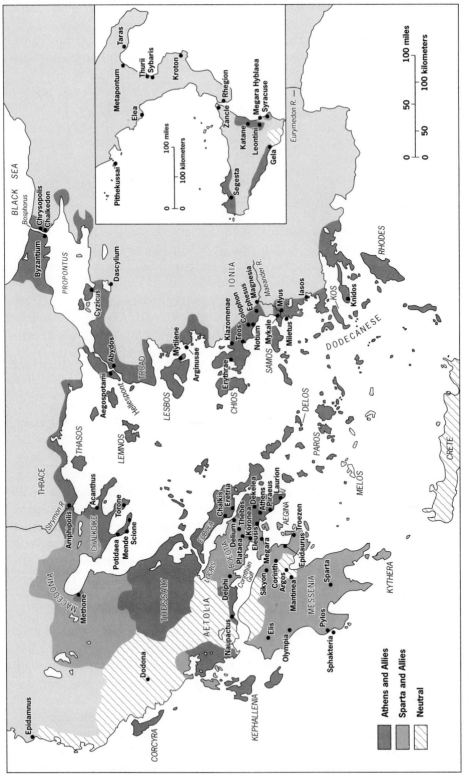

MAP 12   The Peloponnesian War.

Inset (Magna Graecia / Sicily):

Taras
Thurii
Sybaris
Metapontum
Kroton
Elea
Rhegion
Zancle
Megara Hyblaea
Pithekussai
Katane
Syracuse
Leontini
Gela
Segesta

Eurymedon R.

100 miles
100 kilometers

100 miles
100 kilometers

Main map labels:

BLACK SEA
Bosphorus
Chrysopolis
Chalkedon
Byzantium
PROPONTUS
Dascylium
Cyzicus
Abydos
TROAD
Hellespont
Aegospotami
Mytilene
Arginusae
LESBOS
Klazomenae
Teos Colophon
Erythrae
Ephesus
Magnesia
Maeander R.
Notium
Mykale
CHIOS
SAMOS
Myus
Miletus
Iasos
IONIA
KOS
Knidos
DODECANESE
RHODES
THASOS
THRACE
LEMNOS
Strymon R.
Amphipolis
Acanthus
Torone
CHALKIDIKE
Mende
Scione
Potidaea
MACEDONIA
Methone
Dodona
DELOS
PAROS
MELOS
KYTHERA
CRETE
CORCYRA
Epidamnus
KEPHALLENIA
AETOLIA
LOCRIS
Naupactus
Delphi
Corinthian Gulf
EUBOEA
Chalkis
Eretria
Delium
Thebes
BOEOTIA
Plataea
Koronea
Eleusis
Dekelea
Athens
Piraeus
Laurion
AEGINA
Megara
Troezen
Epidaurus
Sikyon
Corinth
Argos
Mantinea
MESSENIA
Elis
Olympia
Sparta
Pylos
Sphakteria
THESSALY

Athens and Allies
Sparta and Allies
Neutral

for he realized that the Spartan general might spare his estates in order to strike at his popularity and effectiveness as a leader by inspiring resentment in the Athenians.

In the winter following the first year of the war, a public funeral was held in Athens for the men who had fallen. It was at this low point in the mood of the Athenians that Thucydides reports Pericles' famous *Funeral Oration* that sums up the greatness of Athens.

S O U R C E A N A L Y S I S

THUCYDIDES 2.34–46 (THE FUNERAL ORATION). Such annual civic funeral orations were traditional in Athens and provided an occasion for the display of patriotic sentiments.[4] Pericles' speech, as reported by Thucydides, was an encomium on Athenian democracy delivered at a particular moment in Athenian history, yet it is often presented as a characterization of all democracy. As we shall see, however, even Athens failed to live up to this picture as the war progressed. To see this most clearly, it is helpful to note the key words that Thucydides uses to express the values of Athenian democracy, and to watch for their recurrence in later passages.

The Plague in Athens

In the following summer, as the Spartans again invaded Attica, an unexpected and unforeseeable blow struck the Athenians. Crowded together in the city, in keeping with the Periclean strategy, they fell victim to a virulent plague that was spreading throughout the eastern Mediterranean. People died in large numbers, and no preventive measures or remedies were of any avail. It has been estimated that a quarter, or perhaps even a third, of the population was lost. The plague returned twice more, in 429 B.C. and 427/6 B.C.; it killed Pericles' two legitimate sons, and the leader himself died during this time, probably as a result of the disease.

Thucydides' account of the plague is a masterpiece that provided a model for later accounts of plagues, ranging from the Roman philosopher-poet Lucretius' poetic account of the Athenian plague to descriptions of the Black Death in early modern Europe. His description was based on personal observation and his own experience as a victim of the illness, but it was framed in terms of contemporary medical theory. His intention was to provide as complete and accurate a description as possible, so that the illness could be recognized should it ever recur. Yet, despite his detailed description, modern scholars are still not able to agree on the identity of the disease. Such investigations consider both the symptoms and the epidemiological pattern of the disease. For example, Thucydides' statement (6.26) that the military rolls were full again by 415 B.C., and his account of large losses among the troops, provide evidence that the illness struck adults more heavily than it did children.

S O U R C E   A N A L Y S I S

THUCYDIDES 2.47–55. Thucydides' detailed description of the plague, following as it does immediately upon the idealism expressed in the Funeral Oration, creates an especially dramatic effect that can hardly have been accidental. What other devices does Thucydides use to enhance the drama of the situation? What elements seem to reflect contemporary medical theory?

The Athenian plague was clearly not the bubonic plague, or Black Death, of the fourteenth century A.D., for the characteristic symptom of the bubo is not found in Thucydides' description. Other candidates that have been suggested are measles, typhus, ergotism, and even influenza complicated by toxic shock syndrome. The case for typhus seems strongest both epidemiologically—the age groups affected fit the pattern—and from the standpoint of the symptoms. Typhus is characterized by fever and a rash, is known as a "doctors' disease" from its frequent incidence among caregivers, confers immunity, and involves gangrene of the extremities. Further, patients during a typhus epidemic in the First World War were reported to have jumped into water tanks to alleviate extreme thirst, which Thucydides describes Athenian victims as doing. But the fit is not exact. The rash is difficult to identify on the basis of Thucydides' description alone (even modern medical texts use pictures to supplement verbal descriptions of rashes), and the mental confusion typical of typhus may not fit Thucydides' description. In the long run, however, all such attempts at identification may prove futile: diseases develop and change over time, and it may be, as A. J. Holladay and J. C. F. Poole argue, that the plague of the fifth century B.C. no longer exists today in a recognizable form.[5]

The social, political, and economic effects of the Athenian plague may be inferred from analysis of studies of the effects of the Black Death in Europe.[6] The loss of perhaps a third of the Athenian population, and the large number of sudden and untimely deaths, must have severely affected normal inheritance patterns. Often distant relatives suddenly became heirs to unexpected fortunes, as Thucydides notes. Similarly, the normal pool of aristocratic candidates for positions of political influence and power was depleted. As noted earlier, both of

Pericles' sons by his Athenian wife, who would have been natural candidates for political leadership, died. Pericles then made a special plea to set aside the citizenship law (which he himself had sponsored in 451 B.C.) so that his son by the Milesian Aspasia could be declared a citizen. Then the leader himself died, probably a victim of the disease or its aftereffects. Although (as noted above) the military rolls were full again by 415 B.C., the older generation that filled offices and provided leadership was not so easily replaced.

THE WAR FROM PERICLES' DEATH TO THE PEACE OF NICIAS

The Rise of the Demagogues

After the death of Pericles, the war entered a new phase, at least in part as the result of the long-term sociological and political effects of the plague noted above. Furthermore, the "new morality" of selfish hedonism described by Thucydides changed the political scene at Athens drastically, and for the worse, at least in the eyes of the historian. He saw the new leaders as lacking in the statesmanlike qualities of Pericles, who had had the intelligence and foresight to formulate the most advantageous policy and the strength to lead the people even when they failed to perceive their own long-term interests. The new political leaders did not so much lead the people as pander to their whims—they were in fact led by the people, *demagogues.*

Of these demagogues, the most notorious in our sources was Kleon. We have already seen Aristophanes' devastating portrayal of the man in *The Wasps,* and Thucydides' depiction essentially agrees with this picture, although it is drawn in the more sober terms appropriate for history. Kleon's actions embodied for Thucydides the unfortunate direction that the Athenian conduct of the war took after the death of Pericles, and so we will focus on Kleon as we consider the course of the war up to the Peace of Nicias in 421 B.C., which followed the demagogue's death. But first a brief outline of the events of the period will provide a context for this discussion.

In 430 B.C., Potidaea surrendered at last, after a long and expensive siege by the Athenians. In the following year the Peloponnesians refrained from invading Attica, fearing a renewed outbreak of the plague; instead they began a siege of Plataea that lasted for two years.

In the summer of 428 B.C., the island of Lesbos, whose largest polis was Mytilene, seized the opportunity to revolt from an Athens weakened by the effects of sustained war and by another attack of the plague. Lesbos was one of the most important subject-allies of Athens, and one of only three that still maintained a fleet. The island's preparations for revolt, which included a *synoikism* (the unification, political or physical, of Greek settlements) of its cities with the largest, Mytilene, were disclosed to the Athenians by Mytilenian dissidents. The Athenians, in their weakened condition, were anxious to avoid war on yet another front, but their attempts to dissuade the rebels, who pinned their hopes on Spartan assistance, were unsuccessful. The Spartans, however, dragged their feet, and finally the Mytilenians were compelled to surrender.

The angry Athenian Assembly voted to punish the Mytilenians by executing the entire male population and enslaving the women and children. If we compare this punishment with those meted out, before the war, to recalcitrant allies, the drastic change in Athenian policy is evident: the Athenian condemnation included even Athenian sympathizers who had informed them of the plot. By the following day, however, many had repented their hasty decision, and it was decided to debate the issue anew in the Assembly. Kleon argued against mercy (see the Source Analysis on page 256), but he failed to persuade the Assembly, which revoked the sentence. After a dramatic race across the Aegean, the ship carrying the report of the change in the Athenians' decision arrived just in time to prevent the executions.

In 427 B.C., after a two-year siege, the Spartans succeeded in taking Plataea when the Plataeans surrendered on the promise of a fair trial. The Spartan "trial," however, consisted of a single question: What had they done to benefit the Spartans? Those who had done nothing to aid the Spartans were summarily executed. In the same year vicious civil strife broke out in Corcyra, and Thucydides described the collapse of traditional values in a set piece intended to illustrate the moral degradation caused by the war.

In 425 B.C., the Athenians obtained a significant edge over the Spartans, by accident, as Thucydides portrays it. One of their generals, Demosthenes, happened to be sailing around the Peloponnesus as a passenger on an expedition headed for Sicily when he suddenly conceived the idea of fortifying Pylos, a site on the west coast of the Peloponnesus in Messenia, about 45 miles from Sparta. Demosthenes established an Athenian camp there (again, as Thucydides portrays it) as a result of serendipity: a storm temporarily stranded the expedition, and the stranded soldiers, bored, spontaneously took to fortifying the spot as a means of keeping busy.

The Spartans, alarmed by this intrusion into their territory, immediately sent a hoplite force to the uninhabited offshore island of Sphakteria, which could serve as a base for an attack on the Athenians. But they were unable to dislodge the Athenians; even worse, they lost control of Sphakteria and their men on the island were marooned, virtual hostages of the Athenians. Intent on getting their men back, the Spartans sued for peace. But the Athenians, following the advice of Kleon, refused the Spartan offers of peace. The Spartans then turned to drastic measures to supply the men on the island, offering freedom to any helot who could get food across to them. Their success in provisioning the men in this way raised concerns in Athens: winter was approaching, and the

Athenians realized that the weather would soon force them to abandon their naval blockade of the island. Now they risked losing the Spartan prisoners without gaining anything. Anger grew at Kleon for his advice to reject the Spartan peace proposal. The demagogue responded with an offer to go himself to bring the hostages back to Athens within twenty days, an apparently rash promise that he was able to carry out successfully (see the Source Analysis, on page 256).

In 424 B.C. the Athenians departed from Periclean policy by attempting to extend their empire into Boeotia, an effort that had been unsuccessful earlier in the century (see Chapter 10). Their plan for a simultaneous attack on three fronts misfired when one of the generals mistook the day of attack. The Athenians did manage to fortify Delium, a Boeotian site on the coast, but the Thebans soon defeated them in battle, inflicting heavy losses and driving them out (Thuc. 4.89–101).

In the meantime, in 424 B.C. a more serious threat to Athenian interests arose when the Spartan general Brasidas marched north to court Athenian subjects in that area. The Greek and local population had been in active revolt since 432 B.C., and recent Athenian successes had alarmed them, for they feared that Athens might now feel free to send a major force against them. They requested assistance from Sparta, and a number of factors contributed to their receiving a favorable response. The Spartans saw an opportunity to enroll some of the more enterprising helots, who had been emboldened by the Spartan defeat at Sphakteria, into Brasidas's army, thus removing a dangerous element from Lakonia. Moreover, some in Sparta perceived Brasidas himself, with his military successes and persuasive abilities, as a threat, and they were happy to see him out of the way, campaigning in the north.[7] Finally, the Spartans hoped that success in the north would gain territory that might be swapped for the prisoners from Sphakteria.

Amphipolis was lost to Athens as a result of the Spartan decision to send Brasidas north, and the loss was a serious one for Athens. As noted earlier, Amphipolis commanded the crossing of the Strymon River, the main east-west route in the north, and the area was a vital source of the timber Athens needed for shipbuilding, as well as the site of lucrative silver and gold mines. At the time Thucydides was serving as a general and was at nearby Thasos with a few ships; his failure to reach the city in time to put down the revolt before the arrival of Spartan support resulted in his exile—and thus inadvertently gave him the opportunity to write his history (Thuc. 4.103–107).

In 423 B.C., Athens and Sparta concluded a one-year truce based on the status quo. Two days later, according to Thucydides, the city of Scione in Thrace revolted from Athens. In contrast to the Mytilenian affair, the fate of Scione is not presented as a dramatic set piece by Thucydides, and its story must be pieced together from scattered references. Yet despite this understated, undramatic presentation, it too represented a significant step in the downward spiral

Thucydides and Aristophanes on Kleon[8]

B oth Thucydides and Aristophanes provide extensive portraits of Kleon, and it is interesting to compare their treatments, bearing in mind the differing aims of the two authors and the different genres in which they worked.

The Mytilenian debate provides a graphic picture of Thucydides' opinions of the new direction in Athenian leadership:

THUCYDIDES 3.36–50.   Note the key words and ideas in these speeches; consider Kleon's views on rhetoric and his interpretation of justice and right and compare his views with those expressed by Pericles in the Funeral Oration.

Thucydides' account of the Pylos affair provides further insight into his attitudes toward Kleon as a political leader, as well as a good example of the way in which historians are able to turn apparent success into failure by the way they present facts.

THUCYDIDES 4.27–41.   Note the role played by Demosthenes, who had originally been responsible for the fortification of Pylos. In particular, consider Thucydides' account of an earlier incident in which Demosthenes had fought during the war: 3.96–98. How might this experience have affected the conduct of Kleon's expedition?

Thucydides was not alone in seeing the demagogue as the undeserving victor in the Pylos situation. We have already met Kleon in *The Wasps* of Aristophanes, produced in 422. Two years earlier, in 424 B.C., the comic poet had made his most sustained attack on the demagogue in *The Knights*, which focuses specifically on the Pylos incident.

ARISTOPHANES' *KNIGHTS*.   How many references are there to Kleon's theft of Demosthenes' victory? Was Aristophanes' satire fair?

When Kleon appears for the last time in the pages of Thucydides' history, he is a general in his own right, fighting in the battle of Amphipolis. Thucydides is merciless to the end in his treatment of the demagogue, portraying him as deserting his troops while they were still resisting the enemy, and fleeing for his life, only to be shot in the back by a barbarian.

THUCYDIDES 5.6–11.   What devices does Thucydides use to influence his readers in this passage?

of Athenian political morality. What was at issue was the timing of the revolt. While the Spartans claimed that the people of Scione had rebelled before the armistice and thus that their claim to independence was part of the status quo protected by the treaty, the Athenians maintained that the revolt had occurred after the agreement. (Thucydides accepted the Athenian claim.) On the motion of Kleon, a decree was passed to recapture Scione and to put its inhabitants to death (Thuc. 4.122). A fleet was sent out, and the city was besieged. When the Athenians finally succeeded in reducing the city in 421 B.C., there were no second thoughts about harsh sentences: the men were put to death, and the women and children sold into slavery (Thuc. 5.32).

In 422 B.C., Kleon carried a resolution in the Assembly to the effect that Amphipolis should be retaken, and the Athenians, under his command, marched against the city. In the ensuing battle, Kleon fell, shot in the back by a light-armed Thracian peltast. In contrast, Thucydides reports that Brasidas fell nobly in the battle, having lived long enough to learn of the victory of his men. He was buried with public honors in the agora of Amphipolis, where the citizens accorded him worship as the true founder of the city, replacing Hagnon, the original Athenian founder (Thuc. 5.11). (See the Source Analysis on the facing page.)

THE PEACE OF NICIAS, 421 B.C.

The deaths of both Kleon and Brasidas during the battle of Amphipolis removed the two chief obstacles to a peace settlement, and both cities felt the need for a respite from war. The Spartans were anxious to regain the hostages taken at Pylos; moreover, their thirty-year truce with Argos, which had been concluded in 451 B.C., was about to expire, threatening them with hostilities on a new front. In Athens, the loss of Amphipolis was added to the city's losses in the battle of Delium in Boeotia. Thus the two sides concluded a treaty, called the *Peace of Nicias* (the text is cited by Thucydides [5.18]). Thucydides remarks that for six years and ten months they abstained from invasions of each other's territory, but in no other way could it have been called a period of peace.

Among the many hostile actions carried out by both sides during the Peace of Nicias, Thucydides picked the suppression of the small island of Melos as a subject for a set piece. While this was apparently a minor affair, by his presentation Thucydides elevated it to a position as linchpin of his history. As we saw in the last chapter, beginning with prewar punishments of medizing Greeks (Greeks who had gone over to the Persians), Athens had moved on to the compulsion of allies, becoming increasingly violent. Mytilene escaped total destruction by a hair. Scione was destroyed. Finally even Melos—a neutral city which simply asked to be left alone—fell victim to what can at this point only be called Athenian imperial greed.

S O U R C E   A N A L Y S I S

T HUCYDIDES 5.84–116.   The dialogue form in which this incident is presented itself serves to call attention to the significance of the passage.
Thucydides nowhere else used this form, which was later employed in reporting
philosophical discussions: the most familiar examples are Plato's Socratic dialogues. In the Melian dialogue a philosophical topic—the nature of justice—
makes the dialogue form especially relevant. Consider the values expressed in
each side's arguments, and compare these values with those expressed in the Funeral Oration and the Mytilenian debate.

THE SICILIAN EXPEDITION

The Sicilian expedition, which was the largest military expedition up to that
time in history, and which led to the greatest disaster Athens faced until its final
defeat, began in a small way. The insignificant city of Segesta in Sicily, with
which Athens was in alliance, hoped to gain some advantage for itself in its local
squabbles with a neighbor by exploiting its relation with its powerful ally.
Athens listened to Segesta's requests for aid primarily because expansion to
Sicily, a rich grain-producing area, had long been a temptation for a city with a
perennial need for grain. Pericles, of course, had warned against expansion during the war, and Athenian involvement in Sicily would signal a major deviation
from his policies (although it could be argued that the city was not at this time
technically at war). Thucydides presents both sides of the question in the form
of a debate in the Assembly between two of the generals who were to lead the
expedition—Nicias, a cautious and conservative older man known for his sponsorship of the Peace of Nicias, and Alkibiades, a wealthy and dashing young aristocrat who had been brought up in the household of Pericles, as his ward. As
Thucydides portrays Alkibiades, he is a charismatic but ambiguous character,
and our other sources suggest that his enthusiastic, but erratic, political adven-
turing left other Athenians puzzled and undecided about him as well. He is portrayed by Plato in *The Symposium* as a young, handsome, but spoiled admirer of
Socrates who tries unsuccessfully to seduce the philosopher. In his efforts to dissuade the Assembly from the expedition, Nicias magnified the forces that he believed would be needed, but the Assembly, swept by enthusiasm for the project,
voted an even larger force—and even that, in the end, proved to be insufficient.

On the eve of the departure, near panic struck Athens when vandals attacked
the Herms throughout the city. These were figures of the god Hermes, in the
form of a pillar with the head of the god and an erect phallus, which stood at

house gateways and crossroads to protect travelers. Accusations were also made that the "Eleusinian Mysteries" had been profaned in secret celebrations. Many were arrested. Alkibiades was among those accused of involvement, but, because of his popularity with the men, his enemies did not dare to have him arrested while the army was still in Athens. They deemed it better to arrest him en route to Segesta and bring him back to Athens to stand trial when the army was no longer there to protest.

In fact, the arrest warrant was served to Alkibiades as the expedition was on its way to Sicily. At first Alkibiades acceded to the arrest, but he later escaped and made his way to Sparta, where he traded advice for sanctuary. He counseled the Spartans to send reinforcements to Syracuse with a capable general and to fortify an outpost at Dekelea in Attica for strategic reasons.

When the expedition arrived in Sicily the remaining generals followed the strategy Alkibiades had proposed, one of sailing around and trying to attract allies, but they had little success. In the first engagement of the war, a battle in the harbor at Syracuse, they did achieve a victory, but Nicias failed to follow it up. Instead he ordered the fleet back to the Athenian camp at Katane, giving the Syracusans the opportunity to prepare their defenses.

In 414 B.C. the Athenians attempted a siege of Syracuse, but their encircling wall was blocked by a Syracusan counterwall. A long, drawn-out, and indecisive contest of wall building ensued, in which the second Athenian commander, Lamachus, was killed. This left Nicias alone in command, and he was sick, suffering from a debilitating kidney ailment. Athenian prospects deteriorated further when the Spartan reinforcements arrived in Syracuse, as Alkibiades had advised, accompanied by a talented general, Gylippus. On mainland Greece the Spartans also followed Alkibiades' advice to fortify Dekelea, which gave them a base for damaging year-round attacks on the countryside of Attica.

Nicias appealed to the Assembly for more forces and for relief from his command because of his illness. The Assembly refused to relieve him, but ordered a second, even larger expedition to sail to Sicily, under the command of the general Demosthenes.

On the day before Demosthenes arrived, the Syracusans won a major sea victory. When Demosthenes landed he saw that the only hope now lay with the capture of the Syracusan counterwall. Hoping to accomplish this, he ordered a daring night battle, but the attempt failed. Demosthenes then concluded that the most reasonable course of action was to withdraw the Athenian troops from Sicily. Nicias, however, fearing condemnation by the Athenian Assembly, and misled by a wishful hope that the Syracusans would soon run out of money, refused to agree. Demosthenes honored Nicias' decision because he believed that Nicias had more information about affairs in Syracuse than he, in fact, had. And so the Athenians' best opportunity to escape was lost through fear on one side and misapprehension on the other.

When Demosthenes finally succeeded in persuading Nicias to withdraw, an eclipse of the moon took place (August 27). The men saw it as an omen, as the soothsayers held, and urged the commanders to wait. Nicias himself, whom Thucydides describes as excessively given to divination, refused even to discuss leaving until the three times nine days had passed, according to the soothsayers' decree. But the soothsayers' advice proved fatal. On September 3, the Athenian fleet fought and lost a battle in the harbor, and the Syracusans began to blockade its entrance. On September 9 the Athenians suffered their final defeat at sea when they were unable to break through the harbor blockade. At this point, the men were so demoralized that they refused to reboard the ships, and the only option was to retreat by land.

But again the Athenian departure was postponed. With the Syracusan troops in drunken celebration, Gylippus realized that the only way to pursue the victory was to delay the Athenian march until his troops had recovered from the aftereffects of their celebrations. Accordingly, he sent a spy to the Athenians with a false warning that the roads were all watched and that they should wait. The Athenians fell for the ruse and waited for two days. As a result, when they finally set out in ignoble retreat, abandoning the sick and wounded and leaving the dead unburied, the Syracusans had recovered and were ready for them. The entire army was soon slaughtered or captured. Both generals were executed.

S O U R C E   A N A L Y S I S

Some Highlights of the Sicilian Expedition

T HUCYDIDES 6.8–32.   The debate of Alkibiades and Nicias in the Athenian Assembly on the wisdom of the expedition to Sicily reveals not only the situation of Athens on the eve of the expedition, but also much about the character of these two men as seen by Thucydides. What characteristics does Thucydides show the two embodying by the speeches that he attributes to them?

THUCYDIDES 6.52–61 (THE MUTILATION OF THE HERMS).   What is the relevance of the story of Aristogiton and Harmodus? Does the historian imply that Alkibiades was in fact involved?

THUCYDIDES 6.30–32, 42–51 (THE DESCRIPTION OF THE DEPARTURE OF THE EXPEDITION).   What were the attitudes of the Athenians as the expedition set out? What responses did the expedition meet en route? What were the various plans put forward by the three generals? Do any forebodings of difficulties appear in this passage?

THUCYDIDES 6.89–93 (ALKIBIADES' APPEAL FOR REFUGE IN SPARTA AND HIS SELF-DEFENSE).   Are Alkibiades' justifications for offering assistance to the Spartans persuasive?

THUCYDIDES 7.10–18 (NICIAS' LETTER SEEKING ASSISTANCE FROM THE ATHENIAN ASSEMBLY).   How many of the problems faced by the Athenian forces had been anticipated by Nicias in his earlier speeches? On the other hand, to what extent had events borne out Alkibiades' predictions?

THUCYDIDES 7.55–72 (THE LAST BATTLE IN THE HARBOR).   Why does Thucydides provide such detail about the participants in the battle? What changes had the Athenians made to their ships, and how had the Syracusans responded? What literary devices does Thucydides use to enhance the account of the battle?

THUCYDIDES 7.72–87) (THE FLIGHT OF THE ATHENIAN FORCES).   To what does Thucydides compare the retreating forces, and how does this affect the force of his description? Since he was not present, what sources might he have used for this passage?

THE IONIAN PHASE OF THE WAR

After the Sicilian disaster, the weakened position of Athens shifted the focus of the war to the east. Three main problems, all essentially economic, faced the Athenians and directed their attention eastward: the vulnerability of their grain-supply route to the Black Sea; the threat of subject revolts in the Aegean; and the depletion of Athenian financial reserves by the expenses of the Sicilian expedition, which made the prospect of Persian gold especially tempting. In the tangle of intrigues that followed, Alkibiades was a key figure, playing all three sides—Sparta, the Persian satraps, and Athens—against each other in an attempt to further his own advantage.

After the Sicilian disaster, Athens' subjects vied with each other for Spartan assistance in their revolts. The first to seek help was Euboea. It was quickly followed by Lesbos and Chios. Meanwhile, exiles from Megara and Cyzicus at the court of the Persian satrap Pharnabazus at Dascylium appealed to the Spartans for help in fomenting revolt in the Hellespont. Sparta thus faced a choice between concentrating attention on the Hellespont or on Ionia.

It was Alkibiades, still in Sparta, who persuaded the Spartans to favor the Chians' request, and the chosen theater of war became Ionia. This may have been a mistaken choice, as was often the case with Alkibiades' advice, for later events showed that the key to victory for the Peloponnesians lay in control of the Athenian supply route through the Hellespont.

In Ionia, the revolt of Chios was quickly followed by those of Erythrae, Klazomenae, and Miletus. Nevertheless, even in the midst of these reverses, Athens achieved some successes. In Samos the demos seized power from the oligarchic rulers with Athenian assistance, and the island became the base for the Athenian navy. The Athenians were quick to rebuild their fleet, and soon other successes followed: Lesbos and Klazomenae were regained, and a base was seized on the island of Chios, from which the Athenians could harass the Chians and provide a refuge for fugitives. Meanwhile, however, Knidos and Rhodes revolted.

THE OLIGARCHIC COUP OF 411 B.C.: THE 400 AND THE 5000

With the war almost at a stalemate and the city desperate for funds, the machinations of Alkibiades again came to the fore. In 411 B.C., he became a primary factor in the instigation of an oligarchic coup in Athens. Hoping to obtain his own recall to Athens, he dangled the prospect of Persian gold before the leading Athenians in the fleet at Samos: if an oligarchic regime were to be established at Athens, he would use his influence with the satrap to secure Persian aid for Athens. In the end he was unable to deliver the promised Persian assistance, but, nonetheless, the revolution proceeded in Athens without him. The conspirators appealed to a fictitious "Constitution of Dracon" and promised to institute a body of 5000 citizens, composed of those who could provide their own arms and who would serve without pay. In fact, however, the 5000 were never chosen, and a *Council of 400* instituted a reign of terror.

Envoys attempting to bring the fleet at Samos over to the cause of the 400 failed, however. Alkibiades now allied himself with the democrats, and Thucydides credits him with doing the city a signal favor by persuading the sailors not to head immediately for Athens to put down the revolution by force. Thereby he prevented a civil war that would have cost many lives. Instead, at his advice they sent a message to Athens that the 400 must go, but that there was no objection to the 5000. This proved to be the turning point: the coup collapsed, and a mixed oligarchic-democratic regime of 5000 was established. Thucydides called it the best government that the Athenians had ever had.

THE WAR IN THE HELLESPONT

In 411 B.C. the Spartans at last transferred their theater of operations to the Hellespont. The Athenians followed, assembling their naval forces for an attack upon the Spartans at Cyzicus, which had revolted. Assisting the Athenian forces was Alkibiades, who played a major role in their victory and the recovery of Cyzicus. The Spartan commander was killed and the Spartans offered peace terms which the Athenians, under the influence of the demagogue Kleophon, unwisely rejected.[9] However, with victory the Athenians were able to exact tribute from the area, which helped their immediate financial difficulties (at this time the Spartans were receiving gold from Persia).

Soon after its account of the Athenian victory at Cyzicus, Thucydides' history breaks off in midsentence. A recently discovered inscription from the island of Thasos suggests, however, that the historian lived at least until 397 B.C. It lists under the year 397 B.C. the name of a local magistrate, Lichas son of Arkesilas. If this is the same man as the Lichas son of Arkesilas whose death Thucydides reports at 8.84.2, it demonstrates that the historian was alive and still writing seven years after the war; many scholars are skeptical about the identification, however.[10] But whether or not the historian lived on, he did not complete his history of the war, and for the period after the victory at Cyzicus, our sources become much less reliable. They include Plutarch, the biographer whom we have already discussed, Xenophon, and Diodorus Siculus. Xenophon, an Athenian aristocrat exiled in the fourth century B.C. by the Athenians for his pro-Spartan inclinations, undertook a continuation of Thucydides' history. His work, however, lacks the accuracy and impartiality of Thucydides' account. Diodorus Siculus was the author of a universal history in the time of Julius Caesar and Augustus, chiefly valuable for its use of the fourth-century B.C. Greek historian Ephorus. Diodorus added his own moralizing passages and was often careless about chronology as he put the material into annalistic form.

Following the victory at Cyzicus, the Athenians succeeded in capturing three sites on the Bosphorus: Chrysopolis, where they established a lucrative customs station, Chalkedon, and Byzantium. Alkibiades played a starring role in these successes, and in 407/6 B.C. the Athenians elected him general in absentia. He seized upon this show of goodwill to return to the city. Although he sailed back with great pageantry and display, he cautiously waited to land until he saw relatives and friends among the crowd; they provided him with a safe escort into the city.

Alkibiades had no need to fear. The Athenian people, fickle as they so often were, welcomed this charismatic figure back as a savior in their time of need. He spoke in the Assembly in his own defense and was cleared of the charges of impiety in the affair of the Herms, and he was even elected Supreme General. As a means of enhancing his public image, he undertook to lead a procession by land to Eleusis in celebration of the Greater Eleusinian Mysteries—the first such procession since the war. His credit and popularity had never been higher, but both he and the Athenian demos were volatile, and his days of glory were to be short-lived.

Before long Alkibiades sailed out again on naval operations off the Anatolian coast. During the course of the expedition, a minor loss contributed to ending his brief period of popularity in Athens. At Notium he left the main body of his fleet in charge of his pilot and drinking buddy, Antiochus, with orders not to risk battle, while he himself set out on a mission with a few ships. The sources do not agree on the facts of the situation. Was Alkibiades engaged in collecting necessary funds to pay the sailors? Or was this an indiscretion on his part? Was Antiochus a reliable choice? Did Antiochus disobey orders and offer battle, or was he caught in an ambush? Whatever the circumstances, a battle and a defeat ensued at Notium in Alkibiades' absence. We do not know whether this alone was responsible for the reverse in Athenian public opinion, or whether there were other difficulties: according to Plutarch, his enemies brought other accusations against him, including his provision for himself of a private fortress in the Chersonese as a possible refuge. At any rate, the demos did not reelect him general in 406/5 B.C., and he prudently withdrew to his refuge in the Chersonese, fearing the wrath of the notoriously fickle Athenian people if he should return again. And it seems that the Athenians were indeed still in a quandary about his true aims, as we can see from Aristophanes' *Frogs*, produced in 405 B.C. In this play, when a poet was to be chosen to be resurrected as savior of the city, a decisive question put to the two candidates (Euripides and Aeschylus) was, "What should be done about Alkibiades?" Their advice, while comic, expresses the ambivalence felt about Alkibiades in Athens:

Euripides: Quickness and brains are what we seek, I know;
              HE'S quick—to harm, but when we need him, slow;
              Brilliant enough to plan his own escape,
              But useless when the City's in a scrape.

Aeschylus: It is not very wise for city-states
              To rear a lion's whelp within their gates:
              But should they do so, they will find it pays
              To learn to tolerate its little ways.

THE BATTLE OF ARGINUSAE, 406 B.C.

The Athenians were to have one more great victory, and to turn it into a disgrace to the democracy, before their final defeat. The victory followed upon a great crisis. A new Spartan commander, Lysander, cleverly appealed to the self-interest of the oligarchic leaders in a number of cities and was able to organize a fleet of 140 ships. He achieved immediate success in an engagement off Lesbos in which the newly elected Athenian general Conon lost 30 of his 70 ships, while the remaining ships were blockaded in the harbor of Mytilene. The situation for Athens was desperate: gold and silver dedications in the temples were melted down, and freedom was even offered to slaves, and citizenship to metics, who were willing to join in the fight. In a month the Athenians managed to assemble a fleet of more than 150 ships, and they were able to defeat the Spartan forces in the naval battle of Arginusae.

After the victory at Arginusae, however, a storm arose, and the Athenian generals decided against staying to recover the dead from the twenty-five ships lost in the battle. This violation of religious custom enraged the people of Athens, and the generals, including the son of Pericles by Aspasia, were executed after being tried en masse, rather than as individuals as the law required. Later many of the Athenians repented of their hasty and illegal action; as was too often the case, the Athenian demos acted first and thought afterwards.

THE FINAL DEFEAT OF ATHENS: THE BATTLE OF AEGOSPOTAMI, 405 B.C.

The Athenians lost the final and decisive battle in the Peloponnesian War almost entirely because of the negligence and internal dissension of their own leaders. They faced the enemy in the Hellespont, but the Spartans, in a strong position, refused to give battle. The Athenian position was weak, and the men had to go a long distance for supplies. Each day the Athenian fleet sailed out and tried to draw the Spartans into battle, and when this failed, they sailed back, disembarked, and the crews scattered in search of food and supplies. Alkibiades, whose refuge was nearby, saw the weakness in the Athenian position and advised them to move. According to Diodorus, he also offered them the assistance of a large Thracian army under his command. The Athenian generals, however, refused his advice and his offer, in part out of jealousy and fear that he would reap the public relations rewards of any success they might have. Eventually the Spartan commander Lysander, remarking the Athenian pattern of behavior, attacked the fleet when the crews had scattered in search of supplies. The result was a massacre. Only 20 of the 180 Athenian ships managed to escape, under the leadership of Conon; the rest were lost, and three to four thousand Athenians perished. Conon sent twelve of the surviving ships back to Athens while he himself took the other eight to seek protection from King Evagoras in Cyprus.

The victory at Aegospotami put Lysander in a commanding position, with nothing to stand in the way of a siege of Athens. He ordered that all overseas Athenians should be driven back home in order to put more pressure on the city's food supplies, and then began a siege. The Athenians held out for eight months, mainly because the demagogue Kleophon resisted acceptance of Spartan terms. (Thucydides was recalled from exile during this time of crisis.) Eventually, however, the Athenians, starving, were forced to capitulate.

The terms of the surrender were not as devastating as some of the Greek cities, notably Thebes, had urged, for almost immediately after Athens' defeat the other Greek cities began to worry about the new balance of power. The Athenians thus did not receive the fate that they had so often meted out to others—their men were not slaughtered nor were their women and children sold into slavery. Instead they were made allies of Sparta, and their fleet was limited to twelve ships. The Long Walls to the Piraeus were torn down, to the rejoicing sound of flutes, and a governing body consisting of thirty men (the "Thirty Tyrants") was established by Sparta. The Thirty were appointed to draw up a new constitution, but instead they ruled arbitrarily, taking advantage of their power to purge the citizen body of their personal enemies. Their harshness was so great that finally, in 403 B.C., the Athenians, aided by exiles who had found refuge in Thebes, succeeded in defeating and expelling them. Democracy was restored, and it was to last for three generations.

IMPORTANT PLACES IN CHAPTER 12

On Chapter Map: Aegina, Aegospotami, Amphipolis, Arginusae, Athens, Bosphorus, Byzantium, Chalkedon, Chios, Chrysopolis, Corcyra, Corinth, Cyzicus, Dascylium, Dekelea, Delium, Eleusis, Erythrae, Euboea, Hellespont, Katane, Klazomenae, Knidos, Lesbos, Megara, Melos, Messenia, Mytilene, Notium, Piraeus, Plataea, Potidaea, Pylos, Rhodes, Scione, Segesta, Sparta, Sphakteria, Strymon River, Syracuse, Thasos, Thebes, Thrace

SUGGESTIONS FOR FURTHER READING

The best source for the events of the war is the account by Thucydides himself, until it breaks off in 411 B.C. Useful general books on Thucydides include W. Robert Connor, *Thucydides* (1984); V. Hunter, *Thucydides the Artful Reporter* (1982); and S. Hornblower, *Thucydides* (1987). The standard commentary on the Greek text, A. W. Gomme, A. Andrewes, and K. J. Dover, *A Historical Commentary on Thucydides* (1945–1981), contains historical as well as textual discussions.

ENDNOTES

1. Aristophanes' *Acharnians* 515–539, 730–835; *Peace* 605–611, 615–618; Andocides III 8; Aeschines II 175; Ephorus, Frag. 196 *ap.* Diod. Sic. xii. 38.1–41.1. For a full discussion, see G. E. M. de Ste.-Croix, *The Origins of the Peloponnesian War* (1972).
2. L. Kallet-Marx, *Money, Expense, and Naval Power in Thucydides' History 1–5.24* (1993), argues that Thucydides did in fact pay a great deal of attention to economic issues.
3. L. Kallet-Marx disagrees with the notion of the use of League funds for the building program; see "Did Tribute Fund the Parthenon?" *Classical Antiquity* 8 (1989), 252–266.
4. See Nicole Loraux, *The Invention of Athens: The Funeral Oration in the Classical City* (1986).
5. A. J. Holladay and J. C. F. Poole, *Classical Quarterly* 29 (1979), 299ff., argue that the plague cannot be identified but that Thucydides should be given credit for the first mention of contagion; in the course of their argument they provide a full bibliography for the various candidates. Nevertheless, new suggestions have been made since that time; for an argument for toxic shock syndrome complicated by influenza: A. D. Langmuir et al., "The Thucydides Syndrome," *New England Journal of Medicine* (1985), 1027–1030; for Marburg-Ebolu fevers: G. D. Scarrow, "The Athenian Plague: A Possible Diagnosis," *Ancient History Bulletin* 11 (1988), 4–8. For another view of the issue of contagion, see J. Solomon, "Thucydides and the Recognition of Contagion," *Maia* 37 (1985), 121ff.; on

the intellectual effects of the plague, see J. Mikalson, "Religion and the Plague in Athens 431–427 B.C.," *Greek, Roman and Byzantine Studies* 10 (1982), 217ff.

6. For example, M. Meiss, *Painting in Florence and Siena after the Black Death* (1951).

7. Thuc. 4.107.7 remarks that the leading men were jealous of him.

8. For another view of Kleon, see W. R. Conner, *The New Politicians of Fifth-Century Athens* (1971).

9. But see A. Powell, *Athens and Sparta* (1988), for a defense of Athens' refusal.

10. For example, S. Hornblower, *Thucydides* (1987), 151–153; P. J. Rhodes, *Thucydides. History II* (1988), 1; P. Cartledge, "A New Lease of Life for Lichas Son of Arkesilas?" *Liverpool Classical Monthly* 9, 7 (1984), 98, 102.

CHAPTER THIRTEEN

Greece in the Fourth Century

I n the century following the defeat of Athens in the Peloponnesian War, Sparta and Thebes—and eventually Athens, as well—vied for power and leadership of the Greek cities. During the fourth century B.C. the balance of power shifted again and again, and with it political alliances, for as one power threatened to gain ascendancy, the others quickly realigned themselves in opposition. Warfare was almost constant, and Persia often entered in the fray as well—usually from the sidelines, but sometimes playing a major role. Meanwhile, in Macedonia, on the fringes of the Greek world, a new power was growing that was soon to engulf the Greek cities and bring an end to the era of the autonomous polis.

No historian of the caliber of Herodotus or Thucydides dominates the historical scene in the fourth century B.C. The principal sources for mainland Greece in the period following the Peloponnesian War are Xenophon's *Hellenica*, in which the pro-Spartan Athenian takes up the account of the Peloponnesian War where Thucydides breaks off, as noted earlier, and the universal history of Diodorus Siculus, a writer of the Roman period who abridged the work of the fourth-century B.C. Greek historian Ephorus. There is also abundant evidence of the nature of social and economic life in the records of private lawsuits. In this chapter we will first consider the political events of the period and then turn to some aspects of the economic and social scenes.

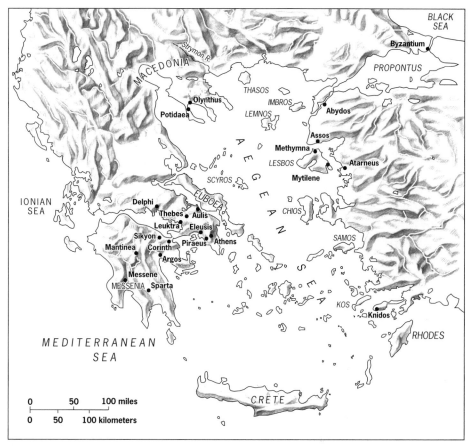

MAP 13 Greece in the fourth century.

POLITICAL HISTORY IN MAINLAND GREECE

The Period of Spartan Hegemony

The fall of Athens left that city with great losses. Perhaps half the adult male citizen body had died in the course of the war,[1] and a large number of women and children, unmentioned in our sources, must have succumbed as well, especially in the famine brought on by the prolonged siege that ended the war. The city's territory had been ravaged, its fleet wiped out, its empire forfeited, and its walls dismantled by the Peloponnesians. With these losses, the city's economic base was shattered. Thebes, in contrast, was much enriched by years of plundering Attica, although it remained angry with its ally Sparta for refusing to share the prizes of victory. Sparta itself emerged as the strongest power in Greece.

But Sparta, despite its victory—in fact, because of it—had an unfulfilled "contract" with Persia hanging over its head: the Persian gold that had made Spartan victory possible had been obtained at the price of a promise to turn over the Greek cities in Asia Minor to Persia. Sparta had a choice: fulfill the contract, or develop a power capable of standing up to the Persians. And the latter choice in effect meant replacing Athens as an imperial power in the Aegean.[2]

The idea of a Spartan empire that could stand up to Persia was not an unreasonable one in some respects. The Spartans had unquestioned military strength and abilities, and they possessed an outstanding military and political strategist in Lysander, who had led them to victory over the Athenians at Notium and Aegospotami, conducted the successful siege of Athens, and been instrumental in establishing the rule of the Thirty in defeated Athens. Moreover, while in charge of Spartan operations in Asia Minor and the Aegean, Lysander had given Sparta a tangible basis for empire building by the establishment of garrisons in many east Greek cities. These garrisons were commanded by Spartan officials, or **harmosts,** and governed by **decarchies** (councils made up of ten local citizens sympathetic to Spartan interests).

But despite the assets that Sparta possessed, the Spartan system itself proved unequal to the demands of securing and maintaining an empire. Its economic base still rested on the continued exploitation of the helots, and this required a continual state of military alert at home; the Spartans could ill afford extensive operations abroad. Moreover, the agoge that the Spartans had created to develop and maintain this state of readiness itself posed problems. It successfully created citizens who could function well within a tightly controlled hierarchical society, but it did not prepare them to face the challenges and temptations of a life free from the oversight of their peers. Spartans had no experience handling the temptations of wealth and individual power, nor were they accustomed to motivating men who had not been raised under the discipline of a similar system. Thucydides, in the speech that the Athenian envoy made to the Spartans in the negotiations leading up to the Peloponnesian War, correctly predicted the troubles that imperialism would bring to Sparta[3]:

> If you were to succeed in overthrowing us and in taking our place, you would speedily lose the popularity with which fear of us has invested you, if your policy of to-day is at all to tally with the sample that you gave of it during the brief period of your command against the Mede. Not only is your life at home regulated by rules and institutions incompatible with those of others, but your citizens abroad act neither on these rules nor on those which are recognized by the rest of Hellas.

Thucydides' prediction was amply borne out by events in the postwar period. The Spartan harmosts in the subject cities were often rapacious, and the Spartan system permitted no appeal from their decisions. Decarchies too often functioned above the law, as collective tyrannies. Individual Spartans, forbidden the possession of gold, silver, and other luxuries at home, found such items irresistible abroad. A striking illustration of this is provided by Gylippus, the Spartan commander who had led the Syracusans to victory over the Athenians in the Sicilian expedition. His conduct of the Sicilian campaign was exemplary, but in 404 B.C., when Lysander entrusted him with the task of carrying back to Sparta a treasure of captured gold and silver, he succumbed to the temptation to steal from the contents.[4]

It is somewhat ironic that Lysander, who was exceptional for a Spartan in his personal incorruptibility and creative ingenuity, was frustrated and eventually defeated by a second fundamental weakness of the Spartan system: its inability to make use of the talents of ambitious men in ways that served both their own and the state's interests. His success in establishing decarchies, garrisons, and harmosts in the East Greek cities appeared to jealous peers back home as steps in the building of a personal following. Nor did he help his cause by his frank celebration of his own achievements—such as commissioning the grandiose monument with his own statue as centerpiece that he dedicated at Delphi. He even accepted being worshiped as a god by the people of Samos—the first Greek to be so honored during his lifetime.[5] Disturbed by this un-Spartan behavior, the Spartans recalled him and repudiated the decarchies as his personal "clients" (although they kept the system of garrisons and harmosts intact). Deprived of his command and kept idle at home, prevented by law from holding the office of Navarch a second time, and ineligible by birth for the hereditary kingship, Lysander saw no constitutional outlet for his ambitions. It was at this point that he apparently began to plot to alter the constitution to allow for an elective kingship. Success eluded him here as well, however; although he consulted (and bribed) a number of oracles, none supported him.

On the death of King Agis II in 397 B.C., Lysander saw still another opportunity. Agis's son, Leotychides, who was next in line for the succession, was widely rumored to be the natural son of Alkibiades, and many opposed his election to the hereditary kingship because of this. The brother of Agis, Agesilaus, was the next candidate for the succession, after Leotychides. He was a mild-mannered man, who had, moreover, been Lysander's boyhood lover. Lysander, hoping to control Agesilaus and through him to influence Spartan policy, encouraged him to put forward his claim.[6] The main obstacle was the fact that Agesilaus was lame—the kingship was a religious as well as a secular office, and physical defects were considered incompatible with service to the gods. In fact, an oracle was circulated that seemed to warn specifically against the accession of Agesilaus[7]:

> Boasting Sparta, be careful not to sprout
> a crippled kingship, you are sure-footed;
> unexpected troubles will overtake you,
> the lamentations of the storm of war
> destroyer of mankind.

Lysander turned the apparently unfavorable oracle to Agesilaus's advantage by pointing out that, correctly interpreted, it referred not to Agesilaus's physical lameness but to Leotychides's suspect birth: if he was not the natural son of Agis, as there were grounds to suspect, he had no right to succeed, and his accession would result in a crippled kingship. Oracles were notorious for their riddles and ambiguities (remember the wooden walls that were to offer protection for the Athenians against the Persian invasion), and Lysander's symbolic interpretation convinced the Spartans. Agesilaus was accepted as king, but Lysander's hopes that he could control him were soon disappointed. Although Lysander was chosen to head the board of thirty advisers who accompanied the king on his expedition to Asia (see below), the king consistently rejected his advice and refused his requests for favors for his friends in the East Greek cities. Sent back to Greece to serve in the Corinthian War (see below), Lysander was killed in the first battle.

The Spartan system itself thus presented three major obstacles to effective control of an empire: its need to maintain a strong military presence at home, the failure of the agoge to instill the society's value system in its citizens, and a governmental structure that made no provisions for the effective use of (and outlets for) outstanding individual talents and ambition. Nevertheless, in 397 B.C., when the Persians demanded the promised submission of the East Greek cities, the Spartans made the imperial choice. The Greek cities in Asia Minor appealed to Sparta for assistance, and the first Spartan "imperial" activity was underway. In 396 B.C. King Agesilaus set out at the head of a Greek force, posing as the new Agamemnon in still another war of Greeks against the "Barbarian East." He planned a dramatic Homeric scenario for his departure, intending to offer sacrifice at Aulis, where Agamemnon had made the fateful sacrifice of his daughter in return for favorable winds as he set out for Troy. But Agesilaus failed to ask permission of the Boeotians, and they, alarmed by an expedition that they viewed as a dangerous display of power by Sparta, stepped in to prevent the sacrifice. It was not a good omen for the expedition.

In the meantime, the Athenian general Conon, who had taken refuge in Cyprus after the disaster at Aegospotami, led a Persian fleet to victory over the Spartan fleet at Knidos. In response, the East Greek cities threw off their Spartan garrisons and declared themselves for Persia—so much for the Spartans' contract and their hopes of "liberating" the East Greeks. At home, moreover, Thebes, Athens, Corinth, and Argos, frightened by the Spartan initiatives, put aside their animosities to unite in opposing Sparta. Facing war in Greece, the Spartans called Agesilaus home, forcing him to abort his planned Trojan War in order to fight a war against fellow Greeks in his own home territory.

This new conflict, the Corinthian War (395 to 387/6 B.C.), was intended to confine Sparta to the Peloponnesus. The Persians, angry at Agesilaus's invasion of Asia Minor, joined the anti-Sparta cause: the satrap Pharnabazus brought Conon and his fleet to Greece to aid the enemies of Sparta and to ravage Spartan territory. When Pharnabazus returned to the east, he left the fleet behind with Conon in Athens, and added money to the treasury of the polis so that the Athenians could rebuild the Long Walls and fortify the port of Piraeus. Athens was thus restored by Persian assistance to a position of potential equality with the other Greek states.

Bolstered by their renewed defenses and restored fleet, the Athenians embarked once again on the imperialistic path. They seized the islands of Scyros, Imbros, and Lemnos and established cleruchies. Soon they won other allies along the route to the Black Sea, including Byzantium, where they reestablished the 10 percent duty on ships sailing from the Black Sea. They imposed a tax of 5 percent on the maritime imports and exports of their allies, but they asked for no tribute as such. This renewal of Athenian imperialism frightened Sparta and Thebes, and they abandoned their mutual enmity to join in opposition to Athens. Peace was achieved only by the intervention of the Persian king, who oversaw a treaty called the *King's Peace* in 387/6 B.C.

The provisions of the King's Peace were generally favorable to Sparta. Spartan control of the mainland of Greece was supported, leagues were forbidden (and hence the dismantling of the Boeotian League, source of Thebes' power), and the Greek cities in Asia were given up to the Persians. In 382 B.C., however, another Spartan blunder turned the other Greeks against Sparta once again. In keeping with the provisions of the King's Peace, Sparta decided to put down the league that the city of Olynthus in northern Greece had gradually built up. Since leagues were outlawed by the terms of the King's Peace, Sparta was justified in sending a force to see to its dissolution. On their march north, however, the Spartans discovered a fortuitous combination of circumstances at Thebes—internal treachery and a **Kadmeia** (the Theban acropolis) that was undefended, having been given over to the women, who were celebrating the festival of the Thesmophoria. The Spartans seized the opportunity and occupied the Kadmeia. The unexpected and unprovoked nature of the attack, the violation of a widely revered religious festival, and continuing Spartan occupation of the Kadmeia roused the feelings of the other Greeks against Sparta.

In 378 B.C. still another example of Spartan high-handedness brought Athens into alliance with Thebes. A Spartan harmost in Thessaly, Sphodrias, set out by night to lead a surprise attack on the Piraeus. Sphodrias underestimated the distance, however, and dawn found his forces only in the vicinity of Eleusis; having lost the advantage of surprise, he turned back, abandoning the attack. Nevertheless, the incident frightened and angered the Athenians, and in 377 B.C., exactly a century after the formation of the Delian League, they formalized their relations with their allies in the *Second Athenian Sea League*.[8] The original members of the League were Thebes, Chios, Mytilene, Methymna, Rhodes, and Byzantium, but eventually there were some sixty to seventy members. In the new League, the Athenians tried to profit by their past experience; they allowed the allies a veto over Athenian actions and promised to establish no new garrisons or cleruchies and to levy no tribute. Within a year, Athens had regained supremacy of the sea.

The Battle of Leuktra and Theban Hegemony

The end of Spartan hegemony—the end, in fact, of Sparta as a major power in Greece—came in 371 B.C. Intent on breaking up the Boeotian League, the Spartans marched toward Thebes. They were met at Leuktra by the Theban army under the command of the general Epaminondas. Epaminondas had reorganized the Theban army to enable it to employ new tactics: a concentration of force on the left in depth (fifty men deep, in contrast to the usual hoplite formation that was eight to twelve men deep); an oblique advance with the right wing holding back; the use of reserve forces, which gave the generals a role throughout the battle and not just at its onset; and the coordination of infantry and cavalry. Already well trained in these innovative tactics, the Theban force of 6000 won an overwhelming victory over a Spartan force of 10,000 hoplites (most of whom must have been perioikoi). Suddenly the renowned Spartan army was revealed to be no longer invincible, and Spartan power itself a discounted mirage.

The Athenians were ambivalent at this revelation of Spartan weakness. While they saw prospects of increasing their empire through alliance with Thebes, they also feared a too-powerful Thebes. The smaller Peloponnesian states had no such qualms, however, and they quickly seized the opportunity to escape from Spartan domination. Farther afield the effect of the revelation of Spartan weakness was an almost universal reaction against Spartan-supported oligarchies. The resulting democratic revolutions flooded Greece with exiles willing to sell their services as mercenaries to the highest bidder.

In the next campaigning season (370 B.C.), Epaminondas followed up his victory at Leuktra by an invasion of the Peloponnesus. The city of Sparta escaped capture only because the river was swollen with winter rains and the bridge was well defended. The Spartans, driven to last resorts, offered freedom to 6000 helots in return for military service; many of the helots deserted instead, as did many perioikoi. Epaminondas, however, did not take advantage of the situation to capture Sparta; instead he turned his forces toward the real heart of Spartan power, Messenia. He permanently freed the Messenians from Spartan control, recalled the Messenian exiles, and carried out a synoikism of Messenia, uniting the many small communities as the new city of Messene. At this point the Athenians, fearing the rising power of Thebes, switched their alliance to Sparta. They sent a force to assure that the Thebans left the Peloponnesus and did not attack Athens as they went.

Thebes, an oligarchy, controlled its new territories with harmosts, as had the Spartans, and, as had been the case with the Spartan harmosts, the rule of the Theban harmosts soon led to discontent.[9] Two more Theban interventions were carried out to put down unrest and fighting in the Peloponnesus. In 362 B.C., in the course of one of these invasions, Epaminondas died while fighting at

Mantinea, in a battle that was in all other respects a Theban victory. The general had been the moving spirit behind the Thebans' military and diplomatic achievements, and after his death they were never again to attain similar successes. Thebes' brief moment as Hegemon of Greece was over, but Spartan power was also broken forever (perhaps Lysander's interpretation of the oracle had not been correct after all).

Athenian Hegemony

After the battle of Mantinea, Athens again enjoyed a brief spell as the leading Greek state. As Athenian power grew, however, the expenses of a growing fleet led it to place more and more demands upon its allies. Moreover, the original justification of the second Athenian Sea League, the threat of Spartan power, no longer existed. Discontent among the members of the League grew, and in 357 B.C. the Social War ("War of the Allies") broke out, led by Rhodes, Kos, Chios, and Byzantium, with assistance from the Carian dynast and Persian satrap Mausolus. Peace came only in 355 B.C. when the Persian king, outraged by Athenian actions in Asia Minor, threatened the city with war. By the terms of the new peace, the independence of the rebellious states was recognized. Lesbos and other East Greek cities soon broke away as well, although a truncated Athenian League continued to exist.

In the same year in which Athens' second attempt at empire was cut back, 355 B.C., a "Sacred War" over control of Delphi broke out in the north of Greece. Before it was over, Philip of Macedon was to play a key role in the first of a series of events that would end in his conquest of Greece.

ECONOMIC HISTORY

The Evidence of the Attic Orators

A large number of speeches written by the Attic orators for private legal cases have been preserved. It is true that these men in arguing their cases must on occasion have bent the truth, if they did not lie outright; nonetheless, the basic structure, if not the specific details, of the trading activities and the transactions that they described must have been reasonably accurate in order to convince a contemporary jury. These speeches offer a rich source of information about daily life and the economy in Athens in the fourth century B.C.[10] What they tell us about trade is especially interesting, since this was a sphere that was central to many political and even military decisions. But the Greek economy was much different from our own modern economy. The Greek economic ideal was self-sufficiency, not, as in the modern world, successful investment for profit. Business and trade were carried on by individuals of relatively low status, most of whom were not citizens, but metics and even slaves. Wealth brought by trade did not automatically enhance the status of these men, for status was determined by family connections and possession of land; as a result, traders were more likely to use gains from business to purchase land than to plough them back into the business. Governments did not involve themselves in trade except to ensure adequate supplies of grain in times of shortage.[11]

The speeches of the Attic orators provide interesting insights into the nature of Athenian trade practices. Athens was far from reaching the ideal of self-sufficiency, even in the most vital matter of feeding its own population. Already, by the fifth century B.C., the city was regularly dependent on outside sources of grain. Other imports were also vital, such as slaves and timber for the building of ships, as noted earlier. Athens paid for its imports primarily by the export of olives, olive oil, and silver from the mines at Laurion.

While the provision of sufficient grain to all citizens at reasonable prices was of first importance to the leaders of the Athenian polis, the actual trade that brought grain to the city was in the hands of private merchants. Some traders, called *naukleroi,* owned their own ships, but they were not big operators, rarely owning more than one vessel. Most traders did not even own a ship, but sailed on board ships owned or captained by others; such men were called *epibatoi* (literally, "those going on board," or passengers). Since there was no credit, most traders used borrowed money to finance their ventures. Maritime loans were usually provided by wealthy citizens or metics who did not themselves engage in trade, but some loans are known to have been made by traders. Such maritime loans had the advantage of including an element of insurance: if the ship and its cargo were lost at sea, a not infrequent occurrence, the lender, and not the borrower, bore the loss. Not surprisingly, considering the risks for the lender, maritime loans carried a high rate of interest: the average interest on a loan for a voyage during the safest sailing season was 20 to 30 percent, but since such a voyage lasted perhaps two to three months, the annual rate amounted to 80 to 180 percent.[12]

Such civic control over trade as existed was exerted through laws and regulations; among the more important of these were laws that set the price and conditions for the sale of grain, forbade the export of any produce except olives and olive oil (a law of Solon), and decreed that no ship under the control of an Athenian metic or citizen should carry grain anywhere except to Athens.

S O U R C E   A N A L Y S I S

T he speech of Demosthenes, *Against Phormio,* is typical of the speeches generated by maritime disputes. In it look for some of the characteristics of the businessman's life in fourth-century B.C. Athens. Who are the naukleros and the epibatos? What were the amounts and conditions governing the loan?

What were the roles of partners and agents, including slaves, in foreign ports? What happened at the Black Sea port (the Black Sea was an area of utmost importance for the Athenian grain supply, although this speech identifies only hides as cargo)? What risks did the businessman run besides shipwreck? The fact that Phormio was apprehended in a perfumer's shop is significant; perfumed oil was an important part of the trade in olive oil, and men hung around the shops, where business was likely. [*Note:* A mina was worth 100 drachmas; an average yearly wage was about 300 to 350 drachmas.][13]

I, men of Athens, lent to this man, Phormio, twenty minae for the double voyage to Pontus and back, on the security of goods of twice that value, and deposited a contract with Cittus the banker. But, though the contract required him to put on board the ship goods to the value of four thousand drachmae, he did the most outrageous thing possible. For while still in the Peiraeus he, without our knowledge, secured an additional loan of four thousand five hundred drachmae from Theodorus the Phoenician, and one of one thousand drachmae from Lampis the shipowner. And whereas he was bound to purchase at Athens a cargo worth one hundred and fifteen minae, if he was to perform for all his creditors what was written in their agreements, he purchased only a cargo worth five thousand five hundred drachmae, including the provisions; while his debts were seventy-five minae. This was the beginning of his fraud, men of Athens; he neither furnished security, nor put the goods on board the ship, although the agreement absolutely bade him do so. . . .

When he came, then, to Bosporus, having letters from me, which I had given him to deliver to my slave, who was spending the winter there, and to a partner of mine,—in which letter I had stated the sum which I had lent and the security, and bade them, as soon as the goods should be unshipped, to inspect them and keep an eye on them,—the fellow did not deliver to them the letters which he had received from me, in order that they might know nothing of what he was doing; and, finding that business in Bosporus was bad owing to the war which had broken out between Paerisades and the Scythian, and that there was no market for the goods which he had brought, he was in great perplexity; for his creditors, who had lent him money for the outward voyage, were pressing him for payment. When, therefore, the shipowner bade him put on board according to the agreement the goods bought with my money, this fellow, who now alleges that he has paid the debt in full, said that he could not ship the goods because his trash was unsalable; and he bade him put to sea, saying that he himself would sail in another ship as soon as he should dispose of the cargo. . . .

After this, men of Athens, the defendant was left in Bosporus, while Lampis put to sea, and was shipwrecked not far from the port; for although his ship was already overloaded, as we learn, he took on an additional deck-load of one thousand hides, which proved the cause of the loss of the vessel. He himself made his escape in the boat with the rest of Dio's servants, but he lost more than thirty lives besides the cargo. There was much mourning in Bosporus when they learned of the loss of the

continued

ship, and everybody deemed this Phormio lucky in that he had not sailed with the others, nor put any goods on board the ship. . . .

Lampis himself, to whom Phormio declared he had paid the gold (pray note this carefully), when I approached him as soon as he had returned to Athens after the shipwreck and asked him about these matters, said that Phormio did not put the goods on board the ship according to our agreement, nor had he himself received the gold from him at that time in Bosporus. . . .

Now, men of Athens, when this man Phormio reached Athens, after completing his voyage in safety on another ship, I approached him and demanded payment of the loan. And at the first, men of Athens, he did not in any instance make the statement which he now makes, but always agreed that he would pay; but after he had entered into an agreement with those who are now at his side and are advocates with him, he was then and there different and not at all the same man. When I saw that he was trying to cheat me, I went to Lampis and told him that Phormio was not doing what was right nor paying back the loan; and at the same time I asked him if he knew where Phormio was, in order that I might summon him. He bade me follow him, and we found the fellow at the perfumery shops; and I, having witnesses with me, served the summons. . . .

Another Aspect of the Economy: Mercenaries

While metic traders speculated and profited, the small farmers who made up the majority of the citizens of the Greek poleis suffered from the consequences of war—now virtually a year-round activity. The continual threat of attack often kept them from carrying out the necessary tasks of the agricultural year, and, when fighting ensued, olive trees and vines that it had taken years to establish were cut down, and buildings were wrecked. Even when the fighting ceased, many small farmers lacked the capital necessary to bring their neglected or devastated land and its structures back to productivity. Selling out to wealthier men who could afford the costs of restoring the land, many small holders drifted into the cities, but, there too, there were few opportunities for making a living. Thus the wealthy accumulated larger estates, and the gulf between the rich and the poor grew. Moreover, constant civil strife brought exile and loss of property to large numbers and transformed men overnight from respectable landowners into wandering, homeless exiles. Tens of thousands of such homeless and destitute men roamed about Greece, often endangering the settled population. Their only hope of employment was to sell their services as mercenaries. The ready supply of mercenaries in itself contributed to the discovery of new uses for their services.

Changes in the methods of warfare in the fourth century B.C. also fostered an increased dependence upon mercenaries. Light-armed tactics became increasingly important, and these called for specialized skills in handling weapons that were traditionally associated with foreigners and looked down upon by the Greek hoplite. The nonprofessional farmer-citizen lacked the time and opportunity, or the incentive, to develop these new skills, and as a result he became less important to the conduct of war, and reliance upon mercenaries who had these skills grew. The reforms of Epaminondas extended this trend toward specialization to the higher ranks: the greater role given to the general throughout the battle increased the need for specialized skills in commanders. While military and political power had previously been inseparable, with election to generalship being an intrinsic part of a political career (Pericles' leadership was based upon his repeated election as general), maintaining the allegiance of a mercenary force called for a full-time commitment that was incompatible with traditional Greek political ambitions. As a result we see a growing split between the military and the political, with professional generals leading mercenary armies loyal primarily to their commanders, while civilian political figures exercised political power without holding military command.

The politics of warfare also contributed to the growing use of, and perceived need for, mercenary service. In the struggle for a balance of power, allegiances became unclear, as yesterday's enemy became today's ally. Goals were also less clear-cut. While the Persian Wars had clearly been a struggle for the survival of Greece in the face of a Barbarian invasion, the frequent wars of the fourth century B.C. often had little justification other than that of advancing the interests of prominent politicians or increasing the profits of a few wealthy men. It is not surprising that ordinary citizens became increasingly reluctant to serve in the military and preferred to provide wages to mercenary replacements.

As mercenary use grew, the expenses of mercenary pay became a real burden on economies already in crisis because of the effects of constant warfare. Unable to pay high-enough wages, the cities attracted mercenaries by offering them the opportunity for loot and plunder, thus adding new victims to the swelling supply of potential mercenaries.

S O U R C E   A N A L Y S I S

A classic account of mercenary warfare is found in Xenophon's *Anabasis*, or *March of the Ten Thousand*, the story of the expedition of the Persian prince Cyrus against his brother Artaxerxes II, who had succeeded to the Persian

continued

throne on the death of their father, Darius. During the Peloponnesian War Cyrus had been commander in chief of the Persian forces in western Asia Minor and satrap of Lydia, a position he had received when he exposed the misdealings of the previous commander, Tissaphernes, who was then demoted to satrap of Ionia. In revenge, Tissaphernes made false accusations against Cyrus to Artaxerxes, who imprisoned his brother and threatened his life. The intercession of his mother saved Cyrus' life, and he was even allowed to return to his satrapy. Nevertheless, he harbored resentment at his treatment and determined that he would never again be in the power of his brother. He therefore began to lay secret plans to seize the kingship for himself. Accordingly he set about gathering a mercenary army, exploiting contacts that he had made while commander of the Persian forces.

What does the following description of these preparations, taken from Xenophon's *Anabasis*, reveal about the motivations of those who collected mercenary forces and those who signed on as mercenaries?[14]

In the first place, [Cyrus] sent orders to the commanders of all the garrisons he had in the cities to enlist as many Peloponnesian soldiers of the best sort as they severally could, on the plea that Tissaphernes had designs upon their cities. For, in fact, the Ionian cities had originally belonged to Tissaphernes, by gift of the King, but at that time all of them except Miletus had revolted and gone over to Cyrus. The people of Miletus also were planning to do the very same thing, namely, to go over to Cyrus, but Tissaphernes, finding out about it in time, put some of them to death and banished others. Cyrus thereupon took the exiles under his protection, collected an army, and laid siege to Miletus both by land and by sea, and endeavoured to restore the exiles to their city; and this, again, made him another pretext for gathering an army. . . .

Still another army was being collected for him in the Chersonese which is opposite Abydus, in the following manner: Clearchus was a Lacedaemonian exile; Cyrus, making his acquaintance, came to admire him, and gave him ten thousand darics. And Clearchus, taking the gold, collected an army by means of this money, and using the Chersonese as a base of operations, proceeded to make war upon the Thracians who dwell beyond the Hellespont, thereby aiding the Greeks [on the European side of the Hellespont, who suffered from the incursions of their Thracian neighbors]. Consequently, the Hellespontine cities of their own free will sent Clearchus contributions of money for the support of his troops. . . .

Again, Aristippus the Thessalian chanced to be a friend of Cyrus, and since he was hard pressed by his political opponents at home, he came to Cyrus and asked him for three months' pay for two thousand mercenaries, urging that in this way he should get the better of his opponents. And Cyrus gave him six months' pay for four thousand, and requested him not to come to terms with his opponents until he had consulted with him. Thus the army in Thessaly, again, was being secretly maintained for him.

Furthermore, Cyrus directed Proxenus the Boeotian, who was a friend of his, to come to him with as many men as he could get, saying that he wished to undertake a campaign against the Pisidians, because, as he said, they were causing trouble to his province. He also directed Sophaenetus the Stymphalian and Socrates the Achaean, who were likewise friends of his, to come with as many men as they could get, saying that he intended to make war upon Tissaphernes with the aid of the Milesian exiles; and they proceeded to carry out his directions.

DIONYSIUS OF SYRACUSE

As the Greeks in the fourth century B.C. squabbled, repeatedly shifting alliances so as to prevent any one polis from becoming supreme, and as they increasingly gave over the job of soldiering to professionals, in the north of Greece, in Macedonia, a power was growing that was soon to sweep over them, demonstrating the irrelevance of their petty disputes and of the polis itself as a political form. The few voices that were raised in alarm, such as that of the Athenian orator Demosthenes, were little heeded; in fact, the leading political thinkers were turning more and more to monarchical ideals. Plato's involvement with the tyrant Dionysius of Syracuse (in Sicily) provides a good example.

In Syracuse the incompetence of the democratic government in dealing with a Carthaginian military threat provided the opportunity for the establishment of a tyranny. Dionysius followed an almost classic pattern in his rise to tyranny. A young man of obscure birth, he first successfully argued in the Assembly for the deposition of the existing board of generals and was himself appointed as one of a new board. Then his demagoguery won him election as sole general with sovereign powers to meet the immediate Carthaginian threat. The final step to the tyranny was the official provision of a bodyguard, voted to him when it was rumored that an attempt had been made on his life. The democracy was never formally overthrown, and, as in Athens under the Peisistratids, the outward forms of democracy were maintained: the Assembly met, passed decrees, and elected magistrates.

As tyrant, Dionysius managed, in the course of four wars, to drive the Carthaginians into the northwestern corner of the island and to gain control himself over all the Greek cities in Sicily. He then extended his rule to southern Italy, creating a western Greek empire. Although many stories of his violent and arbitrary behavior have come down to us (at least some of them the invention of his political enemies), he died of natural causes after a rule of thirty-eight years.

During his rule, Dionysius invited the philosopher Plato to come to Syracuse in order to educate his son and successor, Dionysius the Younger. Plato had strong ideas about ideal government, which he expressed in his dialogue, *The Republic*. Observing the activities of the Athenian democracy (which, not incidently, had put his beloved teacher Socrates to death), Plato firmly believed that the demos (people) was an unruly lot, incapable of governing properly. Just as one needs an expert to build a house or to train a horse, so, Plato argued, one needs an expert to govern a polis. But such an expert, entrusted with the highest office, must be educated to the highest level, and this level Plato described in *The Republic* as that of the philosopher. Beginning with the most fundamental principles of rational knowledge, which Plato saw in geometry, the student would progress to the most esoteric knowledge of *Being-in-Itself*. Plato was intrigued by the prospect of putting his ideas and ideals into practice by making a philosopher-king out of the heir to the tyranny of Syracuse, and he accepted Dionysius' invitation.

Unfortunately, the younger Dionysius was a poor candidate for such a rigorous educational program. While enthusiastic at first—the whole court for a time was immersed in the study of geometry—he soon tired of the effort required. Political intrigues by those opposed to any changes or reforms soon succeeded in making the situation intolerable for Plato, and at last Dionysius let him return to Athens (although the story has it that Dionysius arranged for his disposal en route, an effort that failed).

Plato's transformation of the Syracusan tyranny into a philosopher-kingship was not to be, but the attempt reflects the spirit of the age, with its growing impatience with the ineffectiveness of the polis and its increasing interest in monarchical forms of government. Plato's pupil Aristotle had better luck in a similar job; he was hired to educate the son of Philip II of Macedon, the boy who was to become Alexander the Great. Macedon, being by tradition a kingdom, offered, however, perhaps a better basis, and Aristotle, perhaps, was more practically minded than his teacher.

IMPORTANT PLACES IN CHAPTER 13

On Chapter Map: Abydos, Argos, Assos, Atarneus, Athens, Aulis, Chalkidike, Chios, Corinth, Delphi, Eleusis, Imbros, Knidos, Kos, Lemnos, Lesbos, Leuktra, Mantinea, Messene, Messenia, Methymna, Mytilene, Olynthus, Piraeus, Pontus (Black Sea), Scyros, Sikyon, Sparta, Strymon River, Thebes

On Other Maps: Bosphorus, Byzantium, Carthage, Rhodes, Sicily, Syracuse

SUGGESTIONS FOR FURTHER READING

On the period in general, see S. Hornblower, *The Greek World 479–232* (1983), chaps. 13 to 16. On trials in Athens, a good brief introduction is Mabel Lang, *Life, Death and Litigation in the Athenian Agora* (1994), one of the Picture Book Series of the American School of Classical Studies in Athens; also interesting is a longer work by Virginia Hunter, *Policing Athens* (1994). On mercenaries, see G. T. Griffith, *The Mercenaries of the Hellenistic World* (1935).

ENDNOTES

1. Many of the problems inherent in population estimates are illustrated by this statement. Reports of the war by Thucydides and Xenophon make it clear that casualties were sometimes severe (as in the plague and the prolonged siege at the end of the war), but estimating the overall effect over the thirty years of the war is made impossible both by the paucity of the available numbers and their conflicting evidence. For example, Thucydides 2.13 reports a speech by Pericles in which the Athenians are said to have had 13,000 hoplites in regular service in 431 B.C., plus 16,000 on the walls and garrisons, which included those above and below the age for regular service, as well as metics. In apparent contrast, Xenophon (*Hell.* 4.2.17) reports that the city was able to put 6000 hoplites in the field in 394 B.C. But it is not clear that these numbers are comparable: those reported by Thucydides are given as total forces, while that given by Xenophon is of hoplites mustered for a particular battle, not necessarily the total hoplite force then available to the city.

2. For a discussion of Spartan imperialism, see John V. A. Fine, *The Ancient Greeks: A Critical History* (1983), 537; and S. Hornblower, *The Greek World 429–323 B.C.* (1983), chap. 14; on the Spartan Empire, see P. Cartledge, *Agesilaos and the Crisis of Sparta* (1987), 86–87.

3. Thuc. 1.77 Crawley, tr.

4. Diod. 3. 106.

5. See Cartledge (above, n. 2), 82–84.

6. On Lysander and Agesilaus, see Cartledge (above, n. 2).

7. Pausanias 3.8.9, P. Levi, tr.

8. On the second Athenian Sea League, see J. Cargill, *The Second Athenian League* (1981).

9. On Thebes' problems with its allies, see John Buckler, *The Theban Hegemony 371–362 B.C.* (1980), chap. 8A; on harmosts and garrisons imposed upon the Achaean cities and Sikyon, see Xen., *Hell.* 7.1.42–43; on the garrison at Messene, see Diod. Sic. 67.1; on the harassment of Peloponnesians by Thebans, see Xen., *Hell.* 7.4.36–37; 7.4.40.

10. Speeches from private cases can be found in the Loeb editions of Lysias, Isaeus (who specialized in inheritance cases), and Demosthenes IV–VI, *Private Orations*. On the maritime cases in particular, see Signe Isager and Mogens Herman Hansen, *Aspects of Athenian Society in the Fourth Century B.C.* (1975). On loans and banking, see Edward Cohen, *Athenian Economy and Society: A Banking Perspective* (1992).

11. See M. I. Finley, *The Ancient Economy* (1973), and M. M. Austin and P. Vidal-Naquet, *Economic and Social History of Ancient Greece* (1977).

12. See Isager and Hansen (above, n. 10); and Cohen (above, n. 10).

13. Demosthenes XXXIV, *Against Phormio*, 6–13, A. T. Murray, tr., in *Demosthenes, Private Orations* (1936) IV, 239–247.

14. Xen., *Anabasis* 1.1.6–11, C. L. Brownson, tr., Loeb Library.

CHAPTER FOURTEEN

Philip of Macedon

While the Greek cities engaged in destructive struggles for hegemony, in the north the kingdom of Macedon under Philip II was developing into a power that was to alter the Greek world for all time.[1] The Greek cities either saw temporary advantages for themselves in Philip's activities or were too distracted by their own squabbles to take adequate measures against him. Even though Macedon controlled resources of silver and timber, and the route to the Black Sea, which were all vital to Athenian interests, Macedonia was a long way off, and, in the eyes of many Athenians, the Macedonians were not proper Greeks. Making great sacrifices, as Demosthenes demanded, did not seem all that crucial to many Athenians.

MACEDONIA BEFORE PHILIP

Whether the Macedonians were Greeks was a disputed question even in antiquity.[2] While the Macedonian royal house laid claim to Greek heritage through mythological ancestors, professing to be the descendants of Temenos of Argos, one of the Dorian Heraklids, the Macedonian form of government and way of life differed markedly from those of the poleis of central Greece and the Peloponnesus in the fourth century B.C. In fact, in many ways the Macedonians resembled the Greeks of Homer's epics more than they did their Greek contemporaries. Many were pastoralists, among their upper classes the chief activities were hunting and fighting, and they were ruled by kings who were similar in many respects to Homeric kings.

The Macedonian Kingship

The Macedonian kingship was not a constitutional office like the Spartan king-ship, with well-defined powers and limitations. A Macedonian king's power de-pended a great deal upon his personal strength—in effect, on what he could get away with—yet it was in no way absolute.[3] Power was clan-based—thus from ca. 650 B.C. to ca. 310 B.C. the kingship was hereditary in the line of the Argeadae—but the principle of primogeniture did not hold. A new king was expected to be an Argead, but beyond that there is too little evidence and too great a variety of situations for us to be able to identify "normal" lines of succession. Often the succession was contested among a number of Argead candidates, resulting in a bloodbath—with the succession going to the survivor. As a consequence, the elimination of possible rival candidates was a common first step in a new rule. At other times things went more smoothly, but not as one might expect. Thus when Perdikkas III was killed in 359 B.C. in a disastrous defeat, leaving an infant son, Amyntas, and a demoralized army, his brother Philip took over the kingship and ruled in his own name until his assassination, and Amyntas, when adult, never contested his rule. In contrast, upon the death of Alexander the Great, when the army was still campaigning, his somehow-defective half-brother Ar-rhidaios was chosen successor by the generals. When his widow, Roxane, bore a boy posthumously, the child, as Alexander IV, ruled jointly for a time with Ar-rhidaios, and then later alone until he was murdered at the age of thirteen.[4] It is surely significant that they were the only surviving male Argeads. In fact, it seems that the ability of any given candidate to muster support and maintain his position as king varied widely with circumstances. Even personal weakness or incompetency did not necessarily rule out a candidate, as long as no more-viable Argead candidate was available.

Once the succession was established, the king ruled more or less as he wished. His real power seems to have been limited not by traditional law or an assembly (constitutional measures), but by pressures from various groups within the Macedonian elite. While the king had no formal council, he was surrounded by a retinue of upper-class men—the ***Companions***—with whom he lived on a daily basis and from whom he variously chose his drinking companions in the symposium. Here he received advice and tested out his ideas, for Macedonian custom allowed men to speak freely to the king, and Macedonian drinking cus-toms fostered this freedom (sometimes to disastrous ends). Nevertheless, he was under no obligation to follow the advice offered to him.

The king served as supreme judge of disputes, although he frequently dele-gated this duty, appointing deputies. However, the authority to pronounce the death sentence upon a Macedonian seems to have been entrusted not to the king but to the people as a whole (on campaigns, this was the army).

The nobility—the large, traditional landowners of Lower Macedonia—formed the core of the Companions. Philip brought others—the nobility of the formerly independent Upper Macedonian principalities of Lyncestis, Orestis,

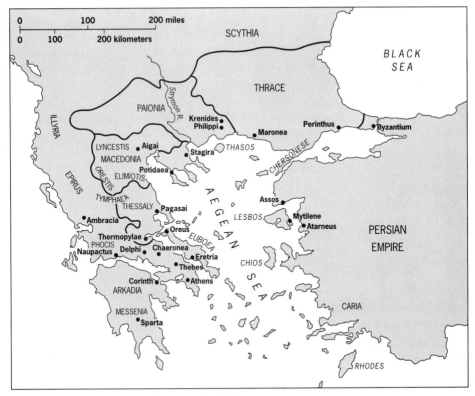

MAP 14 The rise of Macedonia under Philip.

Elimea, and Tymphaea that he had incorporated into the kingdom, and also non-Macedonian Greeks—into the ranks of the Companions as well (there were reportedly about 800 Companions under Philip II). The new men received grants of land with the expectation that they would serve the king, and they probably served as the local governing authority in their home territories. As land was newly acquired in Chalkidike and Thrace, it was allocated to new and old Companions alike.

Philip's Antecedents and Boyhood

Although Macedonia did not play a major role in Greek affairs before the reign of Philip II, some of its earlier kings were noteworthy. The first historically attested Macedonian king was Perdikkas I (ca. 640 B.C.). Alexander I (495 to 450 B.C.) fought with the Persians *against* the Greeks in the Persian Wars; since, however, he had also helped the Greeks with advice (and the Athenians needed his timber for ships), he was rewarded by admission as a Hellene to the Olympic games and with the honor of proxenia (official friendship) in Athens. He sought to emphasize his Greek status by Hellenizing the Macedonian court, to which he invited the poet Pindar. His successor, Perdikkas II (450 to 413 B.C.), took part in the Peloponnesian War, now on one side, now on the other. Perdikkas' son Archelaus (413 to 399 B.C.), who obtained the throne by the murder of his half-brother, continued the work of Hellenization, inviting noted Greek poets and artists to his court. Among these were Agathon, the tragic poet whose contest victory was honored in Plato's *Symposium;* the painter Zeuxis, whose skills were such that his grapes were said to deceive the birds; and Euripides, whose extant play *The Bacchae* was first performed at Archelaus' court, and perhaps written there as well. After Archelaus was killed in a hunting accident (or was murdered), the next noteworthy king was Philip II, the son of Amyntas.

During his boyhood, Philip spent three years in Thebes as a political hostage when his brother, Alexander II, was forced into an alliance with that city. Such political hostages were common; taken in by elite families, they were raised and educated together with the family's own sons. The practice had the double advantage of guaranteeing the loyalty of the family of the hostage and creating in the boy a tie of loyalty to his "hosts" that would be useful after he returned home. Philip was in Thebes during the time when Epaminondas was reorganizing the Theban army, and his later use of Epaminondas' tactics of the deep line and oblique advance suggests that he was an observant student.[5] His later organization of the Greek cities into the Corinthian League may also owe something to Epaminondas' employment of coalitions of self-governing leagues (the Boeotian League cooperated with the Arkadian, Achaean, Lokrian, and Thessalian leagues at one time or another).

Amyntas had three sons: Philip, the youngest; Alexander, who succeeded him as Alexander II; and Perdikkas. Alexander II was murdered by his brother-in-law, Ptolemy, who married the queen and ruled in place of Amyntas' second son, Perdikkas. In 365/4 B.C. Perdikkas killed the usurper Ptolemy and assumed the kingship in his own right as Perdikkas III. In 359 B.C., however, he was killed in a humiliating defeat by an invading Illyrian force—a defeat that cost the Macedonians not only their king but also 4000 men.[6] The army was demoralized, and Perdikkas' son and presumed successor, Amyntas, was only a child. In the face of the crisis, Philip, aged twenty-three, stepped in as king.

On his accession, Philip was faced with several immediate crises. The first and most pressing was the devastating defeat and demoralization of the army. His own position of weakness invited other problems as well: a number of other claimants to the throne were at hand to advance their own causes by military force, one with the help of Thrace, another assisted by Athens. Meanwhile, neighboring tribes to the north took advantage of the situation to cross over the borders and plunder Macedonian territory.

PHILIP'S REORGANIZATION OF THE ARMY

Philip addressed himself first to the problem of morale in the army. He gathered the men together in assembly and, as Greek generals traditionally did before battles, used his rhetorical skills to encourage them, demonstrating control and communicating his own sense of youthful confidence. He also instituted a regimen of intensive training, maneuvers, and reviews. In the meantime, he began a program of reorganization of his forces that probably extended over several years.[7]

Perhaps Philip's most important military innovation was in the equipment and fighting style of the infantry phalanx. In Thebes he had learned the value of the deep line, and he seems to have expanded the smallest unit of the Macedonian phalanx, the *dekad*, from a ten- to a sixteen-man unit, which provided for a line depth of sixteen men. As the main infantry weapon he adopted the *sarissa*, a longer than normal pike, up to 18 feet long. Since it was longer than the Greek spear and could outreach it, his men had the advantage of first contact in the clash of lines. Because the sarissa required the use of both hands, a shield slightly smaller than the standard hoplite model was adopted (the *pelta*, used by the light-armed *peltasts*); like the hoplite shield it rested on the upper arm, but it did not require the left hand for support, leaving both hands free for handling the sarissa.[8] It seems that the men wore no breastplates; G. T. Griffith, an expert on the reforms, suggests that Philip, in increasing the infantry rolls, recruited many men who could not afford the full complement of hoplite armor, and that he took advantage of this circumstance and created a lighter, more mobile force. Another apparent result was that the army had comparatively small numbers of Macedonian light infantry. By raising more men to hoplite status, with its distinctive Greek implications of citizenship participation, Griffith suggests that he brought about "a change in the social character of the people."[9]

Alexander much later reminded the Macedonian soldiers of the benefits that they had received from Philip.[10]

S O U R C E   A N A L Y S I S

ARRIAN, *ANABASIS* 7.9.2–4.   While the context of this passage, a speech to the troops, suggests rhetorical exaggeration, the discipline that Philip imposed was also evident in his military successes.

> Philip took you over when you were helpless vagabonds, mostly clothed in skins, feeding a few animals on the mountains and engaged in their defence in unsuccessful fighting with Illyrians, Triballians and the neighbouring Thracians. He gave you cloaks to wear instead of skins, he brought you down from the mountains to the plains; he made you a match in battle for the barbarians on your borders, so that you no longer trusted for your safety to the strength of your positions so much as to your

continued

natural courage. He made you city dwellers and established the order that comes from good laws and customs. It was due to him that you became masters and not slaves and subjects of those very barbarians who used previously to plunder your possessions and carry off your persons.

Philip also enlarged the Macedonian cavalry, the army's strong suit, by constantly drawing on the expanding resources of his kingdom.[11] While he seems to have made no striking innovations in arms or equipment, he did make one important tactical change. He replaced the square formation of the cavalry squadrons with a wedge-shaped formation, an idea drawn from the Scythians and Thracians. This improved the cavalry's ability to break through the enemy line and added to its flexibility by making it easier for the squadrons to wheel about.

Finally, one of the most important military developments carried out by Philip, at least for the future, was the introduction of the catapult into siege tactics. The catapult had first been used by Dionysius I of Syracuse in the battle of Motya in 397 B.C., but, despite its impressive effectiveness, it was not immediately taken up by other Greek cities. Under Philip, torsion was added to the simple catapult used at Motya, giving it far greater power.[12] The new machines required expert handling, although much of the work of construction and setting up could be done by ordinary infantrymen under direction, and so Philip added to his army a *siege train*. The siege train probably consisted of only a few dozen specialists, who could direct and train ordinary soldiers; Philip attracted them from various parts of the Greek world by his lavish payments.

Another area in which money could buy power was the employment of mercenaries, of which the supply was very plentiful, especially in the Greek states. It seems, however, that, other than the Thessalian cavalry, Philip assigned mercenaries mostly to routine or tedious tasks. Thus they most often served as long-term garrison troops or occupation forces, or were sent abroad on campaigns with limited objectives, rather than playing an important role in the major battles.

Philip was able to expend money and resources upon his newly reorganized and revived army on a scale surpassed only by the Great King of Persia, and had far more of such wealth than was available to any of the Greek states (except the Phocians, who had seized and were spending the treasury at Delphi; see below). Macedonia was rich in timber, and there were enormous resources of silver and gold in the mines around Mount Pangaeum, to which Philip gained access when he took over the Krenides in 356 B.C. (see below). And as he expanded his territories, the dues upon landed property also grew, as did his resources of manpower. But he also spent lavishly. He invited the most prominent figures in the

Greek world, and high-ranking Persian refugees as well, to the court at Pella, where he entertained them in splendid Homeric fashion and showered them with guest-gifts. And he freely expended largess to secure allies, extending his kingdom by gifts as well as by conquest.

EXPANSION OF THE KINGDOM: GREATER MACEDONIA

As he reorganized his army, Philip also took steps to secure his northern borders against encroaching neighbors. In 359 B.C. he suppressed the Paionians, and in the following year annexed Upper Macedonia. In 357 B.C., when the allies of Athens rebelled in the Social War, diverting Athenian attention from the north, Philip took advantage of the situation to capture Amphipolis, an Athenian foundation and ally that controlled the strategic crossing of the river Strymon. This was a sharp blow to Athens and was much resented. As suggested above, not everything was done by military force, however. Gifts played their role, as did marriages. The Macedonian royal house had long practiced polygamy, for political purposes, and Philip continued the practice. Thus he married Audata the Illyrian,[13] who died after bearing him a daughter; Phila, of the Upper Macedonian royal house of Elimea; and two Thessalians, Nikesipolis of Pherae, who bore him another daughter, Thessalonike, and Philinna of Larisa, who bore a son, Arrhidaios. Arrhidaios was probably Philip's first son, but he was somehow disabled, possibly mentally defective.[14] Thus, most important for the future was Philip's marriage in 357 B.C. to Olympias, niece of the king of Epirus, who later bore him a son, Alexander. Subsequently he married the Thracian Medea, and finally, a Macedonian, Cleopatra, niece of his general Attalus, a marriage that proved problematic.

But to return to Philip's establishment of his kingdom, a much needed opportunity to bolster Macedonian finances was offered when the king of Thrace, also hoping to capitalize on Athens' distraction in the Social War, prepared to attack the Krenides, a group of gold- and silver-mining settlements established by Greeks from Thasos. The Krenides appealed to Philip for assistance, and he was successful in fending off the Thracians. Philip then drew the mining communities together into one city (a synoikism), which he named Philippi. Philippi was the first eponymous Macedonian colony to be established. Unlike earlier Greek colonies, however, Philippi was founded specifically to help control territory for its founder, and not as an independent polis. Fortified, and with its population augmented by a large number of Macedonian colonists, Philippi provided Philip with a strong Macedonian frontier outpost and also control over the lucrative mines. By introducing improved mining techniques, Philip was able to draw an annual revenue of more than 1000 talents from the mines,[15] but nonetheless, he spent so prodigiously that the treasury never ran an excess.

Philippi set a precedent for Philip's future city foundations in Thessaly and Thrace, and for Alexander's throughout the area of his conquests. At a time when the city-state was fast becoming obsolete, the city itself was turned into an instrument of the territorial state.

OPPORTUNITIES IN THE SOUTH

With his economic situation greatly improved, his kingdom's northern borders safeguarded, and his army well trained and increased by new recruits from newly acquired areas, Philip could look farther afield. An opportunity to expand to the south offered itself when a political assassination and coup in Thessaly brought chaos and confusion to that area. The Thebans, anxious to bolster their hegemony, which had been faltering since the death of their great general Epaminondas in 362 B.C., took the opportunity to intervene. This provoked the Phocians to seize the treasury of the god Apollo at Delphi to obtain funds to pay for mercenaries to oppose the Theban move.

The Phocian seizure of Apollo's treasury brought on a Sacred War to avenge Delphi (355 to 346 B.C.). (*Sacred War* is a term used to refer to wars declared by the **Delphic Amphictyony,** or coalition of states that controlled the shrine.) Philip played a key role in this war and gained important advantages for Macedonia. Coming to the aid of the oracle, he advanced south, taking control of Thessaly and the Gulf of Pagasai. This gave Macedonia the potential to develop a strong sea power, but the Athenians, temporarily aroused to concern, blocked Philip's advance further south at Thermopylae. Philip then returned north, where he attacked and besieged the city of Olynthus, on the grounds that it had given refuge to two of his half-brothers, pretenders to the throne. In Athens, Demosthenes tried to persuade the citizens to save Olynthus, but they sent only a small and inadequate force. When Olynthus fell, Philip had it destroyed and its citizens sold into slavery.

In 347 B.C. Philip was invited south again to assist in the protracted Sacred War. The war was concluded in 346 B.C. with a formal peace agreement, the *Peace of Philokrates,* that gave Philip Phocis' seat in the Amphictyonic Council, in effect granting him Hellenic status. In fact, he was widely regarded as the "Savior of Delphi," and was accordingly allowed to join in celebrating Delphi's Pythian Games.

ORGANIZATION OF THE KINGDOM

With the problems in Greece apparently settled, Philip again turned his attention to the north. Seriously wounded fighting against the Illyrians in 345 B.C., Philip devoted himself to the organization of his kingdom as he recuperated, and carried out a massive program of population transfers, establishing new towns and augmenting the population of existing ones to bring added security and prosperity to the kingdom. In 344 B.C. he reorganized Thessaly, reestablishing its ancient four-part administration in order to prevent a dangerous concentration of power.

ARISTOTLE AND ALEXANDER

It was probably in 342 B.C. that Philip engaged Aristotle as tutor for his thirteen-year-old son, Alexander. Aristotle was a Macedonian, the son of a doctor who had been employed at the court by Philip's father. Aristotle's father died while Aristotle was still a child; had his father lived, Aristotle would probably have followed him in his profession and become a doctor. As it was, his guardian arranged for him to go to Athens at the age of eighteen to study in the school that Plato had established, the *Academy*. This school was designed to provide an education based on mathematics, along the lines that we saw Plato pursuing in his attempt to educate Dionysius the Younger at Syracuse. Early works of Aristotle, not surprisingly, follow the lines of Plato's thinking: mathematics is the gateway to philosophy, which provides a sound foundation for political action as well as for the conduct of one's personal life.[16]

On the death of Plato in 348 B.C., when the headship of the Academy was given to Plato's nephew, Aristotle left Athens. He went to Assos, on the coast of Asia Minor, where a branch of the Academy had been established under the patronage of Hermias, a local tyrant. Hermias was a man of humble origins who had come to power with Persian support, enlisted a mercenary army, and now controlled an extensive territory. He had appealed to Plato for assistance in legislation and had sponsored the establishment of an Academy in Assos. Aristotle's relationship with Hermias was a close one, for the tyrant gave him his niece, who was also his adopted daughter, in marriage.

After three years, Aristotle left Assos for Mytilene, on the nearby island of Lesbos, probably on a political mission for Hermias. In both Assos and Lesbos Aristotle devoted himself to research that reflected his medical background— the study of living things, both plants and animals. These investigations formed the foundation for his treatises on biology, which constitute over a quarter of his surviving work.[17]

In about 342 B.C. Aristotle returned to Macedonia in response to an invitation from Philip to educate the young Alexander. At the time, Hermias was involved in secret negotiations with Philip to abandon his allegiance to Persia and support the Macedonian king's planned attack on the Persian Empire. The philosopher's move to Lesbos may have been connected to Hermias' plans, for the island, together with Assos on the mainland, could serve as a bridgehead for an invasion. Philip's invitation to Aristotle probably also owed something to the philosopher's role in these negotiations, as well as to Philip's concern over Alexander's education. But shortly after Aristotle's arrival in Macedonia, Hermias was betrayed to the Persians, who seized him and put him to death when he refused to reveal Philip's plans. His friends were distraught, and Aristotle wrote a poem celebrating his martyrdom.

The stories that have been handed down about the relationship between Aristotle and Alexander, and the nature and content of the education that Aristotle provided, are typical of the sources on Alexander in their combination of fact with romantic fantasy. That Aristotle shared his work on biology with his pupil is suggested by Alexander's later decision to take scientists along on his expedition against the Persians so that they could accurately record the many new animals and plants that were encountered. It seems clear, however, that in the main Aristotle followed a traditional aristocratic Greek pattern of education, putting strong emphasis on the Homeric tradition. His pupil, after all, was a descendant of both Herakles on his father's side and Achilles on his mother's, through the royal house of Epirus. The fostering of his legacy from the Homeric hero Achilles was perhaps foremost in what the boy took from his teacher. For example, in his great expedition against the Persian Empire (the final chapter in the battle between Greeks and Barbarians), Alexander saw himself as reenacting the role of the hero Achilles. But the boy did not blindly follow his teacher. In particular, he seems to have rethought his Hellenocentrism, at least if, as report has it, Aristotle advised him to act as a king to the Greeks and as a master to the Barbarians. If this advice was really given, it did not determine the course that Alexander was to follow, as we shall see.

PHILIP AND ATHENS

In 342 B.C., Philip set out on yet another military campaign, moving against Thrace with the aim of completely subjecting it. This threatened the Greek cities in the Hellespont, and in Athens the orator Demosthenes once again harangued the Athenians on the dangers Philip posed to their interests. Philip first besieged Perinthus, perhaps using the torsion catapult for the first time, but he met stubborn and sustained resistance and finally withdrew to besiege Byzantium. While he ultimately failed to take that city, he did capture 230 vessels used in the transport of grain, including 180 Athenian ships. This was a great blow to the Athenian economy and morale, and Demosthenes was finally able to rouse the Athenian demos to declare war. The Persians joined in, alerted by Hermias' plot to the danger Philip posed to them as well.

Philip first turned against the Scythians, to secure the northern frontier before he marched south to carry the war into Greece. In the Scythian campaign he again suffered serious injury, surviving an attack in which a spear passed through his thigh, killing his horse.

As Philip recovered from his latest injury, plans went forward for the march into Greece. The way was opened when, in 338 B.C., the Amphictyonic Council again invited him to take command of yet another Sacred War. The Thebans abandoned their alliance with Philip to join Athens in opposing him, but at the battle of Chaeronea in Boeotia, Theban hoplites, the strongest troops the allied Greeks had to offer, proved no match for the Macedonian cavalry.

Led by Alexander, now eighteen, the Macedonian cavalry broke through the Theban line with the Sacred Band at the fore. The Sacred Band made a last, hopeless stand, fighting until they fell and winning lasting glory for their self-sacrifice in the name of freedom, much as had the Spartans at Thermopylae. Philip then took the Athenians in an assault against which they proved helpless. One thousand were killed, two thousand captured, and the rest fled, including Demosthenes, who had been serving as a hoplite. By this decisive victory, Philip effectively became master of Greece.

After the debacle at Chaeronea, the Athenians expected the worst. Philip indeed punished Thebes severely for abandoning its Macedonian alliance, executing or confiscating the property of his leading opponents, establishing a garrison on the Kadmeia, and breaking up the Boeotian League, thereby giving its cities their independence. But Philip showed surprising leniency toward Athens, in part out of reverence for Athenian culture, but also probably out of practical concern for the Athenian fleet, which his naval forces could not match, and the possibility of a failed siege like those of Byzantium and Perinthus. He sent Alexander at the head of a procession to return the ashes of the Athenian dead, freed the Athenian prisoners, and left Athens in control of several of its island possessions.

The victory at Chaeronea allowed Philip to impose a new political order on the mainland Greeks. Following a pattern set by the Theban general Epaminondas, he created a "league of leagues," the *League of Corinth*. It took the form of a **symmachia,** or military alliance, with Philip as Hegemon. The Greek cities were guaranteed freedom from outside attack, freedom in the conduct of their internal affairs, freedom of navigation, and freedom from tribute or garrisons (with the exception of Thebes). The affairs of the League were to be administered by a confederate council, or *Synhedrion*, in which all the Greek members were represented; it could enact decrees binding on the members, as well as pass judgment over them as a court.

These admirable concessions never got proper exercise, however, for Philip was now in an excellent position to carry out his plans for a panhellenic expedition against the Persians. The time was opportune. Since the beginning of the fourth century B.C., Persia had suffered from succession problems—for example, the failed attempt of Cyrus to seize power, which led to the adventures of the Ten Thousand (recorded by Xenophon). To these difficulties were added widespread revolts in the satrapies, including a general revolt of most of the satraps west of the Euphrates in the 360s B.C. Egypt had asserted its independence in

405 B.C., and was repeatedly successful in repelling Persian attacks. From 358 to 338 B.C. a stronger ruler, Artaxerxes III Ochus, was somewhat successful in curbing revolt, regaining Egypt, although only by the use of mercenaries—Greek mercenaries. But shortly before the battle of Chaeronea, Ochus was assassinated by his vizier Bagoas, who also killed all the king's immediate family—with the exception of his youngest son, Arses, whom he put upon the throne as a puppet (as Artaxerxes IV). Two years later, in 336 B.C., he eliminated him as well, putting on the throne a descendant of Darius II, who ruled as Darius III. Darius III immediately removed the vizier, who was assassinated. Revolt was widespread, and the Persian Empire and Persian military power may perhaps have reached their lowest point, since Darius soon began showing signs of reasserting effective control. The Athenian Isocrates had been advocating a common Greek war against the Persians since the 380s, and in 346 B.C. had written an open letter to Philip suggesting that he lead such a crusade.[18] The projected expedition, by uniting the Greek cities in a common cause, would resolve the problem of their constant internecine warfare.

We do not know when Philip actually decided to take up the challenge posed by Isocrates, but in 337 B.C. the council that administered the affairs of the Corinthian League (the Synhedrion) declared war on Persia. In the spring of 336 B.C. Philip sent an advance force to Asia Minor under the general Parmenio to lay the groundwork for the invasion. Before he could carry out these ambitious plans, however, he fell to an assassin's blow, and the new Trojan War was left to his successor, Alexander.

THE ASSASSINATION OF PHILIP

The assassination of Philip is presented by our sources in the context of extended difficulties in the relationship between father and son.[19] First there was the matter of Philip's seventh marriage, to Cleopatra, ward and niece of his general Attalus. Unlike Philip's other marriages, this one was not a matter of foreign policy, for the bride was Macedonian. This appears to have caused concern about her status with respect to that of the other wives, and it seems to have been seen by Olympias, especially, as a threat to her hopes of preeminence as her son came of age and proved himself by his military achievements to be a worthy heir to the kingship. At the drinking party after the wedding, Attalus exacerbated the situation by proposing a toast to a prospective *legitimate* heir to the kingdom. Alexander protested the insult, Philip defended Attalus, and would have run Alexander through with his sword had he not been so drunk that he stumbled and fell. Alexander taunted him, then both mother and son quickly withdrew from the court. She went to Epirus, and he traveled to one of the Illyrian kingdoms.

After this quarrel was patched up by the intervention of a friend, Alexander returned to the court. (It is not known if Olympias also returned at this time.) He then learned of negotiations for a proposed marriage alliance between the daughter of Pixodaros of Caria, a vassal of the king of Persia, and Alexander's half-brother Arrhidaios, who was somehow disabled (as noted earlier) and never, it seems, considered as a possible successor to Philip. Disturbed at this apparent slight to himself, Alexander secretly contacted Pixodaros and offered to serve as bridegroom instead. When Philip discovered these secret counternegotiations, he was furious, and the deal fell through. Philip exiled some of Alexander's friends, but he continued to try to conciliate Alexander.

Perhaps as part of his efforts to reconcile himself with Alexander and Olympias, in 336 B.C. Philip arranged the wedding of Alexander's sister Cleopatra, also Olympias' child, to her maternal uncle, Alexander, who had been established as king of Epirus by Philip. The wedding celebrations, which were planned to celebrate the departure of the great expedition to Asia as well, were marked by a brilliant display of Greek culture, with dramatic and athletic contests, and many Greek guests. Delphi provided an oracle for the expedition: "Garlanded is the bull. Fulfillment is here. One there is who will strike the victim." But, as was so often the case, the oracle was ambiguous. In fact, the victim turned out to be not the Persian king, but Philip himself, who was assassinated in the midst of the wedding ceremonies.[20] The assassin, Pausanias, was a Macedonian nobleman and member of the King's Guard, and his reputed motive was revenge for an insult. Pausanias had quarreled with and been insulted by another young man, also named Pausanias, both of whom were suitors of Philip. The second Pausanias told Attalus of the insult, and also confided in him that he could not bear the shame and planned to kill himself. He did this by stepping in front of Philip in battle as the king was attacked by King Pleurias of the Illyrians, giving his life for his king's. Attalus blamed the first Pausanias for the second Pausanias' death, and took vengeance by arranging to have his men sodomize Pausanias while the nobleman was drunk. Pausanias complained to Philip, but the king, although angry, declined to avenge the insult by his new kin.

The insult rankled in Pausanias' mind, and he determined to get his revenge. Thus when Philip reached what seemed to be the height of hubris with the grandiose wedding festival of his daughter Cleopatra, even having his statue carried in the procession among those of the twelve Olympian gods, the offended man took his opportunity. As the king entered the crowded theater, he had his bodyguard deliberately stand at a distance in order to display his trust in the goodwill of his Greek guests. Pausanias seized the opportunity to rush forward and plunge a Celtic dagger into the king's chest. He nearly escaped, bolting toward a horse that he had posted at the city gates, but the other bodyguards ran him down and killed him on the spot. Thus a number of vexing questions are unresolved to this day: did he act only for himself, or was he instigated to act by others, and, if so, by whom?

At the time, no complex plot was officially considered. Alexander had two of

Pausanias' friends—brothers from Lyncestis and not candidates for the kingship—executed as accomplices of Pausanias. Alexander also soon eliminated Amyntas, but Amyntas' possible claim to the kingship, rather than any complicity in Philip's murder, seems to have been the motivation. Aristotle accepted the story of Pausanias' motivation, using the death of Philip as one of numerous examples of conspiracies against monarchies brought about by insults.[21] However, according to Plutarch, gossip at the time cast suspicion upon both Alexander and Olympias,[22] and Justin directly implicates Olympias.[23] These sources are, however, strongly tainted by the deep-seated Greek fear of women in control.[24] Thus Plutarch repeatedly blames women in general, and Olympias in particular, for aspects of the problem.

SOURCE ANALYSIS

PLUTARCH *ALEXANDER* 9–10.[25] Consider the allusions to women, and specifically to Olympias, in Plutarch's story of the assassination. How much fact and how much interpretation does each involve?

> But before long the domestic strife that resulted from Philip's various marriages and love affairs caused the quarrels which took place in the women's apartments to infect the whole kingdom, and led to bitter clashes and accusations between father and son. This breach was widened by Olympias, a woman of a jealous and vindictive temper, who incited Alexander to oppose his father. . . .
>
> [On the Pixodaros affair] Alexander's mother and his friends sent him a distorted account of this manoeuvre, making out that Philip was planning to settle the kingdom upon Arrhidaeus by arranging a brilliant marriage and treating him as a person of great consequence. . . .
>
> It was Olympias who was chiefly blamed for the assassination, because she was believed to have encouraged the young man [Pausanias] and incited him to take his revenge.

Many modern scholars have adopted the conspiracy theory. Although most absolve Alexander of complicity,[26] many have looked to Olympias, her alleged motivations being sexual jealousy and/or a desire to protect her son's claim to the succession and her own position as "queen mother." In this, it seems that the ancient Greeks' misogyny has regrettably become part of our own inheritance.[27] For the queen is a fairly poor suspect. If she had not returned to the court, it is unlikely that she could have incited and prodded Pausanias from a distance. This would have required sending letters and messengers—a procedure too complicated and with too great a risk of revelation. Although she did use such long-distance methods in some other cases of influence,[28] none of these cases were so risky. Assuming that she had returned to the court (the evidence suggests this), why would she have chosen this very showy, public scheme, full of potential for both discovery and disaster, rather than utilizing some more sure, private means, for which she certainly had opportunity?[29] And why would Pausanias have sought her help? As described, the "plot" was simple and depended much upon opportunity: Pausanias had his Celtic dagger ready, but he might have carried that many times in hopes of a lucky chance (the Celtic designation is in itself suspicious, suggesting an addition from Hellenistic drama), and he had left his horse nearby (even a child could have watched his horse). He had no need to multiply chances of discovery by involving unnecessary people, especially a woman with Olympias' reputedly mercurial personality.

"PHILIP'S BURIAL" AND OTHER ARCHAEOLOGICAL EVIDENCE

A new mystery was added to the subject of Philip's death by the discovery in 1977 of a funeral mound in the ancient Macedonian capital of Aigai at Vergina, traditional burial place of the Macedonian kings. The tumulus contained two previously untouched chamber tombs, an unusually large cist tomb that had been looted some time earlier, and the remains of what may have been a heroön, or funerary shrine, suggesting worship of one or more of the occupants of the burial tumulus. The three tombs were excavated by the Greek archaeologist Manolis Andronicos.[30] The cist tomb, which is labeled "Tomb I," is the earliest of the three. Although this tomb had been looted, it still contained the inhumed remains of a male "in the prime of life," a young woman around twenty-five, and an infant, said to have been a neonate. Splendid wall paintings cover three of the four walls, portraying the seizure of Persephone by Hades, the lord of the Underworld; the Three Fates; and a seated female figure probably to be identified as Demeter, the mother of Persephone, grieving over her lost daughter.[31]

The larger of the chamber tombs, called "Tomb II," has the form of a typical "Macedonian tomb." Such tombs are subterranean buildings characterized by a vault; they usually contain two chambers—the burial chamber itself and an antechamber with a central door and a facade like that of a building. Tomb II has an impressive facade, its central door surmounted by a painted frieze of triglyphs and metopes, which is in turn surmounted by a frieze that extends the width of the building and depicts a lion hunt. This second frieze is crowned by a cornice. The main chamber showed signs of hasty completion, and the antechamber, more carefully done, may have been added later. Both the main chamber and the antechamber contained gold *larnaces*, or caskets, which held cremation remains, the larger larnax weighing 11 kilograms with its contents, the smaller 8.5 kilo-

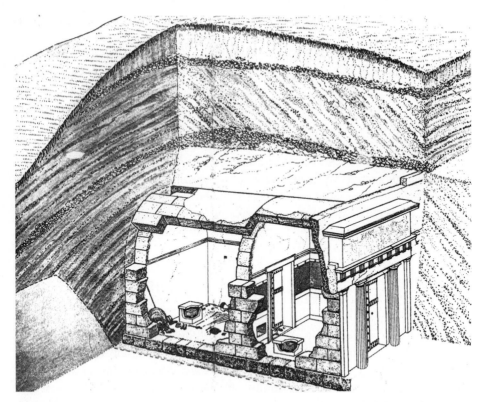

FIGURE 14-1   Tomb at Vergina, speculatively identified as that of Philip II of
Macedon.

grams. The lids of both larnaces were decorated with the Macedonian star, and,
in both cases, the remains were wrapped in purple cloth. In the larger larnax was
also a gold crown of oak leaves and acorns, and in the smaller, a gold diadem.
The inner burial chamber was richly equipped: in it were found a number of silver and bronze vessels and elaborately ornamented armor, including a cuirass of
iron decorated with eight solid gold lion heads. The antechamber with the female burial contained gold greaves and a gold quiver, and near the larnax lay a
gold myrtle wreath of intricate workmanship and a gold diadem of spirals and
scrolls interwoven with flowers, bees, and birds.

The second chamber tomb, "Tomb III," is smaller and of simpler construction than Tomb II. Its exterior frieze appears to have been painted on a panel of
wood of which only traces remain. The walls of the antechamber were crowned
by a frieze of a chariot race. The tomb contained a rich collection of vessels of
various sorts, but of lesser quality than those in Tomb II, some weapons, ivory
relief decorations that probably ornamented a couch, and a large silver hydria
(vessel used for water in symposium) containing the cremation remains, with a

gold wreath placed on its shoulder. The cremated remains were those of a single individual, a male between twelve and fourteen years of age.

The identity of the individuals buried in these three tombs poses a mystery that is still unresolved. The excavator, Andronicos, identified the largest tomb as that of Philip and Cleopatra.[32] Others have suggested Arrhidaios, who succeeded to joint rule with the infant son of Alexander after Alexander's death, and his wife Eurydike. Alexander's general Cassander murdered both Arrhidaios and Eurydike in the autumn of 317 B.C. in order to secure his place as king of Macedonia. He buried them, with funeral games and proper rituals, early in the following year. If Tomb II is that of Arrhidaios and Eurydike, then the occupants of the earlier cist grave—a middle-aged male, a young woman, and an infant—might be Philip, Cleopatra, and their child.[33] However, if the bones of the infant are indeed those of a neonate, this would not fit the reported facts of Cleopatra's death, and there are other questions as well: despite the wall paintings, this tomb does not seem magnificent enough to have been provided by Alexander for his father, nor does it seem likely that he would have interred Philip with the new wife to whom he had so strongly objected. There is also the possibility, suggested by Hammond and entertained, with reservations, by Andronicos, that the female was another of Philip's wives, possibly Meda, who was the daughter of a Getic king.[34] The arms are those of an archer, which fit Getic fighting methods, and the Getae practiced suttee, which would possibly explain the coincidence of the woman's burial with the man.

Most scholars are agreed that the occupant of Tomb III is Alexander IV, who was killed at just the right age to match the cremated remains; nevertheless, the excavator remains silent on this identification.

Of perhaps more lasting significance than the debate over the identification of these members of the royal family—a question which may or may not one day be resolved with additional study of the remains—is the impetus that the finds have given to archaeological investigations in Macedonia.[35] In all, some seventy tombs of "Macedonian" type have been discovered; the majority are in Lower Macedonia, but six are in southern Greece and two in Asia Minor. Among the most interesting of these Macedonian tombs is the "Tomb of Eurydike," the mother of Philip, discovered by Andronicos in 1987. It is the earliest and the largest of the Macedonian tombs, and, while it had been looted, its size and an exceptionally rich throne that it still contained suggest that it was a royal tomb. The throne is a masterpiece, covered with painted and relief decorations on almost its entire surface. The marble back of the throne contains its most important decoration: a picture of Hades and Persephone in their glory, mounted on a four-horse chariot. The tomb has been dated by the initials of an eponymous archon that were found on a sherd of a panathenaic amphora outside the tomb; the initials have been identified as those of a certain Lykiskos, who held office in 344 B.C.

The earliest of the Macedonian tombs dates from just after the middle of the fourth century B.C., but earlier chamber tombs show the development of the internal arrangement and the development of the vaulted roofing, which pre-dated the "Royal Tombs" at Vergina. All, of course, are the monuments of people of great wealth and a very elevated social rank, but they also yield important information about the development of Greek architecture and especially of painting, of which there are few well-preserved examples.

Cemeteries containing the burials of more ordinary people have also yielded masses of information about the culture and funerary customs of the Archaic and early Classical periods. These include a cemetery of a hundred twenty-one tombs near Sindos, 20 kilometers to the west of Thessalonike, and, at Vergina, an Archaic and Classical period cemetery with six tombs, two unplundered, dating from 540 through 430 B.C. to 420 through 410 B.C.

Excavations at sites other than cemeteries have been, or are being, carried out. The more notable include the palaces at Vergina and Pella, and excavations at a number of urban sites: Pella itself, the capital in the time of Philip and Alexander; Dion, the religious capital of Macedonia; and the Athenian colony of Amphipolis, founded in 437 B.C. The way in which the information from such excavations can affect our view of the written evidence is made clear by the case of Aiane, the capital of the Elimea, in Upper Macedonia. There an urban site dating to the fifth century B.C. has been discovered, with agora and terraced stoa. The dimensions of the building and the quality of the construction show that there was organized urban activity at this site a century before our written sources tell us that Philip II incorporated this supposedly backward area into his reorganized kingdom. It gives a different slant to the speech of Alexander from Arrian, quoted above, in which he claimed that it was his father who had brought the Macedonians clothed in skins, down from a rude life in the hills, civilized them, and settled them in cities.

CONCLUSION

In 359 B.C., at the age of twenty-three, Philip took over the kingship of Macedonia after his brother the king had been killed in a humiliating defeat fighting against invading Illyrians. The army was demoralized, the kingdom hedged in and subject to attack by hostile neighbors, and the kingship itself contested. Philip, however, took effective control.

He first reorganized the army, disciplining it and turning it into a powerful instrument of imperial expansion. He used politically motivated marriages as a further means of extending his sphere of influence. Taking advantage of the opportunities at hand, he also became master of the silver-mining region to the east, a rich resource that made possible further military developments and ventures. He then turned his attention south.

Invited to intervene in the Sacred Wars over Delphi, Philip eventually obtained a seat on the Amphictyonic Council of Delphi and gratitude as the "Savior of Delphi." In 338 B.C., he used this entrée to Greece to defeat a coalition of Thebes and Athens at the battle of Chaeronea. This victory made him master of Greece, which he organized into the League of Corinth, with himself as Hegemon.

Philip was on the verge of leading a (nearly) united Greece on a new Trojan War, a great expedition of retribution against the Persian Empire, when he was cut down by an assassin. His son Alexander inherited the kingdom, the newly powerful army, and the cause of Panhellenic war against the Barbarian.

IMPORTANT PLACES IN CHAPTER 14

Places on the Map: Aigai at Verginia, Assos, Atarneus, Byzantium, Caria, Chaeronea, Corinth, Delphi, Epirus, Eretria, Euboea, Gulf of Pagasai, Illyria, Krenides, Lesbos, Macedonia, Mytilene, Pagasai, Paionia, Perinthus, Persian Empire, Philippi, Potidaea, Rhodes, Scythia, Sparta, Thasos, Thebes, Thermopylae, Thrace

SUGGESTIONS FOR FURTHER READING

The basic work on this period in Macedonia is N. G. L. Hammond, G. T. Griffith, and F. W. Walbank, *A History of Macedonia* I–III (1972–1988). Useful works focusing on Philip include E. Borza, *In the Shadow of Olympus: The Emergence of Macedon* (1990), which provides the historical context for his reign; G. L. Cawkwell, *Philip of Macedon* (1978); and J. R. Ellis, *Philip II and Macedonian Imperialism* (1986). On Olympias and the role of women, see the many articles by Elizabeth Carney cited in the notes. On the archaeological remains, R. Ginouvès, ed., *Macedonia from Philip II to the Roman Conquest* (1994).

ENDNOTES

1. The main sources for Macedonian history as it affected the Greeks in the south are Athenian political pamphlets in the form of orations (of Demosthenes, Aeschines, Isocrates); the work of Diodorus Siculus (see Chapter 13); and *The Parallel Lives* of Plutarch, a Greek author of the first and second century A.D. who wrote biographies for the moral edification of a Roman audience.

2. See Ernst Badian, "Greeks and Macedonians," in Beryl Barr-Sharar and E. N. Borza, *Macedonia and Greece in Late Classical and Early Hellenistic Times* (1982), 33–51.

3. On the "constitutional" and "anticonstitutional" positions taken by various historians, see Eugene Borza, *In the Shadow of Olympus: The Emergence of Macedon* (1992), 231–248; Elizabeth Carney, "Women and *Basileia*: Legitimacy and Female Political Action in Macedonia," *The Classical Journal* 90 (1995), 367–391. An anticonstitutional position seems the most persuasive and is the position adopted here.

4. Arrhidaios was killed by order of Olympias, the mother of Alexander the Great, in ca. 317, and Alexander IV was murdered at age thirteen by the Antigonid Cassander in his maneuvering to obtain the kingship. He also killed Olympias, as well as Herakles, the son of Alexander by Barsine, and married Alexander III's half-sister Thessalonike to give himself an Argead connection.

5. This was denied by Ellis because of Philip's youth—he was thirteen–fourteen or fifteen–sixteen years old at the time; however, Philip was only twenty-three at his accession, and his son Alexander (the Great) was only eighteen when he led the hetairoi cavalry to victory over the elite Theban Sacred Band at the battle of Chaeronea in 338 B.C. Even though the adolescent Philip had no assurance of ever becoming king when he was a hostage in Thebes, military matters could not have been far from the mind of a young male member of the Macedonian royal house.

6. Diod. Sic. xvi.2

7. On the reorganization of the army, see N. G. L. Hammond and G. T. Griffith, *A History of Macedonia* II (1979), 405–449.

8. Griffith, 421–424.

9. Griffith (see above, n. 7), 431.

10. Arrian, reprinted by permission of the publishers and Loeb Classical Library from Arrian: *History of Alexander*, 7.9.2–4, Peter A. Brunt, tr. (1976).

11. On the effectiveness of ancient cavalry, see I. G. Spence, *The Cavalry of Classical Greece* (1993).

12. Griffith (above, n. 7), 444–449; E. W. Marsden, *Greek and Roman Artillery: Historical Development* (1969), 5–17, 48–56.

13. The order of some of these early marriages is uncertain; see Borza, *Shadow* (above, n. 3), 206–208.

14. W. S. Greenwalt, "The Search for Arrhideus," *Ancient World* 10 (1984), 69–77.

15. In comparison, on their entrance into the Peloponnesian War the Athenians were collecting an annual tribute of 600 talents and had a reserve on the Acropolis of 6000 talents, laid aside for critical emergencies (they had spent 3700 talents on the building program and the siege of Potidaea); in addition, Thucydides (2.13) notes that they had about 500 talents in the form of dedications in other shrines, and that the gold on the cult statue of Athena weighed 40 talents.

16. Expressed, for example, in the *Protrepticus*, which was addressed to a Cypriot prince around 354 B.C.

17. See D. M. Balme, "The Place of Biology in Aristotle's Philosophy," in A. Gotthelf and J. G. Lennox, *Philosophical Issues in Aristotle's Biology* (1987), 9–20.

18. Isoc., *Philippus*.

19. The basic ancient sources on Philip's assassination and antecedent Pixodaros affair are: Plutarch, *Alex.* 9.3–12; *Mor.* 327c.
Diod. Sic. 16.91–95; "tragic-history" according to Griffith (above, n. 7), 675.
Just. 9.7.10; *P. Oxy.* 1798 = *FGrH* 148.1; cf. A. B. Bosworth, "Philip II and Upper Macedonia," *Classical Quarterly* n.s. 21 (1971), 93–105.
Arist., *Pol.* 5.1311a25–1311.b3.
Satyrus, ap. Athen 13.557d.

20. The oracle story may have been a dramatic Hellenistic addition to the tale, as with many of the other dramatic touches in Diodorus's account.

21. Arist., *Pol.* 5.1311a25–1311.b3.

22. Plut., *Alex.* 10.4.

23. Justin 9.8.1–14.

24. See Elizabeth Carney, "Olympias and the Image of the Virago," *Phoenix* 47 (1993), 29–55.

25. Dryden, tr.

26. But not E. Badian, "The Death of Philip II," *Phoenix* 17 (1963), 244–250.

27. For example, consider the comments of R. Lane Fox, *Alexander the Great* (1973), 22–25, on a passage in Justin (9.7.10–11) accusing Olympias of crowning the crucified head of Pausanias, then cremating the body over her husband's remains, erecting a tomb on the spot, and consecrating the sword with which the king was stabbed to Apollo (using her maiden name): "This may be exaggerated, but there is no reason to dismiss all its details as false or as malicious rumour; its source cannot be checked independently, but Olympias was a woman of wild emotion. . . . (23); similarly W. Heckel, "Philip and Olympias (337/6 B.C.)," in *Classical Contributions: Studies in Honour of Malcolm Francis McGregor*, G. S. Shrimpton and D. J. McCargar eds. (1981), 51–56, only suggests Olympias' guilt but closes with a quotation from a German article published in 1899: "*Dies Teufelsweib hat hinlänglich gezeigt, dass sie zu allem fähig war* . . . ." ("This she-devil has sufficiently shown that she was capable of anything.")

28. Elizabeth Carney, "The Politics of Polygamy: Olympias, Alexander and the Murder of Philip," *Historia* 41 (1992), 167–189, 182, n. 41, mentions various long-distance negotiations carried out by Olympias: marriage arrangements for her daughter, an attempt to seize Harpalus, and quarrels with Antipater.

29. Of many discussions, that of Carney (above, n. 28) is most persuasive on the unlikelihood of Olympias' having played a role and most instructive on the characteristics of polygamous marriage; it also contains a good bibliography on the controversy.

30. See M. Andronicos, *Vergina, the Royal Tombs and the Ancient City* (1984).

31. Andronicos (above, n. 30), 86–95; and Elizabeth Carney, "Tomb I at Vergina and the Meaning of the Great Tumulus as an Historical Monument, *Archaeological News* 17 (1992), 1–10.

32. Andronicos (above, n. 30); N. G. L. Hammond agrees, "The Royal Tombs at Vergina: Evolution and Identities," *Annual of the British School at Athens* 86 (1991), 69–82.

33. An interesting series of articles that brings all these identifications into question appeared in *The Ancient World* 22.2 (1991). The case is still open.

34. Andronicos, (above, n. 30), 231; Hammond (1978), 336; (1991), 67.

35. For these recent archaeological discoveries, see R. Ginouvès, ed., *Macedonia: From Philip II to the Roman Conquest* (1994).

CHAPTER FIFTEEN

Alexander the Great

A fter Philip's assassination in 336 B.C., the question of the succession was paramount. The recent turmoil within the royal family—the quarrel at the wedding, the flight of Alexander and Olympias from the court, and the Pixodaros affair—must have raised some degree of doubt about Alexander's status as heir, despite the fact that he was Philip's only fully competent son, and that Philip had given him military and diplomatic duties that seemed to mark him as the chosen successor. Other candidates stood in the wings. Amyntas, the infant son of Perdikkas III (whom Philip had himself displaced as king), was now grown and provided a viable Argead candidate. He may have been chosen as a potential contestant, even without his knowledge, by the two Lyncestian brothers who were quickly executed as accomplices of Pausanias (see Chapter 14). As princes of the Lyncestian royal house, they were not Argeads and could not have succeeded to the throne themselves, but possibly they sought the prerogatives that would have gone to them as kingmakers. A third Lyncestian brother, Alexander, who declared his support for Alexander immediately, was allowed to live and even received important appointments for a time, although many regarded him as also involved in the conspiracy. Perhaps he provided information helpful in convicting his brothers. Eventually, however, Alexander had him executed as well.

Alexander seems to have been greatly assisted in securing the throne by the advice and support of Antipater, the senior statesman still surviving from Philip's reign. Members of the nobility in the palace at once proclaimed Alexander the successor, and within days he addressed a formal assembly of the people as king, promising to continue his father's policies.

The two Lyncestian brothers accused as accomplices of Pausanias were ritually executed at Philip's funeral to avenge his death. Other potential rivals and

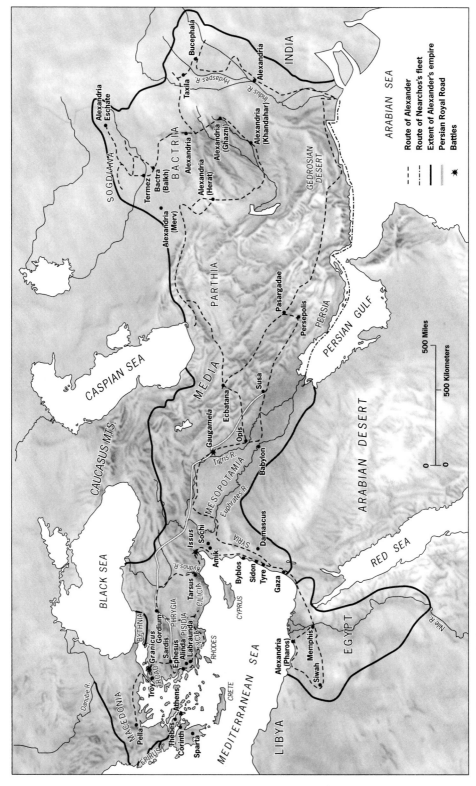

MAP 15 The route of Alexander.

foes were quickly eliminated, as was common practice in Macedonian successions, given their frequent ambiguity. Attalus, who had already alienated Alexander, could not be allowed to continue as a leader in the Asian campaign, and
Alexander sent a friend to arrest or assassinate him. Parmenio, Attalus' senior
general, demonstrated his loyalty to the new king by refusing to intervene, and,
although Attalus tried to bargain with Alexander for his life, the assassination
was carried out before Alexander replied. Amyntas, who had perhaps been the
Lyncestian brothers' candidate for the throne, and who certainly posed a continuing risk, was also eliminated.

Finally, Olympias is given credit for the murder of Cleopatra, Philip's young
widow, and her infant child. The child seems to have been a girl, but even a girl,
as an offspring of Alexander, could have served as a focus of dynastic manipula-
tions through marriage. Olympias is condemned for the cruelty of her acts by
the sources—which are all Greek; however, if she was indeed responsible, she,
too, was acting according to the traditional Macedonian pattern. The only difference was her sex—women, even royal Macedonian women, were not expected to indulge in bloody acts.[1] Alexander is reported to have been angry, but
he had made no moves to protect the victims, nor did he punish the perpetrator.

As he struggled to consolidate his hold on the throne in Macedonia, Alexander faced external challenges from both the north and the south: the tribal peoples to the north, who sensed the prospect of freedom in the weakness of a successor, seized the opportunity to revolt, as did a number of Greek cities, for the
same reason. Late in 336 B.C. Alexander made a quick march south into Greece
to assert his right as Hegemon of the Corinthian League and as leader of the
Asian expedition. He then returned to Macedonia to deal with the northern
tribes, for he could not afford to leave Macedonia insecure and vulnerable to attack as he marched into Asia. But while he was fighting in the north, rumors of
his death began to circulate in Thebes, and the Thebans rose in revolt. Alexander responded with a lightning march south to deliver a lesson in terror to the
Greeks by the destruction of the city (in 335 B.C.). He spared only the house of
Pindar.

THE SOURCES ON ALEXANDER

The sources on Alexander's life and campaigns are difficult, at best: all our extant reports are late and secondhand, even though these are sometimes based on
contemporary accounts. All reports of actual participants are now lost, except
for those fragments that were quoted by or incorporated into the works of later
writers. These eyewitness accounts included the work of Ptolemy, one of
Alexander's generals and later founder of the Ptolemaic dynasty in Egypt; Aristobulus, one of the Greek philosophers, scientists, and technicians who accom-

panied the Asian expedition; Callisthenes, a relative of Aristotle by marriage, who wrote much of the official history of the campaign; Onesicritus, Alexander's helmsman, a source mostly for descriptions of the natural curiosities of India; and Nearchus of Crete, who interlaced fact and romance in an account that disparaged Onesicritus. Another early source, although not a participant in the campaign, was Cleitarchus of Alexandria, who often preferred sensation and drama to the truth. The accounts of all these authors were colored and shaped by the purposes for which they were composed: for example, one can hardly expect an official history of the campaign to be completely impartial; nor was impartiality and the recitation of unvarnished facts recognized as a particular virtue by ancient writers. There were morals to be pointed out, rhetorical flourishes to be displayed, personal grudges to be pursued, a reading audience to be entertained; and the sources we have do all of this, often with abandon. Later writers who used this material often added their own rhetorical and even fantastic embellishments.

Of the extant, well-preserved sources, two stand out for their readability. The first is the account of Arrian, a native of Bithynia in Asia Minor, who lived during the first two centuries A.D. He had a traditional Roman political career, culminating in the consulship and service as governor of Cappadocia; he then retired to Athens where he devoted himself to writing; among his books is an account of Alexander's campaigns, *The Anabasis*. His narrative gives the impression of being a sober evaluation, and he was long considered to be the most dependable and responsible source. In fact, N. G. L. Hammond has suggested that Arrian used direct discourse or attribution by name to present material from what he considered his most reliable sources, Ptolemy and Aristobulus, and indirect means, such as "the story goes" or "it is said," to indicate those sources that he considered less reliable.[2] But it seems that Arrian was sometimes taken in by the subtle bias of one of his major sources, Ptolemy. Ptolemy was one of Alexander's generals; at the king's death he moved to take over the satrapy of Egypt, going so far as to kidnap Alexander's corpse and take it to Alexandria, where he entombed it in great splendor. He used his connection with Alexander to legitimate his rule, and the book that he wrote about the campaigns, and which Arrian used as a source, has been found to often magnify Ptolemy's own role in Alexander's campaign by omitting the acts of others. In other words, Ptolemy's account was part of his propaganda, aimed at an educated audience, just as much as was his possession of the body of Alexander and the tomb he provided for it, although these were aimed to appeal to the masses of the people. But unlike many of the other sources, his bias was subtle and sophisticated; it apparently escaped the notice of Arrian, and only recently has been recognized by modern scholars.[3]

Plutarch, the author of an interesting life of Alexander, was a native of Chaeronea in Boeotia, who spent his life mostly in service to his hometown and in scholarly writing. His *Life of Alexander* formed part of a larger work, the *Par-*

allel Lives, in which he used biographies to provide moral edification for his readers. His aim, to provide his readers with salutary role models while entertaining them, can, unlike Ptolemy's subtle bias, often be fairly easily detected.

Other important ancient sources for Alexander are the seventeenth book of the *Universal History* of Diodorus Siculus, a writer of the first century B.C., and, from the first century A.D., the works of Strabo and Curtius. In each case, the particular information must be assessed for its reliability. This is often a job for the expert scholar, but other readers can be on the lookout for anecdotal material and for the clearly fabulous, and can consider the possible motivations lying behind variant versions of a given incident.

THE EXPEDITION: ASIA MINOR AND THE SEACOAST

While Alexander settled affairs in Macedonia and Greece, Parmenio was in Asia Minor, establishing a base for the invasion, having proven his loyalty by his acquiescence to the killing of Attalus. Moreover, the unstable situation in Greece still called out for a unifying cause, and financial problems were also pressing Alexander toward action. Philip had left debts, and Alexander had added to them by the expenses of his own military campaigns; appropriating the riches of the Persian Empire was a tempting solution. Moreover, there was no time like the present as far as the susceptibility of the Persians was concerned, for the new Persian king, Darius III, was proving a competent ruler who might well revive the unity and strength of the Persian Empire. Finally, Alexander had the momentum of Philip's expansion to maintain, and an army primed to carry it on.

Leaving Antipater behind as regent in Macedonia and Greece, Alexander set out for the Hellespont in the early spring of 334 B.C., with an estimated 43,000 infantry, 6100 cavalry,[4] and a thirty-day supply of grain carried by the fleet.[5] This supply was sufficient to last until the harvest in May, when he would have reached Anatolia, where he could requisition food for his troops from the conquered.

Alexander's arrival on the continent of Asia was carried out with many symbolic acts that called attention to his heroic heritage. (See Source Analysis on page 311.)

The Persians chose to make their stand on the far bank of the Granicus River,[6] and to engage them the Macedonians had to cross the river. Although the water was probably no deeper than a meter in early spring, the problem for the Macedonians was the steepness of the riverbanks, which in places rose sharply 3 or 4 meters, preventing a direct frontal assault in extended line. As the Macedonian phalanx struggled up the banks they would have become disorganized and easy targets for slaughter in the river. There were, however, places along the bank where the gravel had accumulated and these offered relatively

S O U R C E   A N A L Y S I S

 RRIAN, *ANABASIS* 1.11.3–12.1.[7]   Consider in this passage the significance of Arrian's use of direct and indirect discourse:

In early spring he marched to the Hellespont, leaving Macedonian and Greek affairs in charge of Antipater. . . . Arriving at Elaeus, he sacrificed to Protesilaus at his tomb, since he was thought to be the first to disembark on Asian soil of the Greeks who fought with Agamemnon against Troy. The intention of the sacrifice was that his own landing on Asian soil might be luckier than that of Protesilaus.

Parmenio was appointed to see to the ferrying over from Sestus to Abydos of the cavalry and most of the infantry; they crossed in a hundred and sixty triremes and in a good number of cargo boats. According to the prevalent story Alexander made from Elaeus for the Achaean harbour, and steered the admiral's ship himself when he crossed, sacrificing a bull to Poseidon and the Nereids in the midst of the Hellespont strait, and pouring into the sea a drink offering from a golden bowl. They also say that he was the first to disembark on Asian soil [in full armor], that he set up altars both where he started from Europe and where he landed in Asia to Zeus of Safe Landings, Athena, and Heracles, and that he then went up to Troy, and sacrificed to the Trojan Athena, dedicated his full armour in the temple, and took down in its place some of the dedicated arms yet remaining from the Trojan war, which, it is said, the hypaspists henceforth used to carry before him into battle. Then he sacrificed also to Priam at the altar of Zeus of Enclosures (so runs the story), praying Priam not to vent his anger on the race of Neoptolemus, of which he himself was a scion.

When Alexander reached Troy Menoetius the pilot crowned him with a golden wreath and then Chares the Athenian arrived from Sigeum with others, Greeks or natives of the place. . . . Some say that Alexander crowned the tomb of Achilles, while Hephaestion, others say, placed a wreath on Patroclus' tomb; and Alexander, so the story goes, blessed Achilles for having Homer to proclaim his fame to posterity.

easy access. Alexander sent some of his force ahead to utilize these spots; they were directed to ride up in waves in a diagonal line rather than in a direct frontal assault on the banks. The Macedonian vanguard met the enemy cavalry and suffered badly, but by taking the momentum out of the Persian charge, they gave room for Alexander to lead a countercharge. He plunged into the hand-to-hand fighting and, once recognized, became the focus of an attack led by the son-in-law of the Persian king (the king himself was not present). His helmet was shattered, and it was only the intervention of one of his Companions, Cleitus, that saved him from death. Alexander escaped without serious injury, and the Macedonian cavalry soon pushed the Persians back so that the rest of the army was able to cross the river. They then advanced against the Persian mercenary infantry, which had been stationed far back in the foothills and had not yet played a part in the battle. The Persian infantry had to face both the Macedonian phalanx and the cavalry, and although they inflicted heavy casualties on the Macedonians, 9 out of 10 Persians fell in the fighting. The survivors, about two thousand, were taken prisoner. The Persian defeat was overwhelming, and the surviving Persian senior commander committed suicide. From this point on, the Persians recognized that they could not contest the Macedonian occupation of Asia Minor by land.

Alexander now established himself at Ephesus, a major port on the coast, in order to oversee the political organization of the newly acquired territory. At this time he also dismissed his fleet, since he was short on funds and the fleet was not large enough to achieve control of the sea. The problem of control of the sea was one that would determine Alexander's strategy throughout the first stage of the expedition. His solution was to use the Macedonian infantry to seize the ports, thereby gaining control of the Phoenician fleets based in them—these ships, which had provided the naval power of the Persians, were now to serve as the Macedonian fleet. By this strategy, he avoided direct confrontations at sea, where he was at a clear disadvantage, and continually added to the fleet under his control while reducing the Persians' seapower.

Following this strategy, Alexander next headed for the port of Halicarnassos in Caria.

Alexander and Ada

The city resisted, and he undertook his first major siege. He succeeded in taking the city, although some Persian holdouts who took refuge in the citadel were not defeated until months later. The Carian resistance had been led by Orontobates, Pixodaros' son-in-law (not long in the past, Alexander had offered himself for this very position of son-in-law; see Chapter 14). Pixodaros had usurped power from the legitimate ruler, his sister Ada, as noted earlier. Alexander reinstated Ada, allowing her to adopt him as a son. By making her satrap of Caria, he gained the allegiance of her political supporters, and by the adoption he gained a legitimate claim to Caria. (See Source Analysis on pages 313–314.)

The appointment of Ada as ruler of Caria was typical of Alexander's method of organizing conquered territory. Adopting the Persian system of satrapies, he usually kept military control in the hands of Macedonians, while often giving over control of civil affairs to natives who commanded local loyalties, as Ada obviously did, judging by her success in staving off Pixodaros and then Orontobates for seven years (from 341 to 334 B.C.) from the stronghold of Alinda. This policy of sharing rule with local figures stood in contrast to the traditional

S O U R C E   A N A L Y S I S

he story of Ada and Alexander is told by both Arrian and Plutarch. An idea of the differing approaches of these two sources can be gotten from a comparison of their respective treatments of this episode. How would you summarize the two approaches on the basis of the two treatments of this story?
According to Plutarch[8]:

> [Alexander] had also the most complete mastery over his appetite, and showed this both in many other ways, and especially by what he said to Ada, whom he honoured with the title of Mother and made queen of Caria. When, namely, in the kindness of her heart, she used to send him day by day many viands and sweetmeats, and finally offered him bakers and cooks reputed to be very skillful, he said he wanted none of them, for he had better cooks which had been given him by his tutor, Leonidas; for his breakfast, namely, a night march, and for his supper, a light breakfast.

According to Arrian[9]:

> As satrap of all Caria he appointed Ada, daughter of Hecatomnos, wife of Hidrieus; though her brother, he had lived with her in accordance with Carian custom. On his death Hidrieus had handed over affairs to her; from Semiramis down, it had been accepted in Asia that women should actually rule men. Pixodarus, however, turned her out of the government and held power himself. On his death Orontobates, his brother-in-law [this should be son-in-law], was sent down by the king and assumed the government. Ada meanwhile held only Alinda, the strongest fortress in Caria; and when Alexander entered Caria she went to meet him, surrendering Alinda and adopting Alexander as her son. Alexander gave Alinda to her charge, and did not reject the title of son, and when he had taken Halicarnassus and become master of the rest of Caria, made her ruler of the whole country.

Archaeological evidence may also exist for Ada. In 1989 when workmen were laying the foundation for a house in Bodrum (ancient Halicarnassos), they came upon a sarcophagus with the bones of a woman who had died in the mid-fourth century B.C. at about the age of forty. Gold ornaments from her clothing and a golden crown of a myrtle branch and flower design were found in the sarcophagus, as well as three rings, two bracelets, and two necklaces. Other burial goods included a black-glazed wine pitcher and three wine cups. The richness of the burial, the good physical condition of the woman, and the dating of the remains suggest that this was the burial of Ada, although no inscriptions were

continued

found to confirm this. The Bodrum Underwater Archaeology Museum employed experts from Manchester University Museum and the university's medical art department to make a reconstruction of the queen, and they have provided a suitable setting for the exhibit of the burial in a replica of the *Andron* (banquet hall) constructed by King Mausolos, the brother of Hidrieus and Ada, who preceded them in rule, at the shrine of Zeus at Labraunda in 355 B.C.[10]

Greek view of the Barbarians as the enemy, as well as to the reported advice of Aristotle that Alexander deal with the Barbarians as a master over slaves. It demonstrates Alexander's independence and pragmatic sense; if the Persian Empire were truly to come under his control, it could not be held by force of arms alone. He expanded this policy of shared administration as the campaign progressed, until it included the integration of Persians into the army itself. Alexander also adopted some of the dress and customs that his new subjects expected of their rulers. But many of Alexander's followers, especially the older men who had served Philip, did not share his vision of a bicultural future, and a current of opposition developed that at times threatened the campaign itself.

With affairs in Caria under control, the approach of winter required that Alexander find winter quarters for his army (334/33 B.C.). He won popularity with many by sending the newly married men back home to Macedonia, with orders to enroll new recruits during their stay. Parmenio was sent to Sardis with about a quarter of the army, and Alexander marched with the remainder along the warmer coast of southern Lycia and inland through Lycia and Pisidia, capturing or receiving the surrender of many towns. (It was common practice to split up an army in winter, so that no one district was overburdened with their provisioning.)

First Encounter with Darius

In the spring of 333 B.C. the army reassembled at Gordium, where Alexander visited a famous local landmark, the Wagon of Gordius, the mythical founder of the Phrygian dynasty. Tradition held that whoever could unfasten the knot on the yoke of this wagon (the famous Gordian Knot) would rule Asia. There are variant accounts of Alexander's actions. Arrian reports that most authors claimed that he cut the knot with his sword, while Aristobulus says that he removed the pole pin that held the knot together, and so removed the yoke from the pole.[11] In both versions Alexander succeeded in unfastening the knot in a less than direct way, yet in both he still fulfilled the prophecy.

Alexander next marched southeast, passing through the Cilician Gates and encamping at Tarsus. Here he fell seriously ill with a fever after a swim in the icy river. The fever brought Alexander near death, and he was saved only when his doctor prescribed a strong purge. (This was a typical remedy in Greek medicine; Alexander's recovery from this "remedy" suggests that his constitution was quite strong.) This was one of a number of times when Alexander suffered serious illness or injuries during the campaign, episodes that were to culminate in his early death. In this case, the fever was probably a malarial relapse, brought on either by fatigue or by chilling.[12]

Cilicia was Alexander's base for the next several months while he recovered. Meanwhile the Persian king Darius was collecting his forces, which included a large number of Greek mercenaries, and moving toward a confrontation. Alexander marched his forces south along the coast into the narrows between the mountains and the sea, hoping to meet Darius at a narrow site that would give the advantage to his smaller forces. But Darius was encamped east of the mountains at Sochi, in the Syrian plain of Amik. According to the sources, he delayed, at a loss for what to do. Some of his advisers urged him to stay put, since the plain gave his large army the advantage, but finally he decided to move forward. Perhaps delay was making supply of the army difficult, while Alexander was positioned on the sea, where his forces could be easily supplied. But Darius took an unexpected circuitous route northward to a pass over the mountains and then down south again into the Cilician Plain, surprising the Macedonians at their rear.

When he became aware of the situation, Alexander marched the bulk of his forces northward to meet Darius, probably leaving behind the allied infantry in case a second contingent of Persians should approach through the pass directly from Sochi and he should be surrounded. The Macedonians advanced until the two armies met at a relatively narrow spot along the coast, in November of 333 B.C., at the battle of Issus.[13] While the sources give obviously magnified numbers for the army of Darius, it is also clear that Alexander's forces were in fact greatly outnumbered. However, the Persian line soon gave way before the Macedonian phalanx; Alexander's court historians, always on the alert to see the worst in the Persian king, suggested that Darius fled at the very start of the battle, but other sources report that he fought bravely. It is in fact the confrontation of Darius and Alexander at this battle that is depicted on the famous mosaic from Pompeii, probably a copy of a contemporary painting based on eyewitness reports (Figure 15-1).

The battle did not last long, and Darius did soon flee, along with the rest of his army. They suffered terrible losses in the rout, reportedly losing 100,000 men, while the Macedonians lost only 500. The baggage train of the Persian king was also captured, with his treasury and the women of his court, including his wife and mother.

After the humiliation of his defeat. Darius quickly offered terms: if Alexander would restore his family, Darius would make peace and enter into an al-

FIGURE 15-1 Alexander and Darius mosaic from the House of the Faun at Pompeii.

liance. But Alexander was not ready to compromise. He countered with a list of all the grievances that the Greeks had against the Persians and a demand that Darius come to him as a suppliant, acknowledging him as king of all Asia, and that in the future Darius deal with him not as an equal but as an overlord.[14] The war was to continue.

Alexander could not risk pursuing Darius into the interior as long as the Persians had control of the sea and could foment trouble among the restless Greeks at his back. He therefore remained on the coast to continue with his plan of seizing the harbors used by the Persians. This was not to be easily achieved, however. Although the cities of Byblos and Sidon surrendered, Tyre refused to submit, and it required a seven-month siege, from January through August 332 B.C., and all the ingenuity of Alexander and his engineers to capture the island-city.

Alexander began his attack on Tyre by ordering the construction of a mole (raised dirtbank) to provide access to the island for his soldiers. While his men worked, the defenders attacked them by sea. To protect their workers and to provide a base from which to fire down on the attackers, the Macedonians then built two towers covered with a screen of hides and positioned them on the completed portion of the mole. The defenders countered by outfitting and launching an incendiary ship against the mole, setting the towers on fire. People from the city joined in the defense, rowing in and setting alight all the engines not caught by the fire from the incendiary ship. After the destruction, however,

Alexander rallied his forces to build a broader mole with more towers, and ordered the engineers to construct new machines, while he himself went off to collect more ships. The Phoenician naval commanders from Byblos and Sidon, learning that their cities had fallen to Alexander, brought their ships to join him, and commanders from Rhodes, Lycia, and Cyprus added their ships as well. Alarmed by the size of the new armada, the Tyrians refused to give battle, and Alexander set up a blockade of the city. When the mole was completed and the new engines ready, Alexander launched another attack. The city was stubbornly defended but finally fell.

EGYPT AND THE EAST

From Phoenicia Alexander marched south toward Egypt, taking the city of Gaza in a bitterly defended siege (from September to October 332 B.C.) in which he was wounded.

When Alexander entered Egypt he was welcomed as Pharaoh by a people who had been resentful of Persian rule. Two important events marked his stay in Egypt: the foundation of Alexandria in the spring of 331 B.C. and his visit to the oracle of Ammon at the oasis of Siwah (Libya).

Alexandria was the most successful of Alexander's many city foundations.[15] The location was strategically important: by connecting the offshore island of Pharos with the mainland, two good harbors would be provided on a coast where there were no other harbors suitable for a large fleet. This military advantage gave the city a commercial advantage as well, and it later prospered. The foundation of the city as celebrated in the Roman period was April 7, 331 B.C. Alexander reportedly determined the general layout of the town, deciding the circuit of the walls and the location of the agora and the main temples; he also selected the gods to whom the temples would be devoted—Greek gods as well as the Egyptian goddess Isis. Diodorus, who had visited the city, says that the streets were oriented so that the prevailing winds would cool the city and make it more healthful.[16] The original population was mixed, made up of Greek mercenaries, retired or disabled Macedonians, and local people from small nearby native settlements who would provide the menial labor force. Over time, however, the city attracted a large population from all areas of Greece and the Mediterranean.

Alexandria provided a model for many later Alexandrian city foundations, although none proved to be so successful. Seventy foundations were attributed to him by Plutarch.[17] In fact, however, the exact number is not known. Some are mentioned by the ancient sources, others are identifiable by continuing tradition and later claims, and still others have been discovered only by scholarly detective work. Most, like Alexandria in Egypt, were named after him. Unlike Alexandria in Egypt, however, the later foundations were made in isolated areas, east of the

Tigris, in a part of the world that had not yet been urbanized.[18] Many were founded on important trade routes or at their junctions; others were sited to provide protection against the intrusion of hostile tribes into conquered and pacified territory. Some have since disappeared or been changed radically, but five still remain as living cities: the original Alexandria in Egypt, Herat, Ghazni, Merv, and Termez. In addition to the cities, Alexander also established numerous garrisons in strategic locations.

The other significant event that occurred during Alexander's stay in Egypt was his visit to the oracle of Ammon at Siwah. This oracle was already well known and respected in the Greek world, and Siwah was a place of pilgrimage and homage to a god who was regarded by the Greeks as a manifestation of the Greek Zeus. In fact, there was a local branch of the cult not far from Alexander's home, at Aphytis in Chalkidike, whose coinage had long portrayed the horned head of Zeus Ammon. Alexander had long suspected that there was something exceptional about himself—was it possible that he was, like his ancestor Herakles, the son of a god, in his case, Zeus Ammon? This was the question that he was anxious to ask the oracle at Ammon.

The consultation was private, and Alexander kept the details of it to himself. Thus none of our sources can speak with authority about the exact questions that Alexander posed to the oracle, nor about its precise answers. But all agree that the oracle's responses confirmed Alexander's suspicions that he was the son of the god.

What did it mean, to be the son of Zeus Ammon? First of all, that he had a divine father did not mean that Alexander denied his human father, Philip; like Herakles, he had two "real" fathers, one human and one divine. Nor did it mean that Alexander himself was a god. For the Greeks, the offspring of mortals and divinities were heroes and mortal, not gods and immortal. There were, however, a few exceptional cases—heroes who, through extraordinary accomplishments, had become gods, being transported directly to heaven without dying. This was the case with Herakles, whom Alexander considered to be his direct ancestor.

Did Alexander at this point consider himself to be one of these exceptional cases? In Egypt, belief in the divinity of the ruler had been customary from the earliest period. When Alexander entered the country as a conqueror, the Egyptian people had naturally hailed him as Pharaoh and as a god. The pragmatic response for Alexander was not to try to revise thousands of years of Egyptian religious tradition, but to adapt to the expectations of his new subjects. (The same problem was met by the Romans as they expanded into the east, where the common belief that the Emperor as ruler was divine disturbed the Roman Senators, who saw the Emperor as a human being like themselves, albeit the first among equals.) To what extent these two events—his recognition by the people of Egypt and his recognition by the oracle at Siwah—merged in Alexander's mind to solidify his belief in his own divinity, we cannot know. However, it is clear that the nature of his "divinity" was a matter of serious debate among the Macedonians, and that Alexander's belief in his divine ancestry was a source of continuing irritation to some. Despite Herakles, and even despite a few harbingers of the elevation of important political figures to divinity that had already appeared in Greece (for example, Lysander had accepted worship from the people of Samos; see Chapter 13), the Greeks did not traditionally attribute divinity to their rulers, and the idea was troubling to the more conservative men.[19]

When the political settlement of Egypt was concluded and his curiosity about his paternity satisfied, Alexander turned back to the east and the unfinished business of Darius. The king, trying to forestall a military disaster, now offered even more generous terms to Alexander: 10,000 talents in return for his family, all the territory west of the Euphrates, the hand of his daughter in marriage, and future friendship and alliance. Many of his staff urged acceptance at this point, but Alexander was unbending. He demanded again that Darius acknowledge his overlordship by coming to him as a suppliant. This uncompromising reply shows that Alexander was now firmly committed to rule as king over the entire Persian Empire, an idea that had been gradually gaining importance to him since the episode of the Gordian Knot. Requital for Persia's past wrongs was no longer enough.

On October 1, 331 B.C., he met the king in battle at Gaugamela—in Assyria near the Tigris River, not far from Nineveh. Darius picked the battle spot, positioning his forces in a level plain that would offer the best scope for use of his strong point, the cavalry. In addition, he had 200 scythed chariots and had had the battle surface smoothed out in order to assure their most effective use. In the clash of forces, however, the scythed chariots proved ineffective—the Macedonian light infantry attacked their horses, and those few that escaped were allowed to pass harmlessly through gaps that were opened in the Macedonian line. Alexander himself, at the head of a wedge-shaped formation, drove through a gap in the Persian line, continually widening it. Darius, at the center, came under increasing pressure, until finally he turned to escape—and Alexander followed. Alexander pressed his pursuit until evening, becoming separated from the rest of the army, but he failed to catch the king. The battle continued, however, and some of the sources seem intent on exonerating Alexander for his reckless abandonment of the field in the midst of the battle. Nevertheless, a general rout of the Persians followed, and the victory at Gaugamela was the decisive victory of empire. Darius, having fled the field in disgrace, now became a fugitive.

Rather than continuing his pursuit of the king at once, Alexander next turned his attention to gaining control of the various capitals of the Persian Empire to which he now laid claim: Babylon, Susa, Pasargadae, Persepolis, and Ecbatana. In each of these he seized the royal treasury; the total was reckoned at 180,000 talents of gold, an amount equal to 200 years of the income of Athens at the height of its power.[20] This treasure would radically alter the economy of the ancient world in the Hellenistic period as more and more of it was coined and passed into circulation.

Only at Persepolis, the capital associated with Darius I and Xerxes, was the army turned loose to loot, even though the city did not resist occupation. Until that time, the army had been restrained from looting, and the spoils were added to the treasury of the expedition; now the men were allowed their due share of the fruits of victory, and they fell avidly upon the riches in the homes of the Persian nobility, killing the men and seizing the women as slaves.

Alexander remained in the palace at Persepolis for some time, overseeing allocation of the treasury, distributing some of the riches to other centers, and setting some aside to travel with the army. Nothing was to remain in Persepolis; the city was to be downgraded and a new capital established at Babylon. Perhaps as a final show of disparagement, in the spring of 330 B.C., in a dramatic act that aroused great controversy even in antiquity, Alexander burned the great palace. The violent fire left marks that are still visible in the ruins today. Some sources maintain Alexander's motive was symbolic retribution for the destructions caused by the Persian Wars, and that Alexander himself later regretted the act. Other sources provide a less savory picture, reporting that the conflagration was the suggestion of the Athenian courtesan Thais, the mistress of Ptolemy, during a drunken party.

The burning of the palace at Persepolis, whether on an impulse during a drunken party or as a sober act of policy, dramatically symbolized the end of the Panhellenic campaign of retribution against the Persians.[21] Either the campaign was to be declared finished, or it had to take on a new goal. For Alexander, the answer was not in doubt; he had already declared himself Darius' successor as ruler of the Persian Empire, and his restless ambition framed even more ambitious plans for extending that empire. But he faced strong opposition from some of his generals, who were disturbed by his increasing adoption of Persian ways and felt strongly that the army should return to Macedonia. These men are sometimes characterized as the *Old Guard*, men who had fought under Philip and were strongly imbued with the Macedonian ethos, in contrast to the younger men who had come to positions of authority under Alexander and shared his more pragmatic attitudes. It was surely significant that Parmenio, one of the most important of the Old Guard, advised against the burning of Persepolis, for he soon became a key victim in one of a series of events that had the effect of eliminating the central figures of this Macedonian opposition.

Opposition among the Macedonians

The plot that led to Parmenio's downfall is called the *conspiracy of Philotas*. Philotas was the son of Parmenio. Since the visit to the oracle of Ammon, Philotas had been outspoken in his disapproval of Alexander's increasing adoption of the customs and dress of a Persian king and of his claims to be the son of Zeus Ammon. In 330 B.C. an otherwise unknown Macedonian called Dimnos told his lover that he was involved in a conspiracy to murder Alexander. The boy then told his brother, who reported it to Philotas. Philotas, however, failed to pass the information along, apparently not taking it seriously. The brother then revealed the plot to one of the *Royal Pages* (adolescent sons of Macedonian nobles who were enlisted for personal attendance on the king), and the page reported it to Alexander. Dimnos immediately, and conveniently, killed himself (or was killed). The charge against Philotas was that he had failed to warn Alexander of the conspiracy, which he did not deny. There was no evidence that he had played any positive role in a plot against Alexander. Nevertheless, the army judged him guilty and executed him. With the execution of Philotas, the question was naturally raised of the possible involvement of his father, Parmenio. Family ties were strong in Macedonia, and even if Parmenio had played no role in the "plot," he could still be expected to avenge his son's death. Alexander did not hesitate, but sent a letter to the generals under Parmenio's command, ordering them to kill the old general. Because of the obscurity of Dimnos and his compatriots, and Philotas' tenuous role in the action, the plot has been seen by some as a conspiracy *against* Philotas, perhaps even a complex scheme primarily intended to eliminate Parmenio.[22]

Others of a conservative tendency also fell at this time, and Alexander's friends came more to the forefront. The third Lyncestian brother, Alexander (whose brothers had been executed as conspirators in the death of Philip), was executed now, and a member of the King's Body Guard who had been a friend of Philotas was replaced by Ptolemy (who after Alexander's death eventually become Ptolemy I of Egypt, as noted earlier). Aristotle's friend Hephaestion, who had played an active role against Philotas, also received his first important post, sharing the command of the Companion cavalry with Cleitus, who was soon to meet a fate similar to that of Philotas.

Meanwhile Darius had established himself in Ecbatana, the Median capital, still hoping to defend the Iranian heartland. As Alexander approached, Darius moved eastward. But the eastern satrapies, which had been relatively neglected by Darius and his predecessors, were unwilling to accept his leadership, compromised as it was by defeat. Opinions began to be expressed favoring the rule of Bessus, the strongest of the eastern satraps. A split developed in the Persian camp, and, as Alexander gained on the fleeing king, Bessus imprisoned Darius, carrying him along in a wagon, bound in golden chains. When it became clear that Alexander would catch up with them, Darius' captors killed him, preventing his being captured by Alexander and forced into the demeaning role of vassal.

On discovering the body of Darius, Alexander treated it with all the respect due to royalty, sending it back to Persepolis for a royal funeral and burial. He could now truly present himself as the king of all Asia—the last Achaemenid king was dead, and Alexander was in possession of all the Persian capitals, the principal one of which, Persepolis, lay in ruins. Bessus, however, now claimed the throne as Darius' successor and undertook to continue the war against Alexander.

Alexander pursued and finally caught Bessus in 330/29 B.C. Two stories are told of Bessus' death. According to one account, Alexander had Bessus stand, stripped and wearing a spiked dog collar, beside the road as the army passed by, and then had him executed.[23] According to the other account, Alexander had Bessus mutilated—his nose and ears cut off—and then executed.[24] Both stories illustrate Alexander's adoption of Persian customs—in this case, in the treatment of defeated foes. Which, if either, version is true is of less moment than the fact that rumors were circulating that expressed opposition to Alexander's "Persianizing."

Two other stories of the opposition to Alexander among the Macedonians focused on his lack of self-control, or *sophrosyne*. One relates an incident in 328 B.C., which ended with the death of Cleitus. Cleitus was the brother of Alexander's favorite nurse; moreover, he had saved Alexander's life in the battle of the Granicus, and he now shared with Hephaestion the command of the Companion cavalry. He seems to have been among the more conservative men, however, and some sources report that he had just been appointed satrap of Bactria and Sogdiana, probably a form of "honorable exile." When the incident occurred, Cleitus and other friends of Alexander were drinking together with the king in one of the traditional Macedonian drinking parties, where the consumption of unmixed wine often reached heroic quantities. When several of the Companions flattered Alexander, likening him to various gods, Cleitus reproved them for showing disrespect to the gods, caustically remarking that Alexander's achievements were not so great nor had he accomplished them unaided. This angered Alexander, but Cleitus continued taunting him. As the king's anger mounted, Cleitus' friends desperately tried to get him away from the king. Finally, in a drunken rage, Alexander grabbed a pike and ran him through. All the sources report that the king was immediately struck by guilt at what he had done and that he spent three days in remorseful seclusion, without food or water.

The second incident involved Callisthenes, a cousin and former pupil of Aristotle, whose job it was to write the official history of the campaign. Alexander was experimenting with having the Macedonians follow the Persian practice of doing obeisance to himself as king (the Greek term is *proskynesis;* the homage, which was secular and widely practiced among the Persians, was expressed in various ways, ranging from complete prostration before the ruler to bowing slightly and blowing a kiss). Callisthenes refused to do obeisance to Alexander, saying that this was an honor appropriate only to the gods. His arguments against obeisance pleased the more conservative Macedonians, who were uncomfortable with this new practice. But their disapproval greatly provoked Alexander, as did Callisthenes' claim that Alexander's fame did not rest on his own exploits, but on the history that he himself was writing. Alexander, however, bided his time, waiting for treasonous acts rather than mere words. Again, discovery of a plot provided the opportunity.

In 327 B.C. one of the Royal Pages anticipated Alexander in striking a wild boar during a hunt. As a punishment Alexander took the boy's horse away and ordered that the boy be whipped in front of the other pages. Embittered by the insulting punishment, the boy persuaded several of his fellow pages to help him avenge the insult by killing Alexander as he slept. As it happened, however, Alexander did not go to bed that night but instead drank the night away, and the pages' plot came to nothing. The next day, however, one of the boys talked too much, and the plot was revealed. All the conspirators were immediately arrested and confessed under torture, whereupon they were stoned to death by the army, the usual method of execution in such cases. Callisthenes was charged with having encouraged the pages in the attempt. Whether he was any more involved in this plot than Philotas had been in the plot that led to his death is unclear, however. According to some reports, Callisthenes was bound in chains and carried around with the army until he finally sickened and died; according to others, he was immediately racked, then put to death by hanging.

The Campaign Continues

Despite these problems in the Macedonian camp, the campaign went forward. Following the death of Darius and the execution of Bessus, Alexander faced no more counterclaimants to the Persian throne, but stubborn local resistance continued in the remote and mountainous areas of Sogdiana and Bactria (northern Iran, southern Russia, and Afghanistan). Three years of difficult guerrilla warfare were required to subdue these fiercely independent peoples. In the process, Alexander established a number of new cities, settling Macedonians and Greek mercenaries far from their homelands in the midst of an alien and hostile culture. While land and settlement were a customary reward for military service, many of these settlers were, not surprisingly, unwilling and unhappy residents in their new poleis.

INDIA AND RETURN

When he had succeeded in subduing the farthest eastern satrapies of the Persian Empire, Alexander might reasonably have turned back, having made good his claim to the Persian throne in addition to fulfilling his original objective of retribution for the Persian Wars. But he was driven on by a desire to conquer India and to reach the end of the world at Ocean, which, like most Greeks, he believed to encircle and delimit the world.

Once he had crossed the Indus River, Alexander soon met serious opposition from the Indian king, Poros, and it was in India that he fought his fourth— and last—pitched battle. In it his forces first confronted elephants in battle, although they had seen them earlier and Alexander have even acquired some for his own army, using them, however, for parade and display, rather than in battle. He had not trained his horses with the elephants either, and since untrained horses will not face elephants, the job of countering the elephant opposition was assigned to the infantry.

SOURCE ANALYSIS

 RRIAN 5.17.2–7.²⁵ What methods did Alexander use to meet the threat of the elephants to his troops?

Alexander, seeing his opportunity exactly in this redeployment of the cavalry, attacked those on his front, with such effect that the Indians did not even wait to receive the charge of his cavalry, but were broken and driven back to their elephants, as if to some friendly wall. At this point the drivers of the elephants brought up their animals against the cavalry, and the Macedonian phalanx for its part boldly advanced to meet the elephants, hurling javelins at their drivers, and, forming a ring round the animals, volleyed upon them from all sides. And the action was now without parallel in any previous contest, for the beasts charged into the line of infantry and, whichever way they turned, began to devastate the Macedonian phalanx, dense though it was, while the Indian cavalry, seeing the infantry fully engaged, wheeled again and themselves charged the cavalry. But when Alexander's forces had the mastery over them a second time, as they were much superior both in strength and experience, they were again pressed back on the elephants. At this point all Alexander's cavalry had become concentrated in one squadron, not under orders but forced into this concentration in the very conflict, and wherever it fell upon the Indian ranks they escaped only with heavy slaughter. The elephants were now crowded into a narrow space, and their own side were as much damaged by them as the enemy, and trodden down in their turnings and jostlings. Among the Indian cavalry, cramped round the elephants in a narrow space there was great carnage; and most of the drivers of the elephants had been shot down, some of the elephants had been wounded, others were weary and had lost their drivers; they no longer kept their separate formation in the battle, but, as if maddened by suffering, attacked friends and foes alike and in all sorts of ways kept pushing, trampling, and destroying. The Macedonians, however, had plenty of room, and attacked the animals at their own judgement, giving way wherever they charged, but following close as they turned round, and shooting at them with javelins, whereas the Indians who were retreating among the elephants were now receiving most damage from them. As the beasts wearied and no longer made vigorous charges, but merely trumpeted and gradually retired like ships backing water, Alexander himself threw his cavalry in a circle around their whole division, and then gave a signal for the infantry to lock shields, concentrate into the most compact mass possible and advance the phalanx. In this way the Indian cavalry were cut down in the action with few exceptions, while their infantry too were falling, as the Macedonians were by this time pressing them on all sides. At this point, where a gap appeared in Alexander's cavalry, they all turned and fled.

Despite Poros' great defeat, he fought bravely, only retreating from the battle at the end, when he was wounded. After much persuasion, he finally surrendered to Alexander, asking only to be treated as a king. Alexander rewarded his courage by returning his kingdom to him, and even adding to it; in return Poros became a faithful ally to Alexander. The victory was celebrated on coins, including large *decadrachms* (10-drachm pieces) portraying Alexander on horseback, armed with a sarissa and attacking Poros, who is mounted on an elephant, along with the driver. On the reverse, Alexander appears wielding the thunderbolt of Zeus and crowned by a small figure of Victory (Figure 15-2).[26]

After Alexander defeated Poros, the Indian ruler's enemies became Alexander's, and the fighting continued. Alexander's men, however, had finally lost their campaigning zeal. They had been away from their homes for years (it was now 326), local replacements of their worn-out Macedonian clothing seemed even to challenge their Macedonian identity, and monsoon rains had been pouring down upon them for over two months, rusting their equipment and generally making life miserable. To go on would mean more hardships, more river crossings, more battles, more elephants. They simply refused. Alexander tried to change their minds; he threatened to continue alone if necessary, but this threat was now answered only by stubborn silence. Finally he called together his generals and announced that they would turn back. At the news, the men wept and cheered and invoked blessings on Alexander. In the end, it was not the might of enemy forces but the exhaustion and the refusal of his own men to continue that brought Alexander's conquest of the world to an end.

While Alexander did agree to return, he did not take the fastest or easiest route back, choosing instead to use the return journey for further exploration and conquest. The army set out down the Hydaspes and Indus rivers in a trip that lasted from November 326 to July 325 B.C., during which they were faced with numerous hostile tribes and perilous conditions.

Among the local peoples whom they encountered, the Mallians were especially ferocious. The Mallians abandoned their cities and massed their forces for a single stand. When that failed, they took refuge in a heavily fortified settlement. Alexander's forces managed to break into the settlement, but as Alexander took the foremost role in the fighting, he was gravely wounded, his lung pierced by an arrow. As he lay wounded, rumors circulated that he had died. To counter these, Alexander had himself carried before the army on a boat, weakly lifting his hand to greet them so that they would know that he still lived. Once again, he survived.

While Alexander convalesced, his good fortune continued, for the Mallians, apparently convinced of his invincibility, surrendered. New riverboats were built in preparation for the trip downriver. When Alexander had recovered suffi-

FIGURE 15-2 Alexander and Poros coins.

ciently, the joint land and river expedition continued, although he sent Craterus with the elephants and most of the troops by an easier route. Perhaps the worst part of the entire expedition still lay ahead: the Gedrosian Desert. Alexander deliberately chose a dangerous and difficult route for the glory of achievement. It was, however, to have little glory for the many men (and all the accompanying families) who perished along the way.

S O U R C E   A N A L Y S I S

RRIAN, *ANABASIS* 6.24–26.[27]

It is said that the scorching heat and want of water destroyed a great part of the army and most particularly the baggage animals; that the depth of the sand and its heat, burning as it was, and in most cases thirst as well brought about their destruction. . . . Then the lengths of the marches, it is said, did most to distress the army; for want of water, which was found at irregular intervals, drove them to make their marches as necessity dictated. . . . The loss of transport animals was heavy and caused deliberately by the army; for whenever their provisions failed them, they would club together and kill off most of their horses and mules and eat their flesh, saying that they had perished from thirst or collapsed from fatigue; and there was no one to investigate the actual facts, because of the distress and because they were all involved in the same offence. Alexander was not unaware of these happenings, but he saw that the remedy for the situation lay rather in his pretending ignorance than in recognizing and permitting the practice. Nor was it easy any longer to bring along the troops who were suffering from sickness, or left dying on the road from fatigue, as there was a shortage of transport animals, and the men themselves kept breaking up the waggons, which it was impossible to drag along owing to the depth of the sand. . . . And so some were left behind on the roads from sickness, others from weariness or heat or inability to hold out against thirst; there was no one to help them forward, and no one to stay behind and take care of them; for the march was pressed hurriedly on, and in concern for the whole army the welfare of individuals was necessarily neglected. Sleep too overpowered men on the roads, since it was by night that they generally made their stages. In that case on waking, if they still had the strength, they would follow in the tracks of the army, but few out of many were saved: most of them were lost in the sand, like men who fall overboard at sea.

The army suffered also a further disaster, which more than anything else distressed the troops, horses and transport animals. . . . Now the army had bivouacked near a torrent bed with a little water—it was actually for the water that the site was chosen—when about the second watch in the night the stream here, swollen by rains of which the army had seen nothing, came down with so great a spate of water that it killed most of the women and children following the army and swept away all the royal equipment and the surviving transport animals; and indeed the troops themselves were only saved with great difficulty, with their weapons only, and not even all of these. . . .

THE DEATH OF ALEXANDER

After the ordeal in the Gedrosian Desert, Alexander, back in Persia, was met with numerous complaints of maladministration and even treasonous activities on the part of those he had left in charge during his long absence, many of whom had never expected to see him again. Severe punishments followed swiftly. Among those whom he executed were two of the three Macedonian generals who had executed Parmenio—in Alexander's absence they had plundered temples, disturbed tombs, and committed acts of injustice against the subject peoples. Not long after, the third of these generals was also executed for plundering the temple of Susa. Numerous other executions followed.[28]

Alexander next proceeded to Pasargadae, where he repaired and restored the plundered temple of Cyrus, the founder of the Persian Empire. By his reverence to the tomb of the founder, Alexander expressed his own claim to be the legitimate ruler of Persia, heir not only of Darius but of Cyrus as well. He also went forward with the integration of the Macedonians and Persians under his rule. Perhaps the most impressive of these acts of reconciliation and integration was the mass wedding he held at Susa for himself and other high-ranking Macedonians. Following the Macedonian tradition of royal polygamy, he married Statira,[29] Darius' eldest daughter, as well as Parysatis, the youngest daughter of Darius' predecessor (he had previously married Roxane, the daughter of the defeated ruler of Bactria). The Companions were also married to women from among the Persian ruling class (Alexander's closest friend Hephaestion was married to a full sister of Statira; thus, as possible heir or regent, he too would have children by a daughter of the last Achaemenid). The weddings were conducted in Persian style. Alexander gave all the brides dowries, and ordered that the other Macedonians who had already married Asian women be registered as well (Arrian reports that there were more than 10,000), and he gave them gifts. He also paid all the debts that his men had incurred and gave presents to those who had displayed conspicuous courage in battle.

But all did not go smoothly at these ceremonies. Many of the men were angry at being married to the women of a conquered people, and they also resented the reception into the army of 30,000 Persian youths whom Alexander had had raised in Macedonian fashion. These youths were dressed in the Macedonian fashion and trained in the Macedonian style of warfare, and Alexander rather tactlessly called them the *Successors*. The Macedonians saw this as an effort by Alexander to reduce his dependence on them, and it also called to their minds the many other marks of Alexander's accommodation to Persian ways that also angered them: Alexander's adoption of Persian dress and court ceremonies, the use of Persian wedding ceremonies in the mass marriages, and the recent introduction of Barbarians into the army itself and even into the Companion cavalry.

The culmination of the discontent occurred shortly afterwards, in the summer of 324 B.C. at Opis. Alexander announced that he was discharging and sending home those Macedonians unfit for service because of age or disability. They would serve at home as a reserve, and be replaced by fresh troops. This brought to the surface all the soldiers' past grievances, and they demanded that he discharge them all: let him campaign in the future with his father Ammon! Furious, Alexander ordered his officers to arrest the most conspicuous agitators. Around thirteen men were arrested and executed. He then harangued the stunned and silent men on the ingratitude to him and to his father Philip, and told them all that they were free to return home; he himself went into seclusion for three days. This time, however, he did not relent. Emerging from his seclusion, he summoned the most capable of the Persian leaders, divided the commands of the army among them, and made other plans to reorganize the army around his Asian forces. When word that they were being replaced reached the Macedonians, they were struck by remorse. They rushed to the palace and threw down their arms before the doors in supplication. Alexander then forgave them and ordered that a huge banquet of reconciliation be held. Nine thousand men shared in the feast at which Alexander prayed that harmony should prevail between the Macedonians and the Persians as partners in government.

In the autumn of 324 B.C. Alexander suffered a great blow when his closest friend Hephaestion fell ill and died. Alexander was consumed with grief, much like his hero Achilles after the death of Patroclus. Hephaestion was buried at Babylon, and in the spring a funeral was held for him with splendid funeral games. Alexander ordered that heroic honors be paid to Hephaestion, even offering the satrap of Egypt pardon for past and future crimes if he would establish hero shrines for Hephaestion at Alexandria and Pharos. Alexander planned his friend's tomb himself, to be built in Babylon at a cost of 10,000 talents. It was to take the shape of a *ziggurat,* the traditional Mesopotamian pyramidal shrine platform. The walls of the tomb were to be decorated with elaborate friezes of gold, and the base decorated with gilded ship prows seized from the Persians. Diodorus Siculus, who provides the most complete description, states that the monument was completed, but no traces of such a building have been found.[30]

As Alexander recovered from his overwhelming grief, he laid plans for further exploration and conquest. Among these new adventures were an expedition to the Caspian Sea,[31] a voyage to conquer and colonize Arabia, and the construction of a giant harbor at Babylon large enough to anchor 1000 warships.[32] Plans to conquer Carthage and to reach the Pillars of Herakles and Ocean in the west (Gibraltar) have also been attributed to him. Diodorus reports that notes about his future plans, including the western expedition, were found after his death (*The Hypomnemnemata*),[33] but when these were presented to the army, they were rejected as being too ambitious.

As these plans for the future were being laid, Alexander fell ill once more. Again the illness came on after one of the court's prolonged drinking parties. The fever progressed over the course of about ten days, despite efforts to alleviate it. Some sources report that, when asked to whom he was leaving his kingdom, he replied, "To the strongest"; others, that he added that he saw there would be a great funeral contest over him. At the end he lapsed into a coma, and on June 10, 323 B.C., he died. Rumors of poisoning circulated almost from the moment of his death, but both Arrian and Plutarch found them unpersuasive, as do most modern historians.[34]

SOURCE ANALYSIS

 RRIAN, 7.27.1–3.[35]

I am aware, of course, that there are many other versions recorded of Alexander's death; for instance, that Antipater sent him a drug, of which he died, and that it was made up for Antipater by Aristotle, as he had already come to fear Alexander on account of Callisthenes' death, and brought by Cassander, Antipater's son. Others have even said that it was conveyed in a mule's hoof, and given to Alexander by Iollas, Cassander's younger brother. . . . Others again hold that Medius had some hand in the business, as he was Iollas' lover, on the grounds that it was Medius who sug-

continued

gested to Alexander the drinking bout, and that Alexander had a sharp feeling of pain after quaffing the cup, and on feeling this he retired from the carouse. One writer has had the impudence to record that Alexander, feeling that he would not survive, went to throw himself into the Euphrates, so that he might disappear from the world and make more credible to posterity the belief that his birth was by a god and that it was to the gods that he had departed, but that Roxane, his wife, noticed that he was going out and stopped him, when he groaned and said that she was really grudging him the everlasting fame accorded to one who had been born a god. So much for stories which I have set down to show that I know they are told rather than because they are credible enough to recount.

While a recent case has been made for attributing Alexander's death to alcoholism,[36] it seems most likely that he died of malaria,[37] probably aggravated by the heavy drinking of the Macedonian court.

EPILOGUE: MACEDONIA AND THE HELLENISTIC WORLD

The Effects of Alexander's Conquests on Macedonia

Alexander died an untimely death at the age of thirty-three, in the midst of plans for further exploration and conquest. His adaptation of the Persian system to the administration of conquered territory was still evolving, and he had made no arrangements for the succession. Arrhidaios, his disabled half-brother, was the only Aegead successor, although Alexander's wife Roxane was pregnant.

None of the surviving generals claimed the succession. Rather, they agreed that Roxane's unborn child, if it turned out to be a boy, should be king under their combined regency. The army, however, resented the idea of a half-Barbarian king, and pushed for the succession of Arrhidaios. When the child turned out to be a boy, a compromise was reached: he, as Alexander IV, and Arrhidaios, as Philip III, were to be joint rulers, under a regency. The two were, of course, nothing more than puppets, to be eliminated when they were no longer useful.

The generals sought very soon to carve out their own domains. First to act was Ptolemy, who laid claim to Egypt. To support his claim, he kidnapped the body of Alexander, which he took to Alexandria and installed in a reportedly magnificent tomb, yet to be found. Ptolemy fended off one early challenge to his control of Egypt, and from that time on his descendants ruled the rich territory until the Romans took over after the death of Cleopatra in 30 B.C. Struggles for control of the other conquests of Alexander went on intermittently for about fifty years. At the end of this period of chaos and warfare (the Wars of the Successors), the world conquered by Alexander had come to be divided among a number of kingdoms ruled by Macedonian dynastic rulers who had little in common with the people whom they ruled. The most important of these kingdoms were Egypt, in the hands of the Ptolemies; Asia Minor and the Near East under the Seleucids; and Macedonia under the Antigonids, who also controlled Thessaly and some strongholds in Greece. But in the post-Alexandrian world, Macedon never regained its commanding role.

Was Macedonia's weakness in the period after Alexander a result of the depletion of manpower brought on by years of manning Alexander's armies and peopling his new settlements? There is disagreement about this.

A. B. Bosworth blames Alexander's conquests for the manpower weakness of post-Alexandrian Macedonia.[38] During the period 334–331 B.C., he points out, over 30,000 men had been taken out of the country, and few of them ever returned—he calculates, at most, half. Those who failed to return included, in addition to battle casualties and the victims of accidents, disease, and the rigors of the march, the many men who were settled permanently in garrisons and city foundations at the far reaches of the empire. Bosworth concludes that the birthrate in Macedonia must have declined sharply as a result of these manpower losses, as is suggested by an abrupt reduction in recruits that shows up in the accounts of Macedonian military actions after 320 B.C. Bosworth thus gives an assessment of the cost of Alexander's conquests that is quite different from that of Arrian: "He may have led his men to wealth and glory, but those who remained had little profit and lasting grief. . . . the country was set on a path of decline that proved irreversible."[39]

In contrast, Richard Billows argues that Alexander's campaign losses and resettlements did not have a permanent effect upon the ability of the population of Macedonia to muster fighters.[40] Thus, he estimates that in 319 B.C. there were approximately 25,000 Macedonian troops in Asia, and roughly the same number in Macedonia, in contrast to the 30,000 that he estimates Alexander had with him after the battle of Gaugamela. This optimistic view is based upon arguments from population estimates and demographic calculations relying on many unknowns and much supposition. For example, Billows puts the total Macedonian losses of Alexander's campaigns at 5000 to 7000 men, a casualty rate of some 12 to 20 percent.[41] He argues that such losses would be made up comparatively rapidly, since women and children were not, for the most part, casualties of war, many recruits had already started families before they left, many began new families on the campaign, and the citizenry was not a closed body. Yet Billows does not deny that Macedonian manpower declined, and that Macedonia sank to a level of relative unimportance in the post-Alexandrian world.[42] He attributes this decline, however, not to the campaigns of Alexander, but to the Gallic invasions of 280 to 277 B.C., which brought four years of devastation to the country. The Gauls killed not only men, but women and children as well. In the chaos, Philip's Greater Macedonia disintegrated. Many of the border areas that he had added broke away, and Illyrian and Thracian tribes again became a menace, as they had been in the days before Philip. Macedonia never fully recovered. Thus, in Billows' assessment, the campaigns of Alexander actually had little effect on the future of Macedonia, whether for good or ill. The villains were the Gauls.

After the Successors: The Hellenistic World

The world that emerged from the Wars of the Successors was vastly different from the old world of the polis. The descendants of Alexander's generals ruled autocratically over native populations in giant states, replacing the face-to-face interactions of a self-ruled polis by remote rulers approached through vast bureaucracies. A simplified form of Greek called *koine* Greek (common Greek, the language of the New Testament) became the international language. A veneer of Greek culture spread widely, fusing classical Greek and native traditions and creating a new culture, called the *Hellenistic*.

Yet, despite the end of the polis as a city-state, it remained vital as a city. Cities served rulers as capitals and provided the framework of administration; they continued to be the centers of culture and of an expanding commerce. They functioned politically on the local level, bargaining with Hellenistic kings for their "freedom"—from various taxes and other burdens—and exploiting the kings as patrons, lavishing honors and accolades upon them in return for civic improvements. It was a symbiotic relation: kings and cities both needed, and profited from, one another.[43]

This new form of "citizenship," however, failed to enlist the same patriotic devotion that the polis had engendered. Individuals, in reality, had little impact upon their fate, and they knew it. Yet, almost ironically, it became an age of individualism as patriotic devotion to the polis was replaced by the pursuit of personal happiness and salvation. New cults flourished, especially mystery cults that promised individuals a better life in the hereafter. Moreover, in many ways the lives of ordinary people were vastly improved. The period was economically prosperous, as the riches of the Persian Empire came into circulation. There was increased mobility as ties to the polis of birth weakened and economic opportunities appeared elsewhere. Women in particular gained more rights as the family ties that formed the basis of citizenship in the polis slackened. And the activity of Hellenistic kings as patrons of the arts and learning brought libraries and other civic amenities to the cities, and supported scholars who worked to preserve the Greek heritage and to further knowledge, especially in scientific areas such as astronomy and the perfection of the mechanisms of warfare. Medicine in particular made great progress; in Alexandria the practice of dissection, and perhaps even vivisection, resulted in important discoveries in anatomy and physiology.

Alexander and his conquests thus were both an ending and a beginning. The age to come was more than simply post-Alexandrian and post-Hellenic, more than simply a vehicle for the transmission of Greek culture to the Roman world. In it the Greeks joined—in fact, formed the basis of—a wider culture of the Mediterranean, the Hellenistic.

IMPORTANT PLACES IN CHAPTER 15

On Chapter Map: *Major battles*—Gaugamela, Granicus River, Halicarnassos, Hydaspes River, Issus, Tyre

Other significant locations: Alexandria, Alinda, Babylon, Bactria, Byblos, Caspian Sea, Cyprus, Ecbatana, Ephesus, Euphrates River, Gaza, Gedrosian Desert, Ghazni, Gordium, Herat, Indus River, Labraunda, Libya, Lycia, Merv, Opis, Pasargadae, Persepolis, Pharos, Phrygia, Pisidia, Rhodes, Sardis, Sidon, Siwah, Sogdiana, Susa, Syria, Termez, Tigris River

On Other Maps *(use map index to find these):* Carthage

SUGGESTIONS FOR FURTHER READING

A good introduction to the ancient sources is J. Roisman, *Alexander the Great: Ancient and Modern Perspectives* (1995), which also offers modern articles on key topics. Useful general books on Alexander are A. B. Bosworth, *Conquest and Empire: The Reign of Alexander the Great* (1988), and Peter Green, *Alexander the Great* (1974); also very interesting is D. W. Engels, *Alexander the Great and the Logistics of the Macedonian Army* (1978).

ENDNOTES

1. See Elizabeth Carney, "Olympias and the Image of the Royal Virago," *Phoenix* 47 (1993), 29–56.
2. N. G. L. Hammond, *Sources for Alexander the Great* (1993), 189–191.
3. See R. M. Errington, "Bias in Ptolemy's History of Alexander," *Classical Quarterly* n.s. 19 (1969), 233–242.
4. These figures are derived from the various figures given in the different sources by P. A. Brunt, *Arrian* I (1976), 1xix–1xxi. Bosworth also comes up with a figure of about 50,000 at the beginning of the expedition, including the forces already in Asia Minor; see A. B. Bosworth, *Conquest and Empire: The Reign of Alexander the Great* (1988), 35, 259.
5. D. W. Engels, *Alexander the Great and the Logistics of the Macedonian Army* (1978); Engles' book is an interesting example of the application of new questions to existing sources; in it he explores in detail the question of how the troops were provisioned.
6. Arr., *Anabasis* 1.13–16.
7. Tr. P. A. Brunt, *Arrian* (1983).
8. Plut., *Alex.* 22, B. Perrin, tr. (Loeb).

9. Arr., *Anabasis* I 23.7–8, Brunt, tr. (Loeb).

10. Oğuz Alpözen, "The Caria Princess: The Pride of Bodrum," *Hilton Turkey Magazine* vol. 25, no. 97 (1994/1), 6–7.

11. Arr., *Anabasis* 2.3.6–8; Plut., *Alex.* 18.4, also gives both explanations.

12. Peter Green, *Alexander of Macedon* (1974), 220, diagnosed this episode of illness as bronchial pneumonia; the German scholar F. Schachermeyr preferred inflammation of the lungs. *Alexander der Grosse: das Problem seiner Persönlichkeit und seines Wirkens* (1973), 202.

13. Arr., *Anabasis* 2.6–12; section V of J. Roisman, *Alexander the Great: Ancient and Modern Perspectives* (1995), is especially useful.

14. Arr., *Anabasis* 2.14.

15. On Alexandria, see P. M. Fraser, *Ptolemaic Alexandria* (1972).

16. Diod. Sic. 17.52.

17. Plut., *Moralia* 328E.

18. See the study of the eastern foundations by Frank Holt, *Alexander the Great and Bactria: The Formation of a Frontier in Central Asia* (1988).

19. For the sources and various interpretations of Alexander's claims of divinity, see Part VII in Roisman (above, n. 13).

20. Green (above, n. 12), 316.

21. Arr., *Anabasis* 3.19.5.

22. E. Badian, "The Death of Parmenio," *Transactions and Proceedings of the American Philological Association* 91 (1960), 324–338; W. Heckel, "The Conspiracy *Against* Philotas," *Phoenix* 31 (1977), 9–21, finds this rather like the complicated plots of Agatha Christie. If the "plot" had been a ruse to ensnare Philotas, and Philotas *had* reported it to Alexander, the plotters would seem to have been in a serious position themselves. Both articles are reprinted in Roisman (above, n. 13), Part VI.

23. Arr., *Anabasis* 3.30.

24. Arr., *Anabasis* 4.7.

25. Arr. 5.17.2–7, Brunt, tr. (Loeb).

26. M. J. Price, "The 'Porus' Coinage of Alexander the Great: A Symbol of Concord and Community," in S. Scheers, *Studia Paulo Naster Oblata I Numismatica Antiqua* (1982), 75–85, argues that Alexander would not have portrayed Poros's defeat after giving him the kingdom and taking him as an ally, and that the coin must therefore have been minted before the victory; however, this seems to reflect modern rather than ancient behavioral norms, and fails to account for the presence of Victory.

27. P. A. Brunt, tr. (see n. 6, above).

28. Arr., *Anabasis* 7.4.

29. Arrian calls her "Barsine"; he may have confused her with Barsine, the daughter of Artabazus, who was said to have been Alexander's mistress and the mother of his son, Herakles, or Barsine may have been Statira's official name, a fact possibly missed by the other ancient sources. See P. A. Brunt, "Alexander, Barsine and Heracles," *Rivista di Filologia e di Istruzione Classica* (1975), 22–34.

30. Diod. Sic. 17. 115.1–4.

31. Arr., *Anabasis* 7.16.1–4.

32. Arr., *Anabasis* 7.19.3–6.

33. Diod. Sic. 18.4; on these reported last plans, see P. A. Brunt, *Arrian* II, Appendix 23; and A. B. Bosworth, *From Arrian to Alexander: Studies in Historical Interpretation* (1988), chap. 8.

34. But see A. B. Bosworth, "The Death of Alexander the Great: Rumour and Propaganda," *Classical Quarterly* 21 (1971), 112–136.

35. P. A. Brunt, tr. (see n. 6, above).

36. J. M. O'Brien, *Alexander the Great: The Invisible Enemy* (1992). While O'Brien provides a useful bibliography, he makes no distinction between the sources, accepting whatever they report at face value.

37. See D. Engels, "A Note on Alexander's Death," *Classical Philology* 73 (1978), 224–228.

38. A. B. Bosworth, "Alexander and the Decline of Macedonia," *Journal of Hellenic Studies* 106 (1986), 1–12.

39. Bosworth (above, n. 38), 12.

40. Richard A. Billows, *Kings and Colonists: Aspects of Macedonian Imperialism* (1995), chap. 7.

41. Billows (above, n. 40), 188.

42. Billows (above, n. 40), 206.

43. See Billows (above, n. 40), 70–73.

Glossary

acropolis: the defensible hill that formed the nucleus of a Greek city; when the Athenian Acropolis is referred to, it is often capitalized.

Aer: the basic substance of the cosmos according to the philosopher Anaximenes.

agoge: a rigorous system of training and education for Spartan boys that sought to develop courage and collective identity while weakening family ties.

agon: generally, a contest; applied to the formalized contests of an Attic comedy, which often began with a physical fight and ended with a verbal contest.

agora: the civic center of a polis; buying and selling took place there, but the agora was far more than a market.

Agroikoi: three archons, probably of farmer or less than noble status, of the board appointed to resolve the anarchy after the reforms of Solon.

Amazons: literally, *a-mazon*, "without-a-breast"; legendary female warriors and rulers in Scythia, they cauterized one breast in order to be able to fight more effectively with a bow; as non-Greek and nonmale, they served an ideological function for the Athenians, representing the Barbarian "other."

antilogy: a set of paired speeches that argue opposite sides of a given thesis; it was a favorite form of Sophistic teaching.

Apeiron: in the world system of the philosopher Anaximander, the *Boundless* or *Unlimited*, out of which everything arises and into which everything passes away.

Apellai: Spartan Assembly of male citizens; approved or disapproved proposals put before it by the Gerousia.

Archon Eponymous: the Athenian archon whose name was used as a designation of the year.

Areopagus Council: Athenian aristocratic council consisting of men who had served as archons; membership was for life, and the power of the council was apparently great but vague before the reforms of Ephialtes in the early fifth century B.C.; after the reforms it retained mainly its ancient religious prerogatives, notably the trial of homicide cases.

Aristotle: philosopher, pupil of Plato, and teacher of Alexander the Great; founded the school and research institution called the *Lycaeum* in which the constitutions of the Greek cities were collected; historical source on a number of subjects.

astu: the urban center of a polis.

Athenian Tribute Lists (ATL): fragmentary lists inscribed on stone covering several years and listing the portions of the tribute to the members of the Delian League that were paid to the goddess Athena; allows historians to reconstruct the payments of tribute.

Bacchiads: the closed group of aristocrats that ruled Corinth up to the middle of the seventh century B.C.; it consisted of 200 members of a single clan who intermarried only among themselves.

basileus (pl., ***basileis***): Greek word for *king;* during the Mycenaean period it was probably applied to a minor local official.

Building BG: a monumental building at Lerna in the EH II period.

centaur: a mythical creature with the head and upper torso of a man and the body of a horse; the centaur Chiron was famed for his healing abilities and was said to have taught them to Asclepius.

chora: the agricultural territory of a polis, often containing dependent villages.

cleruchy: a settlement of Athenian citizens established in an allied city; the cleruchs kept their Athenian citizenship and were assigned plots of land that were worked for them by the local owners; because the cleruchs were usually of the thetic property class, this mechanism helped to relieve Athens of some of its poorer population and also provided an element of control over the allied population.

Companions: a group of Macedonian nobles, originally cavalrymen, who acted as companions of the king; they received estates in return for their loyalty and service.

crypts: basement rooms with a central pillar in Minoan palaces; a religious significance is suggested by the double axe symbols and offering tables often associated with them.

Cyclopean masonry: Mycenaean building technique using huge blocks that seemed to later Greeks so big that only the Cyclops could have lifted them.

dactylic hexameter: the special meter for Greek epic, consisting of 6 metric feet, each with a pattern of short and long syllables in the form "long, short, short" (the *dactyl*), or its equivalent (two shorts substituted for a long, or vice versa).

damos: Dorian form of *demos,* people.

decarchies: boards of ten local citizens set up by Lysander in a number of cities in Asia Minor after the Peloponnesian War; they served to govern their own poleis under Spartan control.

Delphic Amphictyony: the league of states set up to control and administer the shrine of Apollo at Delphi.

demagogue: a "leader of the people"; a pejorative term applied to the Athenian democratic leaders who held power after the death of Pericles.

demes: villages that were the basis of Kleisthenes's tribal reform; membership in a deme became the official basis of Athenian citizenship.

Demiourgoi: two Athenian archons of craftsman status on the board appointed to resolve the anarchy after the reforms of Solon.

demos: Greek word meaning "people"; probably originally the assembled army, it was applied to the collective of male citizens in a polis.

diolkos: the stone dragway for ships which was built across the Isthmus of Corinth by order of the tyrant Periander in the early sixth century B.C.

Dorians: Greeks who spoke in the Dorian dialect; Greek tradition held that they were driven out of Greece and returned as invaders at the end of the Bronze Age, but contemporary scholarship suggests that they either filtered in after the collapse of the Mycenaean palaces or were the underclass of the palace economy, left behind after the collapse.

Doric order: the simplest of the three orders of classical Greek architecture; characterized by fluted, heavy columns with simple cushion-shaped capitals and by a metope-and-triglyph frieze.

dromos: the long entryway that led into a tholos tomb.

Enneakrounos: the ornamental fountain house built by the tyrant Peisistratus in the Athenian Agora as part of his water supply system.

entablature: in Greek temple architecture, the horizontal superstructure supported by the columns, including the frieze.

ephebes: a Greek term for men between the ages of eighteen and twenty; a period of military training prior to admission to adult citizen status.

Ephetai: in Athens, a special court to try criminal cases.

Ephors: the five annually elected Spartan officials who acted as a check on the kings.

epibatos: a trader who sailed with his merchandise on a ship owned by another; a passenger.

epikleros: literally, "with the estate"; a daughter who was the sole surviving offspring and thus "inherited" her father's *oikos*; her nearest agnatic male relative, her father's brother or brother's son, was obliged to marry her (or arrange a marriage for her) so that she would bear a son who would be the effective heir of the deceased and carry on the *oikos*.

eunomia: orderly conduct of government, having good laws.

Eupatrids: "sons of good fathers"; the term was applied to the old aristocratic families in Athens who originally ruled over the state.

fibulae: safety-pin-type fasteners used by women.

frieze: in Greek temple architecture, a horizontal band on the entablature, decorated by running figures in the Ionic order and by metopes and triglyphs in the Doric order.

genos: the Greek term for *clan*.

Gerousia: Spartan board of thirty elders consisting of the two kings and twenty-eight men over sixty years of age who were elected for life; it put proposals before the Assembly for vote without debate.

Great Rhetra: the Spartan constitution, traditionally attributed to the semilegendary Lykurgus.

Greater Panathenaia: the enhanced celebration of the *Panathenaia* (the annual festival of Athena) that took place every fourth year, traditionally attributed to the tyrant Peisistratus.

Greek Renaissance: the eighth century B.C., the period when Homer recalled the Bronze Age Mycenaean world; also called the *Orientalizing Revolution* because contacts with the East led to adoption of Eastern orientalizing motifs in vase painting.

guest-friendship (xenia): a relationship of mutual hospitality and privilege between two men in different poleis.

harmost: a Spartan governor of a dependent poleis, an office instituted by Lysander; the term was also used by the Thebans.

hebontes: Spartan male citizens between twenty and thirty years of age who played a quasi-parental role in socializing their young charges in the agoge.

hektemoroi: in Athens before the reforms of Solon, men who were "sixth parters," working the land of others for a one-sixth rent; when they failed to pay, they fell into slavery.

Helen: mythical character, wife of King Menelaus of Sparta; her seduction by

Paris, son of Priam of Troy, was the cause of the Trojan War.

Heliaia: the Athenian Assembly when it met as a court of appeal; instituted by the reforms of Solon.

helot: in Sparta, an agricultural worker tied to the land allotment of a Spartan citizen; helots and their families produced food for the Spartans and accompanied them into battle as servers.

heroön: temple or shrine of a hero.

hetaira: a female companion; it usually refers to a woman who entertained men in both a social and sexual sense.

hetairoi: literally, "companions" or "friends"; in the Archaic period, the small circle of aristocratic friends who provided each other with political support; in the Classical period, its meaning became broader and it could be used to refer to political supporters of any social class (thus Kleisthenes was said to take the demos as his hetairoi).

hippeis: the second of the property classes of the reforms of Solon; they were men whose property yielded 300 to 500 bushels, which made them able to support horses; they were eligible for the lesser offices and possibly for the archonship.

homoioi: "equals" or "similars"; status term applied to Spartan male citizens.

hoplites: Greek infantrymen who fought in a line formation using a round shield called a *hoplon;* they had to supply their own armor and weapons, and hence being a hoplite involved having a certain economic status, probably that of *zeugitae.*

Horns of Consecration: Minoan symbol, the stylized horns of an ox.

horoi: "border marker"; one of Solon's reforms was to remove the horoi, freeing the land in Attica; although in the fourth century B.C. horoi marked mortgaged land, their exact legal function in Solon's time is not understood.

House of Tiles: a monumental building at Lerna, constructed over Building BG in the EH II period; it is named after its tile roof; functions of display, storage, and public convenience were apparent, and it perhaps paralleled the proto-palaces on Crete.

Hypomeiones: a Spartan status term, "inferiors"; perhaps men who failed to be elected to a mess, or failed to keep up their required mess contributions.

Hysiae, battle of: battle early in the seventh century B.C. in which Pheidon of Argos defeated Sparta.

Ionian League: a league that was established by twelve Ionian cities founded during the Ionian Migration at the end of the Mycenaean period; its members celebrated their ethnic identity in the festival of the *Panionia.*

Ionian Migration: the movement of Mycenaean survivors from the mainland to the central coast of Asia Minor during the collapse of Mycenaean palace civilization; traditionally assisted by Athenians, they spoke the Ionic dialect.

Ionic order: one of the three orders of classical Greek architecture, characterized by fluted columns with ornamental scrolls on the capitals and by a running frieze.

isonomia: "equality under law"; the term applied to the constitution of Kleisthenes.

Kadmeia: the acropolis of Thebes.

Keftiu: Egyptian word, "People of the Islands," probably referring to the Minoans.

Krypteia: in Sparta, a secret service that consisted of young men up to age thirty; they exercised "control by terror" over the helots, killing those who showed dangerous leadership potential.

laconic: terse of speech, the style adopted by the Spartans (from *Lakonia,* with a Latinized transliteration of the Greek).

Lakedaimonia: see *Lakonia.*

Lakonia: the territory of Sparta.

Lapiths: a legendary Thessalian people of the heroic age, conquerors of the centaurs.

lawagetas: a Mycenaean official lower in rank than the *wanax;* in later Greek the term meant "Leader of the Warhost."

Leuktra, battle of: battle in 371 B.C. in which the Thebans under Epaminondas defeated the Spartans, signaling the end of Spartan military supremacy in Greece.

Linear A: Minoan syllabic script; has not been deciphered yet.

Linear B: Mycenaean syllabic script; deciphered as early Greek; used for palace records.

liturgy: civic expenses assigned to wealthy Athenians, including the provision of choruses for dramatic festivals and the outfitting of triremes; the person assigned a liturgy could enter a suit objecting that he was less capable of affording the expense than another specific citizen and challenging him to either accept the liturgy or exchange properties (the suit was called an *antidosis,* a "giving in exchange").

Logos: measure, proportion, reason; the principle of the cosmos according to the philosopher Heraclitus.

lustral basin: a pool or other container for water used for ritual cleansing.

Lykurgus: Spartan reformer, to whom the constitution (the Great Rhetra) and institutions of Sparta are attributed.

magazine: long, narrow storage room characteristic of Bronze Age palaces.

megaron: a typical building form of the Mycenaeans, consisting of a rectangular room (or rooms) with a porch and entrance on the short side and a central hearth.

Menelaus: Mycenaean king, husband of Helen, whose abduction by Paris, son of Priam of Troy, caused the Trojan War.

mess or syssitia: the fundamental institution of adult Spartan male life; men were elected to a mess at the end of the agoge and lived, fought, and ate together until the age of thirty, after which they could establish individual households, but they continued to eat and fight together; continued membership in a mess was conditional upon making contributions to the common meals and was a prerequisite for full Spartan citizenship.

metic: a legal resident alien; metics were subject to registration and the metic tax, were obliged to serve in the military, and were required to have a citizen-sponsor; metics were not allowed to own land or house and, except in unusual circumstances, neither they nor their descendants could become citizens.

metope: the square area between the triglyphs in a Doric frieze.

miasma: ritual pollution from the shedding of blood; it afflicted not only those who killed another person, intentionally or otherwise, but also women after the shedding of blood in childbirth. If not ritually cleansed, miasma could bring afflictions upon the individual, his or her entire community, and even subsequent generations.

Minyans: name given to first Greek speakers in Greece, traditionally dated to about 2000 B.C.

naukleros: a trader who owned his own ship.

Navarchy: supreme command of a fleet, office held by Lysander in Sparta.

neodamodes: in Sparta, a helot who had been freed for service as a hoplite.

Neolithic Revolution: shift from hunting and gathering to agriculture (plant and animal husbandry); occurred in Greece in about the seventh millennium B.C.

niello technique: "painting in metal," a technique employed on objects in the Shaft Graves at Mycenae; *niello* (a compound of silver, copper, lead, and sulfur) was used to create figures in the metal; the technique appears earlier in Byblos and probably came to Greece from Syria.

nomothetes: a lawgiver; in Athens, a member of a committee charged with revision of legislation.

obai: a political division in Sparta mentioned in the Great Rhetra.

obsidian: a volcanic glass that can take a very sharp edge and was used as a cutting tool (still used today in some surgery); its source in the Greek Neolithic was mainly on the island of Melos.

Odeon: a building on the slope of the Athenian Acropolis in which musical performances took place; it was part of the Periclean building program.

oikistes: the founder of a Greek colony who led the colonization; he became the leading citizen of the new polis and received heroic honors after his death.

oikos: "household," "family"; it encompassed the property of the household as well, including buildings, equipment, animals, and slaves.

oka: a Mycenaean term for military units.

oligarchy: rule of the few.

Oracle of Apollo at Delphi: one of the most important Greek oracles; it offered advice to states more often than to individuals, and is credited with involvement in political decisions such as the constitution of Sparta (Great Rhetra) and the colonization of Cyrene.

ostracism: a ten-year period of exile decided by a special vote of the Athenian Assembly as a precaution against the return of tyranny; the ostracized man retained his citizenship and his property.

Owls: the coinage bearing the image of the owl of Athena introduced by the tyrant Hippias; it remained the basic Athenian coin until the second century

B.C. and was widely used throughout the Greek world.

paidonomos: Spartan official in charge of all males between the ages of seven and thirty.

parabasis: a "stepping aside"; in a Greek comedy, the formal section in which the chorus members shed their cloaks and step outside the framework of dramatic illusion to address the audience directly on behalf of the playwright.

pediment: the triangular gable on a building; on temples the pediment usually bore sculptural decorations.

Peloponnesian War: Greek war between Athens and its allies and Sparta and its allies, 431 to 404 B.C.

Pentecontaetia: the "Fifty Years," the name applied to the condensed account of Thucydides of the period between the Persian and the Peloponnesian wars.

pentecosiomedimi: the highest of the property classes in Solon's reforms; men whose property yielded 500 bushels and who were eligible to serve as archons and treasurers.

perioikoi: in Sparta, "dwellers roundabout," Dorian inhabitants of outlying villages, allied to Sparta and self-governing in local matters, but without citizen rights in Sparta; they served in the Spartan army and probably worked as craftsmen and traders as well as farmers.

Pheidon: tyrant of Argos, early seventh century B.C.; defeated Spartans in the battle of Hysiae.

phratry: a political division in Athens, perhaps a fictive "brotherhood"; acceptance by the phratry of his father was the mark of legitimacy for an Athenian male.

pillar-and-door partitions: an architectural feature of the Minoan palaces, in which walls were made up of a series of pillars with inset doors that could be opened or closed as the weather dictated.

pithoi: large clay storage jars for agricultural products such as grain, oil, wine, and olives.

Plato: Athenian philosopher and pupil of Socrates; his written works took the form of dialogues; although his primary aim was philosophical and not historical, his dialogues are often used as historical sources, especially *The Republic* and *Laws.*

polemarch: in Athens, one of the ten archons, who originally served as the commander in chief of the army; after the reforms of Kleisthenes there were ten generals, one elected from each tribe.

polis: Greek city-state; it was autonomous, and controlled a territory usually consisting of an urban center and countryside (*chora*) with dependent villages. It developed to the point of recognition in the eighth century B.C.

pornai: prostitutes.

Propylaea: the monumental gateway to the Athenian Acropolis, part of the Periclean building program.

proskynesis: the oriental practice of doing obeisance to the king; the act may range from prostration before the ruler to blowing him a kiss.

proxenos: an "official friend" of a state; a local person who served as a representative of Athens in his own polis; a practice especially adopted by the Athenians to control the empire; the office (*proxenia*) was awarded by the Athenians as an honor to the Macedonian king Alexander I.

prytany: the rotating body of fifty members from the Council of 500 that served as the executive each month of the Attic year.

rhetra: a Spartan law; see also *Great Rhetra.*

running frieze: frieze used in Ionic style, uninterrupted by triglyphs.

Sacred Band: elite Theban military unit of male lovers.

satrap: the governor of a Persian *satrapy,* or province.

Sea Peoples: invaders of Egypt who came in search of land to settle: the Egyptian pharoah Ramses III claimed to have driven them back in 1186 B.C. Among them only the Philistines have been identified; some were probably Mycenaean refugees.

Second Intermediate Period: a period in Egyptian history (ca. 1785–1550 B.C.) when the *Hyksos* (foreign princes, probably from the Levant) invaded and took control.

Seisachtheia: in Athens, the "shaking off of burdens" enacted by the reforms of Solon; it removed the horoi, freed those enslaved for debt, and abolished debt-slavery in the future.

Shaft Graves: burials in large rectangular shafts in the ground; at Mycenae a group of especially rich Shaft Grave burials dated to between 1600 and 1500 B.C. with grave goods showing the influence of a wide range of different cultures from Anatolia to central Europe; they were surrounded by two circles of stones in the Mycenaean period.

sophist: a traveling teacher of rhetoric who offered instruction for a fee in a number of different subjects in addition to public speaking, including grammar, music, poetry, and philosophy.

sophrosyne: self-control.

symmachia: military alliance.

symposium: a male dinner and drinking party; symposia served as the central focus of elite male social and political life.

synoikism: the unification, political or physical, of Greek settlements; in the case of Attica, the unification was a political union of towns attributed to the mythical hero Theseus, but probably occurring during the Dark Age.

thalassocracy: control over the seas.

Thesmophoria: the annual festival of the goddess Demeter; the most widely celebrated Greek religious festival, it assured the fertility of the grain and of women by various rituals that lasted for several days (varying according to the polis); it was restricted to women.

thesmothetes: six of the ten archons in Athens, who acted as recorders of judicial decisions and as court officials.

thetes: the lowest of the property classes instituted by the reforms of Solon; men with property that yielded less than 200 bushels, including those without land; they were eligible to attend the Assembly. This class gained significant political rights by the development of democracy in the fifth century B.C.

tholos tomb: a beehive-shaped tomb constructed on the principle of a corbelled arch, found on mainland Greece; they first appeared in Messenia around 1500 B.C.

triglyph: in a Doric frieze, the element between the metopes that is divided into three parts by two vertical grooves.

trittys: a "third of a tribe"; Kleisthenes divided Attica into 30 trittyes, one-third in each region, and constructed the tribes taking 1 trittys from each region.

tyrant: any ruler who came to power by irregular means, whether he was imposed by an outside authority or seized power for himself in conditions of internal political and economic crisies.

Tyrtaeus: Archaic Greek poet, worked at Sparta at the time of the Second Messenian War; perhaps a Spartan.

wanax (pl., wanakes): Greek word for "lord"; in the Mycenaean period it was used of the ruler; in Homer and later Greek it was usually applied only to the gods (but it was used for the sons of the basileus on Cyprus).

Wappenmünzen: "heraldic coins"; they were the earliest Athenian coins, probably instituted by Peisistratus for the payment of mercenaries and long-term contracts in the building program.

zeugitae: the third of the property classes instituted by the reforms of Solon; they were men whose property yielded 200 to 300 bushels; the word perhaps refers to their ability to maintain a yoke of oxen, or to their hoplite status; they were eligible for minor offices.

ziggurat: the traditional Mesopotamian pyramidal platform of a shrine.

Zoroastrianism: the dualistic religion of Persia initiated by Zoroaster, in which the god of Justice and Truth, Ahura Mazda, fought against the god of Evil and the Lie, Ahriman; the religion emphasized the purity and value of fire.

Map Index

Map Exercises

The blank outline maps that follow may be used for map exercises or as practice maps for quizzes.

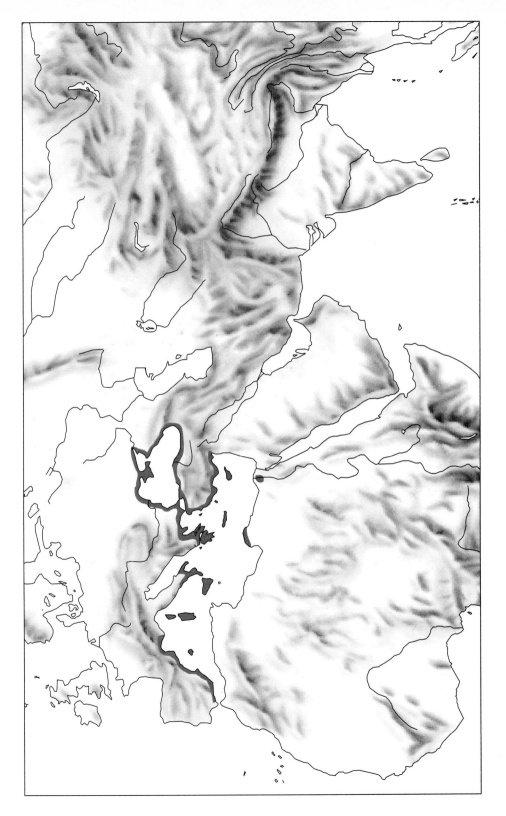

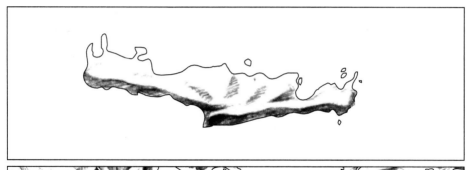

355

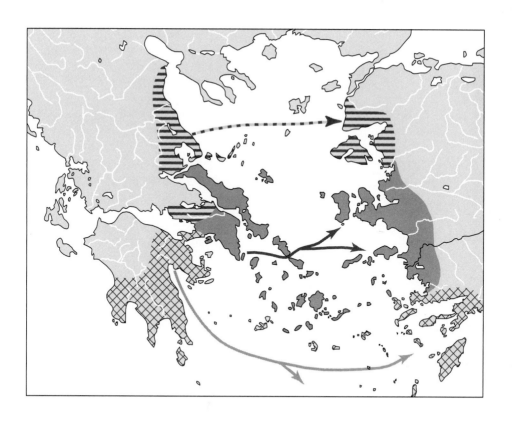

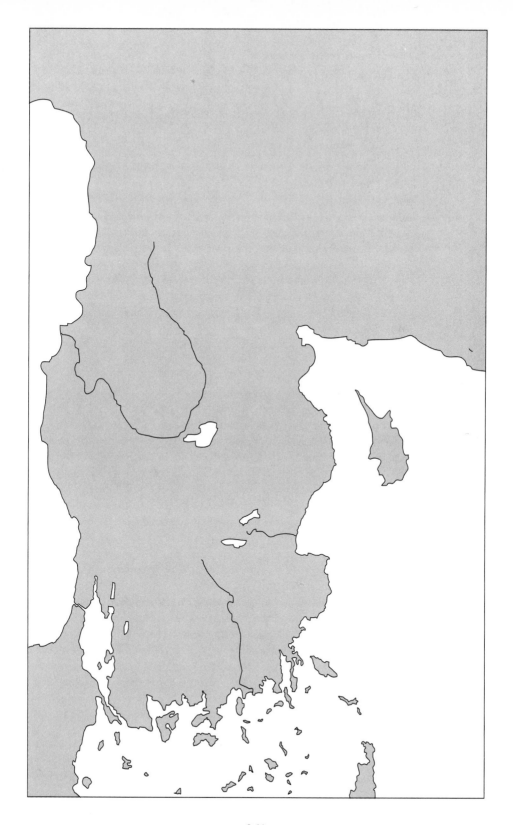

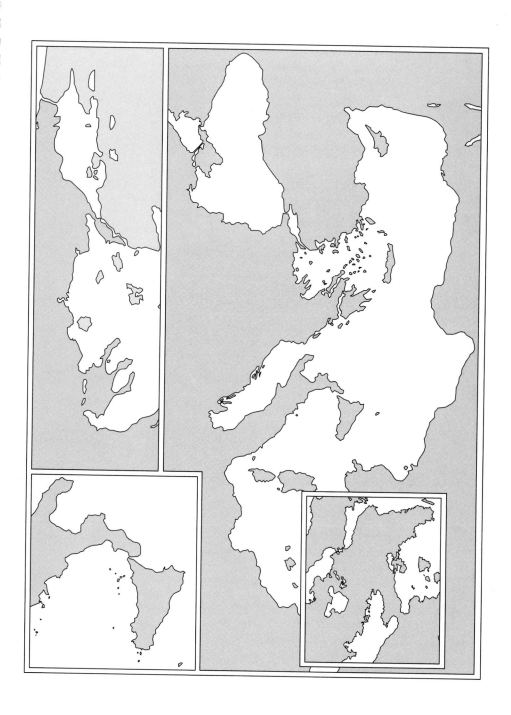

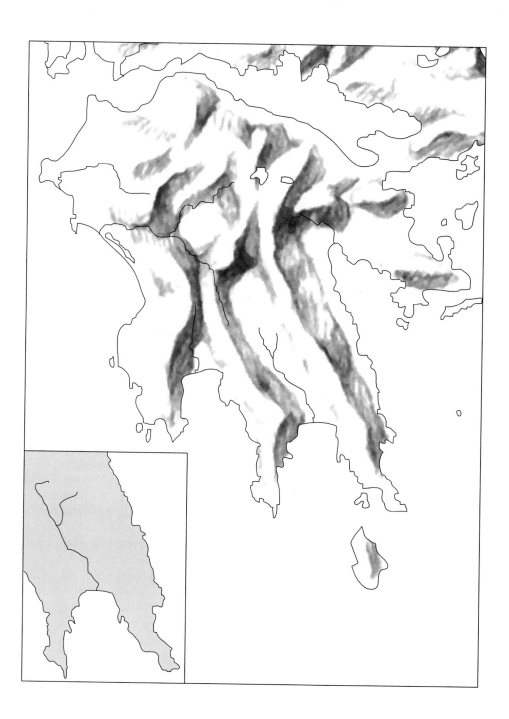

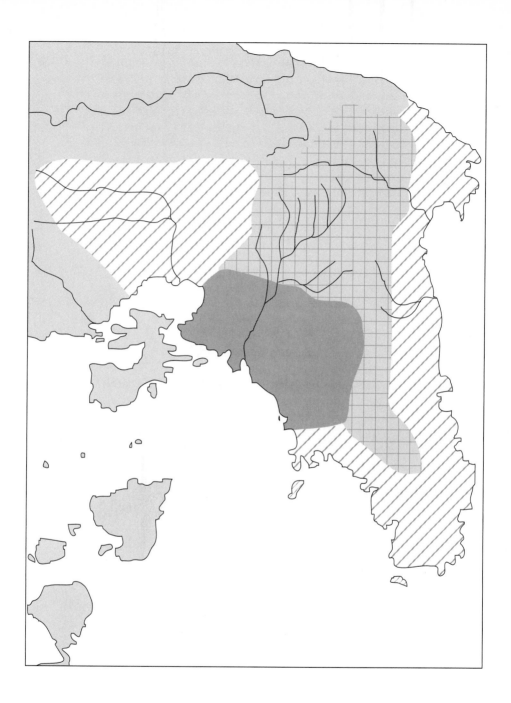

367

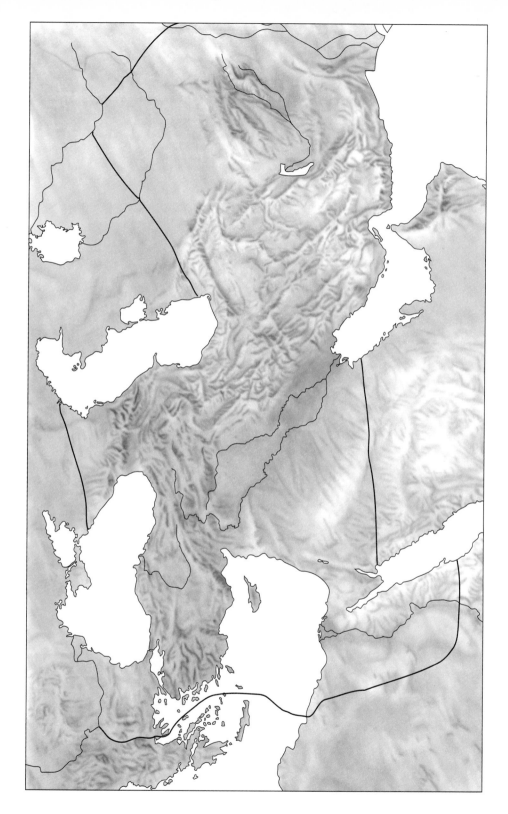

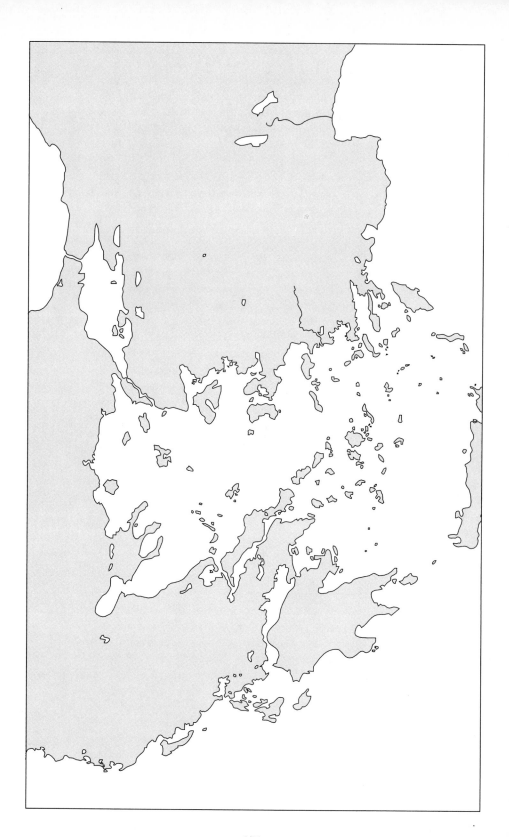

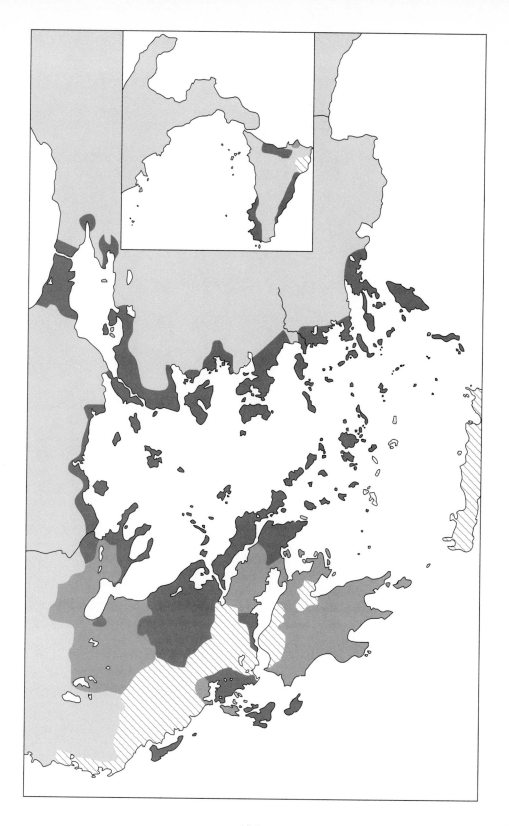

375

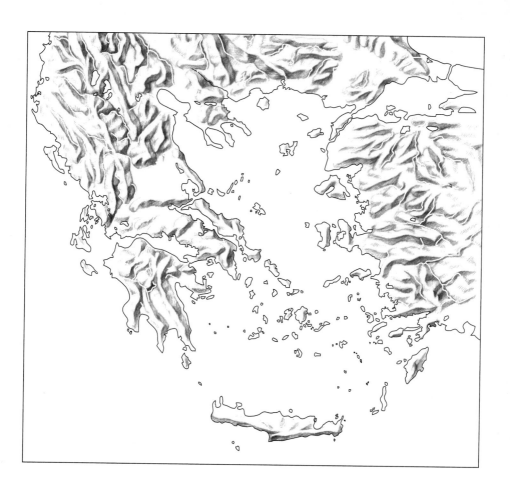

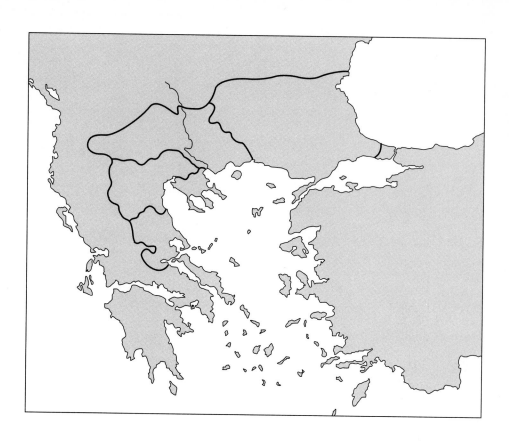

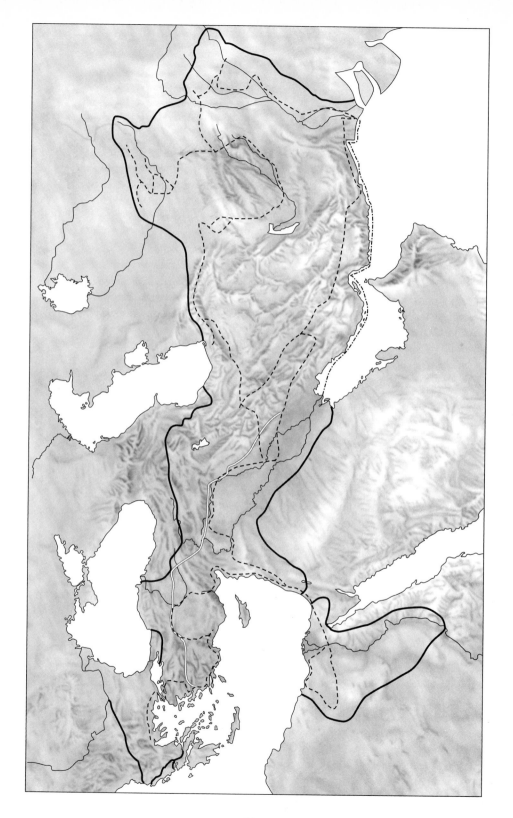

Photo Credits

CHAPTER 1

Page 10: Volos Museum; **p. 11:** From D. Theocharis, *Neolithic Greece* (Athens: National Bank of Greece, 1973), fig. 177; National Archaeological Museum, Athens; **p. 12:** From D. Theocharis, *Neolithic Greece* (Athens: National Bank of Greece, 1973) fig. 178; National Archaeological Museum, Athens; **p. 13:** From D. Theocharis, *Neolithic Greece* (Athens: National Bank of Greece, 1973), fig. 185; National Archaeological Museum, Athens; **p. 14:** From D. Theocharis, *Neolithic Greece* (Athens: National Bank of Greece, 1973), fig. 187; National Archaeological Museum, Athens; **pp. 15** and **16:** National Archaeological Museum, Athens.

CHAPTER 2

Page 18: From *Cambridge Ancient History*, plates to vols. 1 and 2, plate 58; **p. 26:** University of Pennsylvania Museum, Philadelphia; **pp. 27** and **28:** Herakleion Museum; **p. 29:** From Peter Warren, *Myrtos, An Early Bronze Age Settlement in Crete: Annual of the British School at Athens*, Supplementary Paper 7; **p. 30:** From Todd Whitelaw, "The Settlement at Fournou Korifi Myrtos and Aspects of Early Minoan Social Organization," in *Minoan Society*, O. Krzysqkowska

and L. Nixon, eds., 1983; **pp. 31, 32, 33,** and **34:** From Myers, Myers, and Cadogan, *The Aerial Atlas of Ancient Crete* (University of California Press, 1992); **pp. 37, 38,** and **39:** Herakleion Museum; **p. 40:** Myers, Myers, and Cadogan, *The Aerial Atlas of Ancient Crete*, (University of California Press, 1992); **p. 44:** From André Parrot, *Mission Archéologique du Mari Il Le Palais, 1. Architecture*, pl III (Paris: Institut Français d'Archéologie de Beyrouth, 1958); **p. 48:** National Archaeological Museum, Athens.

CHAPTER 3

Page 58: National Archaeological Museum, Athens; **p. 62:** From George E. Mylonas, *Mycenae and the Mycenaean Age*, Princeton; Princeton University Press, 1966, Fig. 1; **p. 13:** After K. F. Müller, *Tiryns III: Die Architektur der Burg und des Palastes*, Mainz: Verlag Philipp von Zabern, 1976; **p. 63:** From Alan J. B. Wace, *Mycenae: An Archaeological History and Guide*, Princeton: Princeton University Press, 1949, fig. 19; **p. 64:** From Carl W. Blegan and Marion Rawson, *The Palace of Nestor at Pylos in Western Messenia*, Princeton: Princeton University Press, 1966, plate 417; **p. 68:** From *The Mycenaeans*, by Lord William Taylor, London, Thames & Hudson, after Blegen.

CHAPTER 4
Page 73: From Deutsches Archäologisches Institut, Athens, in Jeffrey Hurwit, *The Art and Culture of Early Greece 1100–480*, Ithaca: Cornell University Press, 1966, plate 417; **p. 74:** Deutsches Archäologisches Institut, Athens, in Jeffrey Hurwit, *The Art and Culture of Early Greece 1100–480*, Ithaca: Cornell University Press, 1985, fig. 2.7, p. 62; **p. 86:** From M. R. Popham, P. G. Calligas, and L. H. Sackett, *Lefkandi II. Part 2 The Protogeometric Building* (Thames and Hudson, 1990), plates 5, 13, 22b; **p. 88:** Kerameikos Museum; **p. 89:** Deutsches Archäologisches Institut, Athens. Photo by G. Hellner; **p. 90:** Elevsis Museum.

CHAPTER 5
Page 97: National Archaeological Museum, Athens; **p. 112:** Staatliche Antikensammlungen und Glyptothek, München.

CHAPTER 6
Pages 119 and 137: Courtesy of Nancy Demand.

CHAPTER 7
Page 142: Drawing by W. B. Dinsmoor, Jr. and J. Travlos; **p. 151:** Asmolean Museum, Oxford; **p. 152:** Hood Museum of Art, Dartmouth College, Hanover, New Hampshire. Gift of Mr. and Mrs. Ray Winfield Smith, Class of 1918; **p. 153:** Martin v. Wagner-Museum der Universität Würzburg; **p. 155:** British Museum.

CHAPTER 9
Pages 188 and 197: Courtesy of Nancy Demand.

CHAPTER 10
Page 215: From J. Travlos, *A Pictorial Dictionary of Athens*, fig. 91, p. 71; **p. 218:** Carl Frank/Photo Researchers.

CHAPTER 11
Pages 229 and 230: Glyptothek und Museum Antiker Kleinkunst, Munich, 1717(J731); **p. 232** and **233:** British Museum; **p. 234:** National Archaeological Museum, Athens; **p. 239:** Metropolitan Museum of Art; **p. 240:** Princeton University Press; **p. 241:** British Museum.

CHAPTER 14
Page 300: From *The Royal Tombs and the Ancient City Athens*, by M. Andronikos. Ekatike Antheum SA, 1984, 98–99.

CHAPTER 15
Page 316: Art Resource; **p. 326:** British Museum.

Index